Physical Education and Sport:
an Introduction

Physical Education
and Sport:
an Introduction

Edited, with introductory and concluding essays, by

EARLE F. ZEIGLER, Ph.D., LL.D., FAAPE
University of Western Ontario
London, Ontario, Canada

With chapters by
Laura J. Huelster, Harold J. VanderZwaag,
James S. Skinner, A. V. Carron, G. Lawrence Rarick,
Glynn A. Leyshon, Daniel G. Soucie, Ann E. Jewett,
B. Don Franks

Lea & Febiger • Philadelphia • 1982

Lea & Febiger
600 Washington Square
Philadelphia, PA 19106
U.S.A.

Library of Congress Cataloging in Publication Data

Main entry under title:

Physical education and sport.

   Bibliography: p.
   Includes index.
   1. Physical education and training—Addresses,
essays, lectures. 2. Sports—Addresses, essays,
lectures. I. Zeigler, Earle F.
GV341.P465   613.7′1   81-8287
ISBN 0-8121-0795-0   AACR2

PRINTED IN THE UNITED STATES OF AMERICA

Print No. 3   2   1

Preface

The fundamental purpose of this book is to serve as an introduction to the field of physical education and sport—or sport and physical education as it is called within the National Association for Sport and Physical Education, one of the allied professions of the American Alliance for Health, Physical Education, Recreation, and Dance. This volume has been prepared in such a way that it can meet the needs of two different groups of people: (1) those who are using it from the standpoint of their general education, as part of a broad liberal arts and science background; and (2) those who are using it as an introduction to a field in which they will be prepared *professionally*, in addition to the general education function it can serve.

Interestingly enough, it is very difficult to know just what name to give the field at present. The terms "physical education and sport" and "sport and physical education" will be used interchangeably in this text. They are the terms that are recognized to the greatest extent on this continent and around the world. Admittedly, they can probably be regarded right now as "holding-pattern" terms, to borrow from airline nomenclature, although it is true that the entire list of names that one will find applied to the field in North America currently is indeed a long one.

To explain this further, we could have well adopted other terms such as physical education (by itself); health, physical education, and recreation; kinesiology; ergonomics and physical education; human kinetics; physical and health education; sport studies; exercise and sport; and movement arts and sciences. Then there is always the possibility of being innovative and using terms like sport and developmental physical activity, sport and human motor performance, or even developmental physical activity in sport, dance, and exercise—phrases that would each have certain limitations as viewed by some people. Thus, while this struggle over terminology continues, we thought it best to keep the two terms, physical education and sport, in proximity (not worrying about which one comes first).

A new introductory text for the field of sport and physical education offered to the profession by one of the leading publishers of physical education texts merits solid justification. We believe that this volume has been conceived in such a way that it will meet the urgent needs of our field in the 1980s—and even on to the year 2000. Such a text must concern itself forthrightly and strongly with both the "professional" and scholarly dimensions of our work—with the so-called subdisciplinary areas and with the concurrent professional components that we all face. (An example of a concurrent professional component would be management theory and practice.) Diagnosis of the present situation indicates that the field needs redirection and rejuvenation. The American Alliance for Health, Physical Education, Recreation, and Dance has now fully recognized that we are all separate but allied professions.

In Canada there is a separate recreation profession, but health education and physical education remain closely intertwined. This introductory text involves authors from both countries and can therefore be used profitably in both geographical contexts. This approach should help to give direction to the struggling emergence of an entity called the National Association for Sport and Physical Education within the AAH-PERD as presently constituted, and to what is still called physical education (or at times, human kinetics) in Canada.

As the reader examines the table of contents, he will notice immediately that there is a balanced approach between the subdisciplinary areas of our field and what might be identified as the subprofessional or concurrent professional components. By this we mean that what many have called professional writing (e.g., curriculum investigation) will be regarded as scholarly endeavor, just as what many have considered to be scholarly, scientific endeavor (e.g., exercise science) is regarded as professional writing too (writing that should ultimately serve the profession). Some may feel that this tends to redress the present imbalance too much, but we believe that the present rift in the field between the so-called scholars and the so-called practicing professionals must be significantly narrowed at the very least—and largely eliminated if we wish to move toward a relatively ideal state by the year 1990 or, what has become an almost mythical year, 2000. If it is well received, this book may help to close the presently widening gap.

As part of this effort to close the gap or to reverse the direction of present movement, the Editor, with the assistance of Dr. Laura J. Huelster (who explains it more fully in the Prologue), has developed a taxonomical table to explain the proposed areas of scholarly study and research using *our* nomenclature (sport and physical education terms only) along with the accompanying disciplinary and professional aspects. We have agreed upon eight areas of scholarly study and research that are correlated with their respective subdisciplinary and subprofessional aspects in Table 1. Most importantly, the reader will note that the names selected for the eight areas *do not include terms that are currently part of the names, or the actual names, of other recognized disciplines* and that are therefore usually identified with these other (related) disciplines primarily by our colleagues and the public.

Our position is that we must promote and develop *our own* discipline of sport and physical education as described above, while at the same time working cooperatively with the related disciplines (to the extent that interest is shown in our problems). If we continue to speak of *sociology* of sport, *physiology* of exercise, etc., it will just be a matter of time before these other disciplines and professions awake to the importance of what we believe to be *our* professional task—the gathering and dissemination of knowledge about, and the promotion of it to the extent that such promulgation is socially desirable, developmental physical activity through the media of sport, dance, play, and exercise. It is our contention that the present trend, truly a debilitating fractionization, will in time result in our developing profession being regarded as simply another trade, and not a very important one at that. The ultimate goal for our profession should be, however, enriched living and well-being for all people, an opportunity for improvement of the quality of life. We believe that we in physical education and sport should be able to do this—to contribute to the improvement of life quality—best for ourselves with the help of allied professions and related disciplines. If mankind must wait for others to do it *for* us, such development, and possible accompanying recognition of the importance of our function in bringing about greater kinesthetic awareness and improved movement patterns

Table 1. **Professional and Scholarly Dimensions of Sport and Developmental Physical Activity**

Areas of Scholarly Study and Research	Disciplinary Aspects	Professional Aspects
1. Background, meaning, and significance	History Philosophy International and comparative	International relations Professional ethics
2. Functional effects of physical activity	Exercise physiology Anthropometry and body composition	Fitness and health appraisal Athletic and exercise therapy Nutritional application
3. Sociocultural and behavioral aspects	Sociology Psychology (individual and social) Anthropology Political science (geography, economics?)	Application of theory to practice
4. Motor learning and development	Psychomotor learning Physical growth and motor development	Application of theory to practice
5. Mechanical and muscular analysis of motor skills	Biomechanics Neuroskeletal musculature	Application of theory to practice
6. Management theory and practice	Management theory	Application of theory to practice
7. Program development	Curriculum theory Theories of instruction	General education (curriculum and instruction) Professional preparation Intramural sports and physical recreation Athletics Special physical education
8. Measurement and Evaluation (in both the disciplinary and professional aspects of sport and developmental physical activity)		

within the lifestyles of evolving humans on this planet, will come belatedly. It will also be less effective because the present pattern of poor communication and coordination will be continued.

What is needed right now, and is not presently available, is a steadily growing inventory of scientific findings about human motor performance in sport, dance, and exercise arranged as ordered generalizations to help our various professional practitioners in their daily work (be they teachers, coaches, scholars, laboratory researchers, managers, supervisors, performers, or others engaged in positions of a public, semipublic, or private nature (e.g., YMCAs and commercial fitness establishments).

This introductory text is designed to meet the needs of North Americans primarily, although it has relevance for professional practitioners anywhere in the world. As mentioned above, it may be used by students who are beginning a period of professional preparation for physical education and sport or by students who may wish to elect a course in which their general education will be rounded out by such an experience. (It can be studied profitably by students wishing to specialize in either health and safety education *or* recreation and park administration, but it has not been designed to meet their needs as an introduction to either of these developing professions. However, students intending to specialize in dance as a developing profession could use it to advantage as an introduction because the focus in this volume is on human motor performance in sport, dance, and exercise).

What should go into this book was decided (1) by review of the historical development of the field in the twentieth century; (2) by consideration of the material that has been included in earlier introductory texts; (3) by observation of the strong trend that developed in the 1960s in certain quarters that has swung the pendulum too far in many instances in the direction of the related disciplines (and away from the consideration of professional physical education and sport problems); (4) by review of certain of the physical education recommendations of the 1967 Graduate Study Conference (AAHPER); and (5) by conjoint effort of the Editor and Laura J. Huelster (who played one of the two leading roles in the 1967 national professional meeting), who along with the Editor has observed the occurrences of the 1970s with increasing concern.

In any analysis of this emerging field that traces the developments of the twentieth century, three categories or subdivisions of the field should be analyzed: (1) the potential body of knowledge as characterized by its *subdisciplinary areas*; (2) the *concurrent professional components* of the developing field (as exist in all subject-matter fields to a greater or lesser extent); and (3) what may be called *potential related (or allied) professions* (as may exist also in other emerging fields).

In this text, therefore, after a prologue in which Dr. Huelster explains the urgent need for a social relevance perspective for physical education and sport (or SPE as she calls it), the Editor presents a more detailed introductory statement explaining the historical background and present status of the field for which this present volume was designed. Then the first five of a total of eight chapters are presented as the fundamental subdisciplinary areas of the profession: Background, Meaning, and Significance, by Harold J. VanderZwaag; Functional Effects of Physical Activity, by James S. Skinner; Sociocultural and Behavioral Aspects, by A. V. Carron; Motor Learning and Development, by G. Lawrence Rarick; Mechanical and Muscular Analysis of Motor Skills, by Glynn A. Leyshon.

The last three chapters include the various concurrent subsumed professional components: Management Theory and Practice, by Daniel G. Soucie; Program Development by Ann E. Jewett; Measurement and Evaluation, by B. Don Franks.

The Editor concludes the book with a chapter that summarizes, draws some obvious conclusions, and looks to the future.

Interestingly, included in this group of authors are six members of the American Academy of Physical Education (including two Alliance Scholars-of-the-Year), one other well-known scholar/teacher/administrator, and three outstanding Canadian scholars to give the volume a truly North American flavor.

At this point it is important to make clear that the scholars who contributed to this introductory text are anything but a group of people reflecting the philosophical stance held by the Editor. It was tempting to contemplate bringing together a group of people whose writing would state resoundingly the philosophical position held by him. However, it can truly be stated that this collection of scholars represents all positions on the spectrum, that is, from the reasonably far left to the reasonably far right, with a few solid eclectics "thrown in for good measure." Thus, the reader will probably find opinions in one chapter that clash violently with those expressed elsewhere. As I see it, this is a good thing, and it does indeed reflect what is taking place in the field. Further, only a very flexible chapter outline was recommended; I simply did not feel that it would be desirable to attempt to tell these professional leaders exactly how they should handle topics in which they have achieved eminence. I am grateful for their involvement in this exciting development.

It is always pleasurable to express appreciation to the various people who have contributed to the publication of a volume such as this is intended to be. In addition to the chapter authors, I am most appreciative for the direct assistance and continuing encouragement I have received from Dr. Laura J. Huelster, a widely based scholar who has been recognized by the American Academy of Physical Education as a winner of the coveted Hetherington Award. Dr. Huelster is Professor Emerita of Physical Education, University of Illinois, Urbana. Edward H. Wickland, Jr., Executive Editor at Lea & Febiger, offered encouragement with the project and has been helpful at all stages. Thomas Colaiezzi and Alicia Zanzinger of Lea & Febiger, and Agnes Kelly, copy editor, have also helped greatly with the production of this book. Finally, my wife, Bert, has served in so many instances as my personal editor, indexer, or what have you. I thank her for this assistance over a period of more than 30 years of article and book writing.

Earle F. Zeigler, Ph.D., LL.D., FAAPE
Faculty of Physical Education
University of Western Ontario
London, Ontario, Canada

Contributors

A. V. Carron, Ed.D.
Faculty of Physical Education
University of Western Ontario, London, Ontario

B. Don Franks, Ph.D.
Division of Physical Education, School of HPER
University of Tennessee, Knoxville, Tennessee

Laura J. Huelster, Ph.D., FAAPE
University of Illinois, Urbana, Illinois

Ann E. Jewett, Ph.D., FAAPE
Division of Physical Education
University of Georgia, Athens, Georgia

Glynn A. Leyshon, Ph.D.
Faculty of Physical Education/Faculty of Medicine
University of Western Ontario, London, Ontario

G. Lawrence Rarick, Ph.D., FAAPE
Department of Physical Education
University of California, Berkeley, California

James S. Skinner, Ph.D., FAAPE
Department of Health and Physical Education
Arizona State University, Tempe, Arizona

Daniel G. Soucie, Ph.D.
Department of Physical Education, School of Human Kinetics
University of Ottawa, Ottawa, Ontario

Harold J. VanderZwaag, Ph.D., FAAPE
Department of Sport Studies
University of Massachusetts, Amherst, Massachusetts

Earle F. Zeigler, Ph.D., LL.D., FAAPE
Faculty of Physical Education
University of Western Ontario, London, Ontario

Contents

Social Relevance Perspective For Sport and Physical Education

Laura J. Huelster

In a paper on curriculum development and instruction, Jewett stated: "Rarely has physical education been dominated by a social relevance perspective. Since most of us are conservatives, and few are futurists, when we have been influenced by a concept of social relevance, it has been with an adaptive rationale, emphasizing the need for fitness for future survival of the society" (1979, p. 8). How true—the recurring social concept has been that of fitness to fight in a present or pending war and to survive its consequences. The commitment of physical education to society has not been to promote a futuristic goal of enduring peace and its humanistic components. Yet the survival of our society is threatened unless there is fitness to live the quality of life that deemphasizes war and promotes peaceful solutions to national and international social, economic, and political conflicts.

The human and economic costs of past wars are known, and the potential cost to society of nuclear war has been estimated. Research studies have identified the social, economic, and political conditions that cause war and the changes in them that are conducive to peace. However, the resultant body of knowledge tends to be tucked away and treated as if important to relatively few people and certain international organizations. In reality, it is essential that general education include knowledge about the conditions of human societies that are conducive to minimizing wars and maximizing peace. Willingness to accept and act upon that knowledge depends not only upon convincing evidence but also upon having attitudes and ideologies that are compatible with it.

Learning in all school subjects includes acquiring *knowledges* (understandings of and from systematized facts); *skills* (expert abilities); *values* (human desires and means to them); and *attitudes* (persistent mental and emotional readiness to react to situations and propositions). The study of sport and physical education (SPE) is no exception to that definition of learning, and it contains possible educational experiences that are particularly rich in peaceful practices.

I believe (i.e., acceptance of an idea or proposition based on what are considered to be adequate reasons), therefore, that it is possible to formulate a theory of SPE that has relevance to the promotion of peace in society. The ultimate aim would be to further the human desire for peace as an evolving humanistic goal through the development of 'compassionate fitness.' The practicality of this concept depends upon the extent to which you, the readers of this prologue, are sympathetic to its point of view and want to have and provide educational experiences that agree with

Dr. Huelster is from the University of Illinois, Urbana-Champaign. This prologue is an adaptation of a paper presented by the writer at the Curriculum Theory Conference in Physical Education. *In* Conference Proceedings. Edited by A. E. Jewett and C. Norton. Mimeographed. University of Georgia, Athens, 1979, pp. 89–94.

that purpose. (I hope that your present attitudes and ideologies will at least allow you to read to the end of this chapter before deciding.)

STATEMENT OF THE THEORY

A useful definition of theory is that it is a cluster of interrelated assumptions from which a group of principles can be derived as guides to the organization of facts, practices, and the search for new knowledge (Griffiths, 1959, pp. 38–40, 45). The cluster of assumptions below serves as a rationale for principles to be used in structuring plans for SPE that could add to human progress toward enduring peace:

1. War and unrestrained aggression are destructive human forces in our world. It is imperative to reconstruct our society now to minimize war and to maximize conditions for enduring peace if this civilization is to progress and possibly even to survive.

2. There are rational plans that can move nations from war to peaceful means of settling national and international disputes. If adopted, the results would benefit all peoples and nations.

3. Societies have and will change their cultures (social, economic, and political values, institutions, and systems) as well as be changed by them.

4. The will for peace depends basically on the desire for it based upon associated attitudes, ideologies (scheme of attitudes), and behaviors (outward and inward responses to stimuli).

5. Education can prepare people to want to put known requirements for peace into practice through knowledge and the development of supportive attitudes and ideologies.

6. SPE provides experiences in compassionate fitness that are basic to peace.

Brief amplification of the above six assumptions will be stated below. Near the end of the chapter, the concept of 'compassionate fitness' through SPE will be developed, and at the end tentative principles for its promotion in SPE will be stated.

Assumption One. War Is a Destructive Social Force

Noncontroversial human values include survival, justice, and self-fulfillment. War disavows those rights, with the possible exception of self-fulfillment among those working in the military-industrial complex. Our world is full of behavioral violence, war, civil disorders, and terror. Associated with these is the "violence" of starvation, malnutrition, and fleeing to political freedom.

The loss of human lives through wars has been massive. Over 120 civil and international wars erupted from World War II (1945) to 1980, and 95% of those have been fought in Third World countries. Numbers of those resulted in over 1 million casualties each (Bouthoul and Carrère, 1978; "Chronology of Events," 1976–1980). The United States fought in nine wars from 1775 to 1975. The total number of deaths equaled 1,174,808, and 1,584,590 people were wounded. The grand total of over 2.6 million people is more than the population of the Dallas-Ft. Worth, Texas area (1978). The United Nations (UN) World Council reported that 50 million of our estimated world population of about 4.5 billion in 1980 died from starvation (Conti, 1980, p. 56). Of those, 30 million were children as reported by the UN Children's Fund (Righter, 1980, p. 39). Nearly one quarter of the people in the world's population were seriously malnourished, and in the poorest of the Third World nations one half of the population was underfed. Economic upheavals resulting from wars have left 10 million homeless and unwanted. For example, in May, 1980, there were 130,000 persons from Cambodia residing in a refugee camp on Thailand's border as the result of a nonhumanitarian regime in Cambodia (Moritz, 1980, p. 4). And by June 1, 1980, over 91,000 refugees had arrived in Florida from Cuba where they thought they had been economically and politically oppressed. (These figures on the results of war and oppression will have special meaning to you if you have suffered from war and its consequences or know someone who has. Otherwise it is difficult to use numbers as a means of understanding human suffering.)

Future wars would surely cause as much human suffering and probably more than that experienced in the past. A projection of future wars was made by Alcock et al., using a research model of variables known to be associated with past wars from 1951 to 1965 and then by testing that model against the wars that occurred from 1925 to 1939 (1978, pp. 118–135). From the systems analysis data it was concluded that a cluster of future, large international wars would probably peak in 1990, 1992, and 1997 after a relatively peaceful period from 1977 to 1987. Civil wars would result probably as in the past from changes in political regimes and in the status of the economy. Also, as in the past, international wars were predicted to occur as a result of military alliances, armament expenditures, and territorial disputes. If nuclear war breaks out, according to the Stockholm International Peace Research Institute (SIPRI), the weapons available would have 1 million times greater explosive power than the nuclear explosion over Hiroshima, Japan, in 1945. The metric tonnage of nuclear explosions available in 1980 amounted to an average of 3 per person in the world (Arms Control and Disarmament, 1980, p. 50). It has also been widely noted that one of the added dangers to the potential for nuclear war is the proliferation of their availability in an increasing number of nations. The sophistication of delivery systems of nuclear weapons has made even greater the problem of defenses against them. It has been estimated that the Soviet Union (USSR) could launch an attack using only about 10% of its strategic arsenal that would kill half the US population and injure millions. If citizens knew of national evacuation plans, it is doubtful that even their proficient use would save those fleeing. A USA counterstrike from submarine-based missiles could kill an estimated 20 to 100 million Soviet citizens. The greatest danger from reading these, and many other estimations of global disaster from nuclear weapons, is a "psychic numbing," which results in inability to comprehend what would happen to human life and the physical environment in this world (Knox, 1980). Even to use the analogy of the human destruction potential being equal to the elimination of a percentage of the population is not a meaningful device. The count of the numbers of people and the terrible suffering among those who might live does not account for the waste of the quality of those lives and the potential for the good of humanity that they represent. It is impossible to comprehend the effects of nuclear war on humanity. Pictures we have seen that express the imagined bleak world before and after life began may give a notion of the results.

Perhaps it is easier to comprehend the amount of money it costs the people of the world through their governments to prepare for possible future wars. What do plans for war defense and aggression cost nations annually? SIPRI reported that $410 billion would be spent on the world's military forces in 1979. That was the greatest amount in recorded history ever to be spent by humans for the potential destruction of humans (Arms Control and Disarmament, 1980, p. 50). It is possible to translate the size of that amount of money in space (Alcock et al., 1978, pp. 74–77). A 4-inch stack (width of a brick) of $1000 bills contains $1 million. A 24-mile pile of 4-inch stacks of $1 million bills would equal $400 billion. (That can be imagined by considering the distance of a city or town that is about 24 miles from you.) At least $1000 million is spent every day to maintain the armed forces in the world. Brick-thick vertical stacks of that number of $1000 bills would reach as high as a 32 story building. That has been estimated to be the size of a stack of money big enough to pay for the elimination of the world diseases of malaria, leprosy, trachoma, and a contagious tropical skin disease called yaws. However, it would take only slightly more than a day of defense money to eliminate global economic apartheid, unemployment, and poor housing. (The income ratio of the top and bottom 10% of world nations is 40:1.)

The US governmental budget for national defense is the second largest amount spent on its services to citizens. (Income security is first.) It is over 15 times greater than the amount spent for international affairs (Encyclopedia Britannica Book of Year 1980, Federal Administrative Budget, p. 714). The Executive Office of the President estimated $154 billion would be spent for national defense in 1981, or $39 billion more than was spent in 1979 (Information Please Almanac, 1980, p. 65). The increased hawkish mood of the US Senate, due, to the USSR military forces' invasion into Afghanistan and the long retention of the US Embassy hostages in Iran, may result in an additional $4 billion. Also, it is predicted that the budget for international affairs may be decreased. (The International Institute for Strategic Studies, London, has projected that the United States will allocate $225 billion for defense in 1985.) The percentages of gross national product (GNP) spent on defense in the United States in recent years have varied from 5 to 6%. The average GNP spent on defense among nations in the National Treaties Organization (NATO) was abouth 3.5% and for Canada less than 2% (Brit. Book of Year 1978, p. 285).

Armament both reflects and stimulates international tensions. Also, economic deprivation leads to domestic strain, which leads to national violence and the resultant use of armed might. In 1979 at least $20 million was traded among nations. About one half of that amount was traded to Third World nations. Their importations over each previous year have increased approximately 25% (Arms Control and Disarmament, p. 50). In a study of 14 nations, military power was found to be associated with national wars, especially between nations with nearly equal strength (Alcock et al., 1978, pp. 118–128). In the history of modern wars, armament has consistently led to armed aggresssion. Military aid tends not only to reflect social and economic tensions but to promote wars. Those countries receiving armaments become better able to fight against hereditary and neighboring enemies. Balancing armaments among the superpowers of the world may keep the peace for a limited time. Constant effort to equalize the power between superpowers (United States and USSR) has a built-in escalation factor as in a foot race in which each runner is motivated to improve his time or distance in relation to that of the opponent. Disarmament is therefore considered to be a prime means of deterring nuclear and conventional weapon wars (Arms Control and Disarmament, 1980, pp. 52–61).

It seems no easier to comprehend the amount of money spent by humans, through their governments, to defend themselves from aggression by preparing for it than it does to understand what the results of war do to human existence. What does seem clear is that war is a social "disease" that threatens the welfare, and possibly the existence of humanity and of the biosphere, and may make it necessary to "start all over again" (Alcock, 1972, p. 4). People and their social, economic, and political values and systems infect and reinfect societies with aggressive war germs. However, people also have the abilities needed to prescribe remedies and to effect cures of the war disease so that a state of health, called peace, may develop.

Assumption Two. Peace Plans Are Available

There are innovative rational plans for world peace that offer alternative choices for the redirection of societies from the disease of war, civil disorders, and starvation. Those plans encompass global changes in international relationships that are expected to have rehabilitative results. The plans include solutions by which peoples of all nations would compromise. Those that could afford to do so would lose minimally so that those in need would gain maximally. An increasing number of solutions can be found in international peace research journals and books on the subject (see Selected Readings at the close of this prologue for some references). The causes of war have been shown to include military power and alliances, territorial disputes, and conflicting political views. Projected peaceful treatments include worldwide disarmament and economic and political justice.

In 1979 the UN Special Session on Disarmament adopted (by consensus among the representatives of 149 nations) principles for international disarmament strategy (Alcock, 1978, pp. 135–137). The recommendations included balanced and gradual reduction in nuclear and conventional armaments and spending the sums of money saved thereby for the promotion of well-being of all peoples and for an international peace force. It was also noted that progress in disarmament can be made only if it is mobilized by the full support of public opinion (Alcock, 1978, pp. 135–136). (During that conference, US and USSR prestigious leaders were absent. The US delegate was attending a NATO conference where there was an agreement to a 3% increase in armaments.)

The Canadian Peace Research Institute (CPRI) had previously implemented the principles in that UN recommendation in a comprehensive integrative plan. Members of CPRI had been studying the causes of war and requirements for peace since 1961. In 1978 that Institute published a plan for peace intended for the benefit of citizens, leaders, national officers, and the UN (Alcock et al., 1978). The plan was based upon the results of 16 years of systems analysis research among factors that were found to cause wars and of means to deemphasize them. It offers specifications for disarmament and foreign aid and a means of monitoring and enforcing agreements. It is anticipated that the results would bring about greater civil and individual justice and equality and would thereby reduce the occurrence of wars. Tanberger, 1969 Nobel Prize winner in economic science for work in econometrics, stated that the rigors of the methods used to formulate the plan were worthy of extension in the current programs at the International Institute of Applied Systems Analysis, Austria, and worthy as a recommendation for action during the Special UN Disarmament Meeting of the General Assembly, 1982 (Alcock et al., 1978, pp. xi–xii).

The CPRI plan provides first for disarmament (Alcock et al., 1978, pp. 110–140). The United States and other First World nations would disarm steadily beginning in 1982 at a balanced rate of 10% per year until the year 2001, when the world expenditures for arms would be one eighth of the projected 1982 expenditure. The money saved by each nation would be invested in its own economy as desired. In the United States the amount saved would be about 1% of its gross national product. That also could help to counteract the worldwide recession that began in 1973. This overall armament plan would cause hardship to no nation. Although disarmament would not decrease the economic domination of First World nations, the military-industrial complex would contribute less to the total economy. Also, because of disarmament, national border disputes might not decrease, but the following parts of this plan would help to control that. If arms expenditures were decreased in each nation by a consistent 10% annually, then by the year 2001 the nations would be spending only one-eighth as much for military budgets as they did in 1982. "Nations today are like armed knights of old caught in a swelling river: all they needed to do was to slip out of their armor and they could steadily have swum to shore. It was up to the people on shore to shout out encouragement and directions" (Alcock et al., 1978, p. 139).

Second, the CPRI plan calls for a positive program of economic aid from the 12 largest rich nations to 24 of the largest poor nations (Alcock et al., 1978, pp. 64–73). Improvement in the economy of the Third World is necessary if there is to be domestic peace in that world. Such foreign aid includes providing for job-producing industries. The benefits would probably have positive effects in helping civil wars to decrease. The financial aid would be automatically distributed on the basis of need. A new UN agency would be created to conduct the plan for the multi-lateral aid and to give assistance as requested through advisors. It is predicted that life expectancy in the Third World would increase 1 year for each 7.5% increase in GNP per national capita (which is the "economic law of life"). Success of this plan would be proof of increase in life expectancy and would thereby insure that the aid was going to the people. Rising living standards would reduce the rate of increase of populations in poor countries by the year 2000. As disarmament continues until the year 2001, economic aid could then be increased to a greater degree.

Third, a UN active peace-keeping agency would be created with full operational autonomy (Alcock et al., 1978, pp. 150–160). Its purpose would be to supervise agreements among member states and to interpose itself when potential or actual conflicts would arise between member states. Its decisions would be implemented by a peace-keeping force with permanent regional military forces in the world. It would be sent automatically to areas where treaty agreements were in dispute or violation. The UN active peace-keeping agency would probably need a budget of $500 to $600 million, or less than 1/800 of the 1979 world armament budget of $410 billion.

It is possible that the world of nations, such as those in the UN, will adopt and put into operation an agreed-upon plan to promote world peace. (Leadership by the United States would be needed in such an endeavor.) However, the probability of an international plan for peace seems very remote, even if a majority of people want it. While no nation admits that it wants to initiate or engage in a nuclear or conventional war, each seems willing to strengthen its defenses in case other nations might be provoked to attack it. It has been estimated that about $17 billion is the amount spent by the world on armaments every 2 weeks. This is equal to the amount of money required to provide basic food, water, education, housing, and health for everyone in the world (News Report, 1980, p. 5).

It becomes obvious that there are emotional and traditional limits to the use of reason. All people have a vested interest in wanting to live in a world of peace, and yet their governments participate in arms races as a means of buying national security. Somehow, policy makers need to be held accountable not only for military expenditures and trades in arms but for the drift toward war inherent within those policies.

Assumption Three. Societies Have Changed and Will Change

Change is as inherent in societies as it is in the biology of the human beings of which societies are composed. It occurs continuously in social, economic, and political systems and organizations. Not only are humans affected by their cultural environments, but they are also gradually changing them. Changes in each system affect the other, and all are influenced by other cultures in the world. People modify their beliefs and behaviors in response to innovative ideas and technologies they think can benefit them. Choices among alternative inventions lead to preferences that then become consolidated. These preferences are disseminated through individual and group intercommunications and cooperative work. When these preferences are of a political nature they may become part of a legal system of codes and laws. Dominant behaviors gradually emerge, which are gradually adopted by part or all in a given society, and then spread to other cultures (Spicer, 1975).

It is interesting to trace the progress made in the social and political modifications that have influenced improvements in "the rights of man." For example, slavery was an accepted social practice that contributed enormously to the development of colonialism in the Western world for about 300 years (Slavery, Serfdom, etc. 1975, pp. 862–864). At least 15 million people were shipped from Africa as slaves before 1800. The antislavery movement began because of realization of the fact that slavery violated people's human rights and therefore was an inhumane social institution. The slavery abolition movement began in 1671 among Quakers in the British American Colony. All of the states north of Maryland abolished slavery between 1777 and 1804. After a terrible civil war, slaves were emancipated in 1863, and the freeing of all slaves followed in 1865. Slavery as a social institution in the Western world was largely over by 1888. However, forced labor and child labor remain as forms of slavery in Asia and Africa to this day. Forced labor is a means of political coercion and a punishment for political views opposed to the systems where it is used. In 1977 over 50 million children were active in the labor forces of Asia, Africa, and Latin America (Human Rights Report, 1979/80, p. 1).

Since ancient times the need for social innovations in human rights was first expressed by philosophers, poets, and politicians. The first legal codes during the Middle Ages protected nobles and barons from the repression of kings (Schwelb, E., 1975, pp. 1183–1184). In 1215 the English Magna Carta asserted rights for free men as well as for feudal barons. The rights included freedom from imprisonment, exile, and death unless an individual was condemned by law and the judgment of peers. Political bills of human rights were adopted in the eighteenth century in England, France, and the United States. In the nineteenth and twentieth centuries, peoples in all of Europe, the Americas, Africa, and Asia lived under government constitutions that protected political and civil rights. The USSR added economic and social rights to its constitution in 1918. In 1948 the Universal Declaration of Human Rights was made by the UN, and since then it has monitored the evidence of progress and violations among its constituent nations and has held frequent conferences. By 1980, 61 nations had agreed to the International Covenant on Economic, Social and Civil Rights of Citizens, and 59 nations had ratified the International Covenant on Civil and Political Rights.

In the United States the 1964 congressional Civil Rights Act was a landmark decision for progress in equal rights of minority groups and women. It prohibited discrimination against anyone on the basis of sex, race, color, or national origin. By that time liberating movements for women had included voting rights (1920), "freedom" from the kitchen because of technical innovations, the rise of a single-sex code of conduct, and the holding of jobs. In June, 1963, the Equal Pay Act signed into law equal pay for women in any company under the Fair Labor Standards Act, and that has served since as the basis for equal treatment in employment. In 1972 the Educational Amendment Act forbade sex discrimination in educational programs in schools assisted by federal funds. Physical educators and coaches are now all well aware of Title IX, which demands equal treatment in athletics for girls and women with that for boys and men. It went into effect in July, 1978, after at least a 2-year warning period, but it is yet to be completely implemented and interpreted in 1981. The Equal Rights Amendment for Women may or may not be enacted in 1982. That amendment was first proposed in 1923, soon after voting rights were enacted (Sochen, J., 1980, pp. 485–486). All legal acts that followed the Civil Rights Act have been and continue to be challenged by individual and class action suits, but at least the legal standards have been established by which judgments in specific cases can be assessed, thereby interpreting and clarifying the intent of the laws.

Significant social changes are made slowly and painfully. Progress is never a straight-line affair. Although national and international wars have caused major societal, economic, and political changes and reforms, it has usually been during periods of peace between wars that citizens and their political leaders have made changes to improve social conditions for the benefit of humanity. It is during those times that the underdeveloped nations can consolidate efforts to improve the probabilities of survival, economic improvements, the growth of food production and its distribution, and the improvement in the number of jobs and the status of health. Further, it is during peace that the already developed nations work to increase jobs, productivity, welfare among those needing it, and the political freedom to speak out, hold meetings, and organize opposition strategy. It is during peace that global problems are faced concerning population control, materials and forms of energy, distribution of resources, pollution control, and public health. Since a relatively peaceful period is expected to exist until 1989, now is the time to help solve many of these societal problems as a means of improving human conditions and thereby helping to promote lasting peace.

Assumption Four. Peace Depends on Attitudes and Ideologies That Support it

It is increasingly evident that we do not lack the knowledge and reasoning power necessary to make lasting peace a reality. What is missing is the desire to put knowledge and reality into action. People and their political leaders, especially those in the First World nations, must truly want to have peace if it is to happen. A desire for the necessary changes depends upon the extent to which we hold values, attitudes, and ideologies that will promote the desire.

Cantril (1965) found that peace was a desired goal among nations, and Rokeach (1973) discovered that a world at peace and freedom and equality ranked high as values among American white and black youth (11–17 years) and adults (30–72 years). However, a world at peace ranked in the middle range among US and Canadian male college students, while freedom and happiness were in high priority. The qualities of affection and tenderness were greatly valued among all groups and rated highest among the US male college students. Those students were also relatively more supportive of being ambitious, leading a comfortable life, and having social recognition than the Canadian male students. Alcock concluded from the above and other studies that happiness and a world at peace are highly desired and that honesty and courage are the characteristics related to their attainment (1976, p. 41).

As a pioneer in the science of human values, Eckhardt has reported results from measurements of attitudes and ideologies that he and associates have analyzed (1972). His early analyses were based on a 96-item questionnaire that was statistically analyzed to be as value-prophetic-free as possible. The results of repeated analyses made it possible to reduce the 96 items to 12 eight-item scales. Six were related to personality traits, and six measured social attitudes (Eckhardt, 1971). The dominant factors were named compassion (loving, merciful drives) and compulsion (cruel, merciless drives). The subjects used were 104 US and Canadian adults. Table 1 gives a synopsis of comparative compassionate and compulsive personality traits and social attitudes that Eckhardt found (Alcock, 1976, p. 27). The words in parentheses give the comparative Rokeach attitude scale terms (Alcock, 1976, p. 38).

The findings in Table 1 join compassionate personality and social attitudes as follows: independence and internationalism; responsibility and golden-rule religion; self-control and participation; self-confidence and pacifism; faith in people and social consciousness. The opposite compulsive personal and social attitudes are: conformity and nationalism; irresponsibility and authoritarian religion; impulsivity and bureaucraticism; neuroticism and militarism; distrust of people and conventional morality. Some of these matches may seem surprising but probably do not strike you as illogical. It is interesting to pursue the concept of pacifism as a compassionate attitude and militarism as a compulsive attitude, beginning with their emotional foundations.

Love is the basic emotional ingredient of compassion, and hate is the feeling basic to compulsion. Table 2 presents a composite of Alcock's (1976) two-dimensional conceptual love and hate models, based upon the behavioral science (psychology, sociology) value research done by Eckhardt and his associates, and the broad analytical social science (economics, history, political science) research work done by Alcock (1976).

Love is defined as sentiments that help oneself and others, and hate is defined as feelings that harm oneself and others. Loving behavior generates equality and freedom, whereas hateful behavior generates inequality and coercion. In terms of political ideologies, loving attitudes favor socialism (equality), democracy (freedom), and world federation. Hateful attitudes give support to economic and political inequality, militarism (coercion), and world imperialism. The sexual model of love generates sexual equality and freedom, whereas hate generates sexual restraints and inequality (chau-

Table 1
Comparative Compassionate and Compulsive Personality Social Attitudes

Compassion		Compulsion	
Personality	Social Attitudes	Personality	Social Attitudes
Independence	Internationalism	Conformity (Obedience)	Nationalism (National security)
Responsibility	Golden-rule, religion (Altruism)	Irresponsibility	Authoritarian religion (Salvation)
Self-control (Inner harmony)	Participation (Courage)	Impulsivity (Exciting life)	Bureaucraticism
Self-confidence (Sense of accomplishment and happiness)	Pacifism (World at peace)	Neuroticism	Militarism
Faith in people (Honesty)	Social consciousness	Distrust of people	Conventional morality (A comfortable life)

Data from Alcock, 1976.

Table 2
Compassion-Compulsion Models

Model	Love (Compassion)	Hate (Compulsion)
Basic	Behavior that helps oneself and others	Behavior that hurts oneself and others
Operational	Equality and freedom	Coercion and inequality
World	World federation: Socialism (Equality) Democracy (Freedom)	World imperialism: Economic and political inequality Militarism (Coercion)
Sexual	Liberation (Sexual equality) Permissiveness (Sexual freedom)	Puritanism (Sexual restraints) Chauvinism (Sexual inequality)
Transcendental	Love for one another and oneself (Contemplation) Behavior that helps	Alienation from others and oneself

Data from Alcock, 1976

vinism). The transcendental model of love is that of contemplative behavior that helps others and oneself, whereas hateful behavior alienates one from others and self.

It has been said that whom the gods would destroy, they first make mad. There seems to be enough evidence now to state that whom the gods would save they would first make loving. "Maddening" personal attributes (intrinsic qualities and characteristics) have been found to include egoism, hostility, conservatism, acquisitiveness, distrust, authoritarianism, authoritative religiosity, militarism, and nationalism. Associated behaviors include striking back at others physically and verbally and fighting and taking revengeful punitive action as a means of controlling people when in conflict with them. All of those attributes are associated with dogma and fear. "Loving" attributes include confidence, trust, tolerance, empathy, permissiveness, altruism, radicalism, and internationalism. The loving means of influencing people is by reasoning and persuasiveness. Those attributes are associated with imagination, curiosity, and creativity (Alcock, 1971, p. 144).

Research studies have identified (by means of analytical research) ideologies that are clusters of social attitudes and their configurations in political forms of government. Such ideologies include fascism, ultraconservatism, conservatism, liberalism, communism, welfarism, and democratic socialism (Eckhardt, 1972, pp. 76–78). A political model of compassionate ideologies includes democratic socialism, socialism (equality), and democracy (freedom). A political model of compulsive attitudes includes autocracy (coercion), fascism (autocratic capitalism), and capitalism (inequality). A mixture of compassionate and compulsive ideologies was found in communism (autocratic socialism) and conservatism (democratic capitalism) (Alcock, 1976, p. 54). A world order form of compassionate ideologies would include either socialism (equality) or world democracy (freedom). Compulsive forms of world government would be either military imperialism (coercion) or economic and political imperialism (inequality) (Alcock, 1976, p. 78). It probably would require a new form of government to meld socialism and democracy (equality and freedom).

Each of us is undoubtedly characterized by desires, attitudes, and ideologies that range from loving-compassionate to hating-compulsive. We all tend to use a blend of approaches to social problems from an "open to closed" mind (Rokeach, 1960), differing levels of "consciousness" (Reich, 1970), and "radical to conservative" views (Hampden-Turner, 1970).

Those among us who want to promote peace apparently need to confront and correct imbalances and inconsistencies in our compassionate attitudes and behaviors. We would need to promote conditions to minimize war by the nonviolent means of knowing the conditions for peace, and taking stands on them through petitions, demonstrations, and supporting legislation on disarmament and economic and political justice. We would also need to commit ourselves to the related problems of reducing populations, improving the welfare of the poor and oppressed, and improving our ecology. Increased people-power is needed to pressure political leaders to take national and foreign actions in support of enduring peace.

Assumption Five. General Education for Peace

Public schools and universities in the United States make it a point to provide "value-free" education by means of courses in the substantive content of sciences, humanities, arts, and learning tools. The content and accompanying teaching methods are presumably not employed for the purpose of promoting social or political ideologies—at least not those differing from the values held by the majority of those in authority in the community. However, values and purposes are somehow built into the phenomena that are already in existence waiting to be discovered. Value-free science tries to abstract from the universe what is there—as if scientists had no interest in the world. Seekers of knowledge want to discover, but nevertheless their minds shape their discoveries. Research and scholarly work are personally motivated by guiding principles (Bronowski, 1973, pp. 115, 436–437). Nevertheless there continues to be general belief that there is such a thing as value-free knowledge that is accumulated just because the phenomena (objects or events known through the senses) are there and without relation to the purpose it may serve or to any of its physical, biological, social, and artistic uses—and abuses. We act in relation to such knowledge as if that were so. Value-free knowledge is an accumulation of facts that are independent of their effect upon material and resource scarcities and the continuance of life or the biosphere itself. Narrow specializations hold the key to the accumulation of such knowledge. The whole is the sum of specializations. Subjective values are to remain outside of knowledgeable facts.

Value-prone knowledge is accumulated in relation to purposes and physical, biological, social, and artistic uses—and abuses. It is an accumulation of facts and truths closely associated with a growing scarcity of materials and resources, the good life for humanity, and the preservation of the biosphere. Narrow specializations are interrelated, interdependent, and cross-related for the benefit of answering key questions. The whole is greater than the sum of its parts. Value-prone knowledge is the source, method, and authority for personal aspirations and fulfillment.

Education for peace can be as indirect or as subtle as propaganda for war. Knowledge in history, geography, economics, and political science is applicable to war and peace, depending upon the emphasis placed upon the knowledge in each.

Dewey was an early educational philosopher who gave a great deal of thought and energy to the study and promotion of peace, particularly after World War I, which did not serve to free the world for democracy and proved not to be the war to end all wars (1922). (Dewey was undoubtedly less successful in his goal to educate children for global citizenship than he was in the promotion of child-centered learning.) He thought that what was learned in geography could be applied to the study of social and political problems, and that learning geography should include the cultures of all people and develop a world outlook on social problems. Dewey believed that the social meaning of US, Canadian, and world history should be taught and that current national problems in society should be related to the past successes and failures in economic, social, and political problems (1923). History could reveal that certain customs, politics, and economics generated wars. Dewey thought that the teaching of US history left the impression that its military, economic, and political actions were so successful that wars were the inevitable means of solving national and international problems and that the democratic-federation form of government in the United States should be copied by other nations. (Is this the practice today?) His view was that this tended to build international intolerance among students (1940, pp. 112–120, 228).

Many traditional school and university subjects include knowledge that describes, analyzes, and synthesizes content that helps to formulate a worldwide view of cultures, including their values and resultant institutions. Such knowledge is in economics, political science, sociology, psychology, literature, and philosophy. Then there are courses structured to transmit worldwide views: world history, world religion, world public health, future studies, comparative education, and comparative sport and physical education. Other courses are specifically geared to global cultural understanding that is closely associated with potential for peace education and compassionate attitudes. These include social studies or contemporary studies and programs in international student exchanges and travels. Leppert and Payette created sequential social studies courses for intermediate and high school grades to encompass knowledge and understanding of "cultural universals and the relationship within and among the social, economic, political and ethical systems of a culture, and the processes by which cultures persist and change through time"(1970, pp. 38–39). The overall concept is that man makes a culture and culture makes a man and that people are in the center of their social, economic, and political systems—each of which has values and institutions from the past moving through the present to the future—and that all is influenced by the natural physical environment in which the culture exists. Changes in that environment and invention-technological developments cut through the systems as do the values of societies and cultural changes. *Global Insights: People and Cultures* includes the varying cultures in China, India, Latin America, the Middle East, Soviet Union, and sub-Sahara Africa (Leppert and Johnson, 1980). Most significantly, social studies courses can include the development of skills basic to lifelong decisions whereby inferences and hypotheses are tested, and generalizations can be formulated and revised as new information is available. Human values can be judged, and plans of action and their probable sequences can be evaluated. Group experiences include sharing ideas and feelings with others, being considerate of the attitudes and viewpoints held by others, and being willing to compromise and arrive at consensus conclusions.

The concepts in any peace education program include national underdevelopment vs. development; social justice vs. injustice; dependence vs. self-reliance; alternate life styles; liberation vs. opposition; global internationalism; alternative futures; participation and action; social consciousness; and structural violence (violence built into social systems). The areas of study necessary for the formulation of the goal of peace include world population; world wealth vs. poverty; world resources; world food; and urban problems. A study on contemporary global issues contained in United Kingdom teacher training courses ranked those areas high in terms of their appearances in course syllabuses (Hicks, 1978).

It seems clear that international education subject matter content, no matter in what structured form within courses, is a dimension within education that includes a global perspective on world cultures. This tends to promote a global-citizenship perspective on social problems. That, in turn, opens minds to the consideration of nontraditional means of solving world conflict problems. Also, values and attitudes may develop in keeping with social consciousness.

Assumption Six. Sport and Physical Education Provides Experiences Basic to Peace

It is important to define SPE, its meanings, purpose, and body of knowledge before consideration of its potentials for the development of compassionate fitness and tentative principles to attain that fitness.

Definition of SPE, Its Meanings, Purpose, and Body of Knowledge. The word *sport* in the title SPE denotes indoor and outdoor pastimes and games. The words *physical education* indicate that physical activity develops the learner. The common denominator in sport and physical education is movement activities. What may not be understood from the combined terms is that the motor activities must be performed to develop skillful or artistic executions and also to develop the performer. Therefore, to me, developmental motor performance (DMP) seems a better descriptive title for this educational field (Huelster, 1973, p. 28). Sports are one form of motor activity used in DMP as are exercise and dance. The purposes of DMP are to develop the latent motor potentials of students; to adapt and control motor skills in physical space, time, and force; and to perform skillfully in relation to and with others (Jewett and Mullan, pp. 4–5).

The inherent meaning in SPE (or DMP) is the sensory-motor pleasurable awareness of controlled movements in relation to the natural environment of space, time, and force outside of the human body. Significance is contained in the individual's idea-feeling interactions during motor activity (Metheny, 1965, pp. 98–107). Movement and emotions are interrelated and can bring exhilaration. Motor activities that are satisfying can be identified from conscious awareness of interactions within the central nervous system. The neurons and nerve pathways of neuromuscular servo and voluntary chemical impulses are those that are initiated by nonverbal ideation and spatial patterning in the right cerebral cortex. The impulses are coordinated in the cerebellum (center for muscular coordination and balance and the only part of the brain in which the cells multiply after birth) and are given emotional overtones from neural connections with the pleasurable centers in the "old" limbic brain around the brain stem. Muscles contract and stimulate afferent neurons in the sensory area of the brain to produce conscious awareness (Restak, 1979, pp. 176–177, 122–127). This awareness can then be interpreted into verbal meanings. Bronowski noted that "the most powerful drive in the ascent of man is his pleasure in his own skill. He loves to do what he does well, having done it well, he loves to do it better" (1973, p. 116).

SPE performance is a holistic experience for the learner-performer. Fortunately we now know what physical educators and performers long believed: it is impossible to separate bodily movements from psychic and social interactions. That is why there are so many different meanings to be found as the result of performance-learning experiences. Kenyon found that adolescents in Canada, United States, England, and Australia had positive attitudes toward physical education—that is, social intercourse experience, health and fitness, aesthetic experience, catharsis (release of frustrations and tensions), and, to a lesser extent, pursuit of vertigo (risk and thrills) and ascetic experiences (stiff training and competitive demands that require deferment of other personal desires) (1970, pp. 138–155).

Jewett reported that LaPlant and Chapman identified 20 different meanings that performers attached to motor activities and suggested that those values clustered around the qualities of self-actualization (awareness of self in relation to one's potentials) and fitness and performance itself (1977, p. 10). (What meanings do you find in the performance of motor activities?)

It is inevitable that people with inquiring minds have been and are concerned with logical thought in relation to SPE experiences. Many have been stimulated to study because of satisfying and beneficial experiences they have had in SPE that they wanted to identify and explain. The scope of that explanation must be broad to cover holistic motor experiences, e.g., descriptions and bodily analyses of selected motor activities and related bodily, mental, psychological, and sociological involvements and developments. In recent history the body of knowledge resulting from research and scholarly work in SPE has been parceled out as if there were subdisciplines in certain fundamental fields of learning that are independent specializations in SPE. There tends as yet to be little cross-subdisciplinary knowledge. Furthermore, the independent subdisciplines are named to emphasize the fundamental fields of learning that are and can be applied to SPE. This is the scheme used in the *Research Quarterly for Exercise and Sport* (RQES) (March, 1980), published by the American Alliance for Health, Physical Education, Recreation and Dance. Eight of the 14 terms included are biomechanics; history and philosophy; motor learning; neurophysiology; physiology of exercise: strength and endurance; physiology of exercise: cardiovascular endurance; sociology of sport; and psychology of sport. The other six terms included are health; recreation; growth and development; teacher preparation/curriculum and instruction; measurement and research design; and multidisciplinary. It seems reasonable to believe that some control of present fragmentation of knowledge might occur if the subdisciplinary aspects of SPE were named as they are in this textbook. The eight segments used herein allow for inclusion and expansion within the field and for application in value-prone professional knowledge.

Table 3 presents in parallel form the nomenclature of academic segments used in this text and in the RQES.

It seems evident from study of Table 3 that researchers and scholars have a better opportunity to develop generalizations within and among the eight segments of knowledge in SPE through the use of this text's classifications of knowledge than if they use the 14 separated divisions in RQES. It makes it possible to increase a meaningful body of knowledge in SPE rather than to increase knowledge in the fundamental fields of learning that are applied to SPE, i.e., history, philosophy, physiology, psychology, sociology, learning, education, and research design. You are fortunate to be introduced to the field of SPE through the scholarly and professional

Table 3
Segments of Disciplinary and Professional Knowledge in SPE:
Those in This Text Compared to Those in RQES

Segments in This Text (8)	Segments in RQES (14)
1. Background, meaning, and significance: history, philosophy: international aspect	1. History and Philosophy
2. Functional Effects of Physical Activity: exercise physiology, anthropometry and body composition, fitness and health appraisal	2. Physiology of Exercise: Strength and Endurance 3. Physiology of Exercise: Cardiovascular Endurance 4. Health
3. Sociocultural and Behavioral Aspects: sociology, psychology, anthropology, political science, economics, geography	5. Psychology of Sport 6. Sociology of Sport
4. Motor Learning and Development: psychomotor learning; physical growth and motor development	7. Motor Learning 8. Growth and Development
5. Mechanical and Muscular Analysis of Motor Skills: neuroskeletal musculature; biomechanics	9. Biomechanics 10. Neurophysiology
6. Management Theory and Practice: status of administrative theory, application of theory to practice in planning, organizing, staffing, directing and controlling	(omitted)
7. Program Development (Theory and Practice): general education at various levels, curriculum and instruction, programs for exceptional students, professional preparation, intramural sports and physical recreation, intercollegiate athletics, practice of motor performance in sport, dance and exercise	11. Teacher Preparation/Curriculum and Instruction 12. Recreation
8. Evaluation and Measurement: application of evaluation and measurement theory to tools and techniques for assessment of effectiveness of professional and scholarly dimensions of SPE	13. Measurement and Research Design 14. Multidisciplinary

dimensions as organized in this text and developed by the fine academicians who wrote its content.

Compassionate Fitness. The characteristics of compassionate fitness and the parallel compulsive characteristics are summarized in Table 4. They include and add to the compassionate attitudes and ideologies presented in Tables 1 and 2. Compassionate fitness is characterized by (1) the personal affective attitudes of self-competence (leading to empathy), self-acceptance (leading to altruism), and self-control (inner directedness); (2) the social attitudes of faith in people, independence, participation, responsibility, and cooperation; (3) the cognitive patterning of introversion, complexity-creativity, and flexibility; (4) the moral positions of humanitarianism, universality, altruism, and consistency; and (5) the political ideology of justice and equal rights, freedom and equality, pacifism, desegregation, and internationalism. The contrasting compulsive fitness characteristics are listed in the right-hand column in Table 4.

It is important to differentiate between the compassionate and compulsive political ideologies of freedom with equality and freedom without equality and justice based upon equal rights and justice limited to authoritarian rights.

The concept of freedom includes the choice of desired actions that are independent

Table 4
Opposing Characteristics of Compassion and Compulsion

Compassion	Compulsion
Affective Attitudes:	
Self-confidence (leading to empathy)	Egoism (leading to self-centeredness)
Self-acceptance (leading to altruism)	Low self-esteem (leading to self-interests)
Self-control (inner directed-ness)	Aggression (combativeness)
Social Attitudes:	
Faith in people (trustful)	Misanthropy (distrustful)
Independence	Dependence
Participation	Withdrawal
Responsibility	Irresponsibility
Cooperation	Competition
Cognitive Styles:	
Introversion	Egocentricity
Complexity-creativity	Simplism
Flexibility	Rigidity
Morality:	
Humanitarianism	Hatred
Universality	Conformity
Altruism	Dogmatism
Consistency	Inconsistency
Political Ideology:	
Justice based on equal rights	Justice limited to authoritarian rights
Freedom with equality	Freedom without equality
Pacifism	Militarism
Desegregation	Segregation
Internationalism	Nationalism

Data from Eckhardt, 1972

of restrictions, controls, and coercions. Personal freedom may or may not include the concept of freedom for others (Zeigler, 1979, pp. 158–160). (In a strict sense, freedom includes the freedom not to be free if one so desires.) The compassionate ideal of freedom couples it with equality: "All men are created equal." Therefore freedom is desired for those who do not have it as well as for oneself. This includes freedom from social, economic, and political oppressions and freedom for self-goals in an ordered society. This is a difficult ideal to attain, of course. It has greater potential for achievement in times of peace than in war, especially in democratic and socialistic forms of government. The compulsive idea of freedom includes equality among those in favored groups, e.g., the educated elite, the rich, the authoritative, the white race (especially white males). Therefore, among those with compulsive personal and social attitudes, cognitive styles, and political ideologies, freedom is in opposition to equality for all.

The concept of justice is also different among compassionate and compulsive people. Social and legal rewards and punishments relate to the rights of people in an ordered society. Within compassion, those rights are considered to be inalienable and just for all people equally. Social rewards and legal punishments should be given to all deserving and guilty people alike. Among those who have compulsive tendencies, justice is also an inalienable right. However, social rewards may be limited to "privileged groups" divided according to race, color, and creed and limited to one sex. Also, punitive legal decisions are particularly applicable to those outside of the "social establishment" and system of mores. It is believed that they should be minimized among those who have privileged status.

The contrast between the attitudes of self-control and aggression and between cooperation and competition also needs explanation. The tendency toward aggression and competition is undoubtedly in us all. Characteristic conduct associated with those attitudes is nearer the surface in some of us than it is in others—especially those with little self-control and confidence or limited desire to cooperate. It is unimportant to argue whether aggression is an innate biological urge (Ardrey, 1961, pp. 346–354) or a culturally derived urge (Leakey and Lewin, 1978, pp. 278–282). When individuals or groups want to attain the same goals in our material-technological society, it can be expected that competition and fighting back will occur. Yet the urge to be aggressive and competitive is no more generated from our genes or culture than is the compelling force to cooperate. That was the practice among gatherer-hunters over half a million years ago as they exploited resources for communal survival (Leakey and Lewin, 1978, pp. 120–121). In times of war and peace, humans depend upon each other for survival and social satisfaction. Cooperative interactions and reciprocal altruism (no one gains an unfair advantage) are the ingredients of ordered societies and the desire to conform to social values, institutions, and systems. They also are the means of effecting needed changes in cultures.

Compassionate fitness is the state of competence to love oneself and others, to help others and oneself, and to cooperate with others in the promotion of freedom, equality, and justice as elements of enduring peace.

Compassionate Fitness Potentials in SPE. Included in assumption 6 is the supposition that there is rich potential in SPE for the development of the characteristics of compassionate fitness. The supposition is based more upon the results of philosophical reasoning than upon generalizations from research findings on or closely related to this topic. Personal and social attributes of athletes, physical educators and coaches, and professional students have been studied, but usually not within a structured theory of developmental motor performance. For example, Sage stated that, from studies on physical educators/coaches, "available literature is inconclusive as to whether there are unique and consistent personal attributes among the members of this professional occupation. . . . The controversy over physical educators/coaches personal attributes remains. There is little doubt that this is a complex topic" (1980, p. 119). Furthermore, studies on sport have focused on it as a phenomenon to be investigated in relation to sociological theories. Loy stated that researchers on sociological attitudes and values have used descriptive means of research within special social settings, and therefore their findings do not add to the generalized understanding of the "sport phenomenon" (1980, p. 104).

Both compassionate and compulsive behaviors are components of SPE motor performance. A mixture of responses can be expected from individuals and groups of students and professional workers (Table 4). The compulsive-compassionate overt behaviors that probably are most noticeable are those ranging from participation to withdrawal, responsibility to irresponsibility, independence to dependence, and competition to cooperation. The behaviors that teachers and coaches express may be most noticeable in the compulsive-compassionate continuum from desegregation to segregation, loving to hating, justice for all to injustice for at least a few special groups. All who are actively involved may range in their behaviors from trust to distrust, love to hate, altruism to domination, and reasoning persuasion to punitive coercion. A mixture can also be expected in the cognitive, moral, and political qualities listed in Table 4 (e.g., from mind-sets that are rigid and simplistic to flexible and creative, and from nationalistic viewpoints to international ones). The common affective compassionate attitudes that may or may not be apparent in the overt behavior of SPE students, teachers, and coaches are those of self-confidence, control, and acceptance as compared to egoism, low self-esteem, and hostile feelings as compulsive attitudes.

Aggression and competition are classified as compulsive social attitudes, whereas cooperation is associated with compassionate social attitudes. Behavior associated with both of those types of attitudes can be expected among players of sports as they adjust to the restrictions placed upon them. The structure of each familiar individual, dual, and team sport is one demanding conformity. Players must accommodate themselves to a specified playing space; specified sport equipment; performance of motor skills needed to move the object of contention in the specified boundaries; and rules regulating the movements of the object in that space and of players in relation to teammates and opponents. Scoring methods determine the players who win. Team and dual sports provide for competitive and cooperative behavior associated with compulsion and compassion.

Metheny stated that "the concept of 'the good strife' is implicit in the word *competition,* as derived from *cum* and *petere*—literally *to strive with* rather than *against.* The word *contest* has similar implications, being derived from *con* and *testare*—*to testify with another* rather than *against* him" (1965, pp. 41–42). The concept of good sportsmanship represents the code governing good strife in which both winners and losers gain from testing themselves within the rules by doing their best against opponents who also did their best (p. 156). The term *good sportsmanship* includes the concept of neither side taking unfair advantage of the other while playing as well as possible.

Good strife remains the ideal. However, the competitive capitalistic culture in which we live seems to accept "bad strife" and winning without performing as well as possible. During all-out competitive efforts to win, acts may be performed that take unfair advantages of opponents. Violations of the rules governing the sports may be "hidden" from (or not seen by) referees, umpires, and judges. Bad-strife behavior tends to trigger retaliatory reprisals and acts of aggression. Such behavior may also be motivated merely by the very existence of the concepts 'win at any cost' and 'winning is the only thing.'

Highly competitive intercollegiate athletics can be justified inside the realm of SPE if education is the ultimate goal (Zeigler, 1979, p. 134). This may be the purpose of intercollegiate competition in Canada, but it is much less so in the United States: Pressures from alumni and university communities to have winning teams is at the point at which success in recruitment of superathletes determines the amount of financial support in grants-in-aid funds, and there is little freedom for recruited athletes to make curricular choices. It is increasingly being realized by universities that their athletic systems have little to do with their educational systems. In the classification of athletics in the continuum of *players*, from amateurs to semiprofessionals to professional athletic *workers*, it is undoubtedly true that intercollegiate athletes in football and basketball can be classified as semiprofessionals (Zeigler, 1979, p. 204). They extend self-fulfilling, intrinsic, playing awards to monetary, external ones of "scholarship" grants and spectator entertainment income for the university. The intense pressures on universities tend to place the emphasis on winning, even by means of dishonest recruitment and subsidization. That may bring loyalty to the institution on the part of alumni and students if their teams win. Yet each recruiting athlete really needs an education, not exploitation, since very few of them will have lengthy, professional athletic careers. Semiprofessional and professional athletes are a fact in our cultural lives, and universities actually do prepare athletes for professional careers. Yet, in my opinion, except for the basic sport skills in SPE programs, highly competitive athletics should be outside the realm of SPE, particularly when *compassionate* fitness is a goal.

Having considered sports as ambivalent in regard to their compassionate and compulsive potentials, we can now concentrate on developmental motor activities, which by their nature are conducive to compassionate attitudes and behaviors. For those of us who have performed only stylized sports skills of throwing, catching, and striking balls in competition against others, it is difficult to think of the human body moving in ways other than those used in sports. However, the body can move freely and differently from patterned forms of activities in traditional Western use. In fact, it can move in ways often thought to be impossible. This seems evident when watching those trained to reproduce movement compositions created through the use of a movement notation system. Such compositions consciously combine unusual variations in patterned movements of the trunk, upper limbs, pelvis, and lower limbs as the body balances in place and moves from place to place (Eshkol et al., 1973). The movement pattern created in a composition that is notated by movement symbols can be successfully replicated by performers from reading notated scores, just as musicians reproduce musical scores. Also, the Eastern world solo and folk dance patterns may seem improbable to many of us in the Western world. Closer to possible innovative movement patterns have been the changes that have been noticeable during recent years in forms of the high jump, basketball shots, racing starts, and swimming strokes. (Please try to think of additional illustrations.)

The greatest potentials for the development of compassionate attitudes and behavior can probably be found in nonstylized and stylized motor activities that are performed by a single person without relationship to the performance of others and in unopposed relationship to them. These are classified as movement exploration or basic movement, body alignment (posture), relaxation techniques, prescribed exercises, swimming, track and field events, rhythmic gymnastics, informal gymnastics, and modern dance. The competition involved is between self- and desired actualization standards. Included here are lifetime individual and dual sports, e.g., bowling, archery, tennis, badminton, and other racquet games; and risk sports in which performers test their developing motor skills against the external environment, e.g., mountaineering, acrobatic skiing, and aqua-lung diving. Task-setting and problem-solving methods of instruction can be used effectively in unstylized patterns of movement.

It is generally considered that teachers of physical education and coaches of sports tend to have characteristics of those who typically conform and who are conservative. This is possibly understandable since motor skills are based upon the development of inherent motor coordinations, e.g., standing, running, jumping, throwing, and striking, and balance and agility. That development increases the physical functioning of the body and by so doing helps to conserve it throughout life. Yet since the beginning of physical education in North America there have been those who were not content to perpetuate traditional forms of exercise, sport, and dance (Glassford and Redmond, 1979, pp. 119–126; Barney, 1979, pp. 183, 214). Physical educators adapted foreign systems of gymnastics and sports to the culture, and natural gymnastics and dances were created. New sports were invented, e.g., baseball, from the adaptation of English children's ballgames, and basketball. A recent trend is the adaptation of old and the creation of new cooperative games with no losers and collective score games (Orlick, 1978, pp. 159–175). Orlick stated that liking to play them "reflects the degree of conditioning to a competitive or winning ethic" (1978, p. 178). It also seems possible that scoring systems can be invented that will give points for cooperative offensive and defensive plays as well as for successes achieved by the offense team.

Evidently the compulsive-competitive elements in SPE seem assured in our society. It is the compassionate-cooperative qualities that need development if social change toward enduring peace is to be implemented through SPE.

Principles for Structuring the PE Curriculums. The idea that SPE has the potential to help promote enduring peace through emphasis on compassionate fitness is a new social approach. It provides a vantage point from which to review present curriculums when planning new ones. It can detach physical educators from traditional habits of thought and action.

This approach does not change the motor skill achievement objectives of the best of modern physical education curriculums, i.e., the mastery of gross bodily movements in space and water, without and with the use of equipment and objects to be moved in play and sports. As at present, learners would perform by themselves, in cooperation with others, and against opponents. The resultant physical health benefits would continue to be as now: to improve cardiorespiratory and neuromuscular efficiency, strength, and endurance. Also, the setting of performers' self-actualization objective would reach beyond the usual performance expectations. The major change would be to select a breadth of activities beyond those of competitive sports and to emphasize cooperation and fair play within sports. Lesson plans and teaching strategies would be used to effect the development of compassionate attitudes and behaviors toward others and toward oneself. The traditional conscious, and unconscious, approach is to assume that competitive situations will heighten learning and will be more fun. The latter is an important objective in any lesson. However, competition is often used as an easy way to provide motivation without careful planning, and therefore the results may be more recreational than educational. If the competitive device is used constantly, little may be learned except how to compete, and those with aggressive tendencies may primarily learn how to dominate others and act in punitive ways against them.

The study of contemporary as well as historical SPE programs should be included in physical education academic courses to help develop a worldwide view of SPE and to provide comparisons with programs in North America. That understanding may favorably influence compassionate attitudes and the desire for peace. Student foreign exchange courses also extend understandings that are conducive to compassion and peace.

The following tentative principles apply to developmental motor performance as a central focus of SPE. They have compassionate fitness potential as well. They include principles to be applied in general and professional educational curriculums, and they may be used by teachers or coaches and scholars in SPE. They all need to be tested by formulating hypotheses that can be examined by research methods.

1. Select and create basic and exploratory motor skills; exercises for physiological benefits; body mechanics and relaxation techniques; swimming strokes and dives; lifetime individual and dual sports; risk sports; and folk, social, and modern dances.

2. Emphasize and create cooperative play among teammates in competitive sports and fair play against opponents.

3. Include cooperative games, and create ways of scoring sports to make visible the successes that come from cooperation as well as from competition.

4. Encourage students to select freely the motor skills and play forms they want to learn. (These principles do not include solutions to the important problems relating to those who do not want to learn.)

5. Help students to set performance-attainment goals beyond their expectations and thereby to develop self-confidence, control, and acceptance.

6. Use teaching strategies involving task-setting and problem-solving whenever appropriate. Select activities that are adaptable to these methods.

7. Cope with aggressive competitive behaviors by redirecting them into more responsible cooperative ones.

8. Search for knowledge in the academic dimensions of SPE that centers upon the phenomenon of developmental motor performance and its interrelated sociocultural and behavioral aspects.

9. Search for interdimensional and cross-dimensional knowledge in DMP that would result from the use of systems analysis research and computer models.

This social relevance perspective on SPE can serve as a base from which to think, to differ, to concur, and perhaps to revise your outlook. Tennyson wrote in *Locksley Hall*, "Yet I doubt not through the ages one increasing purpose runs." That purpose may indeed be compassionate love that leads to world peace. It may be the great hope for curing the human species of the war disease. Is it not worth trying to help this purpose by promoting compassionate fitness experiences in SPE? We could really claim that our profession helps to improve the quality of life through physical activity and the promotion of enduring satisfaction.

REFERENCES

Alcock, N.Z.: The Emperor's New Clothes. Oakville, Ont., Peace Research Institute Press, 1971.

Alcock, N.Z.: The War Disease. Oakville, Ont., Canadian Peace Research Institute Press, 1972.

Alcock, N.A.: The Logic of Love. Oakville, Ont., Canadian Peace Research Institute Press, 1976.

Alcock, N.Z.: UN special session on disarmament. Peace Research, Canadian Peace Research Institute, 10,4:135–140, 1978.

Alcock, N.Z. et al.: 1982. Oakville, Ont., Canadian Peace Research Institute Press, 1978.

Ardrey, R.: African Genesis. New York, Dell Paperback Publishing Co., 1961.

Arms control and disarmament. *In* Issues Before the 34th General Assembly of the United Nations, 1979–1980, New York, UN Association of the USA: 50–64, 1980.

Barney, R.K.: Physical education and sport in North America. *In* History of Physical Education and Sport. Edited by E.F. Zeigler. Englewood Cliffs, N.J., Prentice-Hall, pp. 171–227, 1979.

Bouthoul, G., and Carrère, R.: A list of the 366 major armed conflicts of the period 1740–1974. Peace Research, Canadian Peace Research Institute, 10,3:83–108, 1978.

Bronowski, J.: The Ascent of Man. Boston, Little, Brown, 1973.

Cantril, H.: The Pattern of Human Concerns. New Brunswick, N.J., Rutgers University Press, 1965.

Chronology of Events. Encyclopedia Britannica Book of Year, 1976:84–103; 1977:84–103; 1978:30–53; 1979:24–51;1980:24–49.

Conti, M.: The famine controversy. World Press Review, Stanley Foundation, New York, 27, 1:56, 1980.

Dewey, J.: Human Nature and Conduct. New York, Henry Holt, 1922.

Dewey, J.: The schools as a means of developing social consciousness and social ideals in children. J. Soc. Forces, 1:514–517, September, 1923.

Dewey, J.: Education Today. New York, G.P. Putnam Sons, 1940.

Eckhardt, W.: CPRI questionnaire. Oakville, Ont., Canadian Peace Research Institute Press, 1971.

Eckhardt, W.: Compassion: Toward a Science of Value. Oakville, Ont., Canadian Peace Research Institute Press, 1972.

Eshkol, N. et al.: Moving Writing Reading. Tel-Aviv, Movement Notation Society, 1973.

Glassford, R.G., and Redmond, G.: Physical education and sport in modern times. *In* History of Physical Education and Sport. Edited by E.F. Zeigler. Englewood Cliffs, N.J., Prentice-Hall, pp. 103–170, 1979.

Griffiths, D.E.: Administrative Theory. New York, Appleton-Century-Crofts, 1959.

Hampden-Turner, C.: Radical Man. Cambridge Mass., Schenkman Co., 1970.

Hicks, D.: Support paper on teacher training survey. Peace Research, Canadian Peace Research Institute, 10,2:66–72, 1978.

Huelster, L.J.: Resolved that "developmental motor performance" shall replace the designation "physical education." Academy Papers, American Academy of Physical Education, 7:28, 1973.

Human Rights Report: United Nations of America Quarterly, Newsletter of the UN Association of the USA, 2,4:1, 1979/80.

Jewett, A.E.: Relationships in Physical Education: A curriculum viewpoint. Academy Papers, American Academy of Physical Education, 11:87–98, 1977.

Jewett, A.E.: Relationships between curriculum development and instruction. Paper for Curriculum Academy Conference, National Association for Sport and Physical Education, New Orleans, March, 1979.

Jewett, A.E., and Mullan, M.R.: Curriculum Design: Purposes and Processes in Physical Education Teaching Learning. Washington, D.C., American Alliance for Health, Physical Education and Recreation, 1977.

Kenyon, G.S.: Attitudes toward sport and physical activity among adolescents from four English speaking countries. *In* The Cross-Cultural Analysis of Sport and Games. Edited by G. Lüschen. Champaign, Ill., Stipes Publishing Co., 1970.

Knox, R.: Nuclear war: what if? Science 80, American Association for the Advancement of Science, 2, 3, 32–34, 1980.

Leakey, R.E., and Lewin, R.L.: People of the Lake. Garden City, N.Y., Anchor Press Doubleday, 1978.

Leppert, E.C., and Johnson, E.: Global Insights: People and Cultures. Columbus, Ohio, Charles E. Merrill, 1980.

Leppert, E.C., and Payette, R.F.: An Evaluative Report of the Sequential Social Science Courses for the Secondary School. Urbana, Ill., College of Education, University of Illinois, 1970.

Loy, J.W., Kenyon, G.S., and McPherson, B.D.: Emergence and development of the sociology of sport as an academic specialty. Res. Q. Exercise and Sport, 51, 1:91–109, 1980.

Metheny, E.: Connotations of Movement in Sport and Dance. Dubuque, Iowa, Wm. C. Brown Co., 1965.

Moritz, F.A.: Thais pull back welcome mat for fleeing Cambodians. Christian Science Monitor, April 18, 1980, p. 4.

News Report. Canadian Peace Research Institute. 18,1:5, 1980.

Orlick, T.: Winning Through Cooperation: Competitive Insanity—Cooperative Alternative. Washington, D.C., Acropolis Books, 1978.

Reich, C.: The Greening of America. New York, Random House, 1970.

Research Quarterly for Exercise and Sport (inside front cover), March, 1980.

Restak, R.M.: The Brain: The Last Frontier. New York, Doubleday & Co., 1979.

Righter, R.: The dangerous imbalance. World Press Review, Stanley Foundation, New York, 27,3:39–40, 1980.

Rokeach, M.: The Nature of Human Values. New York, Free Press, 1973.

Rokeach, M.: The Open and Closed Mind: Investigations into the Nature of Belief Systems and Personality Systems. New York, Basic Books, 1960.

Sage, G.H.: Sociology of physical educator/coaches: The personal attributes controversy. Res. Q. Exercise and Sport, 51,1:110–121, 1980.

[Schwelb, E.]: Human Rights. Encyclopedia Britannica. 15th Ed., 8:1183–1189, 1975.

Slavery, Serfdom and Forced Labor. Encyclopedia Britannica. 15 Ed. 16:853–866, 1975.

Sochen, J.: Women and the Law. Encyclopedia Britannica Book of Year, 1980: 485–486.

[Spicer, E.H.]: Social and cultural changes. Encyclopedia Britannica. 15th Ed. 16:920–923, 1975.

Zeigler, E.: Issues in North American Sport and Physical Education. Washington, D.C., American Alliance for Health, Physical Education and Recreation, 1979.

SELECTED READINGS

Alcock, N.Z.: The Emperor's New Clothes. Oakville, Ont., Peace Research Institute Press, 1971.

Arnold, P.J.: Education, Physical Education and Personality Development. Exeter, N.H., Heineman Educational Books, 1968.

Arnold, P.J.: Meaning in Movement, Sport and Physical Education. Exeter, N.H., Heineman Educational Books, 1980.

Barnaby, F.: The Mounting Prospects of Nuclear War. Stockholm International Peace Research Institute, 1977.

Booth, K., and Wright, M., eds.: Thinking About Peace and War. New York, Barnes and Noble, 1978.

Bulletin of Peace Proposals, International Peace Research Institute, Oslo, 1980.

Camp, E., Jr.: United We Live: Peace for the Nuclear Age. New York, Walton Press, 1978.

Eckhardt, W.: A Manual on the Development of the Concept of Compassion and Its Measurement, 1962–1978. 2nd Ed. Oakville, Ont., Canadian Peace Research Institute, 1979.

Eckhardt, W., and Alcock, N.Z.: Ideology and personality in war/peace attitudes. J. Soc. Psychol., 81:105–116, 1970.

Eckhardt, W. et al.: Measurement of Compassion. Peace Research, Canadian Peace Research Institute, 4,29:31, 1974.

Fabian, L.: Soldiers Without Enemies. Washington, D.C., The Brookings Institute, 1971.

Falk, R.A.: A Study of Future Worlds. New York, Free Press, 1975.

Journal of Peace Research, Peace Research Institute, Oslo, 1980.

Kothari, R.: Footsteps into the Future: A Diagnosis of the Present World and a Design for an Alternative. New York, Free Press, 1974.

Lee, A.: Peace education in Canada. Peace Research, Canadian Peace Research Institute, 10,2:55–59, 1978.

McIntosh, P.: Fair Play: Ethics in Sport and Education. Exeter, N.H., Heineman Educational Books, 1979.

Newcombe, H.: Guaranteed Annual Income Plan for Nations. Bulletin of Peace Proposals, 1975.

Orlick, T.: The Cooperative Sports and Games Book. New York, Pantheon Books Paperback, 1978.

Orlick, T.D., and Botteril, C.: Every Kid Can Win. Chicago, Nelson-Hall, 1975.

Smith, G., Teitler, R., and Boren, L.: Pesonality concomitants of varying attitudes toward the use of violence for settlement of disputes at three different levels: Interpersonal, intergroup, and international. Sociol. Inquiry, 49:83–92, 1979.

Tinbergen, J. et al.: Reshaping the International Order. New York, E.P. Dutton, 1976.

Vanek, J.: The Participatory Economy: A Revolutionary Hypothesis and a Developing Strategy. Ithaca, N.Y., Cornell University Press, 1971.

Introduction

Earle F. Zeigler

In this chapter I will do my best to set the stage for the remainder of this introductory text about the profession of physical education and sport. Dr. Huelster has already set the stage for us importantly as she stressed the urgent need for the profession to adopt a perspective of social relevance that would embody what she has termed compassionate fitness. Now I will draw from a number of my earlier writings concerning the past and the present, and later, at the end of the book, I will attempt to look to the future in the Epilogue.

This is an interesting but also a frightening time to be alive. The "future shock" affecting us currently has occasioned strong waves of nostalgia in many as people seek the dubious security of a return to the good ol' days. For example, a *Time* essay inquired when was "The Best of Times—1821? 1961? Today?" I was pleased by the answer offered by the essayist, Thomas Griffith. He was not definitive in the sense that the reader was urged to seek a return to the past actively. "The question does involve large-scale subjectivity," Griffith stated, yet "the matter with our times is not so much a question of impossibilities, but of complexities that can be faced if only public trust and will are restored" (1975, p. 51). Such a recommendation is actually nothing more or less than the philosophical stance known as positive meliorism, a position that affirms that society has an innate tendency to improve and that people should strive consciously to bring about a steadily improving societal condition. To me this makes much more sense than subscribing to either blind optimism or despairing pessimism.

As the world—this "closed planet"—moves into the last of the twentieth century, the concept of 'communication' has now risen in importance to the point at which its significance is paramount if world society as we know it is to continue indefinitely. Asimov tells us that, along with the increasing tempo of civilization, a fourth revolution is now upon us. It is a different type of revolution from those we are accustomed to on the basis of history. What is referred to here is the fourth revolution *in the area of communications* that is in certain specific ways making the earth a type of global village (1970, pp. 17–20). Moving from (1) the invention of speech to (2) the invention of writing to (3) the mechanical reproduction of the printed word, and now to (4) relay stations in space, all people on earth will very soon be confronted with a blanketing communications network that will make possible personal relationships hitherto undreamed of by our forebears.

This development will have great implications for all levels of education in every country and resultantly will be highly significant for all types of sport, dance, play, and exercise in our society. This will place a new urgency on the topic of international and comparative analysis. Such urgency is needed, according to Asimov, because the world is now faced with a race. This race is "between the coming of the true fourth revolution and the death of civilization that will inevitably occur through

---

Dr. Zeigler is from The University of Western Ontario, London, Ontario, Canada.

growth past the limits of the third." Here we are being presented with a theory, of course, but there is a warning for us that is startling—we must have vastly improved means of communication and put them into use so effectively that the signs of present breakdown will be eliminated.

We can all understand that our world society is indeed precarious for a variety of reasons—wars, poverty, hunger, disease, technology, disturbance of ecological balance. Nevertheless, here in North America we find ourselves semicomfortably ensconced in a society grounded in the Judeo-Christian view of humanity and nature. This society—and now the entire world appears to be adopting Western world science and technology—tends to function on the basis of a series of what Schwartz calls unstated axioms of science whose truths are accepted as an act of faith:*

1. The universe is orderly.
2. This order can be discovered by man and expressed in mathematical quantities and relations.
3. Although there may be many ways of perceiving nature—e.g., art, poetry, music, etc.—only science can achieve "truth" that will enable man to master nature.
4. Observation and experimentation are the only valid means of discovering nature's order.
5. Observed "facts" are independent of the observer.
6. Secondary qualities are not measurable and hence not real.
7. All things on earth are for use by man.
8. Science is neutral, value-free, and independent of morality and ethics.
9. Knowledge will free man from ignorance, superstition, and social ills.
10. Man is not naturally depraved.
11. Reason is the supreme tool of man.
12. The "good" life on earth is not only definable but attainable (pp. 15–16).

A HISTORICAL OVERVIEW OF THE NATURE OF MAN

Even though we may have arrived at a point at which we are prepared to accept these unstated axioms of science as roughly analogous to those assumptions, theory, or both upon which we are grounding our lives, there is still considerable controversy and confusion concerning a definition of the nature of man and woman on a historical time scale. Morris presented a fivefold chronological series of definitions, including analyses as a rational animal, a spiritual being, a receptacle of knowledge, a mind that can be trained by exercise, and a problem-solving organism (1956). Within such a sequential pattern the primary function of the field of physical education and sport could well be to help this problem-solving organism move efficiently and with purpose in such aspects of people's lives as sport, dance, play, and exercise. Such experience would occur, of course, within the context of their socialization in an evolving world (Zeigler, 1975, p. 405).

A more comprehensive analysis of the nature of man was offered a bit later by Berelson and Steiner. They traced six images through recorded history more from the standpoint of the behavioral sciences (as compared to Morris's philosophically oriented definitions). The first of these was the so-called *philosophical image* in which man of the ancient world distinguished virtues through the employment of reason (1964, pp. 662–667). This was followed by what was termed the *Christian image* in which the concept of 'original sin' and possible redemption through the transfiguring love of God was possible for those who controlled their sinful impulses. The third delineation was the *political image* of man during the Renaissance in which man,

*From *Overskill: The Decline of Technology in Modern Civilization* by Eugene S. Schwartz. Copyright © 1971 by Eugene S. Schwartz. Reprinted by permission of Times Books, a division of Quadrangle/The New York Times Book Company, Inc.

through the introduction of his power and will, managed to take greater control of the social environment. In the process, sufficient energy was liberated to bring about many political changes, the end result being the creation of embryonic national ideals that coexisted with somewhat earlier religious ideals. During the eighteenth and nineteenth centuries an *economic image* emerged that provided an underlying rationale for man's economic development in keeping with the possession of property and personal items along with improved monetary standards. There were early efforts to equate the concept of 'individual good' with that of the 'common good.' At the same time the third basic political division, that of class, was more sharply delineated and generally understood.

The early twentieth century saw the development of a fifth image, the *psychoanalytic image* that introduced another form of love hitherto largely misunderstood—the ego and self. The instinctual impulses were being delineated more carefully than ever before. An effort was made to understand the role of childhood experiences in people's lives and how these and other nonconscious controls often ruled their actions because of the frequently incomplete gratification of basic human drives related to libido and sex. Finally, because of the rapid development of the behavioral sciences, Berelson and Steiner postulated the *behavioral science image* of man and woman. This view characterized the human being as a creature who is continually and continuously adapting reality to his or her own ends. In this way the individual is seeking to make reality more pleasant and congenial—to the greatest possible extent *his own* or *her own* reality.

THE INFLUENCE OF THE PIVOTAL SOCIAL FORCES

There have been at least five, and possibly six or more, social forces that have influenced the world's cultures for better or for worse. Accordingly these social forces have shaped our views regarding the present or potential nature of man (Brubacher, 1966; Zeigler, 1977, pp. 6, 20–21). These social forces may be regarded also as persistent historical problems because they have been around since the development of primitive societies, and they will probably be present on into the distant future (or until a utopian state of affairs, perhaps rendering them more or less static in nature, is achieved).

These pivotal social forces, which I have also regarded as persistent historical problems to be confronted by societies and their many collectivities, will be described only briefly at this point:

1. Values and norms. The persistent problem of values and norms seems to possess a watershed quality in that an understanding of those objects and qualities desired by people through the ages can evidently provide significant insight into this particular problem—and also into most if not all of the other recurring problems that will be discussed. (A problem used in this sense, according to its Greek derivation, would be "something thrown forward" for humans to understand and possibly resolve.) For example, throughout history there have been innumerable statements of educational aims (or values), and almost invariably there was a direct relationship with a hierarchy of such values present in the society under consideration. As another example, physical education and sport has been viewed as curricular, cocurricular, or extracurricular.

2. Politics. The influence of politics, or the type of political state, has affected the kind and amount of education offered in a society. Education has varied, depending upon whether a particular country was a monarchy, an aristocratic oligarchy, or some form of democracy. A philosophically progressivistic educational approach can flourish only in a type of democratic society. Conversely, a philosophically essentialistic or traditionalistic type of education, with its definite implications for physical education and sport, may be promoted successfully in any of the three types of political system.

3. Nationalism. The influence of nationalism or patriotism on education and on physical education and sport is obvious. If a strong state is desired, the need for a strong, healthy people is paramount. There have been many examples of this type of influence as far back as the Medes and Spartans and as recently as many twentieth century European and Asian powers.

4. Economics. The influence of economics has been most significant throughout history. The field of education has prospered when there was a surplus economy and declined when the economic structure weakened. Educational aims have tended to vary, depending upon how people made their money and created such surplus economies. Advancing industrial civilization has brought an uneven distribution of wealth, and this in turn has meant educational advantages of a superior quality for some. Education "of the physical" can be promoted under any type of economic system. In largely agrarian societies considerable physical fitness can be gained simply through manual labor. In industrial societies some means has to be developed whereby all will maintain a minimum level of physical fitness and health. The more individual freedom in a society, the more difficult a government will find it to *demand* that all citizens be physically fit.

5. Religion. The influence of organized religion on education has been very strong throughout history, but there is evidence that the power of the church over the individual is continuing to decline in the twentieth century. In the Western world the Christian religion should be recognized for the promulgation of principles in which man was considered valuable as an individual. Today a society must decide to what extent it can or should inculcate moral and religious values in its public schools. It seems reasonable to state that Judaism and Christianity have both hampered the fullest development of physical education and sport in modern times and earlier, but it is also true that a number of religious leaders are at least partially revamping their earlier positions as they realize the potential of sport and physical activity as spiritual forces in people's lives.

6. Ecology. The influence of ecology has been felt in a recognizable and significant way only for the past decade by North American society, so it is not unusual that very little attention has been paid to the environmental crisis by those in the nonscientific fields in education or by those in the field of physical education and sport. Although this problem has not been with us to a similar degree of intensity over the centuries as the five forces listed above, now it seems to be here to stay. Ecology is usually defined as the field of study that treats the relationships and interactions of human beings and other living organisms with each other and with the natural (or physical) environment in which they reside. In this respect the physical educator/coach has a unique role to play in helping individuals to develop and maintain *physical* fitness within a concept of 'total fitness' based on a goal of international understanding and brotherhood.

(Some would argue at this point for the inclusion of other social forces. For example, education itself may be considered a strong social force. More recently, sport itself has mushroomed to a point in this culture at which it has to be reckoned with as a social force—perhaps too strong a one in some instances.)

THE CLASH BETWEEN ECOLOGY AND ECONOMICS

Because of the urgency of the ecological crisis it seems wise to highlight this particular persistent problem at this point. It should be made clear that citizens of our North American society especially, whether from the United States, Canada, or Mexico, will soon be faced with a decision—the need to decide between a continuous-growth economic policy and a no-growth one. According to Murray, an ecologist, it is not simply an either-or matter (1972, p.38).

Unfortunately, however, even today the very large majority of citizens have not a real understanding about the urgent need for such a decision. Even if they understood that scholars are indeed recommending a no-growth policy, they would probably not believe them anyhow or even pay much heed to such advice. Is the United States, for example, not the land of capitalism and democracy where a steadily increasing gross national product is one of the best indicators of economic prosperity? Citizens are apt to wonder, therefore, if it is simply a case of the optimists saying, "full speed ahead, if we ever hope to reduce unemployment and poverty in the United States," and the pessimists responding with the idea that population and economic growth must become steady-state by the next century—if that will not be too late. This brings us back to the concept of 'positive meliorism' mentioned earlier— a position that would indicate the urgent need for careful investigation of the issue along with concomitant awareness of this planet's ecological plight.

Murray examines the concepts of 'growth,' 'movement of materials,' and 'competition' in his comparison of these conflicting models. The ecologist's rule in regard to growth implies that a system will eventually collapse unless it stops growing at some point and recycles; secondly, he is concerned with the biogeochemical cycles operative within nature—the movement within ecosystems for life. Here the serious problem being created by what we call modern man is that both his food requirements and the demands of the vast technological progress are simply not being recycled in such a way as to sustain even a steady-state situation indefinitely. In other words, the movement of materials is largely in one direction—for the temporary service of the earth's population that has been expanding exponentially.

The other fundamental rule of ecology relates to a third concept of 'competition.' The implication here is that sooner or later competition excludes some of the competing agencies (or species). This means practically that if two organisms are competing for an exhaustible resource (and which one is not in a closed system?), one of the competitors will be eliminated by its rival "either by being forced out of the ecosystem or by being forced to use some other resource" (Murray, 1972, p. 64). Thus, we must ask, for how long can the human race expect to proceed with a basic contradiction between the economic theory explaining that competition is supposed to maintain diversity and stability systems and an opposing theory based on the ecological model described above that has been tested in both natural and laboratory situations?

Other notes of gloom and doom could be sounded at this point, but most of us have heard or read so much about local, regional, national, and international problems of greater or lesser magnitude that we are actually beginning to reject such negative information subconsciously. Obviously this could become disastrous before long, especially if all of the grim tidings have not truly alerted us sufficiently and created the motivation to do something right away about the rapidly deteriorating situation. Once again we are faced with the reality of the concept of 'positive meliorism'— striving consciously to bring about a steadily improving ecological status in the world. Cousins sounded just the right note with ample volume and clarity when he argued that perhaps "the most important factor in the complex equation of the future is the way the human mind responds to crisis" (1974, pp. 6–7). Citing Toynbee's famous challenge-and-response theory, Cousins asserted that it is now up to the world culture, and the individual nations and societies within it, to respond positively, intelligently, and strongly to the challenges that are besetting it at the end of the twentieth century. He concluded by declaring that "the biggest task of humanity in the next fifty years will be to prove the experts wrong" (p. 7).

THE STATUS OF EDUCATION

Shifting our focus now from the society in general to the subject of education in particular—no matter which level you may wish to consider—the reports being received are anything but encouraging. Something seems to have happened to the schools, colleges, and universities, to the learning process that is taking place within them typically. The schools accept that bright-eyed youngster at the age of 6 years (or sooner), almost invariably eager and ready to learn, and then in so many cases his desire to learn is quite thoroughly blunted within a few short years. The youngster is indoctrinated into what is, for lack of a better term, called the modern way. This usually involves excessive drill and repetition, competition, speed, dull lectures, tests, quizzes, memorization, final grades, mastery of seemingly useless information, and various types of overt and covert discipline. All along the way a work-hard-to-get-ahead approach is being instilled, the idea being that somehow this will pay off financially when the young adult emerges from the formal educational system at the end of the entire schooling process (if he happens to make it that far). This will enable the man, woman, or couple to purchase sooner or later (usually sooner if one listens to the easy credit arrangements with high interest available) all of the good things that presumably characterize a high standard of living.

Thus, all of this does indeed add up to one of the highest standards of living in the world—based on acquiring material possessions fashioned in an advanced technological age. The recommended plan for all seems to be to get an education so that a person can make enough money to achieve this presumed high standard despite the "stagflation" (i.e., sluggish economy with constant inflation) that has been besetting the economy recently. In this way the man or woman will be able to keep up with relatives, friends, and business associates who are seeking the same goals—ability to purchase all of the modern conveniences becoming increasingly available because of the technological advancements made largely in this century. Somehow such advantages are going to improve the quality of life, although most of us would be hard pressed if we were asked to explain just how such a level of "conspicuous consumption" is going to achieve this desired state for us. (At this point I cannot resist mentioning the plight of people in the Third World nations, who are overworked and underfed [while exactly the opposite is the case for most of us], and reproducing at a much higher rate than people in the developed nations.)

My own analysis of the situation is that we have largely lost track of what education should be all about. The deficiencies of the educational system—often based on deficient curriculum content and poor instructional methodology with an inadequate approach to the achievement of knowledge, skills, and competencies—point out the overall inadequacy of modern education. We should be teaching children and young people how to think logically and how to act ethically on the basis of democratic values and norms. We should be teaching them how to develop active, healthy bodies and how to maintain such a state through joyous physical activity. We should be helping young people to develop a life purpose so that maximum energy for living may be gained and maintained. However, for a variety of reasons these vital topics are not being introduced at the appropriate time, and we do not follow through to help them achieve desirable educational objectives.

Most of us have become quite familiar with Toffler's several volumes of warning and exhortation (1970). His concept of 'future shock' seems to be most apt, but so few seem prepared to examine in any depth the educational values and norms by which they function daily. Far too many want to "circle up the wagons" so that the "slings and arrows" of changing times will not cause us harm while we wait for the "U.S. cavalry to bring us aid from the rear." The good old times are gone; they will never return. What people will need are problem-solving, heuristic abilities that will enable them to adapt and adjust to the changing times and the seemingly increasing tempo of civilization.

Take the case of the university, for example. In 1969 we were told that "the modern university has never been more necessary and central to our national life than it is today," and yet "we must also say in the next breath that no other major institution in this country is now so open to disbalance and in so precarious a state of health" (Gould, 1969). These words were spoken at the end of a very difficult decade for colleges and universities—the 1960s, but who is prepared to argue validly that the 1970s were that much better and that the 1980s will see many of the major problems of this institution resolved? Assuredly the students were ever so much less sullen and openly mutinous in the 1970s; in fact, one wonders how such a transformation came over them in such a few short years. Certainly they are far from being blissfully happy about the university experiences they are receiving, and political clout through vigorous public support has not been apparent in any quarter. Those of us in the teaching profession could complain loudly, but we really do not dare, and it would not do us much good anyhow. The legislators know that the public would not pay much attention to us no matter how loud the protest might be. One is forced to conjecture why the status of university personnel seems so much lower here when studies inform us that the professoriat ranks very high in, for example, the Federal Republic of Germany.

What Gould was telling us above, what he was recommending, was that our colleges and universities should be more democratic, more concerned with social problems, more alert to students' justified demands, and more critical of our own performance. Many of these recommendations have indeed been heeded, to recognizable degrees at least. Nevertheless—and I think there is a relationship here—the social forces have been such that the educational pendulum has swung farther to the right again in the direction of so-called educational essentialism. I view this as highly disturbing, but the social forces are so great that one hardly dares to speak in favor of inclining to educational progressivism, a condition or state that was never really understood and certainly not implemented except in isolated instances.

However, let us put this old argument aside for the present. Of significance now is Toffler's prognostication about education in the future sense (1970, pp. 353–378). As I indicated above, he also affirms that "one of our most critical subsystems—education—is dangerously malfunctioning. Our schools face backwards toward a dying system, rather than forward to the new emerging society" (pp. 353–354). Of course, any student of educational history understands that the schools have never been in the vanguard, that they have never led the way in society. And as long as they are so dependent on the public purse through taxation there is no reason to believe that matters will change significantly. Nevertheless, Toffler's thoughts seem to ring true—that the people preparing for tomorrow's world, those "who must live in super-industrial societies. . . will need new skills in three crucial areas: learning, relating, and choosing" (p. 367). Our task will be that of seeking to provide the answers to the following questions: learning what, relating to whom, and making what choices?

THE STATUS OF PHYSICAL EDUCATION AND SPORT

As might be expected, the field of physical education and sport has not escaped from the serious malaise that has permeated the very fabric of society today. We in this field have one of the most blurred images in the entire educational system. This probably occurred originally because of the many conflicting educational philosophies extant in each of the 60 state and provincial educational systems on this North American continent. Our image with its fuzzy boundaries continues today for essentially the same reason and, of course, because of considerable individual and collective confusion.

Earlier I listed a set of unstated axioms of science whose truth we accept. What has been troubling me lately is a fear that the field of physical education and sport has also been proceeding generally, despite the fact that many do not accord us full curricular status, on the basis of its own unstated axiom: Physical education is so important to people of all ages in our society that the future of the field in our schools is guaranteed forever—no matter whether true professional status is acquired or not. Lest you think that I am being too harsh, I believe there are other unstated axioms that could be listed too. However, let us allow just this one to suffice as a basis for what follows.

By now you no doubt sense that I have serious concerns about what the emerging profession of physical education and sport needs to accomplish by the year 1990— it may even be possible that our period of grace will extend to the year 2000. However, we will need to move forthrightly and strongly along certain lines within the next 5 years. My diagnosis of the present situation is that the field of physical education as we have known it and promoted it is seriously ill. Many people recognize the symptoms of the illness, but most of the group teaching and coaching within the field do not comprehend the severity of the malady that has gradually infected the profession. At least the American Association for Health, Physical Education, and Recreation had the wisdom to substitute the word *alliance* for *association*, and a bit later added the word *dance* to the overall title (AAHPERD). Further, we are also witnessing the struggling emergence of an entity called the National Association for Sport and Physical Education within the AAHPERD as presently constituted. In Canada there has not been the urgency to change the name of the Canadian Association for Health, Physical Education, and Recreation, although it must be stated that (1) health education has not emerged as a separate profession; (2) recreation and park administration is a separate profession; and (3) a great many secondary school physical education teachers and coaches identify more with their provincial teachers' federations than they do with the national physical education association. Further, there is the everpresent need to promote more effective bilingualism than exists at present.

I believe further that there is an urgent need for the application of the techniques of normative and analytical philosophizing to be directed basically to sport and physical activity. Such endeavor is long overdue when we consider our bewildered public often seeking to comprehend what we mean by the conglomeration of terms presently in use such as movement, health, parks administration, campus recreation, leisure studies, physical education and sport, sport and physical education (or physical activity), recreation, rehabilitation education, applied life studies, dance, kinanthropology, recreology, safety education, driver education, physical fitness, movement education, human motor performance, ergonomics, exercise studies, sport studies, human kinetics, kinesiology, anthropokineticology, and, last but not least, the interesting combination of Latin and Greek roots known as homokinetics. If we in the field can laugh at this sampling of terms and combinations thereof in use, just think what people in other disciplines and professions and the general public must think.

To make matters more complicated, while the above developments have been taking place, a large and frightening rift has become apparent between the people in the field with one or more of a number of subdisciplinary orientations and those with what might be called a professional orientation. Still further, there is a split between those with heavier involvement in the biophysical aspects of the field and those with a scholarly interest in the social science and humanities subdisciplinary aspects (social psychology, philosophy, management theory, etc.). Yet despite these controversies of a spoken or unspoken nature, the athletics-oriented ones among us continue on their merry way toward an open future because of our culture's increasing "love affair" with highly competitive sport.

In an effort to improve the clarity of this historical analysis of the twentieth century in North American physical education and its allied professions, and thereby to communicate the present status more effectively, I will explain what I think has happened since 1900 through the use of a series of diagrams (Zeigler, 1979b, pp. 9–19).

Stage 1: Physical Education (and Sport) circa 1900–1930

In this analysis of the emerging physical education field within the public educational system primarily, three categories or subdivisions of the field may be traced:
(1) the potential body of knowledge as characterized by its *subdisciplinary areas;* (2)
the *concurrent professional components* (or subprofessional areas) of the developing
field (such as exist in all subject-matter fields to a greater or lesser extent); and (3)
what are called *potential allied professions* (such as may exist also in other emerging
fields of study).

Subdisciplinary areas include *(A)* physiological aspects, *(B)* historical and philosophical aspects, *(C)* psychological aspects, *(D)* biomechanical aspects, *(E)* sociological aspects, and *(F)* other disciplinary aspects (many of which are not yet sufficiently
identified). (The reader will note immediately the difference between the terminology
employed here in a historical analysis and that used in the Preface and the Prologue—
and basically for the organization of this text. Of course, the reason for the change
is that we now see the basic error involved in using terms from other disciplines in
the past.)

Concurrent professional components (or subprofessional areas) in Figure 1 are *(a)*
administration or management, *(b)* supervision, *(c)* curriculum or program, *(d)* teaching or instructional methods, *(e)* comparative and international relations, *(f)* evaluation and measurement, and *(g)* other components that may be identified.

Potential allied professions are *(1)* competitive athletics, *(2)* health education, *(3)*
dance (education), *(4)* recreation (education), *(5)* adapted exercise (therapy), and *(6)*
safety education.

Analysis of the situation in the field of physical education from about 1900 to
approximately 1930 (designated as stage 1) indicates that the subdisciplinary areas
are blurred and almost indistinguishable within the center of the circle depicting
physical education's body of knowledge (Fig. 1). It is true that professional students
of that time received courses in anatomy and physiology, as well as chemistry and
physics, prior to required professional physical education courses identified, for
example, as physiology of exercise, kinesiology, anthropometry, physical examination
and diagnosis, massage, history of physical training, emergencies, and medical gymnastics (Oberlin College catalogue for 1894). The point to be made here, however,

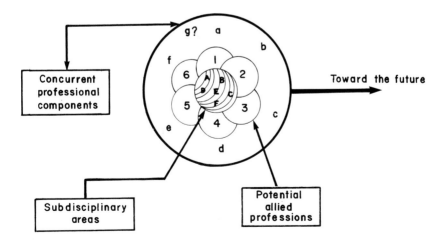

Fig. 1. Physical education stage 1 (circa 1900–1930). See text for explanation. (With
appreciation to Cyril White and Phil Sparling for helpful advice.)

is that there were basic science courses and there were professional physical education courses, but instruction in the so-called academic courses was almost completely lacking. Certain professors had areas of specialization (e.g., Fred Leonard in physical education history; Delphine Hanna in medical gymnastics), but the very large majority of these people saw themselves as physical educators and not as specialists in a disciplinary subject matter within the university. Of course, we must mention the "M.D. phenomenon" in our early history. For instance, James H. McCurdy, M.D., recognized that our embryonic profession needed people with "scientific ability who will increase our knowledge with reference especially to bodily growth, to personal hygiene, to physiology of exercise, etc." (1901, pp. 311–312).

The potential allied professions are also blurred and almost indistinguishable within the center of the circle depicting physical education in Figure 1. (They are isolated in the diagram to the extent necessary for identification, but the overlap was often greater than is shown here arbitrarily.) For example, in the Wellesley College catalogue for 1910, competitive athletics *(1)* is included in the requirements for the bachelor of arts degree in physical education under the heading of "Professional Courses" by virtue of a 2-hour course in organized sports, a 3-hour course in athletics (presumably track and field), and a 3½-hour course in outdoor games and athletics. Health education *(2)* is included as "reg. A.B. hygiene" for 1 hour, and dance (education) or *(3)* is listed as "dancing" for 1 or 2 hours. Recreation *(4)* could conceivably be regarded as physical recreation insofar as sports activities were offered within the physical education curriculum. Adapted exercise (therapy) *(5)* appears as "corrective gymnastics and massage" for 1 hour. Finally, the only reference to safety education *(6)* is a course experience called "emergencies" for 1 hour of credit. Thus if you will check Figure 1 again, you will note that the subdisciplinary areas *(A, B, C, D, E,* and *F)* are very close in the center of the core depicting the body of knowledge contained in physical education; that the potential allied professions *(1, 2, 3, 4, 5,* and *6)* are firmly attached and overlapping, or closely spaced next to, the knowledge core of the diagram, and that the concurrent professional components *(a, b, c, d, e, f,* and *g),* which we later will call the subprofessional components, are simply indicated as belonging in the larger circle that is meant to encompass the entire administrative unit of the field. (These three entities have been explained in detail now because they will appear again with fewer specifics in subsequent diagrams.)

Stage 2: Physical Education (and Sport) circa 1930–1960

In Figure 2, which represents roughly the period from 1930 to 1960 in the United States, we find that there actually was considerable change within the field known as physical education. The subdisciplinary areas, for example, are beginning to emerge from the body-of-knowledge core depicted in Figure 1. The typical tests and measurement course was gradually characterized by an improved laboratory experience, often largely physical fitness-exercise physiological in nature. These were soon supplemented (often in separate courses) by motor learning and kinesiological laboratory experiences as well. There was kinematic analysis of human movement in sport, dance, and exercise, but the first doctoral study involving true kinetic analysis of movement in sport was yet to be carried out. Sport and physical education sociology had not yet come on the scene, nor had the social psychological analysis of sport and physical activity surfaced to any recognizable extent.

There were a great many historical and biographical theses, but by and large the historical studies were not characterized by the use of an interpretive criterion to evaluate the evidence that had been gathered (Adelman, 1970). The biographical studies were interesting and usually substantive, but the subject of such an investigation typically emerged with a large halo around his head. Philosophical studies were primarily normative, although in the mid 40s and in the 50s they were similar

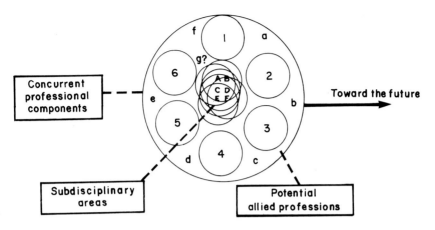

Fig. 2. Physical education stage 2 (circa 1930–1960).

to studies being carried out in educational philosophy (the implications approach, etc.). Occasionally scholars like C.H. McCloy asked how long a field could expect to prosper as a developing profession when the bulk of its research was carried out largely through the medium of doctoral investigations.

In concurrent professional components (subprofessional areas), we find that there were a large number of doctoral studies that could be characterized loosely as administrative in nature. Many of these were helpful and provided useful information, but as Spaeth reported:

> There is an almost total lack of theoretical orientation in the design of research and interpretation of the findings in the sample of administrative research studied. . . . The administrative research in physical education and athletics also generally lacked the methodological rigor necessary for contributions to the development of scientific knowledge about administrative performance" (Zeigler and Spaeth, 1975, p. 44).

With exceptions, of course much the same can be said for the studies carried out in the subprofessional components (as designated here) identified as *supervision, curriculum, evaluation,* etc. It is important to keep in mind, however, that we are describing types of investigation employing a variety of techniques under the rubric of descriptive research methodology. It is often simply not possible or desirable to emerge from such studies with a coefficient of correlation or a multiple correlation— not to mention the employment of a factor analysis technique. International and comparative physical education and sport research was practically nonexistent from the standpoint of the use of even relatively simple social science methodology and accompanying techniques. The final category, evaluation and measurement, was viewed more as part of the subdisciplinary efforts of our scholars at that time (although we are now recommending that it be viewed as a subprofessional component with ramifications for the entire field). It was accordingly employed almost completely by those interested in the physiological, psychological, and kinesiological aspects of physical education. Today it is increasingly being viewed more as a tool subject that may be used by almost any scholar in our field carrying out an investigation in the natural sciences, the social sciences, or even the humanities. Further, we now anticipate that teachers, coaches, and managers will employ evaluation and measurement techniques in on-the-job action research.

Finally, then, in this period from 1930 to 1960, let us consider briefly what happened to the potential allied professions. Examination of Figure 2, designated as stage 2, indicates that the allied professions, which were firmly attached to and part of the physical education core—in the schools, colleges, and universities at least, have now moved away from a position of centrality of what we have been arbitrarily calling physical education. These potential allied professions—*competitive athletics, health education, dance (education), recreation, adapted exercise (therapy),* and *safety education*—have established their own identities. Indeed, in some cases they have even established separate identity within the field of education (not to mention recognition that has been accorded them by the public), and, of course, separate professional associations have been formed.

Stage 3: Physical Education (and Sport) circa 1960–1970

Many will recall vividly the events of the 1960s, both within society in general and within the field of physical education specifically. Our graduate study programs were attacked by Conant; a response was made by Esslinger on our behalf; and our profession developed an incomplete understanding of the need for a substantive body of knowledge to undergird our professional work and related responsibilities. A notable enterprise, for example, was the inauguration of the Big Ten Body-of-Knowledge Project as conceived by Daniels and followed to fruition by McCristal and some of us who were present at the time. The subdisciplinary areas included in this undertaking were (1) history, philosophy, and comparative physical education and sport; (2) sociology of sport and physical education; (3) administrative theory; (4) exercise physiology; (5) biomechanics; and (6) motor learning and sports psychology (Zeigler, 1975a, p. 292). The subdisciplinary areas shown in Figure 3 are similar, the differences being simply that certain subdisciplinary areas are now shown as concurrent subprofessional components.

The significant point to be made, however, is that the subdisciplinary areas themselves have moved away from the central core of the earlier diagrams to a position not too unlike the positions held earlier by the potential allied professions. These subdisciplinary areas (e.g., so-called sociology of sport) were indeed moving strongly away from the recognized physical education field toward the end of the 1960–1970 decade. The position of sport sociology—and this was followed similarly by other subdisciplinary societies being established—reminds one of the floating apex of Peter principle fame. They had gone off to "play by themselves," not wanting anything to do with the field of physical education, even though these people were drawing their

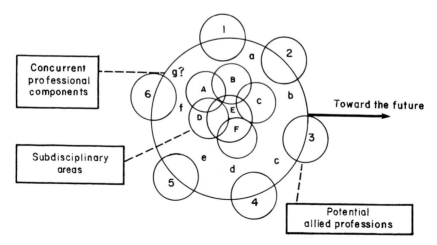

Fig. 3. Physical education stage 3 (circa 1960–1970).

salaries from units with the term physical education in their title. At the same time, however, they were almost completely unrecognized by the societal entities they purported to describe in esoteric, scholarly fashion (e.g., sport or sociology).

Further examination of Figure 3 in regard to the movement of the potential allied professions shows that all six of the fields have moved further in the direction of establishing their own identity even within educational circles. It is impossible, of course, to describe precisely where each of the allied professions was located, but it was clear that there had been further movement away from the field of physical education. Despite the occasional presence of a "professional remnant" within the physical education entity, I believe that historical investigation will soon prove this assertion.

Examination of the concurrent subprofessional components for the period 1960–1970—components that by their very nature are firmly linked to the professional development of any field—brings to light some interesting developments as well. For example, we saw the introduction of a more theoretical orientation on the part of a relatively few graduate programs in physical education. The subject of curriculum received somewhat more attention generally, and several scholars led the way in giving this topic a more theoretical orientation than previously. The idea of competency-based education was receiving consideration in professional education, and this was recognized by several alert people in physical education. The area of instructional methodology was promoted briefly through a "spectrum of styles" by Muska Mosston, but he soon turned to the larger field of education with its many subject matters (Zeigler, 1970, pp. 29–30). Somehow the concept of 'supervision' merged more completely with the larger realm of administration. A few professors reacted toward the end of this decade to what they considered to be the overemphasis being given to a subdisciplinary orientation by their university colleagues. Although the passage of time has proved them correct in their judgment insofar as the existence of a need for scholarly investigation in the subprofessional components of the field, it was nevertheless true that scholarly study in the bioscience, social science, and humanities aspects of sport and physical education was still far from adequate. So perhaps we should commend these leaders for their professional-preparation approach to both undergraduate and graduate education in physical education, because they were indeed arguing for an improved, more precise approach to what the large majority of physical education departments in colleges and universities had been stressing in an inadequate manner for decades.

Stage 4: Physical Education and Sport circa 1970–1980

Stage 4 treats the period from 1970 to 1980 (Fig. 4). We can all readily appreciate the difficulty of gaining a true perspective of the happenings of the decade just preceding the present one. Nevertheless, some of the developments that began in previous decades did indeed continue apace, and so it is possible to describe the present situation with a fair degree of accuracy. The subdisciplinary areas that were moving strongly away from involvement with physical education at the professional conference level continued with their dispersion usually in the direction of the mother discipline (e.g., sport history and sport philosophy). Concurrently we witnessed the beginning of subdisciplinary academies within the National Association for Sport and Physical Education (NASPE) in the American Alliance for Health, Physical Education, Recreation, and Dance (AAHPERD). (Giving the name *academy* to these groupings disturbed me at first because of possible confusion with The American Academy of Physical Education, but after deliberation I now feel that the idea is worthwhile and practical and deserves full support—for reasons that will be more apparent shortly.)

This trend of the subdisciplinary, floating-apex societies (e.g., the Philosophic Society for the Study of Sport) to move away from the physical education core

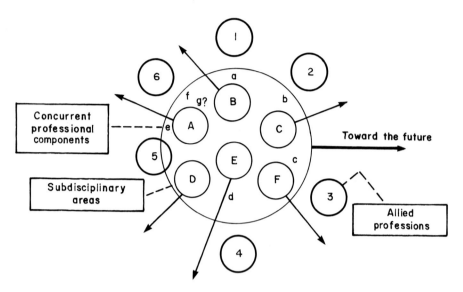

Fig. 4. Physical education stage 4 (circa 1970–1980).

continued despite the fact that the large majority of the members of these societies received their graduate training in the physical education field and, where available, typically received their travel funds to attend many of these scholarly conferences from travel budgets in physical education departments and schools. All in all, it is a very disturbing development, one that in the long run threatens the professional status of physical education. In the final analysis, if it and certain other trends are not halted, physical education will become a trade at best—and could be supplanted by other professions at the worst.

Viewed from an overall basis, it is now apparent that the six potential allied professions have all consolidated their positions outside of physical education departments at the college and university level, although this has not yet been possible officially at the other educational levels. As was mentioned earlier, however, the American Association for Health, Physical Education, and Recreation recognized this growth of the potential allied professions toward full independence by changing its name to the American Alliance for Health, Physical Education, and Recreation and then added the words *and Dance* to the end of the title to give earned recognition to that allied profession. This action culminated a period in which a number of dance units within colleges and universities moved, or sought permission to move, out of the physical education unit per se to some other school or college on campus. Thus, whether we are talking about competitive athletics, health education, dance (education), recreation (education), safety (education), or even adapted exercise (therapy), it is obvious that most of those who identify primarily with these potential allied professions want to be as free as possible from what they overtly or covertly perceive to be the "fizz ed stigma."

During the period from 1970 to 1980, there does not appear to have been any considerable amount of change in the so-called concurrent subprofessional components shown in Figure 4. The term *management* is gaining acceptance along with the term *administration*, but there is no real evidence that the field of physical education and sport is alert to the need for improving *both* the theoretical and practical components of professional preparation in this aspect of our field. In the late 1970s, universities at various points on the continent established sport and physical education management streams within physical education units at both the undergraduate and graduate levels. Several other universities, notably the University of Massachusetts, created graduate programs in sport management quite separate from physical education major programs (i.e., the unit has the name *sport studies*, and undergraduate professional preparation in physical education is not required for admission to this program). Massachusetts has a graduate department in professional preparation for physical education also that is separate from the department of sport studies, and at least one other major university is placing special emphasis on "professional preparation" and methods of instruction in physical education. Furthermore, a relatively small, stalwart band of curriculum theorists continues to strive for careful investigation into the intricacies of this aspect of the professional task. Fortunately for those interested in major emphasis on professional preparation, including curriculum and instructional methodology, all universities are continuing their drive for an improved level of instruction by professors generally, a move that was sparked by the clamor of students in the 1960s and perpetuated by the continuing aim to please them occasioned by the financial constraints of the 1970s and the accompanying need to at least preserve the student head-count at a steady-state level.

The remaining two professional components to be considered in the 1970s—if it is agreed that they should be considered in this broad category—are *comparative and international* and *evaluation and measurement*. Insofar as the international and comparative professional component is concerned, a small, loyal group is keeping this important area alive within the Alliance, but the theoretical component, the amount of scholarly investigation in this aspect of our disciplinary endeavor, is so slight that there is not even a subheading for it listed typically in the annual completed research publication of the Alliance. This lack must be regarded as an indictment of our overall professional growth at a time when we should be moving steadily toward more, not less, involvement with our colleagues abroad.

Evaluation and measurement, formerly known as tests and measurement, is still an important part of undergraduate professional preparation but seems to have become diffused at the graduate level into the various subdisciplinary or subprofessional streams available. At least one major university offers it as an area of specialization at the graduate level, and another major university maintains a "measurement and evaluation professor" to service students and professors needing advice insofar as research design and statistical techniques are concerned.

Stage 5: Sport and Developmental Physical Activity circa 1980–2000

We have now arrived at the point at which we can conjecture about, and possibly prescribe for, the future, circa 1980–2000. You will recall that earlier I expressed serious concern about the field of physical education because I felt that we are not moving rapidly enough to what might be called *true* professional status. Those of us functioning in the public educational system may feel that we will be sheltered indefinitely by the protective arm of the teaching profession. Others in the field may believe that society should not, and probably will not, continue to recognize physical education (even if we officially change our name to sport and physical education) as the profession that can and should be the leading force in human motor performance in sport, dance, and exercise. (For example, in Chapter 1, "Background, Meaning, and Significance," Dr. VanderZwaag offers a clear, vigorous statement in which he envisions quite a different future for sport, dance, and exercise than the one that is being postulated here.) Whatever the future development may be, there is no escaping the fact that we are typically close to the bottom of the totem pole in the schools despite our unique mission. Furthermore, we are presently missing the opportunity to a considerable extent to become the profession of which we are capable—if we will just do the job as it should be done. Societal recognition of our potential and of our accomplishments will take care of itself if we perform our professional task in keeping with our highest tradition.

It is on this basis, therefore, that a stage 5 is being postulated at this point in this book's Introduction. If certain vigorous steps are taken by The American Academy of Physical Education, The American Alliance for Health, Physical Education, Recreation, and Dance, and the National Association for Physical Education in Higher Education, it is conceivable that the beginning of a trend will become evident by 1990 and clearly recognizable by the year 2000. The recommended future development is explained in Figure 5.

You will notice immediately as you examine this diagram that the subdisciplinary areas, instead of continuing along with their movement with greater identification with the related disciplines (e.g., physiology, sociology, philosophy, history), have been brought back within the field of sport and physical education (or developmental physical activity) and are firmly attached to the profession's core—explained as a developing body of knowledge about the theory and practice of sport and physical activity. Obviously it may be extremely difficult, or even impossible, to bring these groups back through some form of affiliation or alliance with the sport and physical education profession. Through persuasion, encouragement, and influence, and even a form of bribery where possible and desirable, we should seek to interest our scholarly people from the various subdisciplinary areas—those who are not averse to a strong, ongoing relationship with the NASPE—in the new academies recently started by the AAHPERD. These should be strengthened immeasurably and given strong encouragement, because we must have the intelligentsia of our field—those who have the background and training to add to the body-of-knowledge core—working and identifying with us in the academy, the alliance, and the NASPE. (In Canada, something similar should be worked out between the Canadian Association for Health, Physical Education, and Recreation and the too heavily bioscience-oriented Canadian Association for Sport Sciences.)

What about the concurrent subprofessional components that have been designated in each diagram? In this instance we are fortunately not in a position in which we

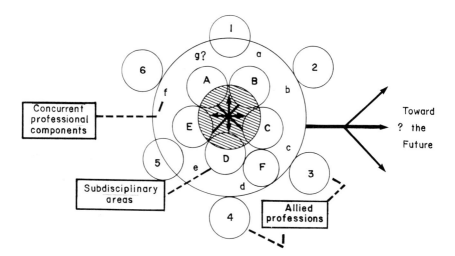

Fig. 5. Physical education stage 5(?) (circa 1980–2000).
The striped circle in the center represents the developing body of knowledge about the theory and practice of sport and physical activity (purposeful human movement in sport, dance, play, and exercise).

will have to retrieve these elements from other scholarly societies far removed from our midst. Our task here is to strengthen the scholarly investigation relative to program development, management, evaluation, etc. We can follow the lead of such people as Jewett, Siedentop, Locke, Mosston, the Howells, Baumgartner, and Spaeth, who have played leadership roles through their endeavors to place, respectively, on a more scholarly basis than heretofore curriculum, teacher competency, professional preparation, instructional methodology, comparative and international physical education and sport, measurement and evaluation, and administrative theory and practice. In the years ahead such efforts should be recognized equally along with the scholarly work and accomplishments of those in the subdisciplinary areas. I say this because I believe they are truly important, and probably even vital, if we hope to achieve true professional status by the turn of the century. Thus these components should gradually assume equal status within the circle that describes the emerging field of sport and physical education (or sport and developmental physical activity).

Lastly we are faced with the continuing problem of our relationship with what have been described as the (potential) allied professions. As mentioned above, we have made significant progress in this regard through the combined efforts of AAHPERD. What we must do in this instance is to make certain that these related or allied professions remain firmly entrenched in their alliance with AAHPERD and the field in general. We can do this best by (1) making the members of these associations feel at home within the alliance, and demonstrating through our actions that we are proud of the role that physical education has played, and will continue to play, in assisting them to promote their own professional status while coexisting with physical education in an alliance that should be beneficial to each and all alike; (2) improving greatly the quality and quantity of our own scholarly endeavor in both the subdisciplinary areas and the concurrent subprofessional areas (i.e., the total body of knowledge about the theory and practice of sport and developmental physical activity); and (3) relating to the scholars in each of the allied professions at those points (or overlapping investigative areas) at which joint research effort can be rewarding to the several professions concerned.

A MODEL FOR THE OPTIMUM DEVELOPMENT OF A PROFESSION CIRCA 1980–2000

I would now like to recommend a model that may be employed for the optimum development of our profession, our allied professions, and, for that matter, any profession. None of us can be certain what most of us will be calling the field by the year 2000. Personally, although I remain loyal to the established physical education profession, I regard *sport and physical education* and *physical education and sport* as holding-pattern terms. What we really need is a term that explains to the public (and to ourselves) what our function truly is. We seek knowledge and understanding about purposeful human movement (or motor performance) in such activities as sport, dance, play, and exercise. (Perhaps, as suggested by Seward Staley years ago, we should invent an acronym such as UNIROYAL, a term that was adopted for tires some time ago.)

The model in Figure 6 includes the following subdivisions: (1) societal values and norms, (2) an operational philosophy for the profession, (3) a developing theory embodying assumptions and testable hypotheses, (4) professional, semiprofessional, and amateur involvement as practitioners, (5) professional preparation and general education, and (6) scholarly endeavor and disciplinary research.

Societal values and norms are placed at the top of the model. This is based on the theory that a society's values and norms have a watershed quality; that in the final analysis progress will be made toward their achievement; and that they exert control and conditioning over the lower levels in the social system as the culture moves gradually and unevenly toward what may be considered progress. Directly below in

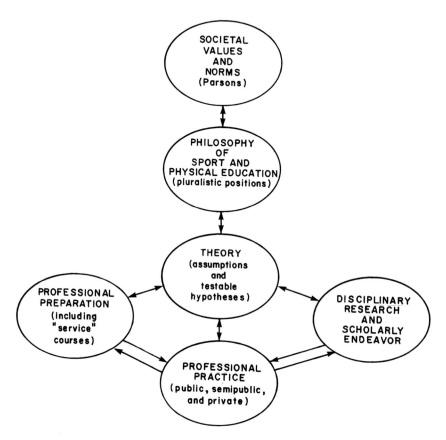

Fig. 6. A model for optimum development of a field called sport and physical education, defined as the field of study that deals with human motor performance in sport, dance, play, and exercise. See text for explanation.

the model is the overriding philosophy of sport and physical education in a society, or the values according to which the profession conducts its practice. At this level we appreciate that especially in a democracy pluralistic philosophies are allowed to exist (Zeigler, 1977, pp. 7–9).

The third level involves the assumptions and testable hypotheses of a steadily evolving theory—a knowledge base upon which professional practice is predicated and executed. This theory should comprise a coherent group of general and specific propositions that can be used as principles to explain the phenomena observed in human motor performance in sport, dance, play, and exercise.

The fourth level in the model is depicted as professional, semiprofessional, and amateur involvement in the practice of the profession. This is subsumed under the categories of public, semipublic (or semiprivate), and private involvement or practice. To the left of this is the area of professional preparation and general education. Professional preparation should include (1) the performer, (2) teachers/coaches, (3) administrators/supervisors; (4) teachers of teachers/coaches, (5) scholars and researchers, and (6) alternative professional careers. So-called general education should now be elevated so that it is regarded as part of a broad liberal arts and science background rather than merely as a "service" course. To achieve this it will be necessary to provide a sound educational experience in the theory and practice of human motor performance in sport, dance, and exercise.

To the right at the fourth level is the area of disciplinary research and scholarly endeavor. The reader should note carefully that by 1990–2000 we are recommending a complete changeover from the use of terms belonging to related fields (e.g., physiology, sociology). Further, the so-called subprofessional areas are included right along with the subdisciplinary areas as legitimate aspects of human motor performance for various types of scholarly investigation. Thus the subareas included in Figure 6 are: (1) background, meaning, and significance, (2) functional effects of physical activity, (3) sociocultural and behavioral aspects, (4) motor learning and development, (5) mechanical and muscular analysis, (6) management theory and practice, (7) program development (theory and practice), and (8) evaluation and measurement (theory and practice).

CHOOSING A CAREER—SPEAKING GENERALLY

Having reviewed a proposed model to help bring about the optimum development of a field called physical education and sport in the title of this book, you, the reader, will now be asked to spend a few moments reviewing at least some of the reasons why you may have expressed an interest in what we have referred to as the field of study that deals with human motor performance in sport, dance, play, and exercise. With a topic such as this we encounter a great deal of confusion on the part of many different people, students included. Society is steadily becoming more complex with greater role differentiation. It has been estimated that there are between 20,000 and 25,000 different occupations from which a person could conceivably choose. We are told, however, that young people are often reluctant to choose some of the newer occupations (e.g., ecology, ethnology, city planning). Why is this so? Lack of information? Insufficient courage? Pressure by parents or friends? Influence of the media? Unwillingness to accept a life style that has not been experienced previously? It is difficult to respond to this question, but my own pet theory is that people tend to follow what they feel is the tried and true route because they are not provided with enough opportunity to "stick their necks out without getting their heads chopped off."

Each decade seems to bring about a change in emphasis, a reordering of priorities, a difference in approach on the part of students. At one point individualism seemed to be in vogue, and then there seemed to be a greater trend toward conformity and a desire to choose the generally accepted occupations. Upward of 50% of college students when asked are quite undecided. I typically ask new students in an introductory course to write down what they expect to be doing with their life 10 years hence, and I get the wildest answers from a large percentage of them and rather stereotyped answers from the rest. This bothers me greatly, but it is very difficult to know what to do about the ideas and attitudes that seem to prevail.

I cannot escape the feeling also that students are not particularly excited about their careers. However, they do seem to be really concerned about the type of life style they are going to be able to afford. A few students want to find themselves, but many more seem to fit into the pattern of the 1970s—a time when young people usually soon became part of the "me generation." "How much will I make at this job?" "What are the hours?" "How long must I go to school to be able to qualify?" I often get the idea that a young person wants to start at the top and work up! And then there is the question that all interviewers dread when a young person is being interviewed early in his career, "What kind of a pension plan does this organization have?"

Some young persons want a life style, while others want to find meaning in their work. Some are antibusiness, while others want to make the most money as soon as possible. Some are really anxious to enter a profession, and others are just looking for a job. Some want to perform a public service, but others are not interested in helping others. Some are quite pampered products of an affluent society, whereas others have worked hard on a farm from an early age. Some want hard science-oriented programs, while others lean to the social sciences and humanities. Some are realistic in the everyday sense, whereas others are (nonphilosophical) idealists of the first order. Some want to be generalists; others are inclined toward specialization as soon as possible. Some have distorted ideas of reality, but others have had "hard slugging" for a number of years already. All in all, what we find is interesting but also quite disturbing to those who have found their purpose in life. Perhaps counselors should not worry. Maybe it is wise to shop around a bit. We used to say, "Try it out; after all, you're not marrying the job" (the latter clause implying a sense of finality and permanence that seems to have vanished in today's world).

CHOOSING A CAREER—SPEAKING SPECIFICALLY

A person who is thinking carefully about choosing an occupation or career should make an effort to examine the proposed field under certain categories or subheadings: (1) definition of the occupation, (2) history and importance, (3) nature of the work, (4) working conditions, (5) qualifications necessary for entry and success, (6) preparation needed, (7) opportunities for advancement, (8) remuneration and security, (9) advantages, (10) disadvantages, (11) how to get started toward the occupation, and (12) related or allied occupations. Quite obviously this entire book could be filled with extensive discussions of each of these categories and appropriate related questions. I do not intend to follow through with such an approach, however, because there is so much basic material about the field that simply must be covered. I do urge, nevertheless, that several class periods be assigned to discuss at some length the various questions that are raised below. The reader will appreciate that the answers to many of these questions will vary and perhaps change often, depending upon the state or province in which a discussion takes place. Some of the answers are self-evident, whereas others will require more specialized knowledge, a reasonable extent of which your instructor will most assuredly possess. There is definite value in asking representative members of the physical education and sport profession to make brief presentations to the class about their particular position, and this can be followed by a question-and-answer period. (At this point I must express appreciation to my colleagues over the years, notably people in both the physical education profession and the recreation profession in Canada, who have contributed many ideas to this type of format.) The following questions (and others) should be considered under the categories presented above:

Definition of the Occupation. After reviewing Figure 6, do you now have a better idea of what the field of physical education and sport is all about? Has the prevailing confusion about terminology disturbed you? Looking at the specific purposes for which we are (and should be) preparing men and women, where do you think you would fit best? Does this thought appeal to you?

History and Importance. Do you have in mind a brief history of the occupation, particularly in North America? (If not, this and many other questions under this heading will be described further by Dr. VanderZwaag in Chapter 1, "Background, Meaning, and Significance.") How does this occupation serve society? Is it ultimately important? How many people, male and female, are employed in this occupation locally, statewide or provincially, regionally, and nationally? Is the number involved increasing or decreasing? Is there wide geographical distribution of workers involved in the field?

Nature of the Work. What does a person involved in the various aspects of the field do (in each of the areas listed)? Consider a typical day. How much time is spent in physical activity? How much time might involve so-called mental activity? Or both combined? Is the work highly repetitive or is it varied? Is the work stimulating, or is it boring? Are there a reasonable number of new problems or challenges to solve?

Working Conditions. Is the work carried on indoors or outdoors? Are you sitting or standing most of the time? Are the working conditions generally sanitary? How many hours do you work? At what time of the day? Do you always work with others, or is some of your work done alone? What kind of fellow workers will you have? Are the work itself and the working conditions well organized? Are there hazards to you or others? Do you and your fellow workers belong to one or more professional organizations? What purposes do they serve? What are the opportunities for recreation, for vacation?

Qualifications Necessary for Entry and Success. What physical qualities are necessary for this profession—strength, endurance, coordination, flexibility, height, weight, good hearing, good eyesight, etc.? What degree of intelligence and emotional stability is needed? What other personality traits are desirable or required—initiative, persistence, leadership, willingness to cooperate, etc.? Are any special aptitudes or attributes required?

Preparation Needed. What general education and specialized professional preparation are necessary or desirable? How can you know the best colleges and universities from which to obtain such training? Is an internship or apprenticeship desirable or necessary? What university degrees will you need now or in the future to be fully qualified? Approximately how much money will all of this cost? Are scholarships available for those with high academic qualifications, for those with exceptional athletic ability, and for those bona fide students with financial need? Where can you obtain information about such scholarships and other information? Will you need any special equipment to get started in this occupation (either at university or after graduation)?

Opportunities for Advancement. What types of positions are available for performers, teachers, coaches, administrators, supervisors, teachers of teachers or coaches or both, scholars and researchers, an alternate career opportunity (such as sports business management, aquatics, athletic specialist, camp director, physical fitness specialist, sports public relations, sports author, sport art)? At what age do you enter any of these occupations? How do you go about entering them? Which of these are blind-alley occupations in the sense that advancement possibilities are limited? If there are levels of advancement in one of these occupations, how long must be spent typically at the various levels? Does a particular occupation seem to be overcrowded? In which of these positions will there be an opportunity for supervisory or administrative responsibility after a period of service?

Remuneration and Security. What annual earning may you expect at first in any of these positions? When you become experienced, what are the average annual earnings? What is the range of salary you might expect? Which of these positions can you remain with for your entire life? How often are you paid (weekly, monthly, etc.)? What provisions are there for pensions and possible early retirement? What other compensations are there (life insurance, dental insurance, unemployment insurance, illness or disability benefits, vacation periods, etc.)?

Advantages. In connection with one or more of the occupations listed above, what would you say are the main advantages of this position (service to mankind, salary, working conditions, opportunities for advancement, etc.)?

Disadvantages. In connection with one or more of the occupations listed above, what would you say are the main disadvantages of this position (salary, repetitiveness of duties, working conditions, period of professional preparation, status of the profession, etc.)?

How to Get Started toward the Occupation. Which subject-matter areas are vital for background prior to specialized professional preparation for one or more of these occupations? Are there hobbies and other activities that would help to prepare you for such involvement? Is there part-time or summer employment that would help to prepare you? What type of extra reading might be of assistance in strengthening your background?

Related or Allied Occupations. If it turns out that you become interested in looking elsewhere for your occupation, what other professions are similar with respect to the nature of the work (e.g., health education, safety education, driver education, related disciplines, recreation manager, park administration)? Are the working conditions of any of these markedly different? What differences are there in regard to personal qualifications (e.g., recreation director)? What differences are there in regard to professional preparation (e.g., health educator)? Finally, if you do not complete the period of professional preparation for one or more of these positions, what opportunities are there for those with lesser qualifications?

CONCLUDING STATEMENT

In this introductory chapter my objective as editor has been to set the stage for the eight chapters and Epilogue to follow. After a statement about the state of the world, we considered briefly the nature of man historically. The coming clash between ecology and economics was stressed. We felt it was important to mention the status of education as a social institution. Then we took a look at the status of physical education and sport as well.

A significant portion of this chapter was devoted to a historical analysis of the development of physical education and the allied professions in the twentieth century. An attempt was made to project our thinking into the future, and a model for the optimum development of physical education and sport was recommended.

Finally, you, the reader were asked to consider (or perhaps reconsider) the bases upon which you may have tentatively chosen your career. You were asked to consider a great many questions, general and specific, perhaps with the help of your instructor in discussion groups in which other experienced professionals in this field might be involved.

REFERENCES

Adelman, M.: An Assessment of Sport History Theses in the United States, 1931–1967. M.A. thesis, University of Illinois, Champaign, 1970.
Asimov, I.: The fourth revolution. Sat. Rev. Oct. 24, 1970, 17–20.
Berelson, B., and Steiner, G.A.: Human Behavior: An Inventory of Scientific Findings. New York, Harcourt, Brace and World, 1964.
Brubacher, J.S.: A History of the Problems of Education. 2nd Ed. New York, McGraw-Hill, 1966.
Cousins, N.: Prophecy and pessimism. Sat. Rev. WORLD, Aug. 24, 1974, 6–7.
Gould, S.B.: The academic condition. In New York Times, Sept. 23, 1969, p. 30.
Griffith, Thomas.: The best of times—1821? 1961? Today? Time Magazine Essay, Sept. 1, 1975, p. 51.
McCurdy, J.H.: Physical training as a profession. Am. Phys. Ed. Rev., 6, 4:311–312, 1901.
Morris, V.C.: Physical education and the philosophy of education. J. Health, Phys. Ed. Rec., 27, 3:21–22, 30–31, 1956.
Murray, B.G, Jr.: What the ecologists can teach the economists. New York Times Magazine, Dec. 10, 1972, pp. 38–39, 64–65, 70,72.
Oberlin College Catalogue, 1894.
Schwartz, E.S.: *Overskill: Decline of Technology in Modern Civilization.* New York, Times Books, 1971.
Toffler, A.: Future Shock. New York, Random House, 1970.
Wellesley College Catalogue, 1910.
Zeigler, E.F.: An analysis of an approach to teaching: Mosston's spectrum of styles. Aust. J. Phys. Ed. 48: 29–30, 1970.
Zeigler, E.F. (ed.): A History of Physical Education and Sport in the United States and Canada. Champaign, Ill., Stipes, 1975a.

Zeigler, E.F.: Personalizing Physical Education and Sport Philosophy. Champaign, Ill, Stipes, 1975b.

Zeigler, E.F.: Physical Education and Sport Philosophy. Englewood Cliffs, N.J., Prentice-Hall, 1977.

Zeigler, E.F. (ed.): A History of Physical Education and Sport. Englewood Cliffs, N.J., Prentice-Hall, 1979a.

Zeigler, E.F.: Past, present, and future development of physical education and sport. The Academy Papers, no. 13. Edited by G. Scott. Washington, D.C., AAHPERD, 1979b.

Zeigler, E.F., and Spaeth, M.J. (eds.): Administrative Theory and Practice in Physical Education and Athletics. Englewood Cliffs, N.J., Prentice-Hall, 1975.

CHAPTER ONE

Background, Meaning, and Significance

Harold J. VanderZwaag

It is difficult to determine where to begin a chapter on the background, meaning, and significance of sport and physical education since much has been written about both topics. Even more has been experienced by those who are involved in sport or physical education in one way or another. Yet there seems to be so much confusion. What are the differences between sport and physical education? Some people would lead us to believe that any differences are largely semantic. One might wish that it were such a simple matter. However, it would seem a bit ludicrous to identify the activity of the National Football League as physical education. By the same token, I seriously doubt whether professional people in dance or movement education consider their work to be part of the sport domain. I contend that the real differences, and ultimate source of difficulty, between sport and physical education can be attributed to organizational confusion. The purposes here are to sort out that confusion and to offer a prospectus for consideration.

BACKGROUND OF SPORT

There are at least two ways to gain a perspective on the background of that human activity we today call sport. The first is an attempt to take a collective look at the development of sport-like activity. It involves a historical analysis of the development of sport in a generic sense. This is the approach I used elsewhere in identifying seven stages in the development of sport as a concept (1972, pp. 22–29):

1. British "field sports"—highlighted in seventeenth century England
2. Organization of other sports in eighteenth century England
3. Mid- to late- nineteenth century sport developments in the United States—particularly the rise of intercollegiate sport
4. Organization of intramural sport programs in the schools and colleges—beginning around 1914
5. Organization of various community sport programs for youth—epitomized by the establishment of Little League baseball in 1939
6. The golden age of sport—roughly covering the period from post World War II to the present—characterized by extensive increase in sport involvement by many people in a variety of sports, both as participants and as spectators
7. Sport as an area for scholarly inquiry—largely a development of the past 15 years—a stage whose impact or future development is still difficult to assess

This outline represents only a cursory look at the development of the total idea of sport. However, it is designed to convey the thought that there is a certain generic

Dr. VanderZwaag is from The University of Massachusetts, Amherst.

sense within which the background of sport can be assessed. In a much more exhaustive manner this is also the basic approach employed by Lucas and Smith in presenting the *Saga of American Sport* (1978).

Even though it is highly desirable to gain insight into the broader perspective in the development of sport, considerably more can be learned from closer examination of the specifics in the development of each sport. That is not to say that the history of sport is nothing more or less than the collective history of the various sports, but at least this would provide a sound point of departure in attempting to gain a better understanding of the total picture. This, however, is an advantage for a sport historian that is not shared by one who desires to investigate the history of physical education. It is possible that the researcher could begin by exploring the history of gym classes; but, beyond that, the various components of physical education do not yield a comparable basis for concrete inquiry as is found in the history of the various sports. More about that will be said later.

In spite of the advantage in probing the history of sports, it by no means makes it a simple matter to gain a firm understanding of the background of sport. For example, Lucas and Smith have included the following entries under their index heading of football:

Football, 300. See also Intercollegiate Football
    American game, 234
    Boston game, 232
    college game, 229–232
    colonial college game, 193, 194
    in Colonial New England, 25
    deaths from, 242
    flying wedge, 240–241
    legislation against, 242
    masculinity factor, 288, 289, 291
    mass plays, 239–242
    rugby game, 230, 232–235, 233
    scoring, 235

Football (professional), 317, 331, 332, 333, 334
    attendance, 325
    Blacks in, 376–378
    Depression and, 321
    integration in, 390–391, 395
    salaries, 331, 335
    Super Bowl, 337

Football equipment, 239, 240
Football rules, 230, 231, 232, 234–235, 240, 243–244, 245
Football stadia. See Stadia   (1978, p. 428)

If one reads the material cited above, one would have a fairly good understanding of the background of football. However, even that would be far from a complete study of the topic. From that point of recognition, the complications are greatly extended when one notes the large number of sports, each with its own history. Nevertheless, in spite of the enormity of the task, the history of sports does offer a viable means for studying the background of that human activity.

BACKGROUND OF PHYSICAL EDUCATION

In contrast to the situation involving sport, the means used to explore the background of physical education are much more obscure. It is necessary to attend to the parts before arriving at an understanding of the whole. However, in the case of physical education, the components, or parts, are not that easily identified.

Spears and Swanson present a definition of physical education. Their definition is one that has fairly general acceptance. "Physical education is referred to as a program of physical activities, usually in educational institutions, including dance, exercise, bodily development activities, and sport" (1978, p. 8). The title of their book was obviously selected to convey the idea that the work is designed to offer more than just background information on sport. In fact, this is made quite clear in the preface: "Dance and exercise, together with sport, are frequently included in school physical education, and therefore, it seems appropriate to include them in this account. The history of physical education as it relates to sport is also appropriate to the text. For these reasons, we selected the title, *History of Sport and Physical Activity in the United States*" (p. xi).

As one examines its content, the work seems to be largely a history of sport in the United States. Yet the authors are consistent in that the analysis is not entirely restricted to sport. With that framework one can glean something with respect to the background of physical education in the United States. My own analysis leads to the following conclusions regarding that background:

1. The establishment of the Round Hill School in Northampton, Massachusetts, in 1823 was a critical turning point in the establishment of the idea of physical education. Spears and Swanson cite earlier examples of organized physical activity in the schools, but the key change may be found in the following statement about Round Hill: "Physical education was made an integral part of the curriculum" (1978, p. 80). The pivotal influence of Round Hill is also reinforced by Lucas and Smith. In their entire work they give only scant attention to the history of physical education. However, the following statement is on target in identifying an early development in physical education:

   > The first volume of the *American Journal of Education* in November, 1826, beamed the good news that qualified instructors of physical education—'men of eminence in science, literature, as well as in the gymnastic art,' were available for hire. Only the year before, Dr. Charles Beck, of Germany, had met these qualifications and was hired to teach physical education at the Round Hill School in Northampton, Massachusetts—the first instructor of gymnastics in this country. (1978, p. 72)

2. It is clear that the earlier programs of physical education in the United States were largely identified with gymnastics. This represents the most direct link between European programs and the development of physical education in the United States. In particular, the German influence is evident. The names of Charles Beck, Francis Lieber, and Charles Follen are somewhat synonymous with the introduction of physical education as a program in the schools.

3. Catherine Beecher stands out as one who was instrumental in advocating the idea that organized exercise programs are beneficial for women as well as for men. Her work also characterizes the train of thought and action that brought physical education into full fledged existence. Beecher's ideas were reinforced through the efforts of Mary Lyon to provide calisthenics for women at Mount Holyoke Seminary. Thus we find that calisthenics can be added to gymnastics as the principal roots of physical education.

4. The first state law requiring physical education was passed in California in 1866 through the efforts of John Swett, who was then the California State Superintendent of Public Instruction (Spears and Swanson, 1978, p. 123). This is also a significant landmark in the background of physical education. There is much evidence that would indicate that physical education has been largely perpetuated through the medium of state legislation.

5. The emergence of physical education as a profession can also be properly identified with the appointments of professors of physical education in various colleges and universities. In this regard, another pivotal action was the appointment of Dr. Edward Hitchcock as Professor of Hygiene and Physical

Education at Amherst College in 1861. His program served as a model for later developments in several other colleges and universities. It is most significant that Hitchcock carefully distinguished between his program and that of "athletic sports" at Amherst College (Weston, 1962, pp. 107–112). At this point in time it was quite evident that there was virtually no effort to provide a marriage between sport and physical education.

6. The last significant landmark in the development of physical education per se is one that still more or less represents the status quo. Spears and Swanson offer a succinct statement of what took place: "During the period between the two World Wars, sport, exercise, dance, and physical activity became integral parts of the education system in the United States" (1978, p. 212). That brief statement basically tells the story. By a variety of means (too complicated to explain in detail here) the earlier roots of physical education in gymnastics and calisthenics were extended to include sport and dance. Furthermore, it is fairly evident that sport became the focus of the men's physical education program, whereas the women's concentrated on sport, dance, and body mechanics (later movement education).

Lewis offers a most insightful analysis of what happened with respect to sport and physical education:

> Well-intentioned administrators, assisted by a tremendous increase in the number and size of physical education programs, forced physical educators to adopt the sports program. From this point formulation of a philosophy was merely a practice in justifying the existence of programs already sanctioned by higher authority. Accommodation then, of varsity athletics, was the key factor in the transformation of the profession. The status of competitive athletics established the location of physical education in high schools and colleges; facilities, equipment, and staff secured for varsity sports determined the content of the curricula and the nature of the programs. (1969, p. 42)

In my opinion there is no more significant statement regarding the recent background of physical education than that in the above quotation. It seems that physical education achieved its real birth as a stepchild of high school and collegiate athletics. By and large this explains many of the current complications. This also prompts the consideration of meaning: What is the current situation involving sport and physical education?

MEANING OF SPORT

Although a logical approach to a discussion of meaning would seem to begin with some sort of definition since we often have to establish the parameters before probing beneath the surface, I shall omit this because the definitional efforts regarding sport have been numerous during the past decade. Furthermore, there is good reason to believe that sport is better experienced and understood than it is defined. Consequently the immediate objective is to review what is known about sport in terms of understanding it as a particular kind of human activity.

I begin by calling attention to three works that have contributed much to such understanding, by Weiss, Novak, and Cady. Although they do not share a common focus, all three authors present ideas that probe the meaning of sport in a deeper sense.

Weiss's *Sport: A Philosophic Inquiry* represents a real breakthrough among efforts to understand sport from a theoretical perspective. Actually, what he did was to call direct attention to a fact that has long been recognized by anyone who has been deeply involved with sport. His opening statement offers the key to everything that follows: "Excellence excites and awes. It pleases and it challenges" (1969, p. 3). One could stop there and make a fairly accurate guess at the central thrust in the work. Weiss sees sport as one of the primary means for the pursuit of and identification with excellence. He is careful to add that it is far from being the only means and not even necessarily the best means. But it happens to be a means that is pursued by many people.

In spite of its significance, two principal criticisms can be levied against Weiss's exposition on sport. The first is that the account has virtually no meaning in terms of explaining the participation of the masses in sport. It can hardly be said that the millions of people who play tennis, racquetball, and golf or who ski, swim, and jog are pursuing excellence through their sport participation. The real meaning of sport for most of these participants has to be found in something other than the pursuit of excellence. One will find that is particularly true after reading Weiss's analysis of what is involved in pursuing excellence.

The second criticism is that his account precludes the majority of women participants. Several statements in Weiss's chapter on women athletes can be used to document his contention that sport participation lacks significant meaning for most women. The following is an example: "A woman, therefore, will typically interest herself in sport only when she sees that will enable her to polish what she had previously acquired without thought or effort" (1969, p. 218). Earlier, after explaining the male need to "turn their minds into bodily vectors" (his description of what the athlete accomplishes), he states; "Normal women do not have this problem, at least not in the acute form that it presents to the men" (1969, p. 217).

In the final analysis, Weiss's treatise seems to disfranchise a very large segment of the sporting world—that is, almost all women and those males who participate in sport for reasons other than the pursuit of excellence. We are left with a splendid account of the meaning of sport for young adult males and the host of spectators who identify with the excellence demonstrated by those athletes. The latter group points to the key significance of Weiss's work in explaining the meaning of sport, in spite of the limitations noted earlier. He has laid bare the meaning of spectator sport that appears to be at the heart of sport as it is known today, at least the kind of sport receiving the vast majority of attention in the sports pages of the various newspapers and in sports magazines such as *Sports Illustrated*. His account of women still seems to be deficient, but he could be given the benefit of the doubt with the suggestion that his treatment might be a bit different if it had written it in 1980 instead of in 1969. However, even then the extent to which he would alter his hypothesis is somewhat questionable on the basis of his relative dismissal of social custom as a prime consideration in explaining the comparatively few women athletes.

Most importantly, Weiss presents an interpretation of the meaning of spectator sport. His approach can be justified on the ground that he analyzes what has been "center stage" in sport during the twentieth century. It might even be said that Weiss interpreted philosophically what Lewis found historically. Earlier reference was made to Lewis's research that led to the conclusion that varsity sport was the dominant factor in shaping the total sport programs in the schools. There is little doubt that Weiss explains the true meaning of varsity sport.

In prefacing this discussion of the meaning of sport I pointed out that the works of Weiss, Novak, and Cady do not share a common focus. They do, however, share a common denominator—all three are heavily oriented toward examination of spectator sport. Differences in focus are to be found in their interpretation of the meaning of such sport.

In an attempt to identify the meaning of sport for Novak, no single word stands out as sharply as excellence does for Weiss. If a choice had to be made it would probably be either fan or rooting. Novak is first and foremost a sports fan. At the outset he indicates that this is the driving factor behind his writing of the book. "How could I be 40 years old and still care what happens to the Dodgers? How could I have thrown away 3 hours of evaporating life, watching a ritual, an inferior dance, a competition without a socially redeeming point?" (1976, p. xi). *Rooting* is another key word in Novak's exposition. It is one of his "seven seals" and is an obvious extension of the focus on the fan. He makes a sharp distinction between a spectator and a fan. Although a fan may be called a spectator, he is a special kind of spectator. A fan is a spectator who really cares. Rooting, thus, can be viewed as the dynamic link in the extension from spectator to fan.

The word *religion* is also critical in Novak's analysis of sport. He uses the term *natural religion* to distinguish sport from what is customarily recognized as being a religion. Furthermore, he carefully points out that sport should not be viewed as a substitute for religion in the traditional sense. Two statements rather dramatically convey his conception of the natural religion: "Going to a stadium is half like going to a political rally, half like going to church" (p. 19). "A ballpark is not a temple, but it isn't a fun house either" (p. 23).

The most penetrating part of Novak's work can be found in his analysis of the seven seals. As I see it, his analysis is right on target if one is seeking an in-depth interpretation of the meaning of sport. In prefacing his explication of the seals, Novak also presents a most convincing argument of why one should come to grips with the meaning of sport:

> There are priests who mumble through the Mass, lovers who read letters over a naked shoulder in love's embrace, teachers who detest students, pedants who shrink from original ideas. So also there are athletes, fans, and sportswriters who never grasp the beauty or the treasure entrusted them. . . . But the failures of human flesh to measure up to the beauties possible in sports should not deter us from pursuing what it is in them that draws so on our love.
>
> Seven seals lock the inner life of sports. They may be broken, one by one. (1976, p. 121)

Novak then proceeds to explicate the seven seals: sacred space, sacred time, bond of brothers, rooting, agon, competing, and self-discovery. I will not go into a detailed discussion of his analysis. However, even from a superficial viewpoint it should be apparent that the seven are most instrumental in attempting to comprehend the fuller meaning of sport. This is true whether one is considering only spectator sport or moves beyond that to include the parameters involving all sport participants. Certainly the seventh seal, self-discovery, is readily recognized as a common point of meaning for all who have any form of extended involvement with sport. To that extent the thrust of Novak's work moves somewhat beyond the focus of Weiss's inquiry.

With Cady the focus is even more restricted in one respect. He does not attempt to explore the meaning of sport in the broader sense. *The Big Game* examines only the meaning of college sports in the United States. That may seem too provincial to grasp anything significant about the meaning of sport. On the other hand, he offers an in-depth analysis of the significance of a segment of sport that is so instrumental in the American sporting scene. It could be argued that collegiate sport serves as the hub for the various manifestations of sport in the high school, professional, and private club sectors. In that regard *The Big Game* may not be as limited as it first appears. Although there would appear to be little in the way of meaning for international sport, it could be that the comparison between the development of sport in North American colleges and universities and that found elsewhere is significant in itself.

Perhaps the most insightful component of Cady's contribution is the manner in which he brings to attention the extended meaning of the college game. The following passage more or less typifies what college sport can mean for those who are involved with it:

> Nevertheless, the collegiate Big Game is different. Nothing elsewhere resembles it. Nothing in professional sport captures, for all the flackery money can buy, the same

glamor or intensity or significance. "I'm filled with wonder every Saturday!" says John Pont, one of the more imaginative coaches. The difference arises from the unique involvement of major institutions of higher education and learning. It locks in symbolic combat the peoples of 'sovereign states': Texas-Oklahoma; Tennessee-Kentucky; Wisconsin-Minnesota. It confronts massive regional and cultural differences: Notre Dame-UCLA; Penn State-Alabama; Virginia-DePaul. It pits life-styles and social convictions: Stanford-USC; Duke-Carolina; Rice-Arkansas. It is symbolically fratricidal: Grambling-Florida A & M; Yale-Harvard; Providence-Marquette. Whole spectra of the national life clash fraternally in the Big Game. (1978, pp. 3–4)

Throughout his work, Cady draws attention to the fact that the fuller meaning of collegiate sport extends far beyond that which takes place on the playing field or court. Much of his analysis centers on those conditions and actions that are external to the actual contest. Yet that can be significant in itself—if one is attempting to get a grasp on the broader interpretation of sport. This is also a primary reason why it is most difficult to probe the meaning of sport. The parameters challenge any attempt to isolate the activity as a particular phenomenon centering around the competition among athletes. Nevertheless, the effort of Cady reinforces the thought that the challenge can be met.

Only one real caution has to be applied in assessing the validity of *The Big Game*. Cady might lead us to believe that the extended meaning of sport is limited to the college game. The cultural context is highlighted in the following of the Pittsburgh Pirates and the Pittsburgh Steelers. At the same time the International Olympic Committee is finding it increasingly difficult to convince the world that the games of the Olympics are only for the athletes.

So what can we conclude about the meaning of sport? From one standpoint that meaning is quite precise. It is precise to the extent that we can identify various sports and readily recognize the kind of activity that takes place within the enactment of that particular sporting event. In other words, sport begins with a fair degree of concreteness. We can even make comparisons among sports that lead to a broader perspective on sport. However, beyond that the road can lead to many paths as one searches for a total understanding of sport. Novak's seven seals offer as complete a reference point as can be cited to date. Nevertheless, a complete examination of the work of Weiss, Novak, Cady, and others would lead to the conclusion that the meaning of sport is a complicated topic. At best we can probably hope to recognize some of that meaning.

Meaning of Physical Education

I am tempted to begin and end by stating that the meaning of physical education can be derived from noting what takes place within the context of gym classes in the public schools. Yet for at least two reasons that hardly seems the right thing to do. Most importantly, such an abrupt beginning and ending would not do justice to the volumes of material written on the nature of physical education. Also, the primary identification of physical education with public school gym classes may merely represent a professional bias of mine. Therefore I will proceed with delineation of that which appears to lie deeper in the meaning of physical education.

Many of the attempts to probe the meaning of physical education date back several years. Among more recent works, Siedentop's *Physical Education: Introductory Analysis* stands out as a legitimate effort in the search for such meaning. Although his efforts to arrive at meaning proceed from a definitional base, he does not stop with mere definition. After assessing other selected efforts to define physical education, Siedentop advances his own source of meaning:

It is my contention that the source of meaning in physical education is best explained by the concept of play and that play is the classification necessary in order to most satisfactorily define the concept of physical education. Further, I will attempt to show that the logical and psychological meaning of our subject matter is best understood and analyzed by classifying physical education as a species of play education. (1976, pp. 217–218)

He then concludes his conceptual effort with a discussion of what he calls the differentiae which define the concept of physical education (p. 226). I suppose his approach here could be considered roughly analogous to the explication of the seven seals by Novak. According to Siedentop the differentiae are

these characteristics that differentiate physical education from other play forms (other members of the same class) such as art, music, and drama (p. 226). He identifies them as (1) an educational criterion for increasing subject matter approach tendencies, (2) an educational criterion for increasing abilities, (3) competitive activities, (4) expressive activities, and (5) activities with a dominant motor emphasis. (p. 232)

Other physical education theorists might not agree with Siedentop's focus on play. Nevertheless, his differentiae strike a familiar cord with respect to other efforts at exploring the meaning of physical education.

The idea that physical education must meet an educational criterion probably is the master key to unlocking the deeper meaning of physical education. Analysis of the background of physical education will reveal that physical educators have usually been preoccupied with their concern that physical education be recognized as an integral part of the educational process. The logic behind such concern is readily understood. Physical educators are employed as part of a school system. Schools are supposed to be first and foremost concerned with the educational process. Therefore, physical educators consider it necessary to secure their place in the sun by proclaiming the educational benefits of their work. After all, who wants to be a second class citizen? With that form of reasoning either consciously or subconsciously operative, the literature of physical education is replete with efforts to justify the existence of physical education from an educational perspective. Even though Siedentop might differ from some of his colleagues in identifying the focus on play, he is careful to add that it should be conceived as play education.

One other key to unlocking the meaning of physical education can also be elicited from Siedentop's differentiae. That is the proposition that physical education involves activities with a dominant motor emphasis. Once again this strikes a familiar tone that is evident in much of the physical education literature. It would appear that this is also a principal reason why many physical educators tend to be quite uncomfortable about the suggestion that sport is the focus of physical education. They will readily point out that physical education includes many activities with a dominant motor emphasis that do not meet the criteria for a sport. Dance, movement education, and various exercise (fitness) programs would be cited as examples of activities with a dominant motor emphasis that are not sports. Hence, in the conception of physical education, sport shares the motor emphasis domain with a number of other activities.

Thus it would appear that the essence of physical education can be readily identified in those school activities that have a dominant motor emphasis and meet certain educational criteria. I would add that the idea of instruction seems to loom large in the fulfillment of those educational criteria. However, another dimension to the meaning of physical education is worth noting, a dimension that lies beneath the surface, but it may be the most significant in explaining why there are conflicts between certain segments of the sport enterprise and physical education.

Physical educators have a mission. As I see it that mission has a twofold thrust. The first objective is to maximize participation by providing opportunities for everyone to benefit from learning through the experience of engaging in these activities with a dominant motor emphasis. The second objective would appear to be a corollary of the first. In attempting to meet their first objective, physical educators are convinced that various controls must be applied to the sport enterprise. Competition is usually the focal point in calling for the control. The literature of physical education and the language of physical educators are replete with references to the need for controlling the extent of competition in sport. Beyond this focal concern about competition we find several related aspects that add spokes to the wheel involving the total mission of physical education. There seems to be inherent resistance to such ideas as sport is entertainment, sport is business, and the commercial nature of sport or that sport should be marketed. Even though physical educators recognize those conditions of sport in our society, they are firm in their conviction that their sport should not be contaminated by such conditions that seem to work at cross-purposes to their principal objectives. This sort of thinking is dramatically revealed in the current posture of the AIAW, which is really a physical education organization. Although the NCAA and the AIAW share a common interest in sport, it is quite obvious that they are far apart in their general orientation toward the conduct of the sport enterprise. The AIAW orientation flows from a mission that undergirds the meaning of physical education.

SIGNIFICANCE

In what direction does this point? Thus far I have attempted to survey those factors that contribute to the background and meaning of sport and physical education, but the past and present need not necessarily dictate the future. 'Significance' is a fairly excessive concept. In defining *significance*, Webster refers to *meaning*. However, significance is extended meaning. The idea of import looms critically in any examination of the significance of a given set of conditions. One might also say that import is what it is all about. While it is helpful to begin with an assessment of background and meaning, we must look beyond this to future possibilities. If that were not the case, progress would be an obsolete concept. For these reasons I have chosen to devote greater attention to the topic of significance.

Before I proceed with this analysis of significance (directional import), one other organizational guide post should also be noted. Proposed changes in structure make it inappropriate to present separate comments on the significance of sport and the significance of physical education. What is suggested is elimination of the field of physical education as such. Thus it would make little sense to discuss significance within that context. At this point many of the readers may be completely "turned off" and feel that it would be useless to continue reading this chapter. I fully realize that such a thought can sound utterly ridiculous and even hostile to one whose profession is physical education. However, I would like to make the case that the significance of present-day physical educators can actually be enhanced through a restructuring that would more clearly delineate their professional identity. It is also important to note that this prospectus is not a mere semantic exercise. Within recent years quite a few people have suggested that the name of physical education should be changed. That in itself would accomplish little. We have to get at the root of the organizational confusion within the profession. There are many capable people in the field of physical education. They have done well in spite of problems associated with organizational identity. However, as we look toward future significance, what can be done to realize some of the untapped potential?

A Sport Management Profession

At present the sport enterprise can be characterized by one word—fragmentation. Sport programs are conducted under many different auspices: in schools, in YMCAs and YWCAs, in community recreation, in industry, in country clubs and other private clubs, in resorts, among professional sport teams. That list is certainly not complete, but it should be sufficient to demonstrate the diversified sponsorship of the sport enterprise. Many of the professional teachers, coaches, and administrators in the broad field of sport have much in common. Yet the irony of the situation is that most of these people have little opportunity to benefit from the accumulated knowledge and skill in the total sport enterprise. They have been shackled by conventions related to their particular professional preparation and professional associations. There is good reason to believe that those who conduct sport programs have more in common than those who currently work under other professional umbrellas. Physical education offers a classic example of the need to search for meaningful professional identity.

In addition to sport specialists, in physical education we find dance specialists, exercise scientists, fitness specialists, movement educators, and health educators. There even are generalists in physical education, whatever may be involved under that classification. The work of all of those people is legitimate in its own right. However, it is difficult to imagine that many of these professionals benefit from the combined expertise of their field. At the same time the sport specialists (and others) are more or less precluded from opportunities to interact with others who are doing essentially the same kind of work. The common denominator is sport. Beyond that, commonality can further be identified through particular interest and ability in one or more sports.

Thus the first pillar for the sport management profession is built on recognition that the focus is on sport, wherever it may be found. Then what about management? How does that fit into the picture? The answer is fairly simple, although it would appear that the basis for the answer has been generally overlooked. The key to the answer can be found by considering those functions that are integral to the management process. These are generally considered to be planning, organizing, staffing, directing, and controlling. From that frame of reference, almost every professional position in sport is of a managerial nature. The athlete is the only notable exception. Beyond that, management is the "name of the game" as we look at the various roles of those who conduct the sport enterprise. This is particularly true when we look at key positions in the sport enterprise such as general manager, athletic director, club manager, and head instructor. However, the significance of management in sport does not stop with the most obvious managerial roles. Even the coach, particularly the head coach, is a manager; it is not merely accidental that the head coach of a professional baseball team is called a manager. As we look back over the five functions of a manager, he is just that.

So we can begin by identifying a common bond among those who have managerial roles in the sport enterprise. Is there a profession? The question is not easily answered. It would probably be safer to say that there could be one than to suggest that it currently exists. However, as Mullin points out, at least the possibilities are there:

> Returning to the Chicken and the Egg questions—When is a profession a profession? We have seen that Sport Executives in the various segments of sport do not necessarily consider themselves as professionals in Sport Management. Yet they undoubtedly are managers in a Sport Industry. To justify the term, Sport Management profession, we must demonstrate a whole body of persons engaged in a calling requiring specialized knowledge. The numbers are clearly there, as an estimated 150,000 organizations in North America are either wholly or substantially involved in Sport. The specialized situation demanding specialized knowledge is also there. The distinguishing characteristics that set Sport Management apart from Management in a general industrial context are also present. (1980, p. 5)

At any rate, regardless of the state of the art concerning a sport management profession, the concept of sport management makes sense. The establishment of academic programs in sport management, the *Sport Management Newsletter*, and the formation of the Sport Management Art and Science Society are partial evidence of the thought that the profession may be emerging. Therefore it would appear that further development of a sport management profession may be one of the significant guidelines as we look toward new directions.

Sport Management Positions

A profession is made up of people who hold professional positions. Earlier reference was made to some of the positions that might be included under the rubric of sport management. However, before proceeding I will discuss a few things about these positions and provide a more complete listing of possibilities. What these really represent is a listing of potential career patterns for those who aspire to work in sport management. Within the past few years I have heard and seen considerable reference to the idea of alternate career patterns in physical education. That proposition seems to be built on the assumption that physical education is the main stem, and related sport positions flow from that stem. The following listing is quite different. None of these positions is meant to be an alternate to another. Priorities are also not implied; as noted earlier, the exclusive relationship among these is work in some facet of sport management.

Athletic Director. It is appropriate to identify the athletic director (AD) first because it is so easily recognized as a sport management position. Most Americans have some idea of the work performed by an AD. It is readily noted that he is first and foremost a manager at the executive level. It is also obvious that the management of several different sport programs is one of the more characteristic features of the position. The fact that he happens to be called an AD (rather than a sport director) is really quite incidental; interscholastic and intercollegiate sport competition is known as athletic competition. This in no way makes it difficult to associate the AD with sports.

Entry into an AD's position is fairly clear-cut but difficult to obtain. I say "fairly clear-cut" because the record shows that most ADs are former coaches and that most coaches are former intercollegiate athletes. Ceglarski's study shows that 95% of the college AD's are former coaches (1979). This study was limited to males. Intercollegiate athletic programs for women are still in too early a stage of development to include women ADs as a significant factor in assessing current qualifications. As more women move into an AD's position it will be interesting to compare their qualifications with those found in Ceglarski's study of males. For instance, he also found that the bulk of the coaching experience among ADs was in either football or basketball.

This suggests one other observation that should be made before leaving the brief discussion of an AD's position. I stated above that AD is an appropriate sport management position to identify first. However, it is appropriate only from the vantage point that has been identified. From another standpoint there would be much better places to begin. As an example, in terms of background information the subject of women ADs has little meaning, but when we move to significance (directional impact) the topic of women ADs moves to the foreground. It is not accidental that a relatively large number of women are now applying and being accepted for admission to the various academic sport management programs. The record will show that many of these women have high-school or collegiate job aspirations or both. In most cases the ultimate goal is to become an AD.

Of course, there is also a limitation in starting with the AD if one is looking at sport from an international perspective. ADs are not limited to the United States, but by and large the AD is an American creation and figure of popularization. The reason for this is quite obvious. For the most part, ADs are found in schools and colleges. I have to assume that the majority of those who read this text will be students who have grown up with an undaunted acceptance of the North American way through heavy emphasis on sport competition among the schools and colleges. Therefore the selection of the AD will come as no surprise when we begin to identify sport management positions.

Assistant or Associate Athletic Director. Size of the institution and nature of the athletic program are the two significant variables in assessing the potential for the position of assistant or associate athletic director. There is also a factor involving women's athletics that currently makes it a viable position for women and in the future is likely to make it a more viable position for both men and women. At present, when men's and women's athletic programs are combined, the AD is still a male in most cases. A fairly customary arrangement is to provide an assistant or associate athletic director for women under the general athletic department. In many cases there is also a comparable assistant or associate AD for the men's program.

Large athletic departments may employ three or four assistant ADs with each one having responsibility for a segment of the total program. That segment may be operations, facilities, finance and budget, marketing, or student advising and eligibility. Particular arrangements will vary, depending on the needs of the department. However, there is increasing evidence that a relatively large number of departments are now employing an assistant AD in the general area of promotions and fund raising.

Traditionally the assistant AD positions have been filled by former coaches. To some extent this practice continues. However, expanded needs in fund raising and the accelerated changes in women's athletics are also creating a new market for special qualifications for assistant AD.

Sports Information Director. The subject of promotion brings to the foreground another position that has long been evident in intercollegiate athletic circles, sports information director, commonly known as the SID. The SID is generally considered to be responsible for publicizing and promoting the entire intercollegiate athletic program. However, as noted earlier, the tendency now is to have a separate position for promotions and fund raising. In these cases it is quite likely that the SID will report to the director of promotions. Of course, the "collapsing effect" should be noted with respect to the organizational matrix for collegiate athletic departments. This collapsing effect is most evident in relatively small athletic departments. Essentially it involves elimination of one or more of the middle management positions. Thus one will find a whole range of organizational arrangements involving functions and personnel related to fund raising, promotions, public relations, and publicity. In the really small college the collapsing effect is likely to be most evident. There we can anticipate that the middle management is eliminated completely with all of these functions being performed by the AD.

At any rate, the publicity need continues for all collegiate athletic departments. Either a full- or part-time SID must provide news releases, home-town features, athletic photographs, publications, special programs, special promotions for special athletes, and appropriate coverage of the athletic contest. It is obvious that some type of background in journalism is very significant for the SID. With respect to training, this feature distinguishes the SID position from any of the other sport management positions.

Intramural Sport Director. In a way, the position of intramural sport director epitomizes the need for a sport management profession. The "intramural people" have grown to be a most significant group in their own right. Yet their very growth has also tended to cut them off from many others who share common interests in the sport enterprise. The history of intramural sport has quite clearly been one that tends to move the programs further away from physical education and athletics. In fact, today, many colleges and universities have a unit called campus recreation, which tends to be an extension of the earlier intramural sport program. The growing independence of intramural sport programs and the extended scope of such programs has been evident for some time. The National Intramural Association was formed in 1950. This organization, known today as the National Intramural Recreational Sports Association (NIRSA), was the first group devoted strictly to intramural sports. Another significant action occurred in 1966 when the National Conference on College and

University Recreation recommended that intramural programs no longer be under the direction of a physical education or athletic department. The further suggestion was that there should be a campus recreation unit that would report to a service-oriented division, such as an office of student affairs.

Regardless of such actions, one cannot deny the fact that the link between campus recreation and intramural sport is still a strong one. Many of the activities are sport activities. There is considerable overlap in the use of facilities among athletics, physical education, and campus recreation. Furthermore, a minority of colleges and universities have followed the 1966 recommendation. In most places intramural sport is still organizationally related to athletics or physical education or both.

There is good reason to believe that an intramural sport director or director of campus recreation could also have much in common with those who manage sport programs through the medium of community recreation. Yet those people have also been limited in their associations because of the conformities stemming from different routes of professional preparation. A developing field of sport management would offer an opportunity to link school and community interests in the broad spectrum of recreational sport.

Business Manager/Ticket Manager. As we look at collegiate athletic departments across the United States, two other types of sport management positions can be readily identified—business manager and ticket manager. They may or may not be separate positions. Duties may also be combined under the rubric of another position, such as assistant athletic director. However, regardless of the specific arrangements, the functions are critical to the management of intercollegiate sport. It is also reasonable to expect that these will exist as separate positions in medium-sized to large athletic departments. As noted earlier, the collapsing effect is also evident in these positions as we survey the small college scene.

It is a bit difficult to pinpoint how people become business managers and ticket managers in collegiate athletic departments. However, it is safe to say that a business administration background is critical for the prospective business manager. In fact, an M.B.A. degree could be considered minimum qualification for such work in a large department. In some respects the situation is akin to that involving SIDs. Whether their background is journalism or business administration, both the SID and business manager must have a form of professional expertise outside the mainstream of professional advancement in sport management at the collegiate level.

By contrast, it is not nearly as easy to make a definitive statement about the specific professional qualification of a ticket manager. I am not aware of any study examining the qualifications of persons who hold positions as athletic ticket managers (of course, that does not mean that the data are not available). My guess would be that they come from diverse backgrounds. Probably some of them are former coaches. More likely they are people who have "worked in the trenches" through a long period of voluntary or part-time service with their particular athletic department. In many cases they have what could be called quasi professional status. But who is to say that this is not still another form of sport management position? They clearly carry out those managerial functions outlined earlier. Furthermore, any AD is likely to attest to the significant role of the ticket manager in carrying out many of the duties associated with the "hands-on" operation of the athletics program. When all is said and done, it is sport management in action.

Sport Instructor. Where does one begin when attempting to discuss the sport instructor in relationship to the total sport enterprise? It might be well to begin with a few observations about the instructor as manager. Without too much difficulty, almost everyone can relate to the idea that a head instructor might be viewed in the role of a manager; the word *head* implies management. We can understand that the basic functions of management are performed by those individuals who have capabilities for heading the various instructional programs. This is true whether they are head ski instructors, head gymnastics instructors, pros in golf clubs, chairpersons of physical education departments, or any one of a number of similar possibilities in which leadership is evident.

It becomes more difficult to relate to the idea that any sport instructor might be considered a manager. However, if we consider the basic functions of management (planning, organizing, staffing, directing, and controlling), it can certainly be argued that any instructor is a manager. The only questionable function among the five might be staffing, and that would depend on how far one would wish to extend the idea of staffing. In a strict sense, only a head instructor is involved with staffing as such. Nevertheless, any instructor has certain personnel responsibilities relative to arrangements for students that, in a broad sense, could also be viewed as staffing. There is no doubt that planning, organizing, directing, and controlling are any instructor's responsibility.

How do people become sport instructors? The answer is not a simple one, yet there is no question or answer more critical to any discussion of the background, meaning, and significance of sport and physical education. The problem is that sport instructors within the context of physical education tend to have one kind of background, whereas other sport instructors have a different kind of background. The common denominator seems to be some form of certification, but there are variances in the source and nature of certification. Physical education certification, of course, is tied in with the whole system of educational certification, which is controlled at the state or provincial level. Thus a bachelor's degree, student teaching, and a certain number of education courses are requisites for physical education certification. By contrast, certification as a professional instructor in a given sport requires rigorous and in-depth evaluation of the individual's ability to teach that sport. For example, the United States Professional Tennis Association requires for certification a resume, three credit references, preferably related to tennis, and a letter of sponsorship from a USPTA professional. Tennis instruction must be a major source of the applicant's income. In addition, the USPTA requires a written test and on-the-court tests of both playing and teaching. After passing, the applicant is rated "Professional," "Instructor," or "Apprentice."

This example of certification for teaching tennis is similar to the certification program for teaching other sports outside the context of school systems. In terms of significance (directional import), it seems to me that it is time for all professional teachers of sport to consider the legitimacy of variances for qualifying as an instructor in a given sport. Is it not reasonable to assume that the standards for teaching tennis (or any other sport) should be of comparable quality whether the instruction is being offered in the school or under some other organizational framework? We cannot expect all sport instructors to hold bachelor's degrees—that is an advantage of physical education—but we can expect that the sport instructor employed by the school (physical educator) be no less qualified in those sports that he is required to teach.

Unfortunately the system of physical education is such that generally well qualified personnel are frequently forced to a situation wherein they are limited by the very structure in which they are required to work. It is clearly a problem in management. The problem seems to stem from an assumption that a physical educator should be able to teach anything involving gross motor activity. The administrator proceeds to schedule the activity. Afterward, it is decided who should teach that activity. That in itself would not be objectionable were it not for the fact that physical educators are also required to teach certain sports for which they are not particularly qualified. Outside the context of the school such a practice would not be acceptable. For example, if a parent registers a son or daughter for instruction in a private gymnastic club, that parent has every reason to expect that the instruction will be given by someone who is well qualified to teach gymnastics. Should that not be the case, I doubt whether the parent would register the child and pay for instruction. At the same time the same parent may see his tax dollar spent for gym classes that represent little more than glorified recess.

Certainly not all gym classes could be so classified. Sometimes we see and hear of quality sport instruction in the schools in spite of the system. This may be attributed to the general professional qualification of dedicated physical educators who do the best they can under difficult circumstances. However, the background of the field would indicate that there is room for organizational improvement. With accelerated inflation and the "tightening" dollar for the school budget, it is also likely that some kind of change will be dictated through external pressures. Sport instruction through the school offers great potential. However, the challenge is there in relationship to all the functions of management. More will be said about that later in this chapter.

The Coach. Another manager is the coach. That point was made earlier. As with the head instructor, it is much easier to identify the head coach as a manager. Nevertheless, various managerial responsibilities can be associated with all coaches. One of the difficulties in attempting to understand the role of the coach is that he is many different things to many different people. A coach may be viewed as group leader, teacher, counselor, trainer, recruiter, or public citizen, or all of these, depending on his own orientation. It would appear that the total role of the coach is indeed a complex variant. However, Sage identified a managerial responsibility that is common to all coaches:

> Leadership is the process of influencing the activities of an organized group toward goal setting and goal achievement (Stogdill, 1950). For most American sports teams, the coach is the appointed leader. While it really is not known to what extent the success or failure of a team is due to the leadership competence of the coach, there is little doubt that it is an important factor in team performance and the coach, as the leader, is held responsible for the team's performance. Thus, the coach serves a function that is similar to management leaders in the business world. (1973, p. 35)

One could extend this idea further by suggesting that coaching is actually a fine place to begin if we wish to observe a concrete example of management in action. What the coach does by way of planning, organizing, staffing, directing, and controlling is under almost constant public scrutiny. In fact, as we look at those functions, it is readily apparent that the coach is indeed a person who has to meet the test of continual public evaluation of managerial effectiveness. If the coach is deficient in his planning the results are there for anyone to observe. I suspect that managers in many other areas might be in a tenuous position if they had to meet a similar test of accountability week in and week out.

Beyond the obvious managerial responsibility there are at least two other reasons for suggesting that a coach should be linked to a sport management profession. The first of these is that coaches are also a fragmented group at the present time. They are fragmented according to their sport and also by virtue of the kind of organization in which they are employed. The coaches in each sport more or less have their own fraternity: Basketball coaches have their professional ties with basketball coaches, as do lacrosse coaches, which is very natural and actually commendable. Beyond that, however, these coaches should also have the opportunity to benefit from broader associations through mutual interest in sport management.

Fragmentation according to type of organization probably occurs to a lesser extent, yet it is also evident: Thus we find high-school coaches, college coaches, coaches of professional sport teams, military coaches, coaches in the YMCA, and Little League coaches. This, too, is quite understandable. Of course, there is also evidence of some overlap and crossover, but one has to think that this form of fragmentation could be alleviated to some extent through mutual identification with a sport management profession. This would in no way negate the grass roots concerns of high-school coaches or any other group of coaches. It would present vistas through the opportunity for professional development in the total sport enterprise.

With regard to the last point, one other observation should also be made concerning the role of the coach in the broader spectrum of sport management. Most coaches have limited careers as coaches. This is particularly true in high-pressure situations involving "big-time" collegiate sport. However, there is also a significant turnover of coaches in small colleges and high schools. What happens to coaches after they leave the coaching position? Many of them move to some other form of managerial position in the athletic department. It was noted earlier that almost all athletic directors are former or current coaches. Beyond that, the ranks of assistant athletic directors, directors of promotions and fund raising, intramural sport directors, and instructional sport directors are replete with former coaches. It makes sense to suggest that these people would also benefit from more complete exposure to the art and science of sport management.

Professional Sport Positions. Thus far, analysis of sport management positions has been largely restricted to those found within an educational context—schools, colleges, and universities. In varying degrees, all seven of those positions have some kind of link, either directly or indirectly, with physical education programs. We now turn to a grouping of sport management positions that have very little, if any, connection with the field of physical education. As far as I can determine, any relationship between physical education and professional sport positions is more incidental than organizationally structured. Yet one cannot do justice to the topic of the background, meaning, and significance of sport without considering professional sport. Furthermore, sport management positions can clearly be identified in professional sport. Consequently, some analysis of professional sport positions seems warranted.

I have chosen to examine these in a collective sense, because there is considerable variance among the kind and extent of such positions as we scan the scope of professional sport organizations. One parameter needs clarification before proceeding. Basically we are considering "front-office" positions as contrasted with those positions involving the field manager or related jobs. There are two reasons for this delimitation. The first is that almost all coaches and field managers in professional sport are former professional athletes. Although exceptions can be noted, as a group they are less likely to identify with the broader scope of sport management. The second reason is closely related to the first. It is not necessary for a professional coach or field manager to hold a baccalaureate degree to be selected for the position, and many of these field leaders do not have that form of qualification. That situation has changed somewhat in recent years and could change even more in the future. Nevertheless, even if there are additional college-educated field managers, there is no particular reason to suggest that entry into such positions would be through a sport management profession.

Somewhat by contrast, there is a potential link between front-office positions in professional sport and a developing sport management profession. Within recent years an increasing number of graduates from sport management programs have obtained positions with professional sport teams. Of course, it is still true that front-office personnel come from a variety of backgrounds. Nepotism has not disappeared, and many of the key positions are held by friends of the family and others who have the necessary significant contacts in professional sport. On the other hand, there is growing recognition that many of the professional sport positions require expertise that cannot completely be learned on the job. These positions represent part of the potential for a sport management profession.

In the larger organization most of the positions are at the level of middle management: finance director/treasurer, director of marketing and promotions, director of public relations, traveling secretary, sales and ticket director, and superintendent of grounds and maintenance. Collectively they are positions that could be classified as being on the business side as contrasted with the player personnel side of a professional sport team. In that regard they are roughly comparable to the positions of business manager, sports information director, ticket manager, director of sports development, and the facilities manager in a collegiate athletic department. This further serves to reinforce the idea that collegiate sport and professional sport share many common denominators in a developing profession of sport management.

Other Sport Management Positions. Sport management is not limited to the context of schools, colleges, universities, and professional teams. In fact, from one standpoint, these aspects of sport management represent but the tip of the iceberg. Sport organizations and sport programs are abundant in a number of other settings. Earlier I referred to some of those settings. However, the parameters are not readily determined. There is considerable difficulty in understanding the total sport enterprise. Part of that difficulty might be called definitional in nature. By definitional, I mean the attempt to identify sport programs within the broad realm of recreation and leisure. What part of it is sport, and wherein lies the potential for sport management?

Management of a civic center, coliseum, stadium, or arena offers a classic example of the gray area that can surround sport, recreation, and leisure. Is the civic center manager a sport manager? Sports are certainly an integral part of the civic center operation. However, it is also well known that civic centers would find it difficult to remain in business if it were not for the scheduling of other events such as rock concerts. It is at such a point that the mix or blend between sport and other recreational pursuits becomes most evident. Yet there is ample evidence to indicate that graduates from academic programs in sport management can be and are viable candidates for positions as managers of arenas, civic centers, coliseums, and stadiums. Facility management is "up front" as an important consideration in sport management. It just so happens that these facilities are also used for other purposes.

Similar examples can be noted in other areas of the sport enterprise. We find organized sport programs in community recreation, service agencies (e.g., YMCA, YWCA, CYO, and Jewish Community Centers), private clubs, industry, and the military services. In addition, there are golf courses, bowling alleys, ski resorts, race tracks, and marinas. Within any one of these organizations we will observe activities that extend beyond the realm of sport. However, that does not detract from the viability of the sport component in any of the organizations. Neither does it negate the need for effective sport management within those operations. Furthermore, there is already sufficient evidence to demonstrate that the entire category represents a potentially significant market for graduates of academic programs in sport management.

DANCE

The past several pages have been devoted exclusively to the topic of sport with the additional recognition that the various professional positions in sport tend to be of a managerial nature. However, even though sport is integral in the realm of physical education, any organizational changes would involve more than replacing physical education with sport management. Therefore it is necessary to discuss those components of physical education that are not part of the realm of sport per se. What are some of the other organizational possibilities?

Just as a sport is an identifiable, concrete activity, so too is dance. Even though dance is manifested in various forms (e.g., modern dance, social dance, and ballet), this does not detract from the centrality of dance when compared with other activities that do not belong within the grouping of dance. Dance specialists have been identified for many years. There are sport specialists, and there are dance specialists.

To some extent the separation of dance from the field of physical education is already in process. Within certain universities, dance programs have left departments or schools of physical education and moved to organizational alignment under fine arts and humanities or some other university unit. Regardless of the particular organizational structure, it is more important to recognize that dance is a viable entity in itself and should be accorded that status by having its own program, department, division, or school, which one depending on the size and general makeup of the institution. Therefore it is relatively useless to comment further on the possibilities in that regard. The most significant factor here is that a professional teacher or professor of dance will tend to lose his or her identity under broad classification as a physical educator. Dance is dance, and sport is sport. It should not be necessary to say more.

EXERCISE SCIENCE

Aside from sport and dance, one other area can be fairly clearly identified with the traditional field of physical education. It is the sphere of exercise per se. Although people exercise when they dance or participate in a sport, they do so within the context of that dance or that particular game or sport. In their actions they are governed by conventions extending beyond exercise as such., Exercise is a means toward an end, whatever that end might be. Conditioning and training are important concepts within the broad domain of exercise.

Within the past 15 years there has been considerable advancement in the body of knowledge related to exercise. Much more is now known about the appropriate means of exercise and the effects of exercise. At the same time there has also been increasing evidence that many Americans are becoming more fitness conscious. This has served to strengthen the connnection between health and exercise. Although there is still need to use caution in advancing claims for the benefits of exercise, some relationship between proper exercise and sound health is now fairly well established.

These points of recognition also have organizational implications. For years the relationship of health and physical education has been generally accepted. However, the history of that relationship also shows a steady trend to separate health education organizationally from physical education. Health education specialists have emerged to a great extent. That development is to be applauded. Now is the time to consider more carefully the significant connection between the emerging field of exercise science and health science. Within the traditional scope of physical education it is most understandable that health education should be viewed as a related but separate area. With the inclusion of sport and dance programs, physical education is too broad to provide a meaningful link with health education or health science. However, identification of sport management and dance as separate programs provides an opportunity for a fresh look at the potential for an organizational link between exercise science and health science.

One other aspect of contemporary physical education programs should also be noted. There are physical educators who focus their work on such activities and programs as movement education, basic movement, or human movement fundamentals. From a conceptual and organizational standpoint, would it not make a great deal of sense to consider such work in movement as a component of the exercise science realm? After all, the efficiency of human movement is an important concern in exercise science. Movement fundamentals are basic to exercise programs. I have heard it argued that movement education is one of the prime reasons a program in physical education should be preserved or advanced. Part of that argument is sound. Beyond a doubt, all people should have an opportunity to learn that which is desirable for the efficiency of human movement. However, that argument should be separated from any organizational claim to retain the identity of physical education. Conceptually and practically speaking, it seems appropriate to consider movement education as an integral part of exercise science.

A PROGRAM FOR SPORT

In the remainder of this chapter I will present some thoughts regarding a program for sport. This is not to imply that there should not be similar plans for dance and exercise science (as a component of health). However, as Zeigler aptly describes, physical education can and does mean many different things to many different people:

> Physical education could be exemplified by a child bouncing a ball on a school playground, an overweight man doing a situp, or a woman taking part in modern dance. From another standpoint, physical education could be explained by a halfback scampering for the goal line in the Rose Bowl, boys and girls playing volleyball in a church recreation room, or a high school boy pinning his opponent in an interscholastic wrestling match. A Ph.D. candidate might be analyzing the contents of a Douglas gas bag full of a runner's expired air in a physical education exercise science laboratory, or a person might be trying out rhythmic exercises at home. Any of these activities could well be designated as aspects of physical education. (1977, p. 1)

It is precisely that kind of recognition that has prompted the approach I have followed in this chapter. One can identify a background for the field of physical education. Also, in spite of difficulties, a certain type of meaning can be ascribed to what is called physical education. However, when it comes to significance (directional import) it does not make much sense to perpetuate organizational confusion. Therefore, I offer a prospectus for sport, with the hope that others who are qualified in those areas might present appropriate programs for dance and exercise science.

This is not the first time that I have outlined a plan for sport. Eight years ago I concluded *Toward a Philosophy of Sport* with such a program (1972). In the interim my thoughts about sport programs have not changed substantially. Some modifications are evident, based on changing times and additional professional insights. Nevertheless, the following are largely extensions of earlier thoughts. The order of these ideas is not of particular significance, so they are offered collectively as possible guidelines for the conduct of sport programs.

Community Sport Programs. Something should be done in an effort to break down the artificial barriers that currently exist among the various sport programs within any given community. In a large measure this is a problem between the school's sport program and the various sport programs offered by other community agencies. Why should junior-high-school sport be separated organizationally from community recreation sport? Or why should Little League or Pop Warner football be administered and coached by volunteer nonprofessionals? These are questions that beg serious consideration. One hears and reads frequent complaints about the way in which youth sport programs are conducted. Yet what is done by trained professionals to improve the situation? Physical educators have been so preoccupied with conducting their gym classes that they have forfeited their claim to a wide segment of the sport enterprise that is in critical need of professional expertise. Also, from a practical standpoint it is evidence of very poor financial planning to continue to duplicate facilities and personnel through the media of public schools and community recreation. It is high time that leaders in these fields take a fresh look at the opportunities for offering an enriched and integrated community sport program.

It is quite likely that the community-wide sport program should be managed under the auspices of the local school system. That is where many of the qualified personnel and facilities are to be found. Furthermore, the precedent involving the significance of interscholastic sports more or less suggests that the school should serve as the central administrative agency. Any change to remove the sport program from the educational framework would require a major shift in American thinking, which has not been evident to date.

As I see it, there should be a community sport director, who would probably be employed by the school system (considering the previous comment). Under the overall director, there would be separate directors for each sport that can be adequately offered by that community. In this case adequacy would be determined by the availability of suitable facilities and qualified personnel. Thus, as examples, there might be a basketball director, gymnastics director, field hockey director, baseball director. All of the instruction, coaching, scheduling, etc., for that particular sport would be centralized under that director on a community-wide basis. This would include the interscholastic competition for that sport. Such an arrangement could accomplish several purposes. For one, it would tend to eliminate unnecessary and even undesirable overlap. Baseball might be used as an example of the situation at the present time. In many communities, interscholastic baseball has an overlapping season with "Babe Ruth" baseball. Some players play in both leagues simultaneously. They may even use the same facility, but the coaching personnel are more likely to consist of two different groups.

Why not have a single, unified baseball program for the community? Such a program could be more appropriately structured to focus on instructional opportunities for elementary age youth. At the junior high level, the program could include some relatively low-keyed intramural sport competition. Under this proposed structure intramural sport would mean community-wide participation for this age group and would actually replace the various youth sport groups that now exist. Interscholastic baseball competition (or interscholastic competition in any sport) would come into full-fledged existence only at the tenth grade level. At the same time, intramural opportunities would continue to exist for those who cannot qualify or who do not wish to participate with the high-school teams. I contend that such a system could be facilitated by a more centralized community sport organization in which there is a sport director who administers a program in which there is a director for each sport offered by the community.

Instructional Considerations and the Sport Experience. In the final analysis, the goal for any sport program can be fairly simply stated: to contribute to each individual's potential for having a positive experience through sport involvement. That goal will meet the needs of those who manage a sport program as a business venture as well as those who manage from a service-oriented perspective. In either case, unless the positive experience is there, other objectives will not be reached.

This may sound all too simple. Certainly one could not refute the need to facilitate a positive sport experience. What is the problem? As I see it, the problem is essentially twofold: (1) the failure to provide a diversified sport program for a large number of youth at early ages and (2) the failure to provide qualified instruction when, and only when, it is needed.

We begin with the recognition that preference for sports is a very individual matter. It is almost impossible to explain why one person likes golf while another prefers tennis. At the same time, a third person may enjoy both of these sports but for different reasons. What is better known is that it is almost impossible for an individual to obtain much enjoyment from golf, tennis, or any other sport unless he acquires some degree of skill in that sport. The particular degree of skill level for enjoyment is also an individual matter. However, that does not negate the basic need for some measure of skill to facilitate a positive sport experience.

It is also known that the only one way to acquire skill in any given sport is by participating in that sport. A program in movement education may be fine for many purposes, but it will not enable one to acquire skills in the game of golf. The same can be said for any other sport.

At the outset of this section on instructional considerations I mentioned a twofold problem in achieving the goal. Those responsible for the management of diversified sport programs should do whatever is possible to maximize the sport options available to any individual. As stated earlier, the only real limitations should be suitable facilities and qualified instructors. I will never know whether I might enjoy lacrosse unless I have had the opportunity to play the game. Obviously everyone cannot have the opportunity to participate in the majority of sports. However, at least an individual should be able to benefit from adequate exposure to several sports. At that point, choices become meaningful.

It is also quite likely that the sport experience will not be facilitated if the instruction is provided by someone who is not particularly well qualified to teach that sport. Obviously this is where much of the traditional gym class structure misses the mark. There is no need to elaborate on this point; enough has been said earlier about the need for qualified sport instruction.

I would like to conclude this section by citing an example of that which should not be done with regard to instructional considerations in facilitating the positive sport experience. Recently I heard a story about a high-school senior who failed to graduate with his class because he received an F grade in a required physical education class as a result of his excessive absences from that class. The failure seems justified unless the circumstances that led to the absences are considered: During his entire life the boy lived near a lake. He learned to canoe at an early age and continued to canoe throughout his boyhood. In his senior-year gym class he was required to take canoeing lessons in the school swimming pool. Because of the boredom of the situation he skipped classes, and the failure resulted. Does such a situation reflect instructional considerations that facilitate positive sport experiences?

College Sport and the Student-Athlete. The front cover of the May 19, 1980, issue of *Sports Illustrated* depicts a condition that has been more or less present in the United States throughout the twentieth century. These words appear on that cover: "The Shame of American Education—The Student-Athlete Hoax—RIP OFF." In this issue is a 36-page "special report" written by John Underwood that is entitled "Student-Athletes: The Sham, the Shame." I commend Underwood for writing the article and *Sports Illustrated* for publishing it. The only surprising thing about the article is that it is written with a tone and content suggesting that the abuses related to academic standards for athletes are a recent phenomenon. As a noted sports writer, Underwood certainly must be aware that the situation he describes has basically existed for 80 years. Nevertheless, his approach can probably be defended on the grounds that he is calling attention to a condition that has deteriorated even more in the past year. He begins by saying: "This is the spoor of an educational system gone mad" (p. 38). After reading the article one begins to wonder whether that educational system is not indeed reaching the end of the trail.

One other limitation of the article should also be noted. One would be led to believe that scholar-athletes are virtually nonexistent and that all schools are more or less equally guilty of the malpractices involving academic standards for athletes. Although the number is undoubtedly far less than desired, some colleges do maintain a relatively high academic standard for their athletes. Also, there are athletes who do demonstrate their abilities as scholars in addition to their athletic achievement. It is only the "numbers game" that causes one to be depressed about the situation. When looking at the total picture, Underwood's analysis seems to be very much on target. This is certainly true when considered from the perspective of the bulk of college sport that is covered by the media. Thus, in spite of a couple of limitations in the account, I am in basic agreement with the treatise presented by Underwood.

This brings me to the point as to why this topic should be included as a general, third part of the program for sport. Cady and Underwood are in basic agreement. Both writers recognize that college sport has been and continues to be an integral part of American life. Many of the attitudes toward sport, of both youth and adults, will continue to be shaped by what takes place at the college level. But that does not suggest that all is well. In this regard, both Cady and Underwood also stress the need for various controls. I tend to agree with the forms of control they suggest. However, in the final analysis, I suggest that the situation will not substantially change unless two conditions are met: (1) college athletes are offered athletic scholarships only on the basis of demonstrated financial need, in accordance with the standards applied to the general student body, and (2) college athletes are academically advised and evaluated like any other student in the college or university. These are simple propositions that have been advanced many times before this writing. However, the situation will not change unless there is considerably more attention to these basic factors in the academic environment.

How is this to be accomplished? For the most part college administrators have not been successful in efforts along that line to date. In fact, Underwood suggests that they are basically at fault for the rapidly deteriorating condition. However, it is quite likely that the potential role of the administrator is limited in this regard because of alumni and other external pressures. I am inclined to concur with Cady's suggestion that strong faculty control offers the only real key to significant change.

It is easy to suggest the need for strong faculty control of an intercollegiate athletic program. However, much work has to be done before that becomes a reality. As I see it, college faculties tend to fall into two extreme groupings in their outlook on athletics. The first group, which would appear to be the vast majority, are inclined to follow the so-called ostrich approach. These faculty members know that the athletic program exists, but they do not wish to be bothered with it. They are convinced that most athletes are "dumb jocks," and they more or less tolerate the athletic program as a necessary evil. In their minds, athletics always has been and always will be secondary to the principal concern of a college or university. One only wishes that they would take the time to read the works of Novak and Cady.

The second group, although smaller, poses an equally critical problem. These faculties are obsessed with one goal—to do whatever is necessary to make their college or university number one on the athletic scene. How that is achieved is beyond their concern. These are the faculties who will quickly criticize the decisions of a coach and who are quick to suggest that a coach should lose his position if a winning team is not produced. Basically, this faculty group has what could be called an identification problem. They identify with the success or failure of their college's teams so strongly that they are completely blinded by the disgraceful conditions outlined in Underwood's article.

Of course, both faculty groups are in error. Yet it would also appear that these people represent the principal hope to reduce the sham and the shame. They will need help. The majority wish that the situation would just disappear. The minority are tunnel visioned in their desire to see their school as number one in athletics.

The help can come only through a process of education and leadership. Who is to provide this? We cannot look to the outside for the answer. Professionals in sport management offer the key to providing the necessary education and leadership. The question is, are we ready to make the necessary organizational changes to facilitate that work?

REFERENCES

Cady, E.F.: The Big Game: College Sports and American Life. Knoxville, University of Tennessee Press, 1978.

Ceglarski, M.A.: A Survey of the Qualifications of Directors of Intercollegiate Athletics. Unpublished paper, 1979.

Lewis, G.M.: Adoption of the sports program, 1906–39: The role of accommodation in the transformation of physical education. Quest, *12*:34–46, 1969.

Lucas, J.A., and R.A. Smith: Saga of American Sport. Philadelphia, Lea & Febiger, 1978.

Mullin, B.J.: Sport management—The chicken and the egg. Sport Man. Newslet., 2, 2:5–6, 1980.

Novak, M.: The Joy of Sports. New York, Basic Books, 1976.

Sage, G.H.: The coach as management: Organizational leadership in American sport. Quest, *19*:35–40, 1973.

Siedentop, D.: Physical Education: Introductory Analysis. Dubuque, Iowa, Wm. C. Brown, 1976.

Spears, B., and R.A. Swanson: History of Sport and Physical Activity in the United States. Dubuque, Iowa, Wm. C. Brown, 1978.

Underwood, J.: Student-Athletes: The sham, the shame. Sports Illus. 52:21–36, 72, 1980.

VanderZwaag, H.J.: Toward a Philosophy of Sport. Reading, Mass., Addison-Wesley, 1972.

Weiss, P.: Sport: A Philosophic Inquiry. Carbondale, Ill., Southern Illinois University Press, 1969.

Weston, A.: The Making of American Physical Education. New York, Appleton-Century Crofts, 1962.

Zeigler, E.F.: Physical Education and Sport Philosophy. Englewood Cliffs, N.J., Prentice-Hall, 1977.

CHAPTER TWO

Functional Effects of Physical Activity

James S. Skinner

One of the best ways to study how the body functions is to increase the demands on its various parts and then see how they adjust. No mechanism is better suited for this than exercise. Muscles can increase the turnover of energy 80 to 90 times their resting rate for a few seconds and 20 to 25 times the resting rate for several hours. By contrast, the highest "nonexercise" rate can be seen in a nude person sitting in a room where the temperature is below zero. When this person shivers uncontrollably, his metabolism is only four times as high as at rest. While it may be argued that shivering is a form of exercise, the comparison is clearer when one considers that the same amount of energy is required to walk at the moderately fast pace of 3.5 mph.

Each of the many forms of occupational, leisure, and sports activities places specific demands on the various systems of the body. Exercising continuously for 20 to 30 minutes, for example, requires adaptations by the nervous, muscular, cardiovascular, respiratory, hormonal, and thermoregulatory systems. There are even adaptations at the cellular level. In short, physical activity puts demands on almost all parts of the body. Likewise, training produces a number of chronic adaptations that are specific to the kind of training involved. These adaptations occur in all the systems mentioned above. By studying how the body responds to and recovers from the many sorts of physical activity, as well as how it adapts to the many kinds of training programs, a better understanding of bodily function can be obtained.

It should be remembered that these adjustments do not occur without good reason. If the reader can perceive and understand the logic of these modifications, then the study of the functional effects of physical activity can be simple, stimulating, interesting, and satisfying. These are the objectives of this chapter.

DEFINITIONS

Two terms that are often used need to be defined. *Work* is the amount of force applied over a distance; it is not related to time in any way. *Power* is the amount of work applied per unit of time. Thus, if 50 kg is lifted 2 m, then 100 kg·m of work is performed (regardless of how much time was needed to do it). If the same 50 kg is lifted 2 m once every 3 seconds or 20 times/min, then a power output of 2000 kg·m/min ($50 \times 2 \times 20$) is performed.

In oversimplified terms, *exercise* is a form of physiological stimulation of the body. In this sense, exercise can be considered any form of physical activity "involving movement, maintenance of posture or expression of force by muscles" (Knuttgen, 1976). The performance of exercise requires the response of a number of functions

Dr. Skinner is from Arizona State University, Tempe.

within the body. The degree to which each of these functions is needed depends on the intensity, duration, and frequency of the activity, as well as on the specific characteristics of the activity performed. In other words, specific forms of exercise produce specific responses in specific people; i.e., identical exercise stimuli produce different responses in different people and even different responses in the same person at different times.

Training is the adaptation (chronic response) by the body to the repeated physiological stimulation of exercise. Adaptation is produced only in those parts of the body that are stimulated to respond (principles of overload and specificity) and is generally of two kinds: structural and functional. Structural adaptations are characterized by changes in the number, size, or both of the functional units within each bodily system involved, while functional adaptations are characterized by modifications in the function of these systems. Muscular hypertrophy as a result of strength training is an example of a structural adaptation, and the reduction in heart rate seen at a given power output after endurance training is an example of a functional change.

The term *physical fitness* implies many things to many people. Its importance to each individual varies during his lifetime and can be influenced by the type of activity he usually does as well as by his motivation to do that activity. Fitness can also be specific to each individual, depending on the physiological challenges that that person will meet in his life. Thus, a marathon runner and a weight lifter both need high levels of specific components that are a part of overall fitness, namely, endurance and strength respectively. Even though the marathon runner may not be strong and the weight lifter may not have much endurance, each athlete is "fit" to do those activities he likes. For this reason a concise definition of physical fitness is not presented. In general terms, however, many changes occur in the body with regular activity. With the increase in the maximal capacity for work or power that usually occurs there is a greater energy reserve. As a result, the same amount of work or power feels easier because it is less strenuous in relation to the increased maximum. If a person's maximum is high enough, he will be able to do his daily tasks and pleasures without fatigue, he will have sufficient energy reserves to meet unexpected emergencies safely, and he will have enough extra energy to enjoy his leisure time.

There is a close relationship between physical fitness and the study of the functional effects of physical activity. Lamb states that

> the improvement in physical fitness could be defined as the application of the principles of exercise physiology to the improvement of man's response and adaptation to life's physical challenges . . . . It is unfortunate that many persons do not see the connection between exercise physiology and physical fitness; for better physical fitness programs could be designed to meet individuals' specific fitness needs if knowledge gained from studies of exercise physiology were more frequently applied to the design of fitness programs. (1978)

The study of the functional effects of physical activity is therefore related to the description and explanation of the acute responses and chronic adaptations of the body to single or repeated bouts of exercise. It is the factor of specificity that makes the study of these functional effects so complex, challenging, and interesting.

PRESENT STATE OF KNOWLEDGE

Basic Concepts

It is important that the reader be aware of certain basic concepts of how the body functions in order to understand this chapter. Examples will also be given throughout to clarify these concepts and to demonstrate how they are used in the study of the physiological functions during exercise.

1. The energy that is used for the functioning of every living cell in the body is

produced by chemical reactions. These reactions are either aerobic (occurring in the presence of oxygen) or anaerobic (without oxygen).

2. A given amount of power output requires a given amount of energy, regardless of whether the energy is produced aerobically or anaerobically. If sufficient amounts of energy are not available the exercise intensity will be reduced.

3. The relative contribution of these two forms of chemical reactions depends on the type, intensity, and duration of exercise.

4. If there are differences in pressure, concentration, or temperature between one part of the body and another, there will be a tendency for movement from areas of high pressure, concentration, or temperature to those areas with lower values in an attempt to reach an equilibrium.

5. The greater the differences in pressure, concentration, or temperature between two areas of the body, the greater the speed of this movement. If no difference exists, movement will cease.

Production of Energy

Energy needed for such bodily functions as muscle contraction, transmission of nervous impulses, and production of hormones is produced by the degradation of several basic raw materials; namely, oxygen, carbohydrates, and fat. For all practical purposes, protein is not used as a direct source for energy production. Proteins are used for the structural components of cells and are a major element of the enzymes that control the speed of different chemical reactions occurring in the cells. If more protein is eaten than is needed, the excess will be converted into either fat or carbohydrate.

Since we live in a sea of oxygen, there is usually not a problem of an adequate supply except at high altitude. After we eat, the stockpiles of the other raw materials are replenished. Fat is stored in fat cells, and all forms of carbohydrates (sugars, starches) are converted by the body to glucose, a simple sugar. This glucose is then transported to various parts of the body (muscle, liver, kidney, heart) where it is stored in the form of glycogen. Once these glycogen stores are filled, any excess glucose is converted to fat and stored as such.

During periods of fasting, liver glycogen is converted back to glucose and released into the bloodstream. Glycogen cannot be released from muscle since the necessary enzyme for its conversion is not present. Thus the liver is the main reservoir for glucose during fasting. This is an important mechanism for maintaining blood glucose levels, especially since the nervous system uses only glucose as fuel for its energy production.

There are no such limitations on the release and utilization of fat by the body. A fat cell contains about 5% water, while each gram of carbohydrate is stored with 3 g of water. (Note: Other than sugar crystals, which are man made, carbohydrates do not normally appear in nature without the presence of water, e.g., orange juice, syrup, potatoes, berries.) As a result, fat can be stored in a more compact, easily transported form (9 kcal eneryg/g fat vs. 4 kcal/g for both carbohydrates and proteins) and is the body's major reservoir of potential energy.

Figure 2–1 is a schematic of the maximal amount of energy that a well-trained athlete can produce over time and of the relative importance of the aerobic and anaerobic mechanisms for energy production during exercise. For comparison, the energy requirement at rest is given a value of 1.

The body does store a very limited amount of energy in muscle for its immediate use. This energy is present in such energy-rich phosphates as adenosine triphosphate (ATP) and the form in which it is stored, creatine phosphate (CP). It is easy to understand the role of ATP and CP if one thinks of these limited reserves as a small battery that can provide energy until the body generates more ATP via aerobic or anaerobic chemical reactions. Even though ATP and CP are formed aerobically, their breakdown occurs very rapidly and does not require the presence of oxygen. They can be utilized for very brief periods during high-intensity exercise requiring energy levels that are 80 to 90 times the level normally found at rest (Fig. 2–1). As an example of the type of exercise that can be performed, it is possible to run at top speed for 8 to 10 seconds without breathing. During this time, the energy comes almost exclusively from that stored in the muscles.

Because these reserves are very limited, there must be continuous resynthesis of ATP if exercise is to continue. Although the aerobic system is the preferred, more efficient, form of energy production, it takes time for the cardiovascular system to pick up and transport sufficient amounts of oxygen to the muscle fibers. As a result, only a fraction of the energy needed is provided by the aerobic mechanism at this time. A faster, emergency supply of energy is needed; this comes from the anaerobic breakdown of glycogen stored in the muscle. Depending on how hard the exercise is, and therefore how much energy is needed, the anaerobic mechanism can provide most of the energy for brief periods of 20 to 120 seconds. Because the resynthesis of ATP takes more time, the supply of energy is not as great and can reach levels of only 30 to 70 times the energy requirement at rest (Fig. 2–1). Therefore, after running at top speed for 10 seconds, a runner has to slow down. This explains why

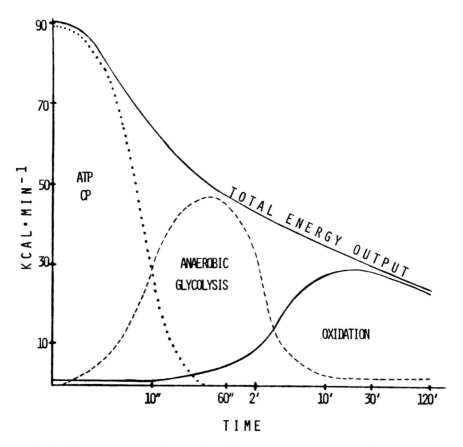

Fig. 2–1. Total energy expenditure and the different sources of energy in relation to duration of exercise.

an athlete cannot run 400 m as fast as he can 100 to 200 m or why a weight lifter can lift more in 1 to 2 repetitions than he can in 4 to 5 lifts without a pause.

This emergency system has its disadvantages, however. Although the method is faster, lactic acid (LA) is produced during the anaerobic degradation of glycogen. If too much LA is present in the muscle cell, it inhibits the efficiency of the aerobic chemical reactions. If this happens, not enough can be produced aerobically, and the person has to either slow down or use the anaerobic system more and more. The use of the anaerobic system is limited, however, by a person's tolerance to high levels of LA. For reasons that are still unclear, the accumulation of LA in the muscle and blood is associated with feelings of breathlessness, fatigue, and heaviness of muscles, forcing the person to stop.

The more efficient method for manufacturing energy is the breakdown of glycogen and fat in the presence of oxygen. Although this aerobic mechanism is slower, its advantage is that the supply of raw materials is essentially unlimited. As more and more oxygen is breathed in, picked up by the blood, pumped by the heart, and carried to the muscles where it is needed, aerobic reactions provide more and more energy. After 3 to 4 minutes these aerobic reactions provide most of the energy needed. The longer the duration of exercise, the more important is the aerobic system. However, if the amount of energy required is greater than the slower aerobic reactions can provide, or if there is a sudden increase in the amount of energy needed, then the faster anaerobic system is once more activated as an emergency, back-up system. As can be seen in Figure 2–1, a highly trained endurance athlete can aerobically produce 20 to 25 times as much energy during prolonged exercise as he needs at rest.

Rest

Since the energy requirements of resting muscle are so low, all of the energy can be provided by the slower, more efficient aerobic mechanism. Fat is the preferred raw material for several reasons: (1) Much more potential energy is stored as fat, while glycogen reserves are small and limited; (2) fat can be broken down only via the aerobic mechanism, while glycogen can be used in both aerobic and anaerobic reactions; and (3) by the use of more fat, the glycogen stores are conserved in the liver (this is important for maintaining blood glucose levels) and in the muscle (muscle glycogen is the predominant fuel for anaerobic reactions during intense exercise).

Onset of Exercise and Recovery

Once exercise starts, extra energy is needed right away. Since the rate at which the aerobic system can increase its production is sluggish, there must be an emergency back-up system that will allow the body to function until the aerobic assembly line speeds up. This is the purpose of the anaerobic system.

By definition, oxygen is needed for aerobic reactions. Therefore, one way of determining the rate of aerobic production is to measure the amount of oxygen taken in by the body. Figure 2–2 shows the typical course of oxygen intake ($\dot{V}o_2$) before, during, and after moderate exercise. At rest, only a small amount of energy or oxygen is used. Once activity starts and a given amount of exercise is performed, however, a given amount of energy is needed at all times; this energy requirement is represented by the solid horizontal line. The anaerobic system (ATP, CP, and muscle glycogen) produces most of the energy at first until the aerobic system becomes activated. The shaded area on the left of Figure 2–2 shows the magnitude of this anaerobic energy supply. This is called the *oxygen deficit* and represents the amount of borrowed energy that must be repaid later.

With activation of the aerobic system, $\dot{V}o_2$ rises until there are no further increases after 3 to 4 minutes. This point is called the *steady state* —i.e., the amount of oxygen taken in is the same as the amount of oxygen being used to produce energy. It is at

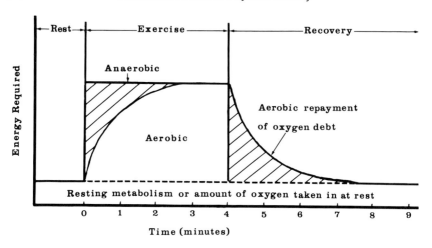

Fig. 2–2. Energy required or amount of oxygen taken in by the body at rest, during exercise, and during recovery from exercise.

this point that measures of $\dot{V}O_2$ are taken to determine the energy cost of an activity. Measures of heart rate, i.e., the number of times the heart beats each minute (HR), blood pressure (BP), and respiration taken at this time also show a tendency to level off and stabilize. This fact is useful when testing people under standardized conditions and when prescribing exercise.

After exercise, HR, respiration, and $\dot{V}O_2$ do not return immediately to their resting levels. The reason for this is that one must pay aerobically for the energy borrowed from the anaerobic sources. The local supply of energy stored in the muscle (ATP, CP) must first be restocked for later use. In addition, the LA produced during the initial part of the exercise must be reconverted into glycogen. Part of this conversion occurs in the muscle itself, but most takes place after the LA is transported via the blood to the liver. Since all of these chemical reactions require energy to proceed, an extra amount of oxygen must be taken in. This is referred to as paying off the *oxygen debt*. In other words, this is the amount of oxygen that would have been used during the first few minutes of exercise if it had been available, plus the extra oxygen needed for the elimination of LA. Like all debts, it takes longer to repay than it does to borrow, and one must pay a charge. In the case of LA, the energy can be borrowed in a few seconds, but the body requires about 15 minutes to eliminate one-half the LA produced. As well, there is an interest rate of about 24%—i.e., 24% more energy is needed just to convert lactic acid back to glycogen. Thus, although the emergency anaerobic system is necessary and useful, it is more expensive to use.

Progressively Increasing Exercise

As the intensity of exercise rises, there is an in increase in HR, respiration, and $\dot{V}O_2$, as well as in the activity of other parts of the oxygen delivery and utilization (i.e., aerobic) system. There comes a point, however, above which the $\dot{V}O_2$ cannot be increased, even though more work is being performed. This point is called the maximal aerobic power or $\dot{V}O_{2\,max}$ and is considered by some to be the best single indicator of "fitness," since it involves the maximal ability of many parts of the body to transport and use oxygen.

Figure 2–3 is a schematic diagram of some of the changes that occur in a normal, untrained person with progressively increasing exercise. There appear to be three

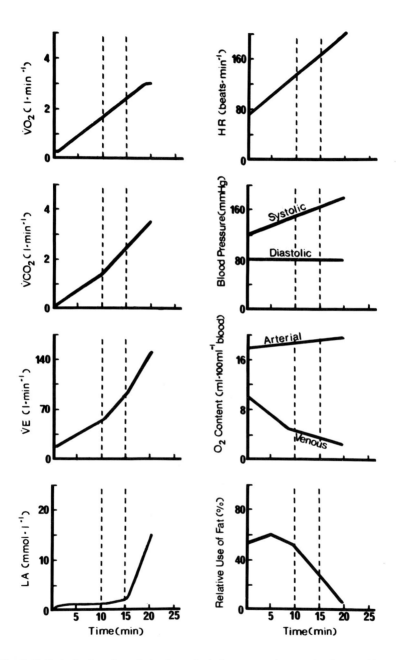

Fig. 2–3. Typical values for untrained people during progressive exercise from rest to maximal oxygen intake.

phases during the transition from rest to maximal aerobic exercise. These phases are separated by the two vertical broken lines in the diagram.

Phase 1 occurs at exercise of low intensity. During exercise, more oxygen (O_2) is being used by the working muscle, resulting in a greater difference between the oxygen content of the muscle and that of the blood passing by. This larger difference causes more oxygen to diffuse from blood to the tissue. Likewise, more carbon dioxide (CO_2) is being produced by the muscles and diffuses into the blood. As the blood is circulated back through the lungs, the greater concentration of CO_2 rapidly diffuses out, and more O_2 from the air diffuses into the blood to offset the low levels. This movement of gases is enhanced by the fact that exercise produces a greater difference in concentration.

In order to increase $\dot{V}O_2$ and eliminate more CO_2 ($\dot{V}CO_2$), the body increases its rate and depth of breathing for a more rapid turnover of air. However, it would make little sense to increase the turnover of air in the lungs if this rise in respiratory ventilation ($\dot{V}E$) were not accompanied by a rise in the rate of blood flow to carry the greater amount of O_2 to the tissues and to transport the greater amount of CO_2 away.

The circulatory system responds in a number of ways to increase blood flow. The amount of blood pumped by the heart per minute (cardiac output) is related to the HR and the amount of blood pumped per beat (stroke volume). Both HR and stroke volume increase during exercise. During the period of contraction by the heart (systole), blood is pumped into the large arteries; the systolic blood pressure (SBP) reflects the force of this contraction. The diastolic blood pressure (DBP) is a measure of the pressure in the muscular-walled arteries during the period of relaxation (diastole). Because there is a drop in pressure within the circulatory system as blood is pumped from the large arteries to the smallest arteries (arterioles), to the capillaries, and then to the veins, blood will continue to flow in this direction. During continuous exercise the heart pumps with greater pressure, while there is a drop in pressure at the arterioles and capillaries. This greater pressure difference produces a faster flow of blood away from the heart. Finally, the body can also control the distribution of blood flow to its various parts by selectively closing and opening the small arterioles. In this way, for example, blood can be diverted from the less active organs (kidneys, gastrointestinal tract) to the working muscles.

During the first few minutes of low-intensity exercise, fat cells release increased amounts of fat into the circulatory system, which is then transported to the working muscles. Since the rate of diffusion of fat across the cell membrane is proportional to the difference in concentration, high levels of fat in the blood ensure a constant supply, making fat the dominant source of fuel for contracting muscles at low levels of exercise. Given the fact that fat can be metabolized only by aerobic chemical reactions and that little or no LA is formed, there is little doubt that this first phase primarily involves aerobic metabolism.

As the exercise intensity increases and reaches a point around 50% of $\dot{V}O_{2\,max}$ (phase 2), $\dot{V}O_2$, HR, and SBP continue to rise linearly, and there is an initial increase in LA to twice resting levels. The acidity produced by LA stimulates the respiratory center, causing a nonlinear rise in $\dot{V}E$. Some excess CO_2 is also blown off, producing a disproportionate rise in $\dot{V}CO_2$ and eliminating part of the acidity caused by carbonic acid ($H_2CO_3 \rightleftharpoons H_2O + CO_2$). Since LA rises only a bit during this second phase, this respiratory compensation appears to be reasonably effective.

LA also has another effect in that its presence inhibits the breakdown and utilization of fat. The small amount of LA at this time probably initiates the reduction in fat utilization and the increased use of carbohydrates. Of course the body does not switch over to the anaerobic system all at once but gradually shifts gears to produce energy faster. This transition seems to occur during the second phase. Above exercise intensities requiring about 70% $\dot{V}O_{2\,max}$, the aerobic system of most sedentary people cannot produce energy fast enough, and they must depend more and more on the anaerobic breakdown of carbohydrates.

With further increases in exercise intensity above 70% $\dot{V}_{O_{2\,max}}$ (phase 3), the linear rises in HR, SBP, and $\dot{V}_{O_2}$ continue until near-maximal exercise, at which time they begin to plateau. At the onset of this phase, blood LA increases very rapidly until the $\dot{V}_{O_{2\,max}}$ is attained. There is also a further disproportionate rise in $\dot{V}_E$ and a continuous rise in $\dot{V}_{O_2}$ in an attempt to compensate for the marked rise in LA. At this point, however, the hyperventilation cannot compensate adequately. In addition, more and more of the $\dot{V}_{O_2}$ has to go to the respiratory muscles performing the increased work of hyperventilation, and less is available for skeletal muscles performing near-maximal exercise. More blood is also going to the skin in an attempt to eliminate the heat being produced during exercise. Thus at near-maximal and maximal levels of exercise there is competition for blood. At this point, however, the heart has reached its maximal capacity to pump blood, and the control system for distributing blood flow cannot adequately supply blood to all parts of the body where it is needed at the same time. As a result, the person cannot do more exercise and has to stop.

The increased use of the anaerobic system at the higher intensities of exercise is not just a function of the speed with which energy must be supplied. It is also related to the amount of blood flowing to the working muscles. In order to sustain high-intensity exercise, muscle contractions must also be stronger. However, when the muscle tension generated by the activation of more muscle fibers reaches 15% to 20% of the maximal force that that particular muscle can produce, the intramuscular pressure around the arteries surpasses the pressure within those arteries bringing nutrients to the muscle. The partial mechanical compression of the arterioles that follows causes a drop in blood flow and deprives the active musculature of a quantity of oxygen. The anaerobic breakdown of glycogen stored within that muscle is then used to furnish some of the necessary energy. Once the muscle contracts at a force of about 60% of its maximal strength (and this occurs around the time of $\dot{V}_{O_{2\,max}}$ in continuous, rhythmical exercise), then the supply of blood and oxygen to that muscle is completely blocked, and the anaerobic degradation of muscle glycogen is the only mechanism available for providing energy.

Thus the third phase is characterized by the breathlessness, fatigue, and discomfort associated with high levels of LA. The rapid rise in LA seen at the onset of phase 3 partially explains why someone can run at a certain pace (e.g., at a speed requiring 70% $\dot{V}_{O_{2\,max}}$) with no problem but will become winded very soon after trying to run a bit faster (e.g., 80 to 90% $\dot{V}_{O_{2\,max}}$).

In summary, phase 1 is predominantly aerobic, while phase 3 has large aerobic and anaerobic components. Phase 2 is a sort of transition between these two extremes. For a more detailed discussion of these phases the reader is referred to the review article by Skinner and McLellan (1980).

It should be mentioned here that most sporting activities require both aerobic and anaerobic production of energy. For example, a soccer player performs aerobic exercise when running 20 to 30 min nonstop. If the activity were not aerobic, he could not run so long. Occasionally, however, he must sprint after the ball. During those brief, high-intensity intervals that are greater than 70% of his maximal aerobic power, he must draw upon his emergency, anaerobic sources once again.

Because of the high level of anaerobic energy production during activities at or near $\dot{V}_{O_{2\,max}}$, most people can exercise at these intensities for only 3 to 6 minutes, the difference in duration being associated with the previous amount of exercise done, as well as with variations in state of training, motivation to continue, and tolerance to high levels of LA. Exercise can be done at intensities greater than $\dot{V}_{O_{2\,max}}$ but for even shorter periods. Given the fact that the energy requirements are greater than the maximal amount that the aerobic mechanism can provide, it is apparent that the overwhelming majority of the energy must come from anaerobic sources.

As mentioned earlier, if one is just beginning to exercise, then the ATP and CP stored in the muscles are used first. If, on the other hand, a soccer player sprints all-out for the ball after running for 15 minutes, then the original stores of ATP and CP have already been exhausted and were replaced by the aerobic and anaerobic synthesis of ATP. Therefore the maximal intensity and duration at which he can now work depends primarily on the rate of energy production by the anaerobic system, the amount of LA produced earlier, and his tolerance for high levels of LA. In general, however, the higher the intensity, the shorter will be the duration.

Anthropometry

One of the axioms in physiology is that form and function are closely related. A concern in the study of physical activity, therefore, is how the performance of exercise may be influenced by the body structure and what influence physical activity may have on the body itself. Anthropometry, literally the measurement of man, has been studied for many years to provide descriptive information in an attempt to explain, analyze, and understand man and movement. The major aspects studied are size, proportion, shape, and composition of the body, each of which describes the body in a different manner.

Measurements of body size include such descriptive information as height, weight, and surface area, while measures of body proportion describe the relationship between height and weight and among lengths, widths, and circumferences of various body segments. It has been found that top athletes in some sports tend to have those proportions that biomechanically aid the particular performance required. In track and field events, for example, good jumpers tend to have longer legs in relation to their height, and good throwers tend to have longer arms.

Measures of physique use subjective terms to describe body shape rather than size to give an immediate impression of the overall appearance of an individual. The system used for body-shape classification (somatotyping) looks at the relative contribution of three basic body types, namely, endomorphy (spherical, round, soft), mesomorphy (cubical, rugged, muscular), and ectomorphy (linear, fragile, delicate). Research by Tanner on Olympic athletes showed that they tend to be more mesomorphic, less endomorphic, and very different from the normal population (1964). Interestingly, athletes in the same events were very similar to each other, regardless of the country from which they came. In other words, athletes with a particular body shape tend to succeed in certain sports. Such information has been used to identify and direct youngsters into sports in which they can reach the greatest level of success. This does not imply that ectomorphic youngsters should not play football or that endomorphs should not compete in distance events if they enjoy these activities. It suggests only that they will have less chance of reaching high levels of performance in them.

Most of the modern physical research in anthropometry involves the measurement of body composition, i.e., lean body mass (bone and muscle) and fat. In turn, since little or no change is seen in bone size (as determined by x-ray techniques and by measurements of bone widths, thicknessess, lengths, and circumferences), most research is focused on muscle and fat.

Muscle mass can be quantified by measuring girths of various muscles. These measurements can then be compared with those from other people (athletes, patients, etc.) or with those from the same person after training, growth, or disuse. Given the fact that the number of muscle cells is determined at birth, any changes must be related to alterations in the size of the individual fibers. Hypertrophy occurs after weight lifting since the muscles are specifically trained for strength development. The increased deposition of protein occurs in the actin and myosin filaments, those portions of the muscle directly involved in development of force during a contraction. Marked hypertrophy does not occur with endurance training since the force of contraction is low in such sustained, aerobic exercise. As a result, the protein deposition that occurs is found in the enzymes, those catalysts that control the chemical reactions in the muscle.

Fat is the most variable tissue in the body and is distributed throughout the body, primarily under the skin and in the abdominal cavity. Measurement techniques include use of soft-tissue roentgenograms, skinfold calipers, and ultrasound to estimate the thickness of subcutaneous fat. Appropriate formulas are then used to estimate the total amount of fat. Total body fat and the pattern of body fat distribution are major interests in research on body composition.

It has been shown that fat patterning is genetically influenced and is different in both sexes, women having more fat on the upper arms and legs and men having more on the trunk. On the average, women are fatter than men. At age 20 years, 12% to 13% of a man's weight is fat, and a woman's is 18% to 20%. Later in life at the age of 30 to 45 years, men have 18% to 20% fat, while women have 25% to 28%. Athletes in training have relatively little fat, males averaging 5% and females averaging 10%.

Since fat is a reservoir in which potential energy is stored, large variations can be found during growth, as well as in the continuum from inactivity to regular heavy training (or from starvation to overeating). Body fat can also influence the performance of various sports. For this reason, research results have also been used to predict a person's optimal weight for such sports as wrestling, boxing, and weight lifting.

Types of Skeletal Muscle Fibers

All skeletal muscle fibers are not the same. Similar to the situation discussed in relation to the types of energy production, there are fibers primarily used in activities requiring speed and strength (anaerobic), and there are fibers especially suited for endurance (aerobic) activities. These two types of fibers have been classified by the time required to complete a contraction. Thus, fast-twitch (FT) fibers can reach their peak tension after stimulation about twice as fast as the slow-twitch (ST) fibers. Table 2–1 is a comparison of a number of structural and functional characteristics of these fibers. Once again, it should be obvious that form and function are closely related.

It can be seen that ST fibers are smaller and have a smaller motor nerve stimulating them. Since the smaller nerves are easier to stimulate and transmit a stimulus more slowly, ST fibers are primarily recruited for moderate levels of exercise, where less speed and strength are needed. ST fibers have more myoglobin (a small, localized reservoir of oxygen), slightly larger intramuscular stores of fat (which can be metabolized only aerobically), more capillaries to bring oxygen to the fibers, plus more aerobic enzymes and mitochondria (the powerhouse of the cell that produces ATP aerobically) to use that oxygen. As a result, low-intensity exercise can be performed for long periods, and these ST fibers are resistant to fatigue. FT fibers, on the other hand, are bigger and have bigger motor nerves; this means that the stronger, faster impulses are used for rapid, high-intensity contractions. The activity of the enzymes in these fibers is especially suited for this kind of anaerobic activity, since myosin ATPase is the enzyme involved in the rapid breakdown of ATP to provide energy, and the glycolytic enzymes are involved in the metabolism of glucose and glycogen. However, since FT fibers do not have a rich blood supply to bring nutrients and to carry away metabolic end products (especially LA), they are easily fatigued.

The recruitment of muscle fibers depends on the kind of activity being performed. At the onset of exercise of moderate intensity, it seems that FT fibers are selectively recruited to get things going, e.g., to overcome the initially high resistance on a bicycle ergometer. After a few seconds, the body is in motion, less force is required, and ST fibers take over. If the exercise continues for a long time, however, then more and more FT fibers are recruited as the glycogen stores in the ST fibers reach a low level. Once the glycogen reserves in FT fibers also reach low levels, the

Table 2–1
Gross Distinction between Muscle Fiber Types

Characteristic	Slow Twitch	Fast Twitch
Size		
Innervating motor nerve	smaller	bigger
Muscle fiber	smaller	bigger
Recruitment		
Light exercise	some	none
Moderate exercise	more	some
Intense exercise	many	many
Contraction		
Speed	slower	faster
Tension developed	less	more
Content		
Myoglobin	more	less
Glycogen	same	same
Fat	more	less
Density		
Capillaries	more	less
Mitochondria	more	less
Enzyme Activity		
Myosin ATPase	less	more
Carbohydrate metabolism	less	more
Fat metabolism	more	less
Oxidation	more	less
Resistance to Fatigue	high	low

individual must either reduce the intensity (thereby allowing the slower aerobic system to metabolize more fat) or stop because of exhaustion. During progressively increasing exercise, as depicted in Figure 2–3, there is also preferential recruitment of specific fiber types. During phase 1, ST fibers are the main fibers being used. With increasing exercise intensity there is a greater recruitment of FT fibers to provide more force. Many ST and FT fibers are used during phase 3.

All skeletal muscles have a mixture of ST and FT fibers. There is a wide range in the relative proportion of these fibers when all muscles are compared in the same person or when the same muscle is compared in different people. Within the same person, for example, ST fibers comprise 40% to 65% of the fibers in the gastrocnemius and 80% to 95% of those in the soleus. The reason for this difference should be clear when one remembers that the gastrocnemius is the larger muscle of the calf used for jumping, while the soleus is the smaller muscle of the calf located closer to the bone and used for walking. The composition of the vastus lateralis muscle (lateral side of the thigh) can be very different among individuals. Although the normal average for ST fibers is 50% to 55% in both men and women, the proportion can range from 10% to 20% in successful male sprinters up to 90% to 98% in male ditance runners. The values for women in the same events are 25% to 30% and 70% to 80% respectively. The reason for the greater variation in men is unknown.

It appears that the proportion of the fiber types is genetically determined. Physical training does not seem to produce any change in proportion, only in the characteristics of the fibers. For example, endurance training will increase the oxidative potential of both ST and FT fibers. This is done by enhancing the capillarization, mitochondrial density, and activity of the aerobic enzymes of both fiber types.

As was the case with differences in body type and body composition, the composition of muscle can play an important role in determining the level of performance attainable by athletes of national and international caliber. In other words, someone who is born with a high percentage of ST fibers will have a better chance of competing successfully in a marathon than one with the average of about 50% ST fibers. Likewise, a person with a high percentage of FT fibers will be better able to compete in weight lifting. However, since most sporting activities require combinations of aerobic and anaerobic energy, an extreme proportion of one fiber type is less important. It should also be mentioned that one cannot compete successfully without training or skills, regardless of the composition of muscle fibers.

Other Factors That Can Modify the Functional Effects of Exercise

If the preceding description of anthropometry, muscle fiber types, and the events occurring during exercise appeared to be logical and straightforward, then it has achieved the objectives of simplification, clarification, and education. As well, the reader should now realize that study of form and function is one of logic, and that nothing occurs within the body unless there is good reason. However, if the reader is left with the impression that the structural and functional responses are simple and uncomplicated, then he should also consider the single and combined effects of some of the many variables and situations that can modify these responses. For example, there are differences when exercise is performed:

1. Rhythmically or statically
2. Intermittently or continuously
3. While lying or standing
4. With arms or legs
5. At altitude or under water
6. In a hot (dry or humid) or cold environment
7. By different kinds of people, e.g.,
    (a) by men or women;
    (b) by children, adults, or the elderly;
    (c) by an untrained person or an athlete who is specifically trained for that activity; and
    (d) by a healthy person or one who has a disease that affects his ability to exercise (heart disease, emphysema, etc.)

Static versus Dynamic Exercise. Activities in our daily lives tend to be of two basic kinds, static and dynamic. Holding a suitcase while walking is an activity combining both of these. This simple classification of activity is based on the predominant type of muscle contraction occurring in a given muscle or group of muscles. A static or isometric contraction is one in which there is no apparent change in the overall length of a muscle, while a dynamic or isotonic contraction occurs when there is either shortening or lengthening of the muscle. Shortening of a muscle (concentric contraction) results when the force of contraction is greater than that of the resistance, and lengthening (eccentric contraction) occurs when the contractile force is less. There is also a special kind of dynamic contraction that can be produced only with a special device. In isokinetic contraction this device allows only a constant rate of movement at all joint angles throughout the range of motion, regardless of the force exerted by the contracting muscle. This quite expensive device has been gaining in popularity recently, but too little research has been done to adequately determine its efficacy in strength-training programs.

It should be mentioned here that few daily activities are purely one type of contraction. For example, in the act of lifting a heavy weight, the first form of contraction is isometric since no movement will occur until there is enough force to overcome the resistance. During the lifting phase, the active muscle fibers are shortening and concentric contraction results. If the weight is held motionless at the top of the lift, contraction is once more isometric. When the weight is being lowered the whole muscle is lengthening. This is considered eccentric contraction, even though some fibers have to be shortening or the weight would drop rapidly. Once the weight is lowered and again motionless, a few fibers are still contracting isometrically.

Regardless of the relative contribution of each type of contraction to the total work performed, the effects on the body depend mainly on their intensity and duration. The general effects of dynamic exercise on various functions can be seen in Figure 2–3.

The effects of static or isometric exercise are quite different. At forces less than 15% to 20% of that seen with a maximal voluntary contraction (MVC), there is little effect on HR, $\dot{V}o_2$, SBP, or DBP, depending on the total size of the muscle mass involved (i.e., the total amount of work being done). A contraction at this intensity can be held indefinitely as the energy requirements are low, while the muscle blood flow is unchanged and more than adequate. As the intensity of contraction rises to 25% to 50% MVC, however, HR, SBP, and DBP increase rapidly, and the duration of the contraction progressively decreases along with muscle blood flow. In this case the heart is attempting to nullify or overcome the rise in intramuscular pressure and subsequent drop in blood flow by increasing its rate (HR) and force (SBP) of contraction. This sudden and marked rise in the work done by the heart is of little consequence to a normal person but makes intense static exercise a high-risk activity for a cardiac patient who already has a weakened heart.

When the force of contraction exceeds 60% MVC, there is a complete block of blood flow to the muscle. Although a small amount of aerobic energy can be provided by the oxygen present in the muscle at the time of blockage, most of the energy must come from the anaerobic degradation of glycogen located within the muscle itself. As a result, the duration of exercise is very short, and the rise in HR, SBP, and DBP is greater and more rapid.

There is a gradual rise in $\dot{V}o_2$ at the onset of an isometric contraction, but it is less rapid than that seen with dynamic exercise (Fig. 2–3). Once the contraction has ended there is an immediate increase in blood flow to those muscles partially or totally deprived of oxygen, resulting in a brief but marked rise in $\dot{V}o_2$. The overall rise in $\dot{V}o_2$ is minor, however, since the duration of exercise is so short, and the total amount of energy used is small.

Although there is a rise in HR, $\dot{V}o_2$, and SBP with high-intensity dynamic exercise, the increases in HR and SBP are less and the increase in $\dot{V}o_2$ is greater than those seen with static exercise since there are alternating periods of contraction and relaxation. During the period of contraction the small arteries, arterioles, and veins are squeezed by the surrounding muscle fibers. The fact that they are emptied reduces the pressure in these blood vessels and accentuates the difference relative to the increased pressure at the heart and large arteries, resulting in an even greater blood flow during the period of relaxation. This explains why DBP does not rise as it does with isometric exercise. The alternating compression and filling of blood vessels ensures an elevated blood flow and thus adequate levels of oxygen and nutrients to the muscles that are working, allowing the person to perform more exercise for longer periods.

Intermittent versus Continuous Exercise. When exercise is done intermittently it can be performed comfortably at high intensity for long periods. If the same amount of exercise is done continuously the duration will be shorter. Thus the two forms of exercise can be very different in their demands on the body.

Even though most occupational, leisure, and sporting activities involve intermittent exercise, more information is available on the effects of continuous exercise. Part of the reason is that once a physiological steady state is reached at a given submaximal work load, there are few changes in the variables normally measured, unless the exercise is continued for so long that body temperature rises or fatigue sets in. As a result, continuous exercise can be controlled, standardized, and described quite easily. In the case of intermittent exercise, however, there are many factors other than energy requirement that can influence response. Some of these follow:

1. Duration of the exercise phase. High-intensity exercise can be performed for 1 to 15 seconds, using primarily the reserves of ATP and CP in the muscle (see Fig. 2–1). If the exercise is stopped, ATP and CP are replenished and become available for the next bout of exercise. If the same exercise is continued for 30 to 60 seconds, the anaerobic system is also stimulated, and LA is produced. After continuation for more than 3 to 4 minutes (probably at a lower intensity), a steady state is reached, and the aerobic system is a major supplier of energy. The duration of exercise is thus the most critical factor in high-intensity exercise, determining whether there will be high levels of LA in the blood, the accumulation of which is associated with fatigue and discomfort. By exercising at an intensity greater than $\dot{V}O_{2\,max}$ for only 20 seconds and then resting for 40 seconds, for example, one can continue to exercise for more than an hour without a buildup of LA. If the same exercise is done for 60 seconds with 120 seconds of rest in between, exercise becomes more difficult after 30 to 40 minutes. Ice hockey teams have found that 1 minute on the ice with 2 to 3 minutes off is the most efficient schedule for their players. Done continuously, the same exercise would have to be stopped after 3 to 4 minutes.

2. Duration of the recovery (rest or low-intensity exercise) phase. Although LA can be produced in a few seconds, it takes about 15 minutes to eliminate one half of that produced. With repeated intermittent exercise of sufficient duration and intensity, more LA will begin to accumulate. Thus, by the third period of ice hockey or the end of the second half of soccer, fatigue is present in poorly conditioned players or in those who pushed themselves too hard or too often. If low to moderate levels of exercise (less than 50% to 60% $\dot{V}O_{2\,max}$ and the point at which LA first begins to accumulate) are done during the recovery phase, as opposed to complete rest, then LA will be removed at a faster rate. The reason for this is that the blood flow to the muscle is higher, allowing more LA to diffuse from the areas of higher concentration in the muscle to the regions of lower concentration in the blood.

3. Average intensity. The intensity of the exercise and recovery phases, as well as the average intensity of the two phases, will affect the responses to intermittent exercise. As with continuous exercise, intensity is a decisive factor for the sources of energy and the muscle fiber types being used.

4. Amplitude. If there is a big difference between the intensities of the exercise and recovery phases, the body will have to make more adjustments. Since there is a delay in the body's ability to respond to varying intensities (see Fig. 2–2), however, the degree to which the responses will oscillate from one level to another depends on the duration of the exercise and recovery phases. For example, if the two phases are only 5 seconds each, oscillations will be small, and the responses will be very similar to those seen during continuous exercise at the same average intensity. On the other hand, if both periods are 3 to 4 minutes, then a steady state may be reached at the end of each phase. The greater the amplitude, the more time will be required to reach a steady state.

Thus, the responses to intermittent and continuous exercise can be very similar or quite different, depending on many factors, those mentioned above plus others. For a more detailed overview of intermittent exercise the article by Saltin, Essén, and Pedersen (1976) is the most thorough.

Effect of Body Position. Changes in body position produce changes in the response to exercise. This is mainly due to gravity, which tends to force more blood into the lower parts of the body. While there will be little effect on the body while it is supine, there is an effect in the upright position.

The energy required to pump blood through the arteries to the extremities and to return the blood through the veins to the heart is much less while a person is lying down. Since the blood is more evenly distributed throughout the body, there will also be more blood returning to the heart. The amount of blood pumped per heart beat will then be greater, and fewer beats will be required to pump the same amount of blood per minute. In addition, the body does not have to use energy to maintain an erect posture. As a result, $\dot{V}O_2$, HR, and BP are lower at rest. In contrast to this, blood tends to pool in the large veins of the legs when the person is standing at rest. Less blood returns to the heart, and more beats are required per minute.

Once exercise begins, a given amount of work requires a given amount of energy or oxygen, regardless of body position. Except for the lower HR while the person is lying down, therefore, there is little difference in the body's responses. At about 40% $\dot{V}O_{2\,max}$ the flow of blood back to the heart is the same in both positions because of the pumping action of the muscles, and the difference in HR disappears. As the exercise becomes more intense, however, there is a point at which standing is the more favorable position. This is true for two reasons: First, if the legs are slightly higher than the rest of the body (as would be the case while pedaling a bicycle in the supine position), gravity will tend to force more blood into the upper and middle parts of the body. As a result, more pressure must be generated by the heart to pump blood uphill. If it cannot provide enough pressure, then the legs work more and more anaerobically and have to stop sooner. Second, the efficiency of exercise is less while the person is lying down, meaning that more energy is required to do the same amount of external work.

Thus, the $\dot{V}O_{2\,max}$ is about 25% to 30% higher in a person who is upright (running) than in one who is lying down (pedaling a bicycle). Values for sitting exercise (bicycle) are about 10% less than those obtained while standing; this is also partially caused by a difference in efficiency.

Exercise Done with Arms versus Exercise Done with Legs. In turning the pedals of a bicycle against resistance, there will be differences in how the body responds to exercise done by the arms or legs. A comparison of the responses must consider three main factors; namely, the absolute muscle mass involved, the relative intensity at which the muscles are working, and the efficiency with which they can work.

First, since the amount of muscle involved in pedaling a bicycle is so different, the legs can produce much more power. It has been shown that the $\dot{V}O_{2\,max}$ with the arms is about 75% of that obtained with the legs. Second, a smaller percentage of the muscle fibers in the legs will be contracting to produce the same power output on the bicycle. In other words, to perform a given level of submaximal exercise, the legs might be working aerobically with more ST fibers at 30% to 40% of the $\dot{V}O_{2\,max}$ attainable with the legs, while the arms will be working more anaerobically with ST and FT fibers at 75% to 80% of the $\dot{V}O_{2\,max}$ that they can attain. As a result, HR, ventilation, and LA concentration will be higher. Third, in order to pedal with the arms at a high intensity, it is necessary to stabilize the muscles of the trunk and shoulders with a series of isometric contractions. The isometric contractions cause the blood pressure to rise and inhibit the rapid breathing needed at this time. In addition, the arms are higher than the heart, so that blood must be pumped at a greater pressure uphill, causing both the SBP and DBP to rise. Because of a decrease in blood flow, LA will also be produced in the muscles contracting isometrically.

Combining arms and legs does increase the total amount of muscle mass that can be involved in an activity. It has been found, for example, that when arms provide 20% to 30% of the total power needed, then the work can be done for longer periods with less overall fatigue. Once the arms have to provide more than 30%, however, fatigue sets in more quickly. In such sports as rowing and kayaking, the strength and endurance of the upper body can be limiting factors for performance, while in cross-country skiing more work is done by the leg and trunk muscles.

Effects of Barometric Pressure. Oxygen diffuses across the lungs into the blood and from the blood to the tissues because there are differences in its partial pressure. The partial pressure of oxygen (PO_2) is determined by multiplying the total pressure of all gases in the environment (barometric pressure) by the relative concentration of oxygen. For example, if the barometric pressure of air at sea level and fully saturated with water, as is the case in the lungs, is around 710 mm Hg and oxygen comprises 21% of that total, then the PO_2 is 710 × 0.21 or 149 mm Hg. Since the PO_2 at the cellular level is around 40 mm Hg, the difference is sufficient to drive oxygen from the lungs toward the cells.

If the PO_2 is changed somehow (either by altering the barometric pressure or the concentration of oxygen in the air), then the availability of oxygen will be affected. For example, if one goes to Mexico City (altitude of 7,600 feet), the barometric pressure drops to such an extent that the PO_2 at the lungs is only 110 mm Hg, and the driving force for the diffusion of oxygen is less. Similarly, the PO_2 in the Andes (14,000 feet) is around 84 mm Hg and only 42 mm Hg at Mount Everest (28,000 feet). Because of these reductions in barometric pressure, an effect would be seen only during exercise at Mexico City but *even at rest* in the Andes. The only way one could exist at Mount Everest would be to increase the concentration of oxygen by breathing from a tank of oxygen.

Given the fact that a given amount of exercise requires a given amount of energy, the body has to use its anaerobic system more when less oxygen is available. Of course this has no effect on those activities lasting only a few seconds or a few minutes, since the energy for these activities comes primarily from anaerobic sources. The longer the duration and the greater the need for oxygen, however, the worse will be the performance. This was the case in the performances at the 1968 Olympic Games in Mexico City. When exercise is continuous at moderate altitude (5,000 to 10,000 feet), HR and ventilation are higher, and more LA is produced. Interestingly, the same amount of LA is produced at the same relative intensity (e.g., at 75% $\dot{V}O_{2\,max}$), but since the $\dot{V}O_{2\,max}$ is reduced, a given work load represents a higher percentage of the maximum.

While altitude causes a drop in barometric pressure, there is a rise in barometric pressure of about 22 mm Hg for every foot that one is immersed under water; this increase is about 760 mm Hg or 1 atmosphere for each 10m. At a depth greater than 1.5 feet the external pressure on the chest will be such that it is not possible to breathe in. That is the reason snorkels are less than 1 foot long. To go deeper one needs a tank of compressed air with a regulator to compensate for the increased external pressure and to provide the air needed to exist.

Other than the sport of scuba diving, most activities in the water are carried out at depths of only a few feet, where the increase in barometric pressure is not the major change. What affects the person more is the fact that he is in an environment where the force of gravity has been removed. As in the case of lying down, less energy is required to stand or sit, and the blood is now distributed evenly throughout the body. With the increased external pressure on the body the superficial veins are compressed so that more blood returns to the heart. Thus HR and $\dot{V}O_2$ at rest will be lower.

During exercise in cool water, less blood goes to the skin to get rid of the heat being produced by the muscles, and more blood is available to the muscles themselves. The HR is about 10 beats per minute lower in the water than while producing the same amount of power on land. The $\dot{V}O_{2\,max}$ in water is about 10% to 15% less; this is partially due to the increased resistance to breathing, thereby reducing the amount of air that can be ventilated. Also, the maximal HR is about 10 beats per minute lower.

Effect of Environmental Temperature. Considered as a machine, man has an efficiency of only 25%; that is, 25% of the energy obtained from food is used for chemical reactions, muscle contractions, nervous impulses, etc., while the other 75% is given off in the form of heat.

The temperature of the body is regulated very closely to stay within a few degrees of an optimal level so that none of the body's functions will be disturbed. This regulation is aided by the fact that the normal core temperature is 37 C (98.6 F), while it is 33 C (91 F) at the skin and usually 21 to 23 C (70 to 75 F) in most buildings. Since heat flows toward the area of low temperature, the body is constantly giving off heat if the room temperature is less than that of the skin. The greater the difference, the more heat will be given off. If the external temperature is less than 20 C (68 F), then the loss of heat can be reduced by adding more clothing; this insulates the skin from the air. On the other hand, if the external temperature is greater than 37 C, then the body can actually gain heat.

The body has little difficulty regulating its temperature at rest in a comfortable environment. Once exercise begins, however, the body can produce 10 to 25 times as much heat as at rest for prolonged periods. Several mechanisms are available to eliminate this extra heat. When a fluid evaporates into a gas, heat is given off; for example, the evaporation of each liter of sweat (2.2 lb water) causes the body to lose 580 kcal heat. Evaporation is thus the main avenue for heat loss during exercise.

The regulatory system is also assisted by the bigger difference in temperature during exercise; the core temperature rises because of increased heat production and the skin temperature drops as a result of evaporation of sweat from its surface. This greater temperature difference promotes the flow of heat from the core to the periphery. There is also more blood flowing to the skin to transport this heat. As a result, the HR rises in an attempt to supply blood simultaneously to the muscles and to the skin. The dilation of many blood vessels at the periphery causes a drop in BP.

At low levels of exercise and heat production, the body has little problem to adjust. This is not the case at higher intensities of exercise, however, when the demands for blood supply to the skin are so great that the amount available to the muscles is less and the person has to stop sooner. Thus the $\dot{V}o_{2 \, max}$ is lower in a hot environment.

An extra problem with exercising in a humid environment is that the skin is saturated with water while the air may be 60% to 80% saturated. As a result, less sweat can be evaporated and less heat can be lost from the skin. The subsequent rise in skin temperature reduces the difference, and less heat flows from the core. Once the core temperature rises more than 3 to 4 F, disturbances occur in the body's functions. At this point the person should (and usually will) stop exercising to avoid problems.

Problems can also arise when exercise of moderate intensity is done for more than 30 minutes, as in a marathon. The hotter the temperature, the higher the humidity, and the longer and more intense the exercise, the greater will be the loss of water. When more than 5% body weight is lost, the blood becomes less dilute, the concentration of minerals and electrolytes is altered, HR goes up, and the temperature-regulating mechanism is impaired. If exercise is continued, the sweating mechanism eventually stops in an attempt to preserve body fluids, body temperature rises quickly, and heat stroke is imminent.

As long as body temperature remains near its desired level, few problems are created by exercising in a cold environment. In this case the major problem is how to control heat loss. This can be done by adding more clothes (insulation) and by producing enough heat to maintain body temperature without sweating. Two winter sports amply illustrate this point. In downhill skiing, the skier wears heavier clothing to insulate himself from the wind and cold mountain air. The intermittent exercise is generally adequate to keep him warm. By contrast, cross-country skiers wear less clothing since they produce much more heat in a continuous manner.

Heat loss can also be reduced by constriction of the blood vessels at the skin; this reduces the gradient between the skin and the environment and keeps more of the blood near the center of the body. With this vasoconstriction there will be a rise in BP. If there is also an attempt to do intense, anaerobic work with the arms (e.g., shoveling a lot of snow in a short period) or intense, isometric exercise (e.g., pushing a stalled car), the combination of vasoconstriction, increased BP, holding the breath while straining, and intensive demands for energy may be too much for the heart of a middle-aged man with arterial disease. Doing mild, aerobic exercise for several minutes beforehand will result in dilation of the blood vessels to eliminate heat, and the aerobic system will be activated, thereby reducing the risk of a heart attack in such a person.

Comparison of Males and Females. Until adolescence there is little difference in size or performance between boys and girls. This similarity ceases with the onset of puberty and the associated alterations in hormonal status. Aside from some obvious qualitative differences, females differ quantitatively in ways that affect their ability to exercise. Some differences may be more related to sociocultural factors than to physiological ones, however. Until recently, women were not considered feminine if they engaged in physical activity. Thus many girls did what was expected and became less active during and after adolescence. While this may now be changing, one must nevertheless consider these sociological factors when discussing possible physiological differences.

Women tend to be smaller and lighter than men. The composition of their weight is different; they tend to have lighter bones, less muscle, and relatively more fat. The strength of their upper body is about 60% to 70% of that of men, while the strength of their legs is 75% to 85% of that for men. The lower values for upper body strength may be more a reflection of the pattern of use and less of a physiological difference. For example, the difference in leg strength disappears when compared per unit of muscle in the legs. This suggests that the quality of the force development is the same, only the quantity is less.

In respect to the aerobic system, women tend to have smaller hearts and a smaller volume of blood (both are related to their smaller body size), as well as less hemoglobin per unit of blood (hemoglobin is the carrier of oxygen). Thus a smaller heart has to beat more often during a standard work load to pump the same amount of oxygen to the muscles. Since men and women of the same age tend to have the same maximal HR, women will reach their maximal value sooner. This decrease in the ability to transport oxygen is matched by a concomitant drop in the ability to use oxygen; i.e., it makes little sense to be able to use a large amount of oxygen if it cannot be delivered.

Accordingly, the $\dot{V}O_{2\,max}$ of women is less than that of men when reported as the total amount of oxygen consumed per minute; this is related to body size. The difference is less when the values are reported as the amount of oxygen consumed per minute for each kilogram of body weight (this eliminates the difference in body weight) and practically disappears when the values are reported as the amount of oxygen consumed per minute for each kilogram of lean body weight (this eliminates the differences in body composition). When reported in this fashion it shows that there are no qualitative differences in the ability of muscle in men and women to extract and use oxygen.

Because of their smaller size and lower $\dot{V}O_{2\,max}$, women are at a disadvantage whenever they have to work against outside resistance (rowing or cycling) or have to transport their own weight (running or jumping). The differences in performance tend to be less in swimming, in which the extra fat and lighter bones help women float, thereby reducing the resistance and work involved in propulsion.

Comparison of Children and Adults. Many people think of a child as a miniature adult. However, many of the functions in a child's body are not fully developed, and he cannot perform exercise as well.

Consider the three sources of energy production shown in Figure 2–1. Children are no different from adults in their ability to perform very intense activities for a few seconds. In other words, their ATP-CP system functions in the same manner. Children do have problems, however, performing high-intensity exercise for 30 to 120 seconds. It seems that children have less of the enzyme needed to produce LA. As a result, they cannot supply as much energy with their anaerobic system and must slow down to allow the aerobic system to provide the required energy. The LA system becomes developed during puberty. The systems for transporting and utilizing oxygen are not fully developed before puberty and put children at a slight disadvantage. Nevertheless, children are able to perform exercise of moderate intensity for moderate periods.

If the intensity becomes too high, there will be problems with the anaerobic mechanism of children. Likewise, if the duration of exercise is too long, there may be another problem peculiar to children. Relative to their body weight, children have a larger surface area. Since the surface is where heat exchange occurs, the greater the ratio of surface area to body weight, the greater will be the exchange of heat with the environment. Thus children will lose more heat during long periods of exercise in a cool environment (e.g., swimming in cold water). If it is hot and humid, children will gain more heat. Children also have less mature sweat glands, and thus loss of heat by evaporation is less effective.

Although children are not aware of these physiological differences, their patterns of play reflect them; that is, children tend toward activities of low to moderate intensity, with very short bursts of intensive activity. Only in competitive situations, especially with pressure from adults, do they attempt high-intensity exercise for any length of time.

Comparison of Young and Old Adults. Once maturity is reached (25 to 30 years of age), the effects of the aging process on a number of the body's functional and structural systems appear. Aging results in a loss in size, number, or both, of functional units within every system of the body, as well as a loss of function in those units that remain. As a result, aging can be characterized by decreased ability to adapt to and to recover from physiological stimuli. It seems that the greater the intensity of the stimulus and the larger the number of physiological mechanisms involved in adjusting to that stimulus, the greater will be the loss of function with age.

As people age, there is a tendency to an increase in body fat and a decrease in the number and size of both muscle fibers and nerve cells. This explains why older people are weaker, slower, and less powerful. Likewise, there is deterioration in those performances requiring the regulating and coordinating functions of the nervous system (e.g., balance, reaction time, agility, and coordination).

Changes in the respiratory system make it more difficult to supply adequate levels of oxygen to the body during intense exercise. The heart has to work harder to pump the same amount of blood, especially against increased BP. When this is coupled with a decrease in maximal HR, it is evident that the maximal amount of blood that can be pumped per minute will also decrease. At the cellular level there is a loss of the units and a decrease in the activity of the enzymes associated with all three mechanisms for producing energy (i.e. ATP-CP, LA, and oxidation). When all these points are considered together, it is easy to understand why older people cannot perform as well in almost any kind of activity, except those of low intensity in which the energy requirements are easily met.

Since aging is characterized by decreased ability to adapt, it stands to reason that the ability to train (adaptation to the repeated stimulation of exercise) will be less in the older person. Although studies have shown that older people can improve, their improvement tends to be less and requires more time.

It appears that training does not affect the aging process per se; that is, the *rate* of change in various functions is probably no different in an active or in a sedentary person. The difference between them is mainly related to the level of function existing at a given time. A well-trained person who continues to train will be in better shape and have a greater functional capacity than others of the same age. The fact that his $\dot{V}o_{2 \, max}$ at 60 years of age may be the same as that of a sedentary person 30 years of age does not mean that he is as young or that he has delayed the process of aging. It means only that he is a well-trained 60-year-old man whose body has undergone many changes and who is still capable of performing a lot of exercise.

The Effects of Training. It is generally accepted in physiology that repeated stimulation (overload) of a system improves its ability to adapt to and recover from that kind of stimulus. This adaptation is the result of both structural and functional alterations within that system, the structural changes usually occurring later. There is also general acceptance of the principle of specificity (i.e., changes occur only in those systems that are overloaded). Some examples will help clarify what is meant by specificity. Even though runners, cyclists, swimmers, and cross-country skiers all may train for endurance, and all may have a high $\dot{V}o_{2 \, max}$, each athlete will excel in his particular activity. Similarly, runners, cyclists, and skiers will do better in activities requiring the use of the legs, while skiers and swimmers will be better in those requiring use of the arms. One can also find specificity in the same activity. In running, for example, a sprinter develops the ability to run fast for brief periods, an activity requiring high levels of strength and speed; all of these are associated with the development of the ATP-CP system. At the other extreme, a marathon runner has the ability to run at moderately high intensity for prolonged periods; i.e., he has developed his aerobic system. Middle-distance runners are somewhere in between (depending on the intensity and duration) and have developed a high tolerance for the LA associated with the anaerobic system. What occurs, therefore, are modifications in the various mechanisms for producing energy.

Figure 2–4 diagrams what happens with training. The solid lines represent values in a sedentary person and are the same as those in Figure 2–3; the dotted lines show the effects of training. As an oversimplification, training causes an increase in the functional capacity of the various systems. With the higher maximum the same absolute power output becomes relatively less strenuous (i.e., the intensity decreases). The $\dot{V}o_2$ is unchanged since the same amount of energy is needed, but there is a reduction in ventilation, $\dot{V}o_2$, HR, and SBP. As well, the average sedentary person begins to produce LA at about 50% $\dot{V}o_{2 \, max}$. After training he is able to do more work before he attains 50% of his increased $\dot{V}o_{2 \, max}$. This is due primarily to the functional changes in his aerobic system. With prolonged training there will also be structural changes in the various parts of his aerobic system. As a result, he will now be able to work at 60% to 65% of an even higher $\dot{V}o_{2 \, max}$ before his aerobic system is not supplying energy rapidly enough. Since fat is the preferred aerobic fuel, more fat is used at the same power output, thereby conserving the limited amounts of glycogen in the muscle and liver. Thus a well-trained person is capable of exercising at higher relative power outputs, and at much higher absolute power outputs, than an unconditioned person of the same age and sex.

It should be mentioned that the body can adapt to inactivity as well as to training. It makes little sense to have the ability to produce large amounts of energy with any of the three mechanisms if large amounts are seldom needed. The changes associated with prolonged inactivity are generally the opposite of those seen with training. A good example of this can be seen in the accelerated changes occurring in a leg that has been put in a cast for 5 to 6 weeks.

Comparison of Various States of Health. A comparison of the effects of health vs. disease or medical problems on the ability to exercise is complicated by the large number and variety of health states. The fact that many people are also older and

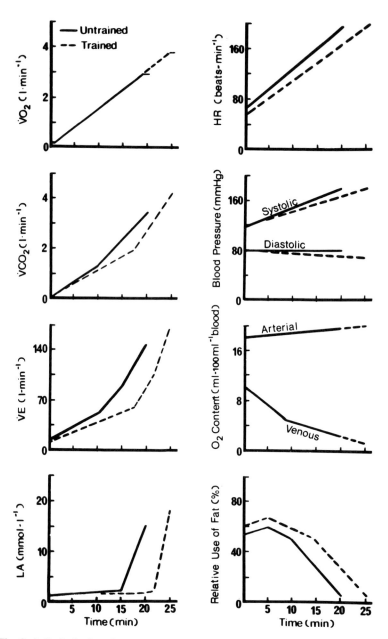

Fig. 2–4. Typical values for trained and untrained people during progressive exercise from rest to maximal oxygen intake.

deconditioned when the symptoms and problems appear makes such a comparison even more difficult.

In order to determine the effects of a particular state of health on the ability to exercise, one should first study the characteristics of that disease or medical problem to see which systems of the body or which mechanisms for producing energy will be affected. For example, the ability to pump blood may be diminished in coronary heart disease, while emphysema alters the exchange of oxygen and carbon dioxide in the lungs. Both of these will affect the ability to do aerobic exercise of moderate intensity.

Knowing which systems have been affected, how they have been changed, and the role that each system plays during specific forms of exercise makes it easier to understand how a particular health state affects and is affected by exercise. Because of the complexity of the various states of health, however, the purpose of this section is only to alert the reader to the wide range of possible responses and not to discuss each of them in detail.

IMPLICATIONS FOR GENERAL EDUCATION

One of the main purposes of education is to help people better understand themselves. In the case of exercise physiology one learns more about the body, how it functions, and how exercise may affect it. This knowledge has implications for one's health and well-being, since a better understanding of the specific effects of specific activities should help one to understand more about such things as fatigue, weight control, and training as well as why physical activity should be an integral part of a healthy life style.

A good program of regular physical activity should consider a person's age, present level of fitness and health, interests and needs, time and facilities available, and reasons (related to physiological or psychological well-being) for wanting to be active. Since any of these factors may change, no one program will always be just right. Therefore, with an understanding of what happens with specific kinds of exercise, why it happens, and how to make it happen, a person should be able to adjust his program of physical activity to the various conditions present at any given time. With knowledge, each person should be able to design a program that is safe, effective, enjoyable, and specifically suited to his life style.

IMPLICATIONS FOR PROFESSIONAL PRACTICE

Although knowledge about the theoretical aspects of exercise physiology would be necessary for anyone interested in research in this area, only a few physical educators will continue with their formal education for this purpose. The vast majority will become more involved in the practical application of knowledge to people of all ages and backgrounds. Given the fact that physical education involves physical activity, however, it stands to reason that a professional (researcher or practitioner) should have a good theoretical background on the functional effects of exercise on the body.

Teachers should know how children and adults adapt to exercise. Dancers should know the kinds of exercise to improve their performance. Exercise leaders need to know what kinds of exercise to emphasize or avoid for certain kinds of people. Coaches need to know about anthropometry, nutrition, weight control, and training in order to select and develop talented athletes for their particular sport. This is an especially complex undertaking since few sports involve just one source of energy or one type of body configuration. If one also considers all of the factors mentioned previously that can modify the functional effects of a given activity, it is obvious that coaching is not so straightforward. Swimming, for example, is performed in the horizontal position in a cool, zero-gravity environment with the arms and legs. Therefore a coach must determine the specific characteristics of the sport and decide on the relative importance of many factors, some of which are more related to skills, tactics, and psychological aspects. He must then try to apply all of this information to athletes with different body builds, muscle fiber composition, and functional capacities.

RELATIONSHIP TO AFFILIATED PROFESSIONS AND PROFESSIONAL OPPORTUNITIES

These two sections have been combined to show that there are a number of relationships with affiliated professions and professional opportunities to work with them.

Exercise physiology draws from and adds to the knowledge of many other sciences. For example, the study of how the body functions is physiology. The energy for the functioning of every living cell in the body comes from chemical reactions. The determination of fiber type and enzyme activities in muscle involves biochemical and histochemical analyses. Information on the amount and type of energy contained in food comes from the science of nutrition. Understanding the effects of a disease or medical problem on the ability to exercise requires knowledge from the field of medicine. Conversely, exercise physiology provides knowledge for all these other sciences about the specific responses and adaptations within the body to specific physiological stimuli.

Many physical educators today work with other professionals to apply the theoretical knowledge of exercise physiology. A few examples should clarify these relationships and opportunities: Physical educators are involved in fitness testing, health appraisal, weight-control counseling, exercise prescription, and in leading exercise programs for government (city recreation departments, fitness programs for government employees), industrial (private clinics, employee fitness and wellness programs), and community organizations (universities, YMCAs). Some are using the same procedures in a clinical setting where they work with physicians, nurses, therapists, etc., in rehabilitation programs for patients with such problems as coronary heart disease, emphysema, diabetes, hypertension, obesity, and cystic fibrosis. Physical educators are also working with physiotherapists and athletic trainers on the prevention and rehabilitation of injuries and musculoskeletal problems. In most of these instances the physical educator is considered an integral part of a team of professionals working on a comprehensive program of life-style modification.

CONCLUDING STATEMENT

The study of the body is a fascinating subject. It is even more interesting to see how it adjusts to the stimulus of exercise and adapts to the influence of repeated exercise. Anyone who works in a profession in which physical activity plays such an important role should be aware of the theoretical and practical aspects of exercise physiology, the science that attempts to explain these responses.

It is a truism in all fields that the more one knows, the more one realizes that there is much more to know. In respect to exercise physiology, there are so many complex factors that can influence how a given individual might respond to a given amount of exercise on a given day that only general guidelines can be formulated. It is then up to the teacher, dancer, coach, exercise leader, etc., to apply these guidelines in the manner that best suits the specific circumstances.

The study of exercise physiology is simplified, however, if one remembers that the responses are logical and specific. This, of course, assumes that there is adequate knowledge upon which to base a judgment. If the reader looks for and finds the logical modifications that must occur, then the study of exercise physiology can also be stimulating, interesting and satisfying.

QUESTIONS FOR POSSIBLE DISCUSSION AND TESTING

1. Select a sport and determine the energy sources involved in its practice.

2. Determine the relative importance of strength, speed, tolerance to lactic acid, endurance, $\dot{V}O_{2\,max}$, skill, and tactics for running 100 m, 800 m, 1500 m, 10,000 m, and the marathon (42,000 m).
3. List the factors that might modify the functional effects of exercise for such sports as ice hockey, channel swimming, weight lifting, and soccer. Briefly describe how each of these factors might affect the responses.
4. Select a modification that occurs with training (e.g., muscle hypertrophy, reduced heart rate at a given power output, increased use of fat as fuel during a given amount of submaximal exercise) and explain the logic of how and why it occurs.

REFERENCES AND SELECTED READINGS*

American College of Sports Medicine: Position statement on the recommended quantity and quality of exercise for developing and maintaining fitness in healthy adults. Med. Sci. Sports, 10:vii–xi, 1978.

American College of Sports Medicine: Guidelines for Graded Exercise Testing and Exercise Prescription. 2nd Ed. Philadelphia, Lea & Febiger, 1980.

Amsterdam, E.A., Wilmore, J.H., and DeMaria, A.N.: Exercise in Cardiovascular Health and Disease. New York, Yorke Medical Books, 1977.

Åstrand, P.O., and Rodahl, K.: Textbook of Work Physiology. 2nd Ed. New York, McGraw-Hill, 1977.

Edington, D.W., and Edgerton, V.R.: The Biology of Physical Activity. Boston, Houghton-Mifflin, 1976.

Holloszy, J.O.: Adaptations of muscular tissue to training. Prog. Cardiovasc. Dis., 43:445–458, 1976.

Knuttgen, H.G. (ed.): Neuromuscular Mechanisms for Therapeutic and Conditioning Exercise. Baltimore, University Park Press, 1976.

Lamb, D.R.: Physiology of Exercise. Responses and Adaptations. New York, Macmillan Co., 1978.

Oldridge, N.B.: What to look for in an exercise class leader. Physician Sportsmed., 5:85–88, 1977.

Pollock, M.L., Wilmore, J.H., and Fox, S.M.: Health and Fitness through Physical Activity. New York, J. Wiley & Sons, 1978.

Saltin, B., Essén, B., and Pedersen, K.: Intermittent exercise: Its physiology and some practical applications. In Advances in Exercise Physiology. Edited by E. Jokl, R. Anand, and H. Stoboy. Basel, Karger, 1976.

Skinner, J.S.: Aging and performance. In Limiting Factors of Physical Performance. Edited by J. Keul. Stuttgart, Thieme, 1973.

Skinner, J.S., and McLellan, T.M.: The transition from aerobic to anaerobic metabolism. Res. Q. Exer. Sport, 51:234–248, 1980.

Tanner, J.M.: The Physique of the Olympic Athlete. London, Allen & Unwin, 1964.

Wilmore, J.H.: The application of science to sport: Physiological profiles of male and female athletes. Can. J. Appl. Sport Sci., 4:103–115, 1979.

---

*This chapter was an attempt to summarize, synthesize, and simplify many facts. As such, it would have been difficult to read if references had been cited for even most of the points made. Therefore, the reader who wishes to know more is referred to any or all of these books and articles.

CHAPTER THREE

Sociocultural and Behavioral Aspects

A.V. Carron

The phenomena of play, dance, games, and sport (which are referred to as *sport* in this chapter) have had a continuous significant impact upon our modern industrial society. This is vividly illustrated by a number of factors. For example, consider the amount of media coverage—radio, television, and newspaper and magazine articles—devoted to sport. Does any other cultural event, including dance, music, or art, receive similar attention? Another example is the amount of time people spend in sport-related activities—either directly as participants or indirectly as spectators, coaches, officials, grounds keepers, concession workers, and so on. A third example is the significant financial expenditures associated with sport. In a comment on this, Loy, McPherson, and Kenyon pointed out that "not only has sport itself become an economic enterprise, it has also stimulated economic growth in a variety of ways, so that sport and sport-related enterprises represent an estimated 100-billion dollar business in the United States alone"(1978, p.256).

In light of the prominence of sport in our society it is not surprising that there has also been a growth in interest in understanding issues concerned with the how and why of sport participation. An example of some of the questions that might come immediately to mind in regard to sport are, Why do so many people become involved in sport—either directly as participants or indirectly as sport consumers? or What psychological and physiological variables are most closely related to performance excellence? or Does a sport experience have any impact upon the social-personal or the anatomical and physiological growth and development of the child?

There are, of course, numerous other issues such as these, issues that have intrigued athletes, coaches, teachers, and researchers for a number of years. The athletes and their coaches and teachers have been interested in the how and the why of sport performance primarily in order to improve performance outcomes and to enhance the quality of the sport experience. While researchers have undoubtedly held similar concerns, they have been principally interested in setting out and analyzing theoretically based interpretations and explanations for sports activity (Snyder and Spreitzer, 1975). Unfortunately, however, research progress, especially in the social-psychological dimension, has been slow.

Although Coleman R. Griffiths of the University of Illinois published a textbook as early as 1922 entitled *Psychology of Athletics*, historically the initial research interest in sport and physical education was in the anatomical and physiological dimensions, not in the social and psychological dimensions. Not surprisingly, the research emphasis and interest were also reflected in the physical education under-

Dr. Carron is from The University of Western Ontario, London.

graduate curriculum where the social-psychological dimension of sport and physical education received little or no attention.

Cratty highlighted these points with the following observations:

> Since before the turn of the century physical education major courses, the primary means of formal training for coaches, contained both practical and applied courses. Coaches were taught how to play and teach traditional sports activities on the one hand, and in addition they undertook various "scientific" courses in which they learned about some basic dimensions of human performance, knowledge of which would purportedly serve them later in good stead. For the most part, these latter courses were based on biomechanics and exercise physiology. Until the late 1950's courses dealing with the psychology of physical activity and the social factors that influence human movement in games and sport were largely absent.
>
> Since the early 1960's, however, interest in the psychological and social dimensions of human athletic endeavor has increased . . . .
>
> In the literature produced by physical educators, psychologists, social psychologists, and sociologists, there is some information that is indirectly relevant to many of the psychological and social dimensions inherent in athletic competition. (1973, pp. 4–5)

This increased emphasis on the social and psychological areas of sport and physical education in the 1960's and 1970's gradually led to its clear separation into a number of different (but interrelated) fields of interest including sociology, psychology, and social psychology. These three are combined in a general way to be the focus of this chapter.

DEFINITIONS

The principal focus of the social and psychological dimension of physical education is, broadly stated, *human social behavior in the context of sport* (where sport, as was pointed out previously, is a broad, umbrella-like term encompassing play, dance, games, and sport). Although this definitional statement seems reasonably straightforward, it should be elaborated upon in order to outline (a) how the general social-psychological dimension differs from other general areas of science, (b) how the specific component areas within the social-psychological dimension (sociology, psychology, and social psychology) are differentiated from one another, (c) how the social-psychological dimension of sport can be examined from a number of different perspectives—what can be referred to as different levels of analysis, and, finally, (d) what is meant by the term *behavior* when we refer to *human social behavior in a sport context*.

The Social-Psychological Dimension as an Area of Science

It is difficult to clearly distinguish between the various areas of science—to distinguish the social-psychological dimension from other dimensions. The boundaries between many areas are not easily differentiated. For example, it has often been suggested that a major difference between the social sciences such as psychology and sociology and the natural sciences such as chemistry and geology is that the former are concerned with behavior (and, as a result, are sometimes referred to as the behavioral sciences) while the latter are concerned with matter or material.

This suggestion is not only an oversimplification, it is essentially inaccurate. All science is interested in behavior. A chemist, for example, may be concerned with analyzing the behavioral properties of gases and liquids under different temperatures, while a geologist may be interested in assessing the behavioral changes that occurred in the earth's surface during significant periods in time. Similarly, the aggressive behavior demonstrated by a sport participant or the behavioral norms present on sport teams may be the subject of study for the social scientist.

Therefore, since all science is interested in behavior, broadly defined, the various areas of science are usually differentiated according to the *type of behavior* they study. From the above examples, it should be clear that the types of behavior focused on by the chemist, geologist, and the social scientist differ dramatically. And it has already been pointed out that the specific behavior that is the focus in the social-psychological dimension of physical education is *human social behavior in the context of sport.*

A Distinction between Components of the Social-Psychological Dimension

Psychology has been defined by psychologists as the science of human behavior—the study of the complex forms of human behavior, including its integration, organization, and manifestation. On the other hand, sociology is considered to be the science of society—the study of human social behavior with emphasis on human interaction. Further, social psychology (which, as its name implies, lies midway between sociology and psychology) has been defined as the science of human behavior in social situations—the study of individual behavior and the social forces that influence it. All of these focuses are very similar and interrelated. Therefore by extrapolation, sociology of sport, psychology of sport, and social psychology of sport are all similar and interrelated. So how can these areas be distinguished from one another?

When areas of scholarly interest have a similar or apparently identical focus, they are often differentiated on the basis of their *unit of analysis.* Thus, for example, the biologist, zoologist, and bacteriologist all have a similar general interest in animal behavior, but their respective specific unit of analysis does differ.

In a discussion on the differences between psychology and sociology, VanderZwaag and Sheehan noted:

> In attempting to clarify areas of scholarly responsibility, two of the most difficult categories to separate are sociology and psychology. One simple way to emphasize the difference between them is to identify each discipline's unit of analysis. Because sociology studies interaction, the basic unit for the sociologist is two or more people. Formal sociological analysis involves the interaction between at least two people who can affect each other directly or indirectly. The basic unit of analysis for the psychologist is the individual. The effect of the social environment on the individual is the primary concern of the psychologist. (1978, p.171)

In terms of the sport situation, then, the sport psychologist might be concerned with the wrestler competing in intercollegiate competition, while the sport sociologist would be concerned with the interaction of the wrestler in the social environment (in which the social environment could constitute the team or the coach, officials, spectators, opponents, and so on). It has been pointed out by Loy that the social environment of sport can also be examined from a number of different perspectives, what he referred to as the *levels of analysis* (1972).

Levels of Analysis in the Social-Psychological Dimension

Drawing upon the work of Caplow (1953), Loy has presented four levels (varying from simple to complex) at which the social factors (i.e., the social environment) influencing human behavior might be examined. These were referred to as the social category, group, organization, and institution.

In the *social category* (the simplest level) the social scientist studies individuals who can be differentiated on the basis of broad social categories such as age, sex, income, sport participation, and race. The general issue of interest is whether those individuals who are in a particular social category possess unique general characteristics. So, for example, if the social category of interest is wrestlers, the researcher might wish to determine what income or education level is characteristic of wrestlers' families.

At the *group level* greater emphasis is placed upon the individual as a unique person interacting with other individuals in the social situation. The association between different individuals and the relationship of that interaction to behavior is the primary focus. As an example, a researcher could be interested in determining whether those wrestling teams that contain members who strongly like one another are the most successful.

At the *organizational level* the analysis is of people as role players (social actors) and not as individual personalities. The coach and athlete, the doctor and patient, the lawyer and client each occupy social positions. (And, in fact, the same individual can occupy a number of social positions. The athlete, for example, could also be the patient and the lawyer in the above situations.) Analysis at the organizational level is concerned with the patterned interactions that occur among social positions regardless of the individuals who occupy them. A question from the sport of baseball that illustrates this type of analysis is, Are team managers recruited more frequently from high interaction positions (infielders) than low interaction positions (outfield)?

At the *institution level* (the most complex level) the analysis is of social positions in enduring organizations. Here the analysis is not concerned with specific competitors on specific teams, but rather with the organization as an abstraction. Thus a researcher might ask, Is sport closely linked with politics?

Human Social Behavior in Sport

A social scientist interested in sport is curious about two general kinds of "outputs" that fall under the classification of human social behavior. These are behavior and performance.

Behavior is the individual's unique way of responding (thinking, feeling, acting, doing) to internal and external stimuli. Within this framework the study of behavior includes the study of personality, attitudes, affective reactions, cognitive reactions, and so on. Some questions about behavior that serve to illustrate this class of sport-related issues are: Are athletes more outgoing, extroverted, confident than nonathletes? Do female athletes more strongly support the concept of sportsmanship than do male athletes? What are the causes of hockey violence? When is a loss most distressing to a competitor? When it results from a lack of ability? A lack of personal effort? An opponent's good play? Bad luck?

Performance is instrumental or goal-directed behavior that may or may not be effective. Within this framework the study of performance includes analysis of the factors that influence the quality and quantity of the athlete's output in games and competitions. Some questions about performance that serve to illustrate this class of sport-related issues are: Does the presence of spectators result in improvement or decrement in performance? Do children learn more quickly after observing the performance of a highly competent model? Does a team play better for an autocratic or democratic coach? Are cohesive teams more successful than noncohesive teams? It may be apparent that behavior and performance are highly similar constructs. Since the definition of behavior includes the concept of doing, performance is simply a very special type of behavior. But despite their similarity the two should be distinguished because

> the basis for evaluating the two is markedly different. In sport and physical activity, the criteria for performance effectiveness are usually well defined—performance, as goal-directed behavior, may be improved or worsened, more or less successful, and so on. Thus, the question of what detrimental or beneficial effect social [factors] have upon performance is significant . . . .
>
> On the other hand, with the possible exception of those instances where behavior fails to conform to broad social norms (e.g., deviancy), value-oriented judgements are not appropriate for behavior. Behavior is the unique response of the individual participant within the sport situation. (Carron, 1980a)

The social scientist studying behavior and performance may treat them as either an independent or a dependent variable or both. As the name suggests, a variable is a factor in the experiment that can vary over a range of values. In an experiment the independent variable is usually the causal factor (the factor that is manipulated—the antecedent condition), while the dependent variable is the effect (the product or outcome of the manipulation—the consequent condition). Thus, in the last illustration presented above—Are cohesive teams more successful than noncohesive teams?—cohesion would be the independent variable; performance success, the dependent variable. In order to answer the question posed, the researcher would have to compare the level of success of a number of teams that possessed differing degrees of cohesiveness.

However, this same question also could be reversed to ask, What is the effect of team success on cohesiveness? In this instance, success would be the independent variable; cohesion, the dependent variable. In order to answer the second question the researcher would have to analyze the degree of cohesiveness present within teams that had demonstrated different levels of performance success.

In the social-psychological dimension, human social behavior in sport has been examined from both of these perspectives—as a dependent behavior (or consequence of social psychological influences) and as an independent variable (or antecedent condition). The former perspective has been by far the most extensively researched. In the next two main sections of this chapter, evidence from some of the research oriented toward these two perspectives is presented.

HUMAN SOCIAL BEHAVIOR IN SPORT: ANALYSIS OF SOME SELECTED ANTECEDENTS

Personality

In any discussion of the antecedents (or consequences) of human behavior in sport, personality is among the first topics that arise. An interest in personality or personality-related questions has dominated the social-psychological dimension. In fact, the only topics that might rival personality in terms of the emphasis placed upon it are motivation- (and stress-) related issues.

The interest in personality is not too surprising when we consider that personality is assumed to be one of the significant, underlying causal factors for behavior. For example, the behavior of people that we know very well never seems to be random or unpredictable; there is an apparent consistency in their response in certain types of situations. Those aspects of the person that lead to that apparent behavioral consistency are referred to as personality. Therefore, if we could assess an athlete's personality accurately, we would be in an excellent position to understand and predict that athlete's behavior in the sport context.

Kroll pointed out that there have been two predominant strategies in analyses of the interrelationship of personality to sport participation (1970). In one of these the focus is on whether there is a specific set of personality factors that lead individuals to participate in certain sports. Do outgoing individuals show a preference for team sports, for example? In the second the focus is on whether sport participation leads to the development of specific personality factors in the athlete. A question that illustrates this is whether participation in a team sport leads to the development of an outgoing personality. In the first of these approaches, personality is examined as an antecedent condition for sport participation; in the second, as a consequence.

Despite the interest and emphasis on determining the relationship of personality and sport participation, the research results to date have been inconclusive. No clear pattern of personality factors has emerged from the many studies that have been undertaken. This led a number of sport psychologists to conclude that the personality domain and the sport domain are not related. As a result of these rather gloomy findings a number of sport researchers have recently advocated changes in the methodological approaches used to examine personality in sport.

One alternative that has been strongly suggested has been the development and utilization of personality inventories or measurement techniques more closely related to the specific context of sport. It has been suggested that the behaviors or behavioral situations that typically are assessed by general personality tests have only a very superficial relevance to sport. As a result, sport-specific inventories are now available to assess facets such as attitudes toward physical activity (Kenyon, 1968), incentive motivations of young athletes (Alderman and Wood, 1976), and sport competition anxiety (Martens, 1977).

A second proposal is that greater attention must be given to the classification of subjects:

> Essentially, this issue revolves around the question of what is an athlete, a question which may be as fundamental (and as perplexing) as the question of what is sport (e.g., are the Sunday jogger, the senior citizen lawn bowler, the high school basketball player, the professional race driver, etc., all athletes?) but also could include the questions of the degree of affiliation required (e.g., should the individual who practices with a team but is not sufficiently skilled to compete be classified as an athlete?) and the multiple group participant (e.g., is the boy who boxes and plays basketball a team versus individual versus combative versus noncombative athlete?). (Carron, 1980a, p. 30–31)

Until this basic problem in definition is resolved satisfactorily, any research concerned with the relationship of personality and sport participation will be difficult to interpret.

Motivation

In the previous section it was pointed out that motivation-related and stress-related issues, along with the topic of personality, are among the most extensively researched in the sociopsychological dimension. Motivation, which is derived from the past participle of the Latin word *movere*, to move, is the psychological construct used to represent the energy, the selectivity, and the direction for behavior. Motivation is usually considered to lie along a continuum of arousal or activation that includes sleep at one of the extremes and high stress at the other, motivation being in the mid regions. Although there is no clear dividing line between stress and motivation the two constructs are usually considered separately.

Factors Affecting Motivation Level. There are numerous, diverse sources that contribute to the *energy* aspect of an athlete's level of motivation. One way to consider these numerous, diverse sources of motivation is to subdivide and categorize them into separate dimensions or classes. Four broad catergories are identified in Figure 3–1: dimensions within the athlete, performance consequence dimensions, athletic competition dimension and task dimension. These dimensions largely differ according to whether they can be manipulated (readily influenced) by a coach or teacher.

The *dimensions within the athletes* are factors specific to the athlete that contribute to the total level of motivation. Among others, these factors include the athlete's personality, aspiration level, and intrinsic interest. This is a source of motivation largely independent of the coach or teacher.

The two major personality factors most frequently associated with motivation level are anxiety and need for achievement. Martens identified a sport-specific anxiety that he referred to as sport competition anxiety: a tendency to perceive competitive situations as threatening and to respond to these situations with feelings of apprehension and tension (1977, p. 23). When individuals who have high levels of sport competition anxiety are placed in competitive situations, it has been observed that they perceive those situations to be much more stressful than do individuals who have low levels of sport competition anxiety. Similarly, individuals who have a high need for achievement bring a high level of innate motivation to all achievement situations.

Since sport competition anxiety and need for achievement are personality traits, they influence the total level of motivation in all sport situations. The level of intrinsic

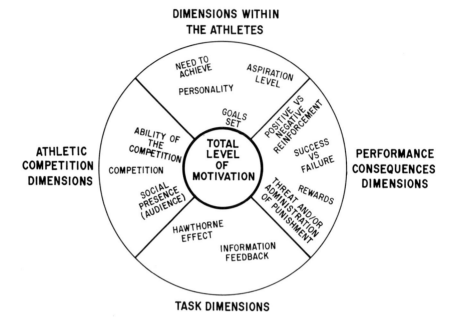

Fig. 3–1. The dimensions of motivation that affect the total level of motivation with the athlete. (Carron, A.V.: Motivating the athlete. Motor Skills, 1:23–24, 1977)

motivation present, however, depends upon the specific situation. Deci proposed that behavior that is intrinsically motivated results from the individual's innate need to feel competent and self-determining in dealing with the environment (1975). This is substantiated by Halliwell:

> Therefore, the more people feel that their actions are self-determined and provide a sense of personal competence, the higher will be their level of intrinsic motivation. On the other hand, if people feel that they are being pushed around by others or if their performance results in constant failure and negative feedback, they will be less intrinsically motivated to participate in that activity. (1978, p. 68)

The *athletic competition dimensions* reflect the dynamics of the athletic situation. Factors such as the relative importance of the event, the presence of an audience, the composition of that audience, and the ability of the competition are potential sources of motivation. The influence of spectators upon performance is discussed subsequently. The motivation resulting from athletic competition dimensions is generally available and relatively independent of the actions of the coach or teacher.

The outcome or performance results (*performance consequences dimension*) also affect the total level of motivation. For example, the outcome of performance usually includes some rewards or punishment, and the possibility of those rewards or punishments serves as a potential source of motivation for the athlete. The coach or teacher has very direct control over this dimension.

Finally, the task itself, *task dimensions*, contains the potential to be motivating. Information feedback refers to the information pertaining to the discrepancy between the completed response and the goal (or target), or between the movement as planned and the movement as executed. Unlike praise, encouragement, or criticism, information feedback is neutral; it is an objective summary of performance. Nonetheless the most common effect of information feedback is to increase motivation (Ammons,

1956). Athletes receiving information feedback tend to pursue the task with greater application and diligence. This may be partly due to the attention given the athletes, but it is also due to the fact that the feedback gives the athletes a yardstick by which progress, or lack of it, may be measured.

Another aspect of the task dimension that is a potential source of motivation may be referred to as the Hawthorne effect. This effect is named after a classic series of studies carried out at Western Electric Company's Hawthorne plant in Chicago. The purpose of the experiments was to examine the effect of the amount of plant illumination on work output. It was initially observed that the productivity of the workers increased when the illumination was increased. When the illumination was then decreased, however, productivity showed a further increase. Thus it was concluded that the level of illumination was not a factor of importance, but rather the change and special attention given the workers produced dramatic changes in motivation. In athletics, coaches have used this principle repeatedly. By introducing different drills and changing the nature of their practices throughout the year, coaches contribute to increased motivation levels in their athletes.

Incentives Associated with Sport Participation. There are also numerous, diverse incentives associated with sport participation that contribute to the selectivity aspect of an athlete's motivation for sport participation. Alderman and Wood in 1976 identified what was referred to as the *incentive systems* for sport, that is, "what it is about the sport itself (particularly its nature and demands) that motivates a young athlete to persist in his participation" (Alderman, 1978, p. 52).

The seven incentive systems in sport are referred to as affiliation, aggression, excellence, independence, power, stress, and success, names that aptly summarize each one. The *affiliation* incentive refers to the fact that children enter into sports to make friends or to maintain existing friendships through participation. The *aggression* incentive system acknowledges the fact that some children use sport as a medium in which to intimidate others, while the *excellence* incentives reflect the motivation that people have to do something well (e.g., to excel in sport). The underlying basis of the *independence* incentive system is to do things alone without the help of others, whereas the *power* system reflects motives to influence and control others in the sport context. *Stress* incentives revolve around opportunities for excitement, tension, pressure, and action. Finally, the *success* system is related to the desire for the extrinsic rewards in sport such as status, recognition, prestige, and social approval.

There is firm evidence that children are most strongly motivated by the affiliation and excellence incentives associated with sport participation. Children are attracted by the social aspects of sport and the opportunity to acquire sport skill and become proficient. Conversely, aggression, power, and independence are considered by children to be the least important incentives in sport. Alderman points out that these results have strong implications for coaches inasmuch as a sports situation must be kept very social in nature and each athlete must have not only the opportunity to become excellent but also must be constantly encouraged toward a personal level of competence (1978, p. 53).

Stresses Associated with Competition. There are three general questions relating to psychological stress in sport. One is concerned with what causes the feelings of apprehension, anxiety, and stress prior to competition. The second is whether there are wide differences among individuals in the degree to which competition is perceived as threatening. The final question is concerned with the impact that stress, apprehension, and anxiety have upon skilled performance.

Kroll has begun to identify the sources of stress-anxiety in athletic competition. His research was designed

to find out what caused the nausea, sweaty hands, pounding heart beat, trembling, and other somatic complaints . . . to find out what caused the feelings of uneasiness, irritability, general restlessness, being afraid and other psychological manifestations. If manifest anxiety was caused by unknown fears, then we wanted to know what specific fear was causing the anxiety seen in athletes prior to competition. (1979, p. 215)

As a result of his interviews with athletes, Kroll isolated 125 causes. These causes clustered together in five major categories (Table 3–1): somatic complaints, fear of failure, feelings of inadequacy, loss of control, and guilt.

The category of *somatic complaints* reflects the fact that many athletes find the precompetition physical manifestations (the physiological reactions associated with the flight or fight response) disturbing. The physical manifestations include an accelerated heart rate, increased sweating, upset stomach, and even throwing up.

Fear of failure includes the concerns an athlete has about losing, letting the team and coaches down, "choking," living up to expectations, and so on.

Feelings of inadequacy arise in some athletes prior to competition. These feelings are associated with concerns such as getting tired during competition, being unable to concentrate, and having insufficient motivation to play well.

Some athletes also may become anxious prior to and during competition because of factors beyond their control. For example, an athlete might experience an equipment problem, unfair officials, bad luck, unfavorable weather conditions, and so on. As a result, an athlete who is extremely well prepared might be unsuccessful.

Finally, some athletes are concerned with what they might do during the heat of competition—play dirty, hurt an opponent, swear too much, or act in an unsportsmanlike fashion. Anticipation of the possibility of these actions also leads to feelings of apprehension, anxiety, and stress.

To date, Kroll has simply identified these sources of precompetition stress. Thus there is no indication at this point whether any one of the five categories is more characteristic of one group of athletes than another. Some interesting possible comparisons might include male and female athletes, team and individual sport athletes, combative and noncombative sport athletes, and athletes of different ages.

In terms of the second stress-related issue presented above, Martens has identified the personality trait referred to previously as *sport competition anxiety* (1977). As was pointed out, this trait is related to the tendency on the part of individuals to perceive competitive situations as threatening and to respond to these situations with increased feelings of apprehension and stress. There are wide individual differences in the degree to which different athletes possess this trait. Martens considers these differences to be largely due to the nature of the athlete's previous experiences in competitive situations: The accumulated results of engaging in competition that

Table 3–1
Sources of Anxiety–Stress in Competitive Situations.

Category	Characteristics
Somatic Complaints	Tightness in neck, upset stomach, nervousness, trembling, throwing-up, accelerated heart rate
Fear of Failure	Making foolish mistake, letting coaches and teammates down, losing, choking up, making a critical mistake
Feelings of Inadequacy	Getting tired, lack of desire, feeling weak, being afraid, inability to "psych up," unable to concentrate
Loss of Control	Equipment failure, unfair officials, bad luck, temperature and weather
Guilt	Hurting opponent, playing dirty, swearing too much, poor sportsmanship, losing temper

Adapted from Kroll, 1979.

are self-imposed or acquired from others, tangible or intangible, or rewarding or punishing.

An important consequence of Martens' predictions is that individuals who possess higher levels of the personality trait of sport competition anxiety have a greater tendency to view competitive situations as most threatening. As a result, they exhibit the greatest apprehension, anxiety, and tension in competitive situations.

The third issue, the impact of stress, apprehension, and anxiety upon skilled performance, is far from resolved. It has been frequently suggested that motivation and performance are related in an inverted-U fashion; as motivation progressively increases from very low levels to extremely high levels, performance will improve, reach a plateau or optimal level, and then deteriorate. While this inverted-U hypothesis has been observed in a number of experiments (Klavora, 1977; Martens and Landers, 1969) there are some limitations in its general applicability for sport. The most desirable (optimal) level of motivation is almost impossible to determine prior to competition. It is only after the competition is completed that the optimal level of motivation can be determined through analysis of the best performances.

The personality dimension of *trait anxiety* has an influence upon the desirable level of motivation. Klavora found that while it is generally assumed that "high-anxious" individuals should be relaxed prior to competition and "low-anxious" individuals should be motivated, this is not the case (1977). In Klavora's study, both types of individuals needed to be motivated to achieve an optimal level (the optimal level for the high-anxious individuals being much greater than that of the low-anxious individuals).

The task being performed also has an impact on the optimal level of motivation (Landers, 1978; Oxendine, 1970). This is illustrated in Figure 3–2. Greater levels of motivation are beneficial in tasks that are very simple or very well learned. This may be a result of the simplification principle or the habituation principle. The former refers to the fact that with repeated exposures, stimuli or situations become less complex and less stimulating. Thus athletes who are highly experienced at a task find it less stressful. The habituation principle, which is related to the simplification

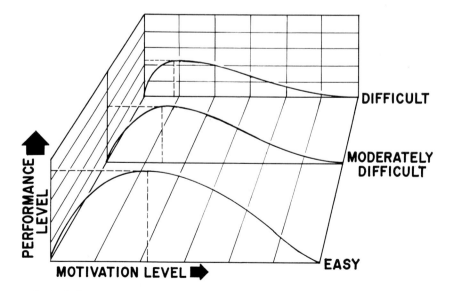

Fig. 3–2. The interaction of motivation and task difficulty (adapted from Eysenck).

principle, refers to the fact that individuals who are most experienced with a stimulus or situation show the greatest preference for an increase in complexity. Thus experienced athletes prefer the pressure of play-off competition in contrast with the routine of the regular schedule.

Team Dynamics

The term *dynamics* implies activity, force, energy, and change. When Kurt Lewin originally introduced the expression *group dynamics* it was intended to represent the processes underlying the changes associated with group involvement. Lewin placed particular emphasis on two general processes or categories of forces within the group: cohesiveness and locomotion. The former is considered to be particularly important because it represents a property contributing to the development and maintenance of the group—group unity and solidarity. The latter is the group's raison d'être, the reason or purpose behind the group's existence.

Cohesiveness. In sport it is held to be almost axiomatic that team success is improbable without high levels of cohesiveness. It is assumed that feelings of togetherness, team spirit, and team unity lead to greater cooperation and, therefore, ultimately to more effective performance. And yet there are examples of teams that have been highly successful despite the visible presence of animosity and team tension. Well-publicized examples include the German rowing team that became Olympic and world champions (Lenk, 1969) and the victorious World Series champion baseball teams of the Oakland Athletics and the New York Yankees.

Two factors seem to be critical in determining whether tension and animosity (low cohesiveness) will detract from performance (Carron, 1980a). The first is the nature of the sport. If members of a team are able to carry out their task performance without the necessity of a great deal of cooperation (e.g., baseball, bowling, track and field, swimming), then the level of team cohesiveness is unimportant. In fact, there is even strong evidence to suggest that when cooperation is not required among team members, feelings of rivalry and competitiveness among team members are better for team performance (Hill, 1975; Landers and Lüschen, 1974; Miller and Hamblin, 1963). No effort or energy is wasted on attempts to maintain a positive group atmosphere; the individual athletes not only compete against opponents, they compete against each other. Studies showing a positive relationship between cohesiveness and team success have generally included sports such as basketball, hockey, and volleyball (Arnold and Straub, 1972; Ball and Carron, 1976; Bird, 1977; Martens and Peterson, 1971) in which a great deal of team play and cooperation are necessary for optimal team performance.

The second factor is the predominant underlying motives that individual athletes have for joining the team. Cohesion can enhance performance only if the team is motivated toward performance and productivity. A team might be highly cohesive but not perform successfully or to an optimal level if individual athletes were participating to fulfill an affiliative- as opposed to a task-oriented motive. In the former instance the cohesive force would be associated with the development of friendships or cliques within a team. These cliques would, in turn, result in less effective performance in those sports that required task cooperation among team members. In studies of both basketball (Klein and Christiansen, 1969) and soccer (Yaffe, 1974) there is evidence that athletes who like each other tend to pass to one another to a greater extent than to less-liked teammates.

Locomotion. An important aspect of group locomotion, i.e., the behavior of the group toward its objective or goal, is the level of motivation and aspiration present. No one would deny that individuals have aspirations and motivations. In addition, as Zander has pointed out, groups/teams also have aspirations and motivations that are more than the simple summation of the motivations and aspirations of the individual members. The welfare of the group as a totality is also a primary and often independent concern of individual members; "members often suppress any inclination to put their own needs first . . . . They concentrate instead on what the total group should do . . . what is 'good for the group' " (Zander, 1971, p. 2).

Zander identified two group-oriented motives. One, the *desire for group success,* is a disposition on the part of a group member to feel pride and satisfaction with the group if it successfully accomplishes a challenging group task. The second, the *desire to avoid group failure,* is a disposition on the part of a group member to feel embarrassment or dissatisfaction with the group if it fails on a challenging task.

While Zander reported mixed results from experiments carried out with groups in laboratory settings, in nonlaboratory research he found that groups with the greatest desire for group success showed the most effective performance (1978). For example, a greater desire for group success was associated with more sales of insurance policies in the different districts of a large company (Bowers and Seashore, 1966), with more speed and skill when groups of military officers were on a 4½-day trek in the snow (Thomas and Zander, 1959), and with more production on a factory assembly line (Zander and Armstrong, 1972).

The effect of success and failure upon group level of aspiration has been examined in a number of experiments with a variety of group tasks (Zander, 1971). The effects that success or failure have upon the aspiration that members have for their group follows a consistent pattern; that is, group success leads to an increase in group aspiration, and group failure, to a decrease. Further, the amount of absolute change is greater with success.

Spectators

An issue that has very real significance to the social-psychological domain is the impact that the presence of spectators or fellow competitors (often referred to as coactors) has upon performance. The research in this area has been categorized as social facilitation research, social facilitation referring to "the consequences upon behavior which derive from the sheer presence of other individuals" (Zajonc, 1965, p. 269).

A considerable number of investigations have been carried out on social facilitation, the earliest of which is attributed to Triplett in 1897. He used official data from the Racing Board of the League of American Wheelmen to compare cycling times under three conditions: *unpaced* (the cyclist raced alone against time); *paced* (the cyclist raced alone against time but in conjunction with a "pacer", a tandem bicycle manned by three or four confederates); and *paced competition* (the cyclist raced against another competitor, but both cyclists were paced). Triplett found that the paced and paced-competition conditions were 39.55 sec/mile and 34.4 sec/mile faster respectively than the unpaced condition.

While subsequent research has not been as unequivocal—in some instances the presence of coactors or an audience has resulted in an improvement in performance, but in others, a decrement—there does appear to be a fairly consistent pattern: In those instances in which the task being performed is either very complex or not well learned, the presence of others is detrimental to performance; on the other hand, in those instances in which the task being performed is either very simple or very well learned, the presence of others is beneficial to performance.

HUMAN SOCIAL BEHAVIOR IN SPORT: SOME SELECTED CONSEQUENCES*

Aggression

Possibly one of the most misunderstood consequences of sport involvement is the relationship of participation in sport to aggressive behavior. For example, one source

---

*It may be somewhat misleading to present the material in this section as a consequence or effect of sport performance. What is presented here are some social psychological parameters that are related to/associated with/correlated with athletic involvement. There is an adage in statistics that states that correlation does not imply causation: Just because two factors are related to each other is no assurance that one is the cause of the other. For example, lighting of the sign FASTEN SEAT BELTS in an airplane may precede and be associated with a turbulent ride. However, one would never suggest that it causes the disturbance. A similar analogy should be kept in mind with sport findings.

of confusion concerns the term *aggression* and what types of behaviors it represents. Aggression, in the sense that it has been analyzed by social scientists (e.g., Bandura, 1973), is not a synonym for motivation, or assertiveness, or dominance; rather, it is a synonym for violence. As such, aggression is always negative, undesirable behavior.

There is also some confusion about the causes of aggression in the sport context. In fact, there are essentially three myths that have arisen in regard to aggression by an athlete in a sport situation: (1) It is an instinctual response; (2) it is a natural by-product of frustration; and (3) it serves as catharsis to drain away the possibilities of future aggression (Carron, 1980b).

Smith has written extensively on the topic of aggression in sport, particularly on aggression in hockey. In an article entitled "Hockey Violence: Interring Some Myths," he dismisses many of the fantasies (including the above three) that have developed around violence in hockey (1974, 1978, 1979a, 1979b). His general conclusions are equally applicable to violence in baseball, basketball, football, and other sports. As Smith pointed out:

> Modern research repudiates instinct theory. Men—and beasts generally speaking—learn to be aggressive and use aggression for specific purposes, usually to get or keep something they want. Frustration theory has a scientific basis, but even its chief proponents don't claim that frustration always leads to aggression or that aggression is always caused by frustration. Anthropologists have shown that people in some societies simpler than ours are willing to suffer frustration indefinitely without ever resorting to aggression. Like most human behavior, responses to frustration are contoured by learning and culture. Violence in hockey undoubtedly is sometimes a response to frustration—but because it's tolerated, not because it's in our genes. Finally, there's almost no reliable evidence in support of catharsis (or "flush toilet") theory; on the contrary, numerous studies show that behaving aggressively, or viewing others behaving aggressively, tends to lead to more aggression, not less. (1978, p. 142)

Violence in sport is a learned social behavior. Through the process of socialization the child learns to model and imitate the behavior of primary socialization agents such as parents, coaches, teachers, peers, and older, more skillful athletes (e.g., professional athletes). The learning of violence results from the observation, imitation, and social reinforcement of certain behaviors.

The development of aggressive behavior in the young athlete can occur in any (or all) of three ways (Bandura, 1973). The first is through *observational learning.* The athlete learns new patterns of behavior by watching others perform, e.g., the skillful, undetected use of the illegal elbow in hockey or basketball or the use of the hockey stick as a weapon might be two illustrations. The young athlete does not naturally acquire these techniques as part of some developmental process; they are learned responses.

Second, there is *disinhibition.* A model serves to strengthen or weaken inhibitions to particular behaviors. If a young athlete observes violent, illegal tactics, and these are either implicitly or explicitly condoned by coaches, parents, television commentators, teachers, and peers, there is a reduction in inhibition. The athlete has not only learned "how to" through observation, but also that it is an acceptable (possibly even approved) way of responding.

Finally, modeling influences behavior through *response facilitation:* Behaviors that are not illegal—aggressive rebounding in basketball, body checking in hockey, base running in baseball, tackling in soccer—are prompted or facilitated through the appearance of similar behaviors in esteemed models such as professional athletes. The result is that the behavior has a much greater likelihood of appearing in the young athlete's performance and then being expanded. Violence in sport can be eradicated if there is sufficient motivation on the part of sport policy-makers.

Psychosocial Consequences of Competition

Depending upon personal experience, the type of articles read, or research examined, it is possible to hold two contrasting views of competition, namely, that it is a beneficial activity or that it is a negative activity in terms of the psychosocial development of the child. The facts (based upon the empirical evidence available) would seem to be that competition is largely value neutral; it can be positive or negative, depending upon the nature of the specific situation.

In terms of its impact upon the development of positive sociopsychological behaviors (and it must be emphasized that these are short-term effects and not permanent changes), the most dramatic case against competition is made when it is contrasted with cooperation. In well-controlled experiments (Deutsch, 1968; Dunn and Goldman, 1966; Julian, Bishop, and Fiedler, 1966; Myers, 1962), cooperation has been found to be clearly superior to competition in terms of such factors as increased communication and attentiveness, increased friendliness and friendship development, enhanced favorable perceptions of the group and its product or output, and improved cohesiveness and feelings of closeness.

The differences between competition and cooperation in terms of performance is largely task specific (Miller and Hamblin, 1963). In tasks requiring a great deal of mutual dependence, cooperation among group members leads to more effective performance. On the other hand, when the group's tasks can be subdivided, or readily completed by individuals working alone, or both, emphasis on cooperation leads to less effective performance.

In organized sport it is difficult to clearly differentiate between competition and cooperation. Both are present to a degree in most situations. Also, it has been observed that competition between groups (intergroup competition) is responsible for improved cooperation within groups (intragroup cooperation) (Sherif, 1970). This resulting intragroup cooperation subsequently results in all of the positive psychological behaviors listed above. In fact, it is largely for this reason that Julian, Bishop, and Fiedler suggested that competition can serve as a potential therapeutic tool to enhance the psychological adjustment of the individual (1966).

The competitive experience has the potential to assist the child in the development of a positive self-identity. Children enter into sport situations primarily to satisfy affiliation needs and the need to do something well (Alderman and Wood, 1976). Further, athletics are the single most important factor contributing to status among adolescents (Coleman, 1961; Eitzen, 1976). This was true in 1961 when Coleman first examined the question, and it was still true in 1976 when Eitzen replicated Coleman's work (Table 3–2). A final psychosocial factor that is related to participation in sport is that individuals involved in sport have higher levels of self-esteem than do nonparticipants (Hyland and Orlick, 1975; Purdon, 1978). However, whether competition specifically and sport generally are positive or negative is largely a function of the rewards available to the child in the specific situation.

Causal Attributions. Attribution theory has been called a *common-sense* or *naive psychology* because it is basically concerned with the "theories" that all of us use in everyday situations to understand, explain, and predict why particular events have occurred. For example, an athlete after competition, a student following an examination, and a person returning from a social engagement all share a common desire to understand why the particular outcome occurred as it did.

Weiner proposed that when individuals attempt to account for an outcome they typically draw upon the four principal explanations in Figure 3–3 (1972): ability, effort, the degree of luck experienced, and the difficulty of the task, assignment, or opponent. The first two are, of course, personal factors within the individual, while the latter two are external factors over which the individual has no control.

It has been repeatedly demonstrated that individuals are extremely self-serving

Table 3–2
Relative Ranking for Various Criteria for Status in Adolescent Males and Females

Criteria for Status	Average Ranking Coleman (1961)	Eitzen (1976)
Ranking to Be Popular with Boys		
Be an Athlete	2.2	2.06
Be in the Leading Crowd	2.6	2.10
Leader in Activities	2.9	2.82
High Grades, Honor Roll	3.5	3.73
Come from Right Family	4.5	3.98
Ranking to Be Popular with Girls		
Be an Athlete	2.2	1.94
Be in the Leading Crowd	2.5	2.12
Have a Nice Car	3.2	2.81
High Grades, Honor Roll	4.0	3.87
Come from Right Family	4.2	3.89

Adapted from Eitzen, 1976

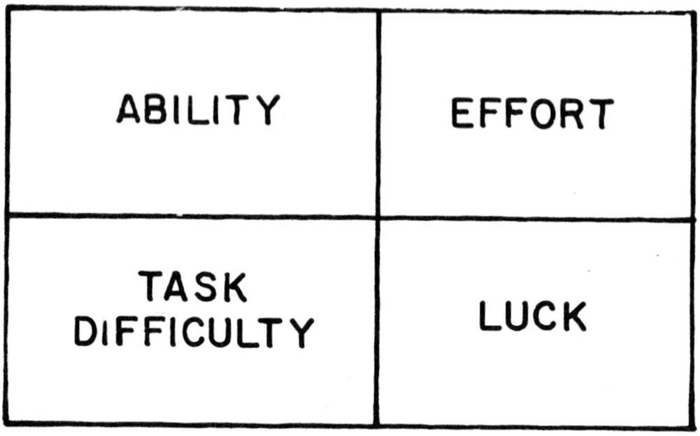

Fig. 3–3. Weiner's model of causal attribution (1972).

in their explanations of an outcome (Carron, 1980a). If the outcome was successful the individual perceives the causes for this success to be personal—the level of his personal ability and the amount of effort expended. On the other hand, if the outcome was unsuccessful, the individual perceives the causes for this to be outside of personal control—the amount of bad luck experienced and the extreme difficulty of the task.

A similar self-serving bias occurs when individuals attempt to account for group outcomes (Carron, 1980a). Individuals who are members of a successful group have a greater tendency to assume responsibility for the group's performance than do individuals who are in unsuccessful groups. Also, individuals who are members of a successful group tend to view their own relative contribution as being greater than that of the "average" group member, whereas individuals who are members of an unsuccessful group tend to view their own relative contribution as being less than that of the average group member.

Team Dynamics

Cohesion and Satisfaction. It was pointed out previously that it is held to be almost axiomatic that team cohesion is essential for team success. However, it also seems reasonable that the relationship is reciprocal—that when a team has been successful it becomes more cohesive. Athletes who have been on highly successful teams fondly recollect the feeling of camaraderie that developed. In turn, athletes who have been on highly unsuccessful teams recollect the lack of general rapport that was present and how happy they were to see the season end.

These subjective feelings have been supported by research by Carron and Ball (1977) and Bakeman and Helmreich (1975). Both studies were interested in determining which relationship was the stronger; i.e., whether cohesion leads to performance success or performance success leads to cohesion. Carron and Ball tested intercollegiate ice hockey teams, while Bakeman and Helmreich examined aquanaut teams that lived and worked in an underwater habitat. In both studies it was observed that there was a considerably greater tendency for success to lead to cohesion than the reverse.

This is by no means an either-or situation. Martens and Peterson found that teams that were more cohesive were more successful, and, in turn, the more successful teams expressed greatest satisfaction with participation (1971). On the basis of their findings Martens and Peterson proposed that a circular relationship exists among cohesion, performance, and satisfaction. This increased satisfaction then contributes to cohesiveness, and the cycle continues.

Leadership. One particularly interesting consequence of sport participation is that the player's position (e.g., catcher versus outfielder in baseball or running back versus lineman in football) can have a significant impact upon his chances of obtaining organizational rewards and benefits; that is, individuals in some positions have a much greater chance of being elected captain, of being recruited as manager or coach after their playing career is over, or of being selected most valuable player.

Table 3–3 is a summary of a number of studies carried out on the sport of baseball. Similar studies have also been conducted with football (e.g., Sage, 1974; Massengale and Farrington, 1977), hockey (Roy, 1974), and basketball (Klonsky, 1978). In Table 3–3 the playing positions are subdivided into three categories: catchers, infielders, and outfielders. In terms of the organizational rewards listed in the footnotes of Table 3–3, on the average a catcher was the recipient 21.8% of the time; an infielder 12.7%; and an outfielder 4.4%.

A number of explanations have been advanced to account for this phenomenon. Chelladurai and Carron suggested that this inequity in rewards and benefits is a function of two aspects of the athlete's playing position (1977). These were referred to as *task dependence* and *propinquity*. Task dependence refers to the fact that some positions in sport involve a considerable amount of task interaction while others do not. The catcher who handles the ball on almost every pitch can be contrasted in this regard with an outfielder who might not have any fielding chances in a full game.

Propinquity, the second dimension, consists of two combined attributes: *observability* (the extent to which the player in a position has knowledge of the ongoing action, including the locations and movements of those in other positions, the strategic decisions being utilized, and so on) and *visibility* (the degree to which the player is seen and watched by those in other positions on the field, including the opponents). Again, the catcher who serves as a highly visible defensive leader can be contrasted in this regard with an outfielder who is relatively removed from the hub of activity and plays a passive role in defensive decision making.

Chelladurai and Carron felt that positions in sport have different amounts of actual and ascribed status, prestige, and importance, depending upon the extent to which they possess propinquity and task dependence. The catcher is high in both, the infielder is average in both, while the outfielder is low in both. As a result, the organizational rewards and benefits are available to individuals in each of these three categories in decreasing degrees. This is highlighted in Table 3–3.

Table 3–3

Recruitment of Managers/Coaches and Selection of Team Captains and Most Valuable Players on the Basis of Playing Position

Categories	Grusky (1963)[1]	Sage, Loy & Ingham (1970)[2]	Loy & Sage (1968)[3]	Sage, Loy & Ingham (1970)[4]	Sage, Loy & Ingham (1970)[5]	Average from All Studies
I Catchers	26.2%	27.0%	27.3%	15.5%	12.9%	21.8%
II Infielders	12.2%	11.0%	16.7%	13.3%	10.4%	12.7%
(First Base)	(11.2)	(12.6)	(0.0)	(9.9)	(8.9)	(8.5)
(Second Base)	(10.3)	(8.6)	(20.0)	(13.8)	(9.8)	(12.5)
(Shortstop)	(14.0)	(17.1)	(40.0)	(14.6)	(11.8)	(19.5)
(Third Base)	(13.1)	(5.8)	(6.7)	(14.8)	(11.1)	(10.3)
III Outfielders	5.3%	1.8%	2.2%	6.4%	6.4%	4.4%
(Left Field)	—	(1.0)	(0.0)	(6.1)	(4.9)	(3.0)
(Center Field)	—	(4.5)	(6.7)	(10.5)	(11.5)	(8.3)
(Right Field)	—	(0.0)	(0.0)	(2.5)	(2.9)	(1.4)

Reprinted with permission from Chelladurai, P., and Carron, A.V.: A reanalysis of formal structure in sport. © 1977. Canadian Journal of Applied Sports Sciences.
[1]Recruitment of professional baseball managers.
[2]Recruitment of collegiate coaches.
[3]Selection of interscholastic team captains.
[4]Selection of intercollegiate team captains.
[5]Selection of most valuable players.

Spectators

Unfortunately, sporting events are sometimes marred by incidents of spectator violence. The soccer riot that occurred in 1964 in Lima, Peru, during which 318 people lost their lives in the stadium, is among the best known examples (but, by no means, the only one). Numerous reasons have been advanced to account for the phenomenon of spectator violence, including strong spectator identification with the participants or teams, excessive crowding, consumption of alcohol, lack of player control by coaches, inadequate officiating, and, in combination with the above, a negative performance outcome. In short, spectator violence is seen as a sociopsychological consequence of performance outcome in combination with some specific moderating variables.

Smelser advanced a sociological framework within which to understand collective violence (of which a sport riot is one example) (1962). In his *value-added approach*, five determinants of collective behavior are necessary: (1) structural conduciveness, (2) structural strain, (3) growth of a generalized hostile belief, (4) mobilization of participants for action, and (5) operation of social control.

The concept of 'value-added' is borrowed from economics. It denotes that

> each determinant of collective behavior adds its value to the prior determinant, increasingly specifying the nature of the collective episode. Each of the determinants is said to be necessary for an incident of collective behavior; together, they are said to be sufficient. (Smith, 1975, p. 300)

Thus each of the five determinants must occur in the prescribed order; for example, structural conduciveness must be present and be followed by structural strain, and so on. Each succeeding determinant then adds "value" to the previous one, and when all have been added, collective behavior, such as the soccer riot in Peru, results.

Structural conduciveness develops when the specific situation is composed of numerous distinct or socially divergent groups of individuals—young-old, racially mixed, rich and poor, etc. This is certainly a characteristic of most sporting events.

Structural strain is simply an acknowledgment of the sources of strain or tension existing in society as a whole. Further, the tensions or strains that exist in society between young and old, rich and poor, and different racial groups are also present in the sport crowd.

The growth of a generalized hostile belief occurs when the crowd individually and collectively develops a common belief or fear. Examples could include the belief that the officials are unfair, that the opponents are attempting to injure, or that a favorite is being deliberately humiliated. This developing, generalized hostile belief serves as a preparatory force for action.

The next stage, mobilization of participants for action, occurs with the actual onset of the riot. It may have what Smelser referred to as a *real* or initial *phase* that derives from a specific situation such as a referee's decision or a participant's injury, or it may have a *derived phase* in which crowd violence erupts from factors not directly related to the previous three conditions. The riots that occur in the streets following sporting events are an example of the latter.

In the final determinant, operation of social control, force is used in an attempt to control the collective behavior. The use of riot police and guard dogs to control crowds illustrates this phase.

IMPLICATIONS FOR GENERAL EDUCATION

What implications does the social-psychological dimension of sport have for education? Learning that occurs in the actual school environment is of three general types: *cognitive, psychomotor, and affective* (VanderZwaag and Sheehan, 1978). Cognitive learning encompasses the traditional view of education with its emphasis on the development of intellectual skills such as the three R's. The psychomotor domain includes those learning experiences reflected in the development of skilled bodily movements through art, music, drama, industrial arts, and physical education. Finally, the affective domain centers around the acquisition of attitudes, values, and interests through the total educational curriculum.

Sport generally and the social-psychological dimension of sport specifically have always been considered an essential medium through which affective learning can occur. Consider, for example, the objectives for athletic programs listed in *The Athletic Director*, a publication of the National Council of Secondary School Athletic Directors:

1. To provide opportunities for competition
2. To provide activities that involve the whole school
3. To instruct students in good health, personal hygiene, and safety habits
4. To provide instruction in sport skills and to offer opportunities to improve those already acquired
5. To provide opportunities for friendship development with both teammates and opponents
6. To provide students with opportunities in leadership-training
7. To provide opportunities for the development of good sportsmanship
8. To provide opportunities for students to work in groups and to learn self-discipline for the overall benefit of that group
9. To provide opportunities to learn to follow rules
10. To provide the student opportunities to gain satisfaction from self-sacrifice as a result of contributions to development of esprit de corps, a feeling of unity, belonging, pride in the team, team work, and the respect for authority
11. To provide extended opportunities for grant-in-aid scholarships and professional athletic or associated careers for all participants
12. To provide the general community with an understanding that the competitive athletic program has been designed to promote sportsmanship, citizenship, and a wholesome relationship between school and community

13. To provide for opportunities to develop approved social patterns of conduct for both individuals and groups
14. To provide for opportunities to develop skills and attitudes that will lead to participation in sports throughout life
15. To encourage the development of the highest standards of moral and spiritual character

It is apparent that the great majority of these objectives relate to affective learning, i.e., the learning of values, interests, and attitudes. In fact, it is the affective domain in which the social and psychological dimensions of sport have had their most significant impact. However, sport does not naturally contribute to the development of positive values, interests, and attitudes. As Orlick and Botterill observed, "Sports are not inherently or necessarily good, as once supposed, nor are they inherently bad; rather they have the capacity to be either" (1975).

VanderZwaag and Sheehan have suggested that at least two important changes must be made before sport can serve as a social learning environment in general education:

> Both affect the teachers. First, teachers who are responsible for providing social learning experiences through sport must have the ability to do so. A good background in psychology, sociology, and social psychology (especially group dynamics) is indispensable. They must become applied social scientists to obtain productive results. Sport studies educators who are equipped with knowledge and skills acquired from the type of teacher-preparation program in sport studies are well prepared to provide social learning experiences through sport.
> Second, student expectations must be changed. Typically, students entering a gym class do not expect to be challenged to learn social behavior. In many cases they expect to learn nothing at all—gym class to them is no more than "recess" or a "fun" class. It is absolutely necessary that teachers redirect these attitudes. (1978, p. 260)

In short, teachers must become familiar with the social and psychological dimensions discussed previously. With an understanding of these dimensions, it may be possible to achieve a positive affective learning environment.

RELATIONSHIP TO AFFILIATED PROFESSIONS

What is the relationship of the social and psychological dimensions of sport to affiliated professions? Carron, in a discussion of the relationship of sport psychology to general psychology, suggested that

> As a science psychology is comprised of a number of subdisciplinary areas including the *developmental, clinical, social, personality, experimental* and *educational.* Even minimal familiarity with these subdisciplines clearly shows that each has some relevance to the study of athletic behavior in sport. Thus, while many researchers in sport consider sport psychology to be another subdiscipline within general psychology, it seems preferable to consider it as a specific type of applied psychology which embraces aspects of all of the areas within psychology. Also, as an extension of this perspective, sport psychology can be defined as a study of the complex forms of human behavior in the specific context of play, games, and sport.(1980b)

This same viewpoint is applicable to the sociology of sport, social psychology of sport, and so on. More than 16 years ago, Henry, in a discussion on the evolution of physical education as an academic field of study, pointed out that physical education evolved because sciences such as sociology and psychology failed to view sport as a sufficiently significant social phenomenon for scientific inquiry (1964). The result was the development of what can broadly be referred to as *sport sciences.*

Since the sport sciences are relatively young the prevalent pattern has been to adapt theories and research strategies that originated in the parent discipline and test their application in the sport context. This is a natural, logical approach. Howerver, it has now become apparent that, while there are some notable exceptions, theories of behavior that have their major application in innocuous social settings are not particularly explanatory in sport settings. The development of theoretical explanations for behavior in sport is one of the major challenges facing researchers interested in the social and psychological dimension of sport.

SUMMARY AND CONCLUDING STATEMENT

The social-psychological dimension with its concern for the behavior and performance of individuals engaged in play, games, and sport plays a predominant role in physical education and athletics. For example, in terms of behavior, the perceived importance of the social-psychological dimension is clearly illustrated through examination of the behavioral objectives listed for physical education and athletics. Sportsmanship, cooperation, social interaction, cohesion, and a variety of personality traits are frequently proposed as desired objectives of participation in sport. Whether they are developed or not is, of course, a function of the dynamics of the situation. Nevertheless the sport environment does offer the potential if it is used effectively.

Gaining an understanding of the social-psychological dimension also has implications for sport performance. Ryder, Carr, and Herget analyzed the factors that could potentially affect future performance in track events (1976). On the basis of their analysis of the performances of runners who held world records over the previous 50 years and the physiological parameters that affect sprint and endurance events, they concluded that the limits to future performance were psychological rather than physiological in nature. They also pointed out that the critical considerations were those affecting daily training, not those present in the actual event itself.

Ryder, Carr, and Herget's suggestion notwithstanding, it is certainly premature to suggest that our understanding of the social-psychological dimension is highly advanced. It is true that we now have some insight into many issues such as why children get involved in sport (Alderman and Wood, 1976); why they drop out of sport (Orlick and Botterill, 1975); the stresses associated with competitive sport (Kroll, 1979), and so on. However concentrated research efforts have only been initiated relatively recently and the number of questions and issues that remain unanswered (or even unexamined) is considerable. This represents a target for social scientists in our field.

QUESTIONS FOR POSSIBLE DISCUSSION AND TESTING

1. Does sport play a significant role in society? What are some general factors that could be used to support your view?
2. What are some of the commonly cited social-psychological antecedents (causes) for skilled athletic performance?
3. What are some of the commonly cited social-psychological consequences (results) of performance in sport?
4. Each of the following factors could be examined as an antecedent or a consequence of sport performance: personality; spectators; team cohesiveness; aggressiveness. Select one of these factors and by means of illustrations show how it could be first an antecedent and then a consequence of motor performance.

REFERENCES

Alderman, R.B.: Incentive motivation in sport: An interpretive speculation of research opportunities. *In* Psychology of Sport. Edited by C. Fisher. Palo Alto, Calif., Mayfield, 1976.
Alderman, R.B.: Strategies for motivating young athletes. *In* Sport Psychology: An Analysis of Athlete Behavior. Edited by W.F. Straub. Ithaca, N.Y., Mouvement, 1978.
Alderman, R.B., and Wood, N.L.: An analysis of incentive motivation in young Canadian athletes. Can. J. Appl. Sport Sci. 1:169–176, 1976.

Ammons, R.B.: Effects of knowledge of performance: A survey and tentative theoretical formulation. J. Gen. Psychol. 54:279–299, 1956.

Arnold, G.E., and Straub, W.F.: Personality and group cohesiveness as determinants of success among inter-scholastic basketball teams. Proceedings Fourth Canadian Symposium on Psycho-Motor Learning and Sport Psychology. Ottawa, Health and Welfare Canada, 1972.

Bakeman, R., and Helmreich, R.: Cohesiveness and performance: Covariation and causality in an underseas environment. J. Exp. Soc. Psychol., 11:478-489, 1975.

Ball, J.R., and Carron, A.V.: The influence of team cohesion and participation motivation upon performance success in intercollegiate ice hockey. Can. J. Appl. Sport Sci., 1:271–275, 1976.

Bandura, A.: Aggression: A Social Learning Analysis. Englewood Cliffs, N.J., Prentice-Hall, 1973.

Bird, A.M.: Team structure and success as related to cohesiveness and leadership. J. Soc. Psychol. 103:217–223, 1977.

Bowers, D., and Seashore, S.: Predicting organizational effectiveness with a four-factor theory of leadership. Adm. Sci. Q., 11:238–263, 1966.

Caplow, T.: The criteria of organizational effectiveness. Soc. Forces, 32:1–9, 1953.

Carron, A.V.: Motivating the athlete. Motor Skills; 1:23–24, 1977.

Carron, A.V.:Social Psychology of Sport. Ithaca, N.Y., Mouvement, 1980a.

Carron, A.V.: Sport Psychology: Fact and fantasy. Rec. Res. Rev., 8:28–37, 1980b.

Carron, A.V., and Ball, J.R.: Cause-effect characteristics of cohesiveness and participation motivation in intercollegiate hockey. Int. Rev. Sport Sociology., 12:49–60, 1977.

Chelladurai, P., and Carron, A.V.: A re-analysis of formal structure in sport. Can. J. Appl. Sport Sci., 2:9–14, 1977.

Coleman, J.S.: The Adolescent Society: The Social Life of the Teenager and Its Impact on Education. New York, Free Press, 1961.

Cratty, B.J.: Psychology in Contemporary Sport. Englewood Cliffs, N.J., Prentice-Hall, 1973.

Deci, E.L.: Intrinsic Motivation. New York, Plenum, 1975.

Deutsch, M.: The effects of cooperation and competition upon group process. In Group dynamics: Research and theory. 3rd. Ed. Edited by D. Cartwright and A. Zander. London, Tavistock Publications, 1968.

Dunn, R.E., and Goldman, M.: Competition and noncompetition in relation to satisfaction and feeling toward own-group and nongroup members. J. Soc. Psychol. 68:299–311, 1966.

Eitzen, D.S.: Athletics in the status system of male adolescents: A replication of Coleman's The Adolescent Society. In Sport Sociology: Contemporary Themes. Edited by A. Yiannakis, T.D. McIntyre, J.J. Melnick, and D.P. Hart. Dubuque, Iowa, Kendall/Hunt Publishing Co., 1976.

Eysenck, H.J.:The measurement of motivation. Sci. 208:130–136, 1963.

Grusky, O.: The effects of formal structure on managerial recruitment: A study of baseball organization. Sociometry, 26:345–353, 1963.

Halliwell, W.: Intrinsic motivation in sport. In Sport Psychology: An Analysis of Athlete Behavior. Edited by W.F. Straub. Ithaca, N.Y., Mouvement, 1978.

Henry, F.M.: Physical education—An academic discipline. Proceedings of National College Physical Education Association for Men. Washington, D.C., AAHPER, 1964.

Hill, R.E.: Interpersonal compatibility and work-group performance. J. Appl. Behav. Sci. 11:210–219, 1975.

Hyland, H., and Orlick, T.D.: Physical education drop outs: Some related factors. In Mouvement. Edited by J. Salmela, et al. Quebec, Association de Professionnels de L'Activité Physique du Québec, 1975.

Julian, J.W., Bishop, D.W., and Fiedler, F.E.: Quasi-therapeutic effects of intergroup competition. J. Pers. Soc. Psychol. 3:321–332, 1966.

Kenyon, G.S.: Six scales for assessing attitudes toward physical activity. Res. Q., 39:566–574, 1968.

Klavora, P.: An attempt to derive inverted-U curves based on the relationship between anxiety and athletic performance. In Psychology of Motor Behavior and Sport. Edited by D.M. Landers and R.W. Christina. Champaign, Ill., Human Kinetics, 1977.

Klein, M., and Christiansen, G.: Group composition, group structure and group effectiveness of basketball teams. In Sport, Culture and Society. Edited by J.W. Loy and G.S. Kenyon. New York, Macmillan Co., 1969.

Klonsky, B.: The effects of formal structure and role skills on coaching recruitment and longevity:

A study of professional basketball teams. Cited in Loy, J., McPherson, B., and Kenyon, G.S.: Sport and Social Systems. Reading, Mass., Addison-Wesley, 1978.

Kroll, W.: Current strategies and problems in personality assessment. *In* Psychology of Motor Learning. Edited by L.E. Smith. Chicago, Athletic Institute, 1970.

Kroll, W.: The stress of high performance athletics. *In* Coach, Athlete, and the Sport Psychologist. Edited by P. Klavora and J.V. Daniel. Champaign, Ill., Human Kinetics, 1979.

Landers, D.M.: Motivation and performance: The role of arousal and attentional factors. *In* Sport Psychology: An Analysis of Athlete Behavior. Edited by W.F. Straub, Ithaca, N.Y., Mouvement, 1978.

Landers, D.M., and Lüschen, G.: Team performance outcome and the cohesiveness of competitive coaching teams. Int. J. Sport Sociol. 9:57–71, 1974.

Lenk, H.: Top performance despite internal conflict: An antithesis to a functionalistic proposition. *In* Sport, Culture and Society. Edited by J. Loy and G. Kenyon. New York, Macmillan Co., 1969.

Loy, J.W.: Sociology and physical education. *In* Physical Education: An Interdisciplinary Approach. Edited by R. Singer et al. New York, Macmillan Co., 1972.

Loy, J.W., McPherson, B.D., and Kenyon, G.S.: Sport and Social Systems. Reading, Mass., Addison-Wesley, 1978.

Loy, J.W., and Sage, G.H.: The effects of a formal structure on organizational leadership: An investigation of interscholastic baseball teams. 2nd International Congress of Sport Psychology, 1968.

Martens, R.: Sport Competition Anxiety Test. Champaign, Ill., Human Kinetics, 1977.

Martens, R., and Landers, D.M.: Coaction effects on a muscular endurance task. Res. Q., 40:733–737, 1969.

Martens, R., and Peterson, J.A.: Group cohesiveness as a determinant of success and member satisfaction in team performance. Int. Ref. Sport Sociol. 6:49–61, 1971.

Massengale, J., and Farrington, S.: The influence of playing position centrality on the careers of college football coaches. Rev. Sport Leisure, 2:107–115, 1977.

Myers, A.E.: Team competition, success, and adjustment of group members. J. Abnorm. Soc. Psychol. 65:325–332, 1962.

Miller, L.K, and Hamblin, R.L.: Interdependence, differential rewarding, and productivity. Am. Sociol. Rev. 28:768–777, 1963.

Orlick, T.D., and Botterill, C.: Every Kid Can Win. Chicago, Nelson Hall, 1975.

Oxendine, J.B.: Emotional arousal and motor performance. Quest, 13:23–32, 1970.

Purdon, J.: Athletic Participation and Self-Esteem. M.A. Thesis, University of Western Ontario, London, 1978.

Roy, G.: The relationship between centrality and mobility: The case of the National Hockey League. M.S. Thesis, University of Waterloo, 1974.

Ryder, H.W., Carr, H.J, and Herget, P.: Future performance in foot racing. Sci. Am. 234:109–119, 1976.

Sage, G.: The effect of formal structure on organizational leadership: An investigation of college football teams. National AAHPER Conference, Anaheim, California, 1974.

Sage, G., Loy, J.W., and Ingham, A.G.: The effects of formal structure on organizational leadership: An investigation of collegiate baseball teams. National AAHPER Conference, Seattle, 1970.

Sherif, M.: Group conflict and cooperation. In Group Processes. Edited by P.B. Smith. New York, Penguin Books, 1970.

Smelser, N.J.: Theory of Collective Behavior. New York, Free Press, 1962

Smith, M.D.: Significant others' influence on the assaultive behavior of young hockey players. Int. Rev. Sport Sociol. 9:45–56, 1974.

Smith, M.D.: Sport and collective violence. *In* Sport and Social Order. Edited by D.W. Ball and J.W. Loy. Reading, Mass., Addison-Wesley, 1975.

Smith, M.D.: Hockey violence: Interring some myths. *In* Sport Psychology: An Analysis of Athlete Behavior. Edited by W.F. Straub. Ithaca, N.Y., Mouvement, 1978.

Smith, M.D.: Social determinants of violence in hockey: A review. Canadian Journal of Applied Sport Sciences, 4:76–82, 1979.

Smith, M.D.: Towards an explanation of hockey violence: A reference-other approach. Can. J. Sociol. 4:105–124, 1979.

Snyder, E.E., and Spreitzer, E.: Sociology of sport: An overview. *In* Sport and Social Order. Edited by D.W. Ball and J.W. Loy. Reading, Mass, Addison-Wesley, 1975.

Thomas, E.J., and Zander, A.: The relationship of goal structure to motivation under extreme conditions. J. Individ. Psychol. 15:121–127, 1959.

Triplett, N.: The dynamogenic factors in face-making and competition. Am. J. Psychol. 9:507–533, 1897.

VanderZwaag, H.J., and Sheehan, T.J.: Introduction to Sport Studies: From the Classroom to the Ball Park. Dubuque, Iowa, W.C. Brown, 1978.

Weiner, B.: Theories of Motivation: From Mechanism to Cognition. Chicago, Rand-McNally, 1972.

Yaffe, M.: The psychology of soccer. New Soc. 27:378–380, 1974.

Zajonc, R.B.: Social facilitation. Science, 149:269–274, 1965.

Zander, A.: Motives and Goals in Groups. New York, Academic Press, 1971.

Zander, A.: Motivation and performance in sport groups. *In* Sport Psychology: An Analysis of Athlete Behavior. Edited by W.F. Straub. Ithaca, N.Y., Mouvement, 1978.

Zander, A., and Armstrong, W.: Working for group pride in a slipper factory. J. Appl. Soc. Psychol. 2:193–207, 1972.

SELECTED READINGS

Alderman, R.B.: Psychological Behavior in Sport. Philadelphia, W.B. Saunders Co., 1974.

Carron, A.V.: Social Psychology of Sport. Ithaca, N.Y., Mouvement, 1980.

Gruneau, R., and Albinson, J. (Eds.): Canadian Sport: Sociological Perspectives. Reading, Mass., Addison-Wesley, 1976.

Klavora, P. and Daniel, J.V.: Coach, Athlete, and the Sport Psychologist. Champaign, Ill., Human Kinetics, 1979.

Loy, J.W. and Kenyon, G.S. (Eds.): Sport, Culture and Society: A Reader in the Sociology of Sport. New York, Macmillan Co., 1969.

Martens, R.: Social Psychology and Physical Activity. New York, Harper & Row, 1975.

Sage, G.H.: Sport in American Society. 2nd Ed. Reading, Mass., Addison-Wesley, 1974.

CHAPTER FOUR

Motor Learning and Development

G. Lawrence Rarick

Development of a broad repertoire of motor skills is an important part of growing up. Skill acquisition is often taken for granted, since many of the motor skills that are normally acquired in infancy and childhood seem to develop naturally with little or no adult assistance. However, sight is often lost of the effort that infants and young children exert on skill development, and also of the failures and limited successes that are part of acquiring such self-sufficiency skills as walking, feeding, and dressing. With advancing age and a broadened environment, children are called upon to test their developing motor capabilities in new and different situations. This requires skills as yet untried or modifications in those already established. The diversity and range of such behaviors are impressive for, according to Barker and Wright, they amount to as many as 2200 distinct transactions using over 660 objects in a 24-hour period (1955). It is self-evident that involvement in motor activities constitutes most of the waking hours of the young child, is largely self-directed, and might rightfully be considered basic to the normal development of children.

This chapter has been written to provide the reader with information about the motor development of children and adolescents and their motor-learning capabilities, information that should be helpful in understanding why children differ in these aspects of development. Thus, this chapter focuses on understandings and insights rather than specific instructional strategies. Inflexible physical activity programs, no matter how carefully planned, are seldom successful, for children vary so widely in their motor capabilities that such programs rarely meet the needs of more than a few.

GROWTH, DEVELOPMENT, AND LEARNING

Growth and development are characteristic of all living things. While the biological expression of growth and development may vary among living forms, the basic phenomenon is essentially the same, namely, an orderly transition from a single fertilized cell to a mature being whose mature state is a reflection of genetic endowment and environmental forces.

Growth and development are terms often used interchangeably and have come to have much the same meaning. For some, however, growth is used in a narrower sense, namely, with reference to increases in size as reflected by the number and size of body cells, in the weight of the body and its component parts, and in the linear dimensions of the body and its segments. Development, on the other hand, is often referred to in qualitative terms such as changes in the biological makeup of cells and tissues and as alterations in the hormonal, metabolic, and functional characteristics of organisms as they mature. Thus the assessment of development requires measurements that are indicative of the organism's integrative, behavioral, and phys-

Dr. Rarick is from the University of California, Berkeley.

iological characteristics. Such measurements are designed to gain insight into the changes in the adaptive powers and response capabilities of the organism as it progresses toward maturity.

Learning is generally held to mean changes in behavior of a more or less permanent nature (i.e., those that occur as a result of practice in which there is an intent to improve performance). Learning has traditionally been assessed by the results of performance tests, i.e., the score achieved on a task following prescribed practice sessions rather than by the form or the style the learner uses in performing the task. Clearly, learning can be assessed only in part by a performance score, for improvements in the manner of executing the task, while difficult to assess, are an important indication of learning.

METHODOLOGICAL APPROACHES FOR STUDYING MOTOR DEVELOPMENT

Longitudinal and Cross-Sectional Methods

As suggested above, growth and development imply change, an ongoing phenomenon terminating at maturity. Thus, to study growth and development effectively, repeated observations should be made on the same individual at specified periods throughout growth. Such an approach is known as the longitudinal method, a procedure that is difficult to follow on humans. In view of the constraints of time and funds, longitudinal studies have usually been restricted to observations of a few characteristics or functions on a limited number of subjects. In only a few instances have such studies followed the same group of children from birth to maturity (Bayley and Espenschade, 1941).

Longitudinal investigations can be conducted on animals with relative ease. Since their life spans are short, environmental conditions and genetic factors can be controlled, and experimental treatments can be used that in many instances would be inappropriate for use with humans. With humans, developmental studies pose problems. Not only is it difficult to apply the necessary controls, but there is always the problem of dropouts, which may distort the nature of the sample. This, in part, explains why much of the longitudinal research on humans to date has been done on infants, a captive group. Furthermore, developmental changes in infancy are rapid and clearly defined, thus simplifying measurement problems.

Most studies of the motor behavior of school-age children have used the cross-sectional approach. Such investigations employ large samples of children categorized by chronological age and sex and thus provide norm-referenced data for evaluating the motor proficiency of children. The findings from such investigations are in no sense developmental and may in fact mask developmental changes that would be apparent from longitudinal data. For example, the dramatic growth in stature of the adolescent is masked when data on early- and late-maturing children are pooled in cross-sectional studies.

Clearly, then, the longitudinal method is the preferred approach in that it enables the investigator to examine differences among children in their rates of physical and behavioral development, as well as the influence of environmental factors upon developmental functions. This method is, however, not without its problems, for the mobility of families today is substantial, making it difficult to maintain intact groups of children over long periods. Dropouts can distort the characteristics of the sample and may materially affect the findings. Decisions regarding the frequency with which the repeated observations need to be made present another problem, one that is particularly critical during periods of rapid growth, namely, in infancy and adolescence, when the risk of missing the impact of significant developmental changes becomes great.

Measurement Procedures

Essentially two kinds of measurement procedures are employed in the study of motor development. The most frequently used method employs performance scores obtained from motor performance tests such as those designed to measure strength, power, balance, flexibility, and performance of such basic skills as running, jumping, and throwing. Some have labeled such scores as product data, since the scores are a quantified expression of the results of the performer's efforts, i.e., distance jumped, time of a run, or weight lifted.

The second approach is one that examines in detail how the skill is executed, namely, analysis of the movement patterns that are used as the skill is performed, usually through the use of high-speed photography. When such an approach is employed in longitudinal investigations the technique is known as developmental kinesiology.

Both methods have their place in motor development research. Norms are often calculated from performance test data, thus providing a data base for comparing a child's performance with that of other children of the same age and sex. Such information, however, gives little insight into why the performer scored at the recorded level. The score, if low, may have been distorted by lack of motivation or it may have been a reflection of excess body weight, inadequate muscular strength, or poor biomechanics. Information on the mechanics of performance obviously gives the teacher much more insight into the problems related to poor performance than the score itself.

DEVELOPMENT OF MOTOR BEHAVIOR IN INFRAHUMANS

Much of our knowledge of the nature and origins of motor behavior has come from animal investigations in the fields of developmental anatomy, developmental physiology, and developmental psychology. For example, the research of Coghill, an early developmental anatomist, is illustrative of how investigators in the biological sciences have utilized observations on the anatomical and behavioral development of animals as a means of studying the relationship between the growth of the nervous system and its developing integrative functions (1929). Shortly after the turn of the century Coghill began to chart the growth and development of the nervous system of the Amblystoma (salamander), demonstrating in a series of detailed investigations that the anatomical growth of the animal's neural mechanisms is intimately related to its initial movements and to subsequent movement sequences.

As Coghill noted, there is a critical period in the embryonic development of the Amblystoma when the first movement response occurs (namely, a slight movement of the head to the right or to the left). As development continues this response gradually becomes more generalized, one that involves lateral bending of the embryo so that it momentarily assumes a position resembling the letter C, giving the appearance of an exaggerated coil, sometimes aligned to the right, sometimes to the left. While the coil gives the animal no locomotor power, it is nevertheless a first step in the cephalocaudal progression of movement leading up to the whiplike S reaction characteristic of swimming behavior. As one C contraction aligned to the left moves from head to tail, another C contraction toward the right is initiated in the head region before the first movement has reached the tail (Fig. 4–1). Furthermore, Coghill observed that, as the limbs appear, the first limb movements are an integral part of the animal's total response mechanism, and it is only at a later point in development that independence, or individuation, of limb action occurs. Thus, as the limbs appear, their movements are not isolated but rather are an integrated part of the whiplike swimming motion of the salamander, a phenomenon that is characteristically seen in the early development of many higher animals. Such movements, according to Coghill, are first generalized following a cephalocaudal pro-

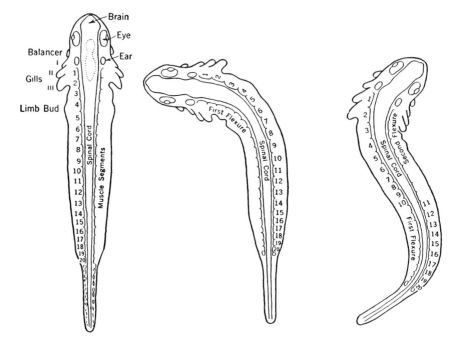

Fig. 4—1. The stages in the development of swimming movements in the Amblystoma. (Left) Early development stage with no body movement. (Center) the onset of swimming behavior, first flexure of anterior muscle segments. (Right) The passing of the first flexure tailward as the second flexure begins in the anterior region, essentially the movements required in swimming. (Carmichael, L.: Manual of Child Psychology. New York, John Wiley & Sons, Inc., 1946, as adapted from G.E. Coghill, Cambridge University Press, 1929. By permission of the publishers)

gression in which the forelimbs gradually gain autonomy, to be followed later by movements of the hind limbs, although the movements of both are in essence a coordinated extension of the time-motion relations of the initial swimming movement.

All of this led Coghill to conclude that movement of the trunk as the salamander first begins to walk is essentially a swimming motion with marked reduction in speed, the movement of the trunk becoming less pronounced as the walk assumes the characteristics needed for land locomotion. The neurological control mechanisms are, according to Coghill, suggestive of a biological inheritance that has given expression to the movement patterns used in quadripedal and bipedal locomotion in higher forms. His work provided the impetus for others to investigate the relationship between the growth of the nervous system and movement in animals and likewise influenced the thinking of those concerned with the early behavioral development of humans.

The research of Coghill and other early twentieth century investigators laid the foundation for what has become known as the law of developmental direction. This law is applicable in general terms to both physical and behavioral growth and development of vertebrates and is stated as follows: Growth proceeds (1) from the cephalic to the caudal pole; (2) from the proximal to the distal parts of body segments; and (3) from the general to the specific (from fundamental to accessory muscle control).

Support for the law of developmental direction comes from observations of embryonic and early postembryonic development of a wide range of vertebrates, including observations on the early development of humans. That physical growth is concentrated first in the head end of the body in all vertebrates is widely recognized. Not only is the head proportionately large, but as the limb buds are formed they appear earlier in the pectoral than in the pelvic region. Proximal to distal development is evidenced by the orderly sequence in which differentiation of the limb segments occurs, namely, differentiation of those segments nearest to the trunk prior to those more distally located.

The third part of the law, which states that development is from the general to the specific, is based on Coghill's observations of individuation of movement; i.e., movements of the body segments early in life occur only in conjunction with already established more generalized movements, and only at a later period of development when the nervous system is sufficiently mature are discrete independent movements possible. Carmichael, in particular, emphasized that one should be cautious in drawing a close parallel between the embryonic pattern of behavioral development in man and other vertebrates, for many of the early behavioral characteristics are in fact quite different (1946). For example, the individuation of movement responses so clearly discernible in the sequential development of locomotion in the embryo salamander is not so readily discernible during the development of the human fetus.

PRENATAL DEVELOPMENT

Information on the motor behavior of humans during the prenatal period has come from observations on fetuses that have been taken from mothers for medical reasons. There is no clear-cut consensus whether the earliest motor responses are general in character or whether they begin as isolated reflexes. For example, Minkowski reported that contraction of the quadriceps can be elicited by patellar tendon percussion as early as the eighth week of prenatal life (1922). While specific reflexes may be relatively isolated at this time, the evidence points to a generalized pattern of response as early as the ninth week of prenatal life. For example, Hooker reported that cutaneous stimulation of the mouth and nose brings about simultaneous hip rotation and body flexion (1939). Further support for the concept that early patterns of motor behavior involve the total organism has come from the early research of Minkowski (1922). He noted that cutaneous stimulation of the face resulted not only in such responses as flexion of both arms and opening and closing of the mouth, but also in other unorganized movement responses that spread throughout the body. Movement patterns that clearly indicate the presence of reciprocal innervation have been noted in 16-week-old fetuses: Stimulation of one foot results in movements of the arm on the opposite side of the body. Such diagonal reflexes are held by Minkowski to be precursors of the establishment of the "trotting reflex," which some authorities believe is a movement pattern that is later built into creeping and walking.

With advancing fetal age, responses gradually become more localized, such localization initially becoming more pronounced in the head than in the foot region. That this gradual localization of response is not under the control of the higher centers has been shown by studies reporting that electrical stimulation of the cortex during the fifth month results in no response whatsoever. Further motor responses are not elicited by stimulation of the basal ganglia. While there are segmentally coordinated movement responses, these are controlled at this time at the level of the spinal cord with no help from the higher centers.

It is not until the seventh month that clearly defined movements involving synergic muscles have been observed. At this time percussion of limb muscles results in responses limited not to single muscle groups but to a rapid spread of responses to synergists. For example, percussion of the pectoral muscles results in adduction and inward rotation of the arm with flexion of the forearm, while pressure applied to the palm of the hand brings about grasping movements like those seen in the newborn.

Thus behavioral development of the fetus follows a rather well defined pattern, characterized by gradual synthesis of diffuse behaviors into ones that are relatively integrated and purposeful.

MOTOR DEVELOPMENT IN INFANCY

Expression of Intrinsic Forces

As indicated in the previous section, the prenatal period witnesses the development of a rather broad range of reasonably well coordinated movement responses, some of which will later be built into the child's movement repertoire. For example, stepping movements that can be elicited when the newborn is held upright with the feet resting on a supporting surface are essentially the movement patterns used in walking. Postural reflexes can be activated by momentary changes of the neonate's body position, and creeping movements occur when the infant is placed in the prone position and pressure is applied to the feet. The result is alternate movement of the arms combined with vigorous thrusting of one or both legs with simultaneous bending of the body from side to side. Likewise the grasping reflex is firmly established at birth, so that a rod placed in the newborn's hand is held with sufficient strength to support the body weight for several seconds (Peiper, 1929).

All of the above movements are controlled at the subcortical level of the brain. Such behaviors are retained until approximately the end of the fourth month; retention for longer periods may indicate central nervous system dysfunction. Thus those motor patterns, which are held by some to be phyletic in character, are organized at the subcortical level, gradually becoming suppressed as the motor area of the cortex assumes dominance.

Among the more dramatic indications that intrinsic factors play a major role in shaping human motor development early in life is the orderly sequence of events that occurs in postural and locomotor development. The gradual and orderly progression of those primary motor abilities that lead to the establishment of erect posture and walking are evidenced by the research of Shirley (1933). The cephalocaudal sequence of motor development is clearly apparent here, for motor control is first established in the region of the head and neck, passing next to the upper trunk and arms, and still later to the lower trunk and inferior extremities (Fig. 4–2).

The above is consistent with the general concept of developmental change proposed by McGraw in which the first 2 years of life may be divided into four periods, each representing a progressive reduction in subcortical control as the motor cortex and the association area of the brain gain dominance (1939). The first 4 months of postnatal life, according to McGraw, are characterized by reduction in rhythmic movements and gradual loss of the reflex responses present at birth. The second period, the fourth month through the ninth, witnesses the development of voluntary movements in the upper spinal region and reduction of unilateral movements in the pelvis and lower extremities. The third period, extending through the 14th month, is characterized by increased control of the lower body and inferior extremities; and the final 10 months (fourth period), by development of the association centers of the brain giving rise to symbolic and language expression.

The development of manual coordination and prehension skills in infancy likewise follows well-defined and orderly developmental changes. The first evidence of budding prehension skills is noted at about the 20th week of postnatal life when the infant reaches out simultaneously with both hands, often without making contact with the object. Between the 24th and the 34th week the infant attempts to "corral" small objects, using a palmar grasp in a scooping motion. It is not until nearly the end of the first year that the pincer movement, thumb against forefinger, is routinely and effectively used. Thus, both gross and fine movement patterns follow well-defined sequences in their development during the period of infancy.

Fig. 4–2. Sequences in gross motor development in infancy. (Shirley. © 1933. By permission of the University of Minnesota.)

Although there is a characteristic sequence in the development of structural and behavioral traits early in life, infants may differ widely in the chronological ages at which these phenomena occur. Such differences are attributed largely to variations among children in their rates of anatomical, physiological, and neurological maturation. Maturation is a term that is freely used but difficult to define. Most authorities attribute maturation largely to biological factors. Thus it is held to be a function of the organism's intrinsic regulatory mechanisms that guide the course of development. These regulatory mechanisms, however, are sensitive to a wide range of environmental forces, and thus the rate of maturation is influenced by such factors as diet, diseases, and use. While structure may set the limits of function, use does in turn affect structure, and thus plays a significant role in affecting maturational status.

The impact of maturational status on the performance and development of motor skills early in life has over the years received considerable attention. One of the most frequently cited studies of the role of maturation and training in the acquisition of motor skills is the classic investigation of McGraw on the twins, Jimmy and Johnny (1935). Johnny, the less mature of the twins, was given special training in a variety of motor activities from the age of 21 days until he was 20 months old, whereas no special training was given during this time to Jimmy. When the performance capabilities of the twins were compared at the completion of the experiment, it was concluded that special exercise in no way altered the age of extinction of the subcortical responses that normally are lost during the early months of life, nor were the developmental trends of such phylogenetic activities as crawling and walking materially speeded up by the special training. However, with those activities of a more specialized character, marked changes were brought about through training. For example, the trained twin roller skated shortly after he was able to walk, and by 14 months the child was highly proficient. While roller skating is a complicated skill it required locomotor movement patterns with which the child was already familiar. In a like manner the trained twin rapidly developed skill in climbing incline boards, commencing this activity while in the creeping stage. It should be noted that in both roller skating and climbing the child was using basic movement patterns into which he was able to build, with little difficulty, the additional elements involved in the new activities.

The possibility that early training might affect aspects of motor development not directly included in the training program was also investigated. While the sequence leading up to walking occurred at approximately the same time for the two infants, not only did the trained twin appear to move more gracefully and maintain better carriage during the early stages of walking, but these differences were still noticeable at 6 years of age.

Studies on both animals and humans have presented evidence showing that critical periods are reached in the development of the organism when physical and behavioral characteristics are most susceptible to modification. As the organism matures the accompanying growth changes result in a higher degree of organization of bodily functions equipping it to cope more effectively with increasingly complex environmental situations. Recognition of this has focused attention on the concept of 'maturational readiness' and what this means for educational programs. The evidence clearly indicates that maturation and the capacity to learn are closely related during the developmental period, although the relative influence exerted by maturation may be greater in the acquisition of certain skills (whereas learning may predominate in others).

The futility of attempting to force children to acquire motor skills at an early age has been the focus of many early studies. For example, Gesell and Thompson trained one of a pair of identical twins in block handling and climbing activities over a period of 6 weeks beginning at 46 weeks of age (1929). At the end of the 6-week period, conditions were made as nearly alike as possible for both twins. The control twin during the first 3 weeks made greater progress than had been made by the experimental child during the preceding six weeks of special training. Similarly, Hicks in studying children in the age range $2\frac{1}{2}$ to $6\frac{1}{2}$ years found that those given experimental practice in hitting a moving target gained no more in this skill than was gained by a matched group given general practice involving elements of this skill (1931).

That deprivation of opportunity prior to the maturity level at which a skill or behavior would normally develop is not necessarily critical was shown by Dennis (1940). He demonstrated that the cradle-binding practice of the Hopi and Navajo

Indians that restricted physical activity during the first 6 to 12 months of life (except for approximately 1 hour each day) had little if any effect on the age of walking.

The foregoing has stressed the importance of intrinsic factors in shaping the course of motor development. As Schneirla pointed out, the tendency has been to overlook or ignore the matrix of factors that affect development (1966). Thus the traditional point of view that behavioral development early in life is purely an endogenous unfolding process has tended to hold sway. Evidence to the contrary comes from the research of Coghill (1940, 1943) and Hamburger (1963), which points out the subtle ways in which the interaction of maturation and experience may alter behavioral development early in life. As pointed out earlier, maturation itself is susceptible to modifying influences that can either nurture or impair the unfolding process. Thus, to say that behavior is solely or primarily a function of maturation is a gross oversimplification.

Postural and Locomotor Development

Of the behavioral traits emerging in infancy, those that are perhaps the most human in character are the development of upright posture, walking, use of the opposable thumb, and the beginnings of speech. Attainment of upright posture and the development of bipedal locomotion constituted major steps in the evolution of humans and are equally important landmarks in the development of the child. Not only is walking the basic movement pattern from which other forms of locomotion emerge, but it frees the hands for the development of a broad range of manipulative skills.

Walking is in no sense a simple unitary skill for, as pointed out earlier, it is the end point in a series of motor experiences that span some 12 to 14 months. It is a complex activity requiring the coordinated action of the many muscle groups needed for eliciting stepping movements and also for maintaining posture and balance as the center of gravity shifts with each step. Thus the development of skill in walking requires integration of information from many feed back loops, which requires the child's undivided attention so that undue response to one source of information is not made at the expense of others.

The age of onset of walking varies widely among children, the mean age being 13 to 14 months; onset occurs as early as 9 months and as late as 17 months in children who are developing normally. As implied earlier, there is no well-founded evidence to indicate that the onset of walking can be speeded up by practice or special exercises. This illustrates once again the important role that intrinsic factors play in the early motor development of children.

There are, however, factors that may postpone the age of onset of walking, such as excessive body weight, clothing that restricts freedom of movement, shoes without the proper support, slippery floors, and overly protective parents. There is also some evidence that physique-associated factors may affect the age of onset of walking. For example, Shirley reported that muscular and small-boned infants walk at an earlier age than those of heavy weight (1933). Similarly, large leg-muscle mass is associated with early standing and walking, whereas there is delay in the acquisition of this capability in infants with small muscles (Garn, 1963). While there are only limited data on the role that physique plays in the motor development of young children, the evidence points to a higher energy output and more vigorous childhood in those of sturdy body build in contrast to obese children and those of extremely slender build (Walker, 1962). In any event, most infants begin to walk when they are ready, and one or more of the foregoing will probably be of only limited consequence on the age at which this activity begins.

THE CHILDHOOD YEARS

Childhood is divided into early and later periods. Early childhood includes ages 18 months to 5 years; later childhood, ages 5 to 10 years in girls and 5 to 12 years in boys. Such divisions are entirely arbitrary, the one constituting the period from infancy to the age at which formal education begins and the other extending over the early school years. While infancy is a time of a rapid but declining rate of physical growth, childhood is one of relatively slow and steady growth, terminated by the begining of the adolescent growth spurt.

Early Childhood

Motor development during this period is characterized both by refinements in already existing movement patterns, building new patterns into those present, and by exploring ways of adapting and altering movements to meet the requirements of tasks as yet not tried. The complexity of the tasks attempted increases as the child matures and as movement experiences provide a base on which to build. As Bruner pointed out, most complex movements are made up of basic units or subroutines that must be organized into the proper sequence and properly timed in such a way that the total movement occurs smoothly and without interruptions (1970). Accomplishment of this is a laborious operation, one that requires time, effort, and previous experiences upon which to draw. In this sense maturation and practice both play a role. The question invariably arises, When can the learning of a skill be accomplished with the least amount of practice? This is a question that still has no satisfactory answer. The fact that maturation at this stage of development cannot be ignored is indicated by a few illustrations from research on skill development.

Let us look first at the evolution of the behavioral changes seen in the development of the standing long jump as reported by Hellebrandt and co-workers (1961). A schematic illustration of the transition from infantile to more mature performance of the standing broad jump in a 3½-year-old child is shown in Figures 4–3 and 4–4. These investigators hold that jumping per se is a phylogenetic skill, its primary set being present at birth, awaiting central nervous system maturation for an unfolding of the total response pattern. As the skill becomes established the sequence and timing of muscle action are essentially involuntary. Thus these investigators propose that this skill does not develop by synthesis of fragments of the act but rather by the expanding pattern of central nervous system integration resulting from the growth and development of the controlling mechanisms.

The sequential stages that occur in the development of the mature pattern of the overarm throw were described more than 40 years ago by Wilde (1938). Using

Fig. 4–3. (Top) Performance of the standing broad jump by a 37-month-old boy. (Bottom) Full-blown "winging" at 41 months. The poise is that of a bird in soaring flight. (Hellebrandt, F.A., et al.: Physiological analysis of basic motor skills. Am. J. Phys. Med., 40:14, 1961. Copyright 1961, The Williams & Wilkins Co., Baltimore.)

Fig. 4–4. At 43 months of age there is transition from infantile to more mature arm positioning during a jump from a two-footed takeoff. The first attempt to bring the arms forward during the propulsive phase of the jump was disastrous. The second was successful. (Hellebrandt, F.A. et al.: Physiological analysis of basic motor skills. Am. J. Phys. Med. 40:14, 1961. Copyright 1961, The Williams & Wilkins Co., Baltimore.)

cinematography this investigator reported that the earliest and least mature pattern of this skill appears at 2 to 3 years of age and is characterized by movements of the arm and trunk in the anteroposterior plane with no displacement of the feet. In the second stage (ages 3½ to 5 years) there is introduction of arm and body movements in the horizontal plane without transfer of weight and without the forward step. Stage three (5 to 6 years) introduces the step forward as the throw is executed, but the step is ipsilateral with respect to the throwing arm; hence there is little trunk rotation or transfer of body weight. The throw at this stage has both anteroposterior and horizontal features, but it lacks power because of limited rotation of the trunk with little adduction of the throwing arm. The fourth and mature stage appears at approximately 6½ years of age in boys and is characterized by well-established opposition of limb movement with transfer of weight accompanied by trunk rotation, horizontal arm adduction, and elbow extension as the throw is executed. These clearly defined age-related sequences strongly suggest that development of the overarm throw is dependent on maturational processes and is not solely a function of practice. Support for this comes from the research of Dusenberry, who found that specific short-term practice of this skill accomplishes little prior to 5 years of age, but with the same amount of practice substantial gains are made during the fifth and sixth years (1952).

Running is generally considered to be a natural activity, but it is not until the fifth or sixth year that the adult pattern of running becomes well established. Prior to this age there is a gradual but well-defined increase in length and frequency of the stride as the child's leg strength and balance capabilities develop. With advancing age the relative rise of the center of gravity during the run becomes less, and the pelvic rotation increases with each stride as the propulsive force in leg extension becomes greater and the arm action becomes stronger and more uniform.

While boys are on the average slightly taller and heavier than girls in early childhood, girls are approximately 1 year more mature physically as indicated by their advanced bone age. Sex differences in motor performance are not significant at this age, although boys on the average are slightly stronger (Metheny, 1941), run faster, and throw farther than girls, whereas girls tend to be more proficient in balance-type activities. Such sex differences would seem to be more a reflection of sex-oriented interests in childhood than of differences in basic motor aptitudes.

Early childhood is a period in which the motor repertoire expands rapidly, partly a function of the child's enlarged environment and partly a reflection of a motor control system that is rapidly developing. Significant advances occur in locomotor development from late infancy throughout the period of early childhood as is evidenced from the early findings of Bayley (1935) and Wellman (1937). The findings of these investigators point to performance age trends that in each instance are indicative of a gradually maturing motor mechanism that permits the child to master progressively more difficult tasks such as (1) a gradual improvement in walking skills as indicated by age-level improvements in the ability to maintain balance while walking a narrow line, and (2) stair-climbing ability as evidenced by a gradual but consistent change in the manner that the child negotiates stairs (first by marking time on each riser and then, some 12 months later, by alternating feet on successive risers). Descending stairs in each instance is accomplished at a later age than is ascending.

The following gives the average age at which the above can be expected to occur (Wellman, 1937):

Stair-Climbing Ability	*Age in months*
Ascends stairs with help	20.3
Descends stairs with help	20.5
Ascends stairs, marks time	24.3
Descends stairs, marks time	24.5
Ascends stairs, alternating feet	35.5
Descends stairs, alternating feet	50.0

Hopping on one foot is a skill that requires elements of strength and balance, improvements coming with advancing age and experience as evidenced from the following age trends (Wellman, 1937):

No. of steps hopped	*Age in months*
1 to 3	43
4 to 6	46
7 to 9	55
10 or more	60

Ball-throwing performance as measured by the distance a child can throw a $9\frac{1}{2}$-inch ball likewise improves with age (Wellman, 1937):

Distance Thrown in Feet	*Age in months*
4–5	30
6–7	33
8–9	44
10–11	52
12–13	57
14–15	65
16–17	72 plus

It should be noted that the foregoing tells us something about expected levels of performance, but no information is given as to how these skills are executed, nor are any data provided on such factors as background of experience, level of maturity, or sex, each of which might well affect the performance achieved by an individual child.

Later Childhood

During later childhood the urge for physical activity remains high. This is in part a reflection of the continued growth of muscle tissue. During the elementary school years there is a 35- to 40-pound gain in weight, some 50 to 60% of which is attributed to muscle tissue. Thus this continues to be a period of physical restlessness, one in which the energy stores of the muscles are pulsating for release.

Physical growth in later childhood continues at a relatively steady pace with a yearly increase of 2 to 3 inches in stature and 3 to 6 pounds in body weight. Boys continue to be the taller and heavier throughout this period and have on the average more muscle tissue and less body fat than girls, although these differences are not great (Reynolds, 1944; Stuart and Dwinell, 1942).

Motor Performance. Muscular strength and performance of most basic motor skills increase linearly with chronological age throughout this period, the performance of boys being slightly superior to that of girls. The linear increases in both strength and motor performance of both sexes during this period is a reflection of steady physical growth and a general similarity in movement experiences. This is not to suggest that the motor performance of children is highly predictable from one age to another, for this is not necessarily true, but rather to point out that uneven individual gains in performance tend to be averaged out, thus yielding group gains that parallel the gains in height and weight. Actually the between-year correlations of motor performance at this age level are only moderately high as indicated by the longitudinal research of Glassow and Kruse in which the correlation between broad jump scores in grade 1 with jump scores 6 years later was .739 and the correlation on the 30-yard dash with the same children was .70 (1960).

While the motor performance of boys in later childhood is generally superior to that of girls, recent research points to a remarkable similarity in the basic components that underlie the motor abilities of the sexes. For example, when 47 motor performance tests were given to 71 boys and 74 girls in the San Francisco East Bay Region and resulting test scores were factor analyzed, six basic components (factors) accounted for a major proportion of the variance in both sexes (Rarick and Dobbins, 1975). Not only was there a striking similarity in the factor structures of the sexes as reflected by the pattern of factor loadings, but the relationships between corresponding factors as indicated by their respective cosines (conceptually interpreted as correlations) were consistently high, two being in the mid .90s, three in the high .80s, and one in the .70s (Fig. 4–5).

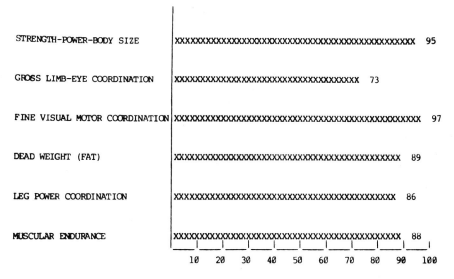

Fig. 4—5. Similarity among factors of the motor performance of 6- to 10-year-old males and females as reflected by the cosines of the factor axes derived from the principal components' solution.

Body Build and Motor Performance. In the childhood years the relationship of body build to strength and motor proficiency is neither great nor well defined. In the sense that ultimate body size and rate of physical growth are regulated by genetic factors, and that physique in adults is important in accounting for individual differences in strength, there is reason to believe that body build and strength have more than a chance relationship during the growing years. In children of linear frame (late maturers) there is a preponderance of endochondral bone formation resulting in accentuation of the linear component of growth with the formation of long slender bones. In children of mesomorphic build (early maturers) appositional bone formation predominates with resulting heavier and shorter bones and relatively more muscle mass. That the mesomorphic individual, particularly the male, is in later childhood and in adolescence stronger per unit of weight than the ectomorph and endomorph is shown when strength-weight ratios of males of these three body types are plotted against chronological age (Fig. 4–6). Note that while the differences at the age level 9 to 11 years are negligible when comparing the mesomorphic and ectomorphic groups, thereafter the superiority of the mesomorph is clearly evident.

Metabolic Functions and Motor Performance. While sex differences in strength and motor performance in childhood are not great there is evidence that there are differences between boys and girls in the metabolic and functional characteristics of their muscles. For example, Garn and Clark showed that when the sexes were equated on the basis of muscle mass, the basal metabolic rate in boys was greater than that of girls, pointing to a higher concentration of active tissues in males (1953). Further support for the foregoing comes from the research of Rarick and Thompson,

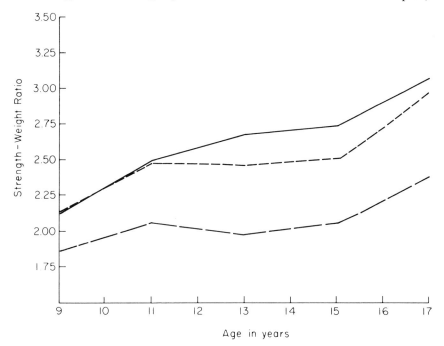

Fig. 4–6. Longitudinal strength-weight ratios of adolescent males grouped by physique categories (strength score: sum of right and left grip, pull, and thrust): (——) = endomorph; (—) = mesomorph; (———) = ectomorph. (Malina, R.M., and Rarick, G.L.: Growth, physique, and motor performance. *In* Physical Activity: Human Growth and Development, edited by G.L. Rarick. New York, Academic Press, Inc., 1973.)

which showed that as early as 7 years of age boys have more strength than girls when proper allowances are made for differences in muscle mass (1956). It is conceivable that strength and performance sex differences at this age level may in part be a reflection of cultural influences, since the role models of the sexes differ in that strength and power are more highly valued and more sought after by males than females at this age.

STRENGTH AND MOTOR PERFORMANCE IN ADOLESCENCE

Adolescence is the time in life when the individual gradually assumes the physical characteristics of the adult, a period that extends in the male from approximately 13 to 15 years to 20 to 21 years, and in the female from 11 to 13 years to 18 years. It is a period of rapid physical growth and marked psychological and emotional change.

The beginnings of adolescence are characterized by a rapid spurt in physical growth occurring in males from ages $12\frac{1}{2}$ to 15 years and in females some 2 years earlier, from $10\frac{1}{2}$ to 13 years. The $2\frac{1}{2}$-year age range during which this phenomenon may occur means that the variability in body size at this time is indeed substantial. Among like-age children there may be a difference of as much as 10 inches in height and 20 to 30 pounds in body weight.

Physical Growth

Growth at adolescence is believed to be under the control of a sequence of endocrinological events that affects the entire body. The growth spurt in both sexes is accompanied by increases in all body dimensions, by the appearance of the secondary sex characteristics, and by a rapid growth of the reproductive organs. There are also changes in body proportions, rapid lengthening of the limbs early in this period, followed by a compensating growth in trunk length later in adolescence. Individual characteristics of body build in childhood tend to be retained in adolescence, such differences being related to the onset of the adolescent growth spurt. Children of linear frame tend to have a delayed growth spurt but usually grow for a longer time than children of more stocky build. Thus intrinsic factors that determine the individuality of physique seem to affect the onset and duration of the adolescent growth spurt.

Growth in Muscular Strength and Motor Performance

While strength of both sexes increases in early adolescence, it is more evident in males than in females. This difference is largely a reflection of the more rapid growth of muscle tissue in males brought about by increased blood levels of testosterone and the androgens. There is a corresponding loss of body fat in males, whereas in females there is a tendency to accumulate adipose tissue. These differences have a direct bearing on motor development and motor performance in adolescence. This is evidenced when body weight and strength data are plotted for both sexes (Fig. 4–7). The strikingly close parallel of growth in weight and in strength of boys in the age range 9 to 19 years will be noted, whereas in girls growth increases in strength on the average cease at approximately age 13 years, and increases in weight level off at about 16 years of age. Similarly, increases in performance of those motor activities that call primarily on elements of strength and power continue to increase in boys throughout adolescence, but as in the case of strength, motor performance in girls levels off at about age 13 years (Fig. 4–8). This rather clearly indicates that the long-recognized differences in strength and motor performance of the sexes in adolescence are to a large extent biological, although cultural factors cannot be ignored.

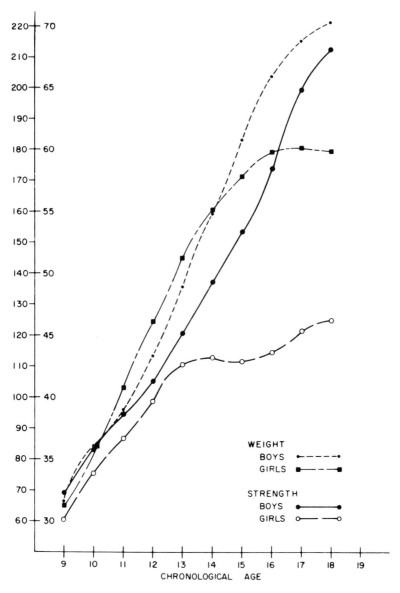

Fig. 4–7. Annual growth in weight and muscular strength of boys and girls, ages 9–18 years.

Sexual Maturation

The differential effects of sexual maturation on the development of strength in males and females is nicely illustrated by the research of Jones in which strength data were obtained semiannually on the same group of boys and girls from 11 through 17 years of age (1949). When these data (right-hand grip) of early- and late-maturing boys and girls were plotted against chronological age the impact of maturational

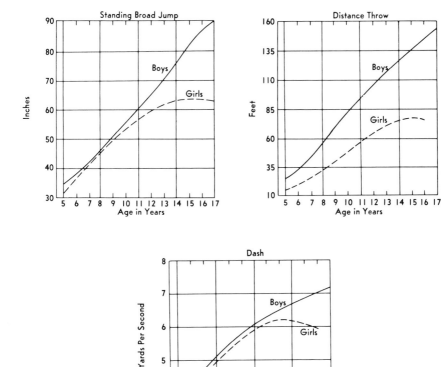

Fig. 4–8. Mean performance of boys and girls, ages 5 to 17 years, on standing broad jump, distance throw, and running speed. (Espenshade, A., and Eckert, H.: Motor development. *In* Science and Medicine of Exercise and Sport. Edited by W.R. Johnson. Hagerstown, Md., Harper & Row, 1960. Reprinted by permission of publisher.)

status on strength development was clearly evident (Fig. 4–9). Maturational status in the boys was evaluated in terms of skeletal age (development of the bones of the hand, wrist, and knee) and in girls as menarcheal age. In the boys the difference in mean strength between the early and late maturers was greatest at age 15, being more than 2 standard deviations. It is interesting that the age of maximum strength difference in males was coincident with age differences in the creatine-creatinine ratio, an index frequently used as a chemical puberty indicator in this sex. In the girls the strength differences between early and late maturers was less dramatic than in the boys, yet the role of menarche as the differentiating factor was clearly evident.

It is perhaps worthy of note that, when the writer used body weight data on this sample of boys and girls and plotted age-weight curves, differences in the weight between the early and late maturers were of approximately the same magnitude as the differences in strength recorded by Jones. Thus the strength difference obtained by Jones would seem to be largely a reflection of differences in body size, a finding that is not surprising since it has long been recognized that size and strength are

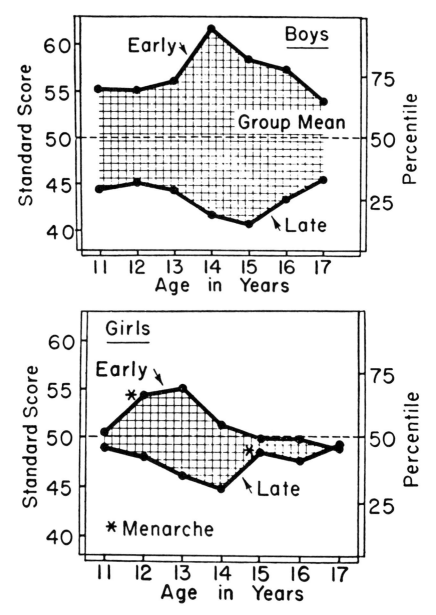

Fig. 4–9. Growth curve scores (right grip) for early and late maturing boys and girls. (Jones, H.: Motor Performance and Growth. Berkeley, University of California Press, 1949. By permission.)

related. Thus it is during the period of rapid physical growth that the variability in strength and body size becomes greatest, a reflection primarily of the age difference in the initiation of the growth spurt for both sexes. In the male, however, it is not size alone that makes the differences. As Jones points out, the big, early-maturing boy is not as strong as his size would suggest, for his data indicate that there is at least a 6-month lag before the early-maturing male's strength is commensurate with his body size.

Body Build

Body weight is important in adolescence in accounting for individual differences in strength, but body build is a factor of considerable consequence as well. The importance of physique to strength was shown by the research of Jones in which he demonstrated that 75% of the variance in strength of adolescent males was attributable to the proper weighting of five factors, namely, height, weight, mesomorphy, endomorphy, and ectomorphy (1949).

Body build is also important in accounting for individual differences in strength, both within and between the sexes, as shown by the research of Bayley (1951). Static muscular strength data were collected on adolescent boys and girls grouped into somatic androgeny classifications, a scale based on masculinity and femininity morphological characteristics. The findings suggest that not only is body build important in accounting for differences in strength when conventional methods of body typing are used, but also that rather dramatic strength differences both within and between the sexes have been obtained when adolescent males are grouped into androgeny classifications. Thus Bayley reported that mean strength per pound of body weight for the boys was substantially greater than that for girls and similarly greater in all androgeny classifications with the exception of bisexual feminine and bisexual masculine categories (1951). Similarly, as one moves from the hyperfeminine to the hypermasculine category, strength per pound of body weight becomes progressively greater (Fig. 4–10). Such data strongly suggest that body build as reflected by somatic androgeny scores is an important factor in accounting for individual differences in strength both within and between the sexes.

ETHNIC AND CULTURAL FACTORS IN MOTOR DEVELOPMENT

Investigations of the influence of ethnic origin and cultural background on the motor development of children in the United States have for the most part compared motor performance data of blacks and whites. These studies have used samples of children within well-defined age categories, including infants, children, and adolescents, in which a wide range of motor tasks has served as the data source. Most studies, but not all, agree that black children early in life are slightly advanced over white children in the accomplishment of common motor tasks (Bayley, 1965; Knobloch and Pasamanick, 1953; Williams and Scott, 1953). The superiority enjoyed by them in the first 2 or 3 years of life, however, becomes less evident in the latter part of early childhood. It has been proposed by Bayley that black infants may by nature be motorically more precocious than whites, although there is no concrete evidence in support of this (1965). They are, however, slightly advanced in such physical maturity indicators as age of dentition and time of appearance of the bony ossification centers. Whether the performance differences noted at this early age can be attributed to biological factors or to differences in child-rearing practices must await further study.

Reports of the comparative motor performance of black and white children of school age, while mixed, generally show overall superiority of black boys and girls. Again, the reason for this trend is not apparent from the data. In activities in which the body weight must be propelled as in running and jumping, the findings of Malina suggest that such differences may be attributable to the lesser quantity of adipose

THE RELATION OF STRENGTH TO ANDROGYNY

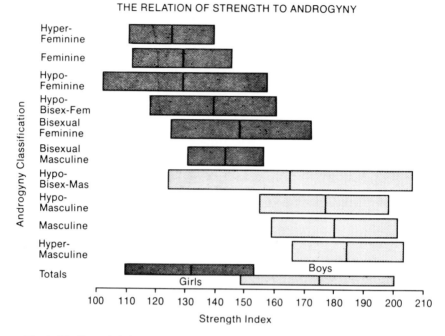

Fig. 4–10. Strength index scores according to somatic androgeny classifications (strength scores: sum of right and left grip, pull and thrust). (Bayley, N.: Some psychological correlates of somatic androgeny. Child Dev., 22:47, 1951. © The Society for Research in Child Development, Inc.)

tissue in black boys and girls (1968). At all ages from 6 to 13 years, Malina reported that the skinfold thickness (log transformation) was on the average greater in whites of both sexes than in blacks.

That cultural factors play a significant role in motor performance levels of children is shown by the results of the AAHPER physical fitness test given to American and British children and adolescents. The average performance of the British males exceeded that of American males on all items of the test, with the exception of the throw for distance, an activity not often used in British sports (Campbell and Pohndorf, 1961).

INTELLECTUAL DEFICITS AND MOTOR DEVELOPMENT

It is well known that the relationship is low between motor performance test scores and measures of intelligence of children and adolescents of normal intelligence. In other words, intelligence as measured by standard intelligence tests is of little value in differentiation between the skilled and unskilled performer in the IQ range of 90 to 130. However, the motor performance capabilities of mentally retarded children are decidedly substandard—the more pronounced the mental deficiency, the poorer the motor performance.

The lag in motor development of the mentally retarded is noted early in life when such motor functions as sitting, creeping, crawling, standing, and walking are considerably delayed. Among school-age children those who are moderately retarded (IQ 50 to 70) are on the average 2 to 4 years behind intellectually normal children in motor skill development. With advancing age the difference becomes greater.

The magnitude of the motor deficiency across the broad spectrum of motor abilities is evident when motor test scores of the retarded are expressed in standard deviation units using data on intellectually normal children of the same age for comparative purposes (Rarick, Dobbins, and Broadhead, 1976). The average of the standard deviation units of some 39 motor performance tests, grouped according to five components of motor performance, places the retarded girls 1.83 SD units below the mean of intellectually normal girls. In the case of the boys the same procedure places the retarded males .96 SD units below those of normal intelligence. Thus the average performance of the retarded girls would be expected to be exceeded by 95% of normal girls, and the mean performance of the retarded boys by 87% of normal boys.

It is worthy of note that both retarded males and females on the average have substantially more body fat than their intellectually normal counterparts, a factor that adversely affects their gross motor performance. The excess body fat of the retarded would seem to be primarily due to lack of physical activity, since no well-defined metabolic deficiencies have been identified in populations of mentally retarded children.

The poor motor performance of the retarded, while in part related to inadequate motor opportunities, is primarily a function of their limited learning capability. Research findings to date indicate that with the mildly retarded, problems of motor learning are largely those of comprehending and attending to the specific requirements of the task rather than to execution once the task requirements are clearly understood. With proper instructional help and with practice under nonstressful conditions, the motor performance level of many mildly retarded boys and girls can approximate that of intellectually normal children of the same age level.

PREDICTION OF MOTOR ABILITIES

The accuracy with which human structural and behavioral characteristics can be predicted from one age level to another has been a matter of considerable interest to child development specialists. Accuracy of prediction is reduced as the time between measurements increases, for individual differences in growth and varying environmental factors are given longer to operate. Even so, adult stature can be predicted with reasonable accuracy from height in childhood. Weight is less predictable, since it is highly susceptible to variations in food intake and to changes in life style.

Most behavioral phenomena, including motor skills, are not highly predictable from one age level to another. For example, Clarke reported that the interage correlations of strength tests used in the Medford boys' growth study were generally only low to moderate, ranging from .413 to .787 for adjacent ages, and from .013 to .723 for age spans of 5 years (1971). It should be kept in mind that strength and body size are related, so that these correlations are in part a reflection of changes in body size. The correlations over the 5-year span were generally higher in the preadolescent years than in the adolescent groups, a reflection of the relatively steady growth rate in the former. Similarly, when longitudinal motor performance data on such fundamental skills as running, jumping, and throwing are used for predictive purposes, predictions are generally poor. For example, in the Wisconsin Growth Study, between-year correlations, ages 7 to 17 years, for males on jumping, running, and throwing performance were .60, .18, and .29 respectively, and for girls .50, .56, and .13 (Rarick and Smoll, 1967). With between-age correlations of this magnitude it is evident that the chances for relatively good performers at age 7 to be among the best at 17 is not very likely.

The prediction of athletic potential from childhood to adolescence is equally hazardous as evidenced by the findings of the Medford Growth Study (Clarke, 1971). The findings showed that many of the participants on interscholastic athletic teams in this Oregon community, who at an early age exhibited athletic potential, did not become outstanding athletes. For example, only one fourth of these individuals were considered outstanding in both elementary school and junior high school. Approximately 45% were listed as outstanding in elementary school but not in junior high school, whereas only 30% were named as outstanding in junior high school but not in elementary school. The reasons for such ability shifts may well have been as much a function of changing interests as a reflection of changes in basic performance capabilities.

MOTOR LEARNING IN CHILDHOOD

The processes that are involved in the learning of motor skills are not as yet well understood. We know that as children grow and develop their ability to perform motor tasks improves. This is in part a reflection of neurological maturation, increasing muscular strength, and experience, but we have only limited insight into how motor skills develop.

It has long been known that movement patterns such as walking, running, jumping, and throwing once acquired are for the most part executed with little if any conscious direction. Herrick (1931) labeled such movements acquired automatisms, for once initiated the movements continue automatically, although the specific muscle groups controlling the act can, in whole or in part, be controlled by the will. The motor area of the brain serves as the ultimate control mechanism for so-called voluntary movements, although other areas of the central nervous system serve to modulate and control the action of muscles.

Patterned movements are characterized by an ordered and properly timed sequence of subroutines that, when viewed in total, give the movement its quality or form. Each movement subroutine is dependent upon those that precede it. The degree to which the subroutines are synchronized in their time-force-directionality relationships is the basis for skillful, well-coordinated movements. The significance of the body's feedback mechanisms in serving as modulating control systems (servomechanisms) in the many motor activities of daily life involving relatively slow controlled movements is self-evident. However, it has been known for some time that rapid movements of a ballistic character are carried out with such speed that, once the movement is initiated, the feedback control mechanisms do not have time to affect the course of the movement (Hubbard, 1974; Stetson and McDill, 1923). In such cases the error-detecting mechanisms monitoring such movement must play their role in succeeding movements (Schmidt, 1975). That the subroutines of complex rapid (ballistic) movements operate without conscious direction once the act is under way is generally recognized. Thus the centrally stored movement commands or motor programs that are generated by practice are believed to be subject to modification in subsequent trials through the action of peripheral sensory mechanisms. The question whether movements are peripherally controlled by a combination of feedback systems, as proposed by the closed-loop concept (Adams, 1971), or are directly under the control of centrally stored commands (Schmidt, 1980) has yet to be answered.

The problem of the seat of movement control is further clouded by the findings of Kelso, who reported that a limb-positioning task could be accurately executed without vision after removal of the joint capsule (the source responsible for position sense) (1977). This would suggest that the command system is able to direct movements with reasonable accuracy without calling on sensory input. However, Kelso's results are contrary to the findings reported by Laszo and Bairstow, who reported inaccurate finger movements following deadening of tactile and kinesthetic sensations in that region (1971). Most of the research at this point suggests that motor learning is dependent on an effective error-detecting system that would appear to function differently in slow, as contrasted with fast, movements but would in either case result in modifications in the command system.

One of the most promising process-oriented concepts that has both developmental and practical implications is Schmidt's schema theory of discrete motor learning (1975). In essence this theory proposes that through many different motor experiences one establishes a set of rules or strategies for solving a broad range of motor problems. For example, the theory suggests that variable practice that requires variable response specifications results in the development of a motor schema that facilitates transfer to similar but unfamiliar tasks. While there is limited support for this theory from research on adults, evidence is accumulating that the theory may well have credence with children. For example, Kelso and Norman reported that variable practice on a simple novel motor task by young children (2 years and 11 months to 4 years of age) resulted in greater transfer to an unpracticed task of the same response class than occurred following constant practice (1978). Similar findings were reported by Moxley using a complex gross motor task with older children, ages 6 to 8 years of age (1979). Schmidt believes that the theory holds promise for the teaching of motor skills to children; the findings to date reaffirm the belief of those in movement education that the instructional emphasis with children should be placed on the development of a variety of movement patterns, thus leading to the establishment of a generalized motor schema (1975).

A factor of considerable importance in the motor learning of children is the amount of information that must be processed and the speed with which this can be done. As tasks become more complicated the amount and kind of information increases. If it can be assumed that a central command center is the source of motor memory, then information from the sensory mechanisms must in some way be processed before a motor response is made. Such a memory system is believed to include mechanisms for encoding and storing incoming information and retrieval of information previously stored. Thus the effectiveness with which such a system can function depends on the kind of information that is to be processed and the information load that can be handled. That older children can process more information than younger children and do this at a faster rate is well known. The reasons underlying this difference are not clear at this point. Pascual-Leone would attribute this to a greater "mental space" in older children (1970); others would say that "strategies and control processes (software) become more sophisticated and are employed more efficiently, creating an ability to handle increased information loads" (Thomas, 1980).

Support for the foregoing comes from the research of Todor in which it was found that 5- to 6-year-old children do not possess the cognitive capacity to coordinate the components of a complex motor task, one that can be handled effectively with limited practice by children 9 years of age and older (1979).

No one would question the value of practice in motor learning. The frequency and duration of practice sessions obviously depend on maturity level and the skill level of the child. Hard and fast rules regarding practice schedules just cannot be set, because learning is such an individual matter. The fact that learning rates vary widely among individuals is shown by the systematic decline in correlations between the initial trial and succeeding trials on a motor-learning task. Fatigue, reduced attention, and loss of interest are factors that adversely affect performance and learning. Clearly one wants to reduce the frequency with which incorrect movements are practiced. The limited attention span of children, and the tendency for them to lose interest rapidly, require that practice sessions be kept brief.

As mentioned previously, most movements are patterned. Many motor skills require the organization of movements that have already been programmed into new and as yet untried combinations. Thus, in many instances, the child is building on an already present motor base. Practice in which the learner is given cues designed to call into action already familiar movement patterns can do much to facilitate learning. Motor learning is an active process, one in which the learner must in the initial stages of learning focus attention on the details or subroutines of the task. Smoothing out the subroutines as the task is practiced is in most instances better than practicing isolated parts, since under these conditions the routines must later be blended smoothly in the complex movements of the total task.

SUMMARY AND CONCLUDING STATEMENTS

This chapter has focused on the significance of innate and environmental factors in motor development and motor learning. In early life, motor development, like other aspects of human growth, is largely controlled by endogenous forces. Thus, the futility of forcing children to acquire complex motor skills before they are maturationally ready is widely recognized.

The acquisition of motor skills in early childhood is a gradual process characterized by refinements in existing movement patterns and the incorporation of new patterns into those already present. In middle and later childhood, muscular strength and motor proficiency increase linearly with age, with boys performing slightly better on the average than girls.

In early adolescence, there is in both sexes an increase, greater in males than in females, in body size. The accelerated growth in males carries with it substantial increases in muscle mass and muscular strength. In females, adipose tissue rather than muscle mass tends to accumulate, and there is a leveling off of the development of those motor skills that require strength and power. Individual differences in motor performance are substantial at all ages, but they are particularly dramatic in early adolescence. Thus, the prediction of motor performance from one age level to another is hazardous at this time.

The processes involved in the learning and retention of motor skills are not well understood, and as yet no single theory of motor learning has gained complete acceptance. Although we have only limited insight into the mechanisms that control complex movements, we know much of practical significance about motor learning during the growing years. Practice with the intent to learn is essential, although the nature, frequency, and duration of practice sessions vary with the maturational level. Fatigue, reduced attention span, and loss of interest adversely affect motor learning, such factors being of particular significance in young children.

REFERENCES

Adams, J.A.: A closed-loop theory of motor learning. Res. Q. Exercise Sport, 51:122, 1971.

Barker, R.G, and Wright, H.F.: Midwest and Its Children. Evanston, Illinois, Row Peterson and Co., 1955.

Bayley, N.: The development of motor abilities during the first three years. Monogr. Soc. Res. Child Dev., 1:26, 1935.

Bayley, N.: Some psychological correlates of somatic androgeny. Child Dev., 22:47, 1951.

Bayley, N.: Comparisons of mental and motor tests scores for ages 1–15 months by sex, birth order, race, geographical location, and education of parents. Child Dev. 36:379, 1965.

Bayley, N. and Espenschade, A.: Motor development from birth to maturity. Rev. Educ. Res., 11:562, 1941.

Bruner, J.S.: The growth and structure of skill. In Mechanisms of Motor Skill Development. Edited by K. Connolly. New York, Academic Press, 1970.

Campbell, W.R., and Pohndorf, R.H.: Physical fitness of British and United States children. In Health and Fitness in the Modern World. Chicago, The Athletic Institute, 1961.

Carmichael, L.:The onset and early development of behavior. In Manual of Child Psychology. Edited by L. Carmichael. New York, John Wiley and Sons, 1946.

Clarke, H.H.: Physical and Motor Tests in the Medford Boys' Growth Study. Englewood Cliffs, N.J., Prentice-Hall, 1971.

Coghill, G.E.: Anatomy and the Problem of Behavior. Cambridge, Cambridge University Press, 1929.

Coghill, G.E.: Early embryonic somatic movements in birds and mammals other than man. Monogr. Soc. Res. Child Dev. 5:25, 1940.

Coghill, G.E.: Flexion spasms and mass reflexes in relation to the ontogenetic development of behavior. J. Comp. Neurol. 76:463, 1943.

Dennis, W.: Does culture appreciably affect patterns of infant behavior? J. Social Psychol. 12:305, 1940.

Dusenberry, L.: A study of the effects of training in ball throwing by children ages three to seven. Res. Q. 23:9, 1952.

Garn, S.: Human biology and research in body composition. II. Body Composition. Ann. N.Y. Acad. Sci. 111:429, 1963.

Garn, S., and Clark, L.C., Jr.: Sex differences in metabolic rate. Child Dev. 24:215, 1953.

Gesell, A. and Thompson, H.: Learning and growth in identical twins. Genet. Psychol. Monogr. 6:1, 1929.

Glassow, R.B., and Kruse, P.: Motor performance of girls, ages 6 to 14 years. Res. Q., 31:426, 1960.

Hamburger, V.: Some aspects of the embryology of behavior. Q. Rev. Biol. 38:365, 1963.

Hellebrandt, F.A. et al.: Physiological analysis of basic motor skills. Am. J. Phys. Med. 40:14, 1961.

Herrick, D.J.: An Introduction to Neurology. 5th Ed. Philadelphia, W.B. Saunders Co., 1931.

Hicks, J.A.: The acquisition of motor skills in young children. 1. A study of the effects of practice in throwing at a moving target. Child Dev., 2:156, 1931.

Hooker, D.: Fetal behavior. Res. Publ. Assoc. Nerv. Ment. Dis. 19:237, 1939.

Hubbard, A.W.: Homokinetics: Muscular function in human movement. In Science and Medicine in Exercise and Sports. Edited by W.R. Johnson. New York, Harper & Row, 1974.

Jones, H.: Motor Performance and Growth. Berkeley, University of California Press, 1949.

Kelso, J.A.S.: Motor control mechanisms underlying human movement reproduction. J. Exp. Psychol., 3:529, 1977.

Kelso, J.A.S., and Norman, P.E.: Motor schema formation in children. Dev. Psychol., 14:153, 1978.

Knobloch, H., and Pasamanick, B.: Further observations on the behavioral development of Negro children. J. Genet. Psychol., 83:137, 1953.

Laszo, J.I., and Bairstow, P.J.: Accuracy of movement, peripheral feedback and reference copy. J. Motor Behav., 3:241, 1971.

Malina, R.M.: Growth, Maturation, and Performance of Philadelphia Negro and White Elementary School Children. Ph.D. dissertation, University of Pennsylvania, Philadelphia, 1968.

McGraw, M.B.: Growth: A Study of Johnny and Jimmy. New York, Appleton-Century, 1935.

McGraw, M.B.: Behavior of the newborn infant and early neuro-muscular development. Res. Publ. Assoc. Nerv. Ment. Dis., 19:244, 1939.

Metheny, E.: The present status of strength testing for children of elementary school and preschool age. Res. Q., 12:115, 1941.

Minkowski, M.: Über frühzeitige Bewegungen, Reflexe, and muskulare Reaktionen beim menschlichen Fötus und ihre Beziehungen zum fötalen Nerven und Muskelsystem. Schweiz Med. Wochenschr., 52:721, 751, 1922.

Moxley, S.E.: Schema: The variability of practice hypothesis. J. Motor Behav., 11:65, 1979.

Pascual-Leone, J.A.: A mathematical model for the transition rule in Piaget's developmental stages. Acta Physiol., 32:301, 1970.

Peiper, A.: Die Schreitbewegungen der neugeborenen. Monatschr. Kinderheilkd., 45:444, 1929.

Rarick, G.L., and Dobbins, D.A.: Basic components in the motor performance of children six to nine years of age. Med. Sci. Sports, 7:105, 1975.

Rarick, G.L., Dobbins, D.A., and Broadhead, G.D.: The Motor Domain and Its Correlates in Educationally Handicapped Children. Englewood Cliffs, N.J., Prentice-Hall, 1976.

Rarick, G.L., and Smoll, F.L.: Stability of growth in strength and motor performance from childhood to adolescence. Hum. Biol., 39:295, 1967.

Rarick, G.L., and Thompson, J.J.: Roentgenographic measures of leg muscle size and ankle extensor strength of seven year old children. Res. Q., 27:321, 1956.

Reynolds, E.L.: Differential tissue growth in the leg during childhood. Child Dev., 15:181, 1944.

Schmidt, R.A.: A schema theory of discrete motor skill learning. Psychol. Rev. 82:225, 1975.

Schmidt, R.A.: Past and future issues in motor programming. Res. Q. Exer. Sport, 51:122, 1980.

Schneirla, T.C.: Behavioral development and comparative physiology. Q. Rev. Biol. 41:283, 1966.

Shirley, M.M.: The First Two Years: A Study of Twenty-Five Babies. Vol. 1. Postural and Locomotor Development. Minneapolis, University of Minnesota Press, 1933.

Stetson, R.H., and McDill, J.A.: Mechanisms of the different types of movement. Psychol. Monogr., 32:18, 1923.

Stuart, H.C., and Dwinell, P.H.: The growth of bone, muscle, and overlying tissue in children 6 to 10 years of age as revealed by roentgenograms of the leg area. Child Dev., 13:195, 1942.

Thomas, J.R.: Acquisition of motor skills: Information processing differences between children and adults. Res. Q. Exer. Sport, 51:158, 1980.

Todor, J.I.: Developmental differences in motor task integration: A test of Pascual-Leone's theory of construct operators. J. Exp. Child Psychol., 28:314, 1979.

Walker, R.N.: Body build and behavior in young children: 1. Body build and nursery school teachers' ratings. Mongr. Soc. Res. Child Dev., 27, 3:1, 1962.

Wellman, B.L.:Motor achievements of preschool children. Child. Educ., 13:311, 1937.

Wilde, M.R.: The behavior of throwing and some observations concerning its course of development in children. Res. Q., 9:20, 1938.

Williams, J.R., and Scott, R.B.: Growth and development of Negro infants IV. Motor development and its relationship to child rearing practices in two groups of Negro infants. Child. Dev., 24:103, 1953.

CHAPTER FIVE

Mechanical and Muscular Human Function

Glynn A. Leyshon

The human body is a machine of wondrous complexity capable of strong and violent movements or delicate and precise movements. This machine is made up of slightly more than 200 bones to which are attached better than 600 muscles. The latter produce movement under the control of the brain, whose complexities continue to defy understanding even after centuries of study. To properly appreciate the smooth and integrated functioning taken for granted in the body, let one aspect malfunction; the interdependence then becomes apparent. Suppose, for example, you suffer a mild but not uncommon condition known as jumper's knee or chondromalacia. The articulation (joint) between the thigh bone (femur) and shin bone (tibia) will malfunction. This will cause a limp, which causes muscles to contract differently; which in turn causes the stride to change; which affects the fashion the foot strikes the ground; and which in turn may cause other problems in the good leg or even the back.

To fully appreciate the movement of the human body, one must dissect it—if not literally, then figuratively. One needs to know the major skeletal parts, the major muscle groups, which nerves do what, and how the blood supply plays its role. In addition, an understanding of the heart and lungs and their role in movement is essential. Since no one part functions in isolation or apart from the others, all parts should be studied in their integrated roles; however, there is a critical point in the degree of the detail of all the systems beyond which lies only confusion. It is wise, therefore, to limit oneself to studying regions of the body, or segments, and linking them together later.

In studying any region or segment as it concerns movement, one looks at bone, muscle, nerve, and blood supply. No actual line of demarcation exists between segments, so it is necessary to keep in mind that the segments are a study convenience only.

PRINCIPLES AND TERMINOLOGY OF HUMAN MOVEMENTS

Prior to study of the human body as it functions one should have an understanding of certain basic anatomical principles and terminology.

Anatomical Position. In all references to the body it is assumed that the body is standing erect with palms facing forward (Fig. 5–1).

Terms of Direction. From the anatomical position, directions for the location of muscles, bones, etc., are given as follows:

  medial: structures near the midline of the body or of the segment
  lateral: structures away from the midline

Dr. Leyshon is from The University of Western Ontario, London.

143

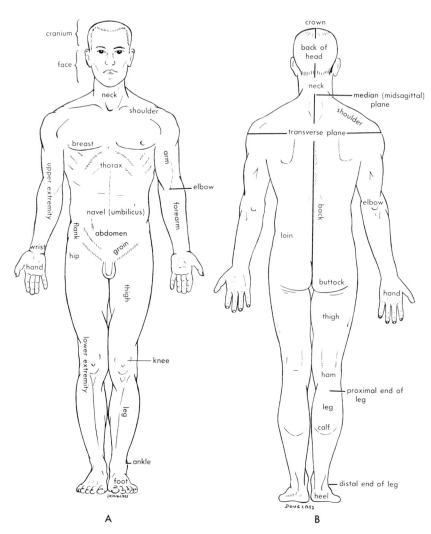

Fig. 5–1. Human figure in the anatomical position. A, Anterior view; B, posterior view. (Crouch, J.E.: Functional Human Anatomy. 3rd Edition. Philadelphia, Lea & Febiger, 1979)

superior: toward the head
inferior: toward the feet
anterior: to the front
posterior: to the rear
proximal: near the center of the body
distal: away from the center of the body

Reference Planes. In dissection, certain viewpoints are necessary to comprehend the relationship of various structures. Thus, for example, a limb may be cut through to show the relationship of the superficial muscles to the deep.

Sagittal plane: any plane parallel to the median plane

Frontal: a plane at right angles to the median plane

Transverse: a plane at right angles to both sagittal and frontal planes. Also called the horizontal plane.

Movements. While movements are varied and complex, they are basically some form or some combination of the following. The terms are related to the body in the anatomical position.

Flexion: a decrease in the angle between two bones, e.g., bend the elbow

Extension: an increase in the angle between two bones, e.g., straighten the elbow

Abduction: movement away from central axis, e.g., lift arm laterally

Adduction: movement toward central axis, e.g., returning arm to the side

Rotation: movement around a long axis—lateral or medial rotation

Circumduction: an action including all of the above, as when the arm is swung in a full circle

Supination: palms turned forward

Pronation: the opposite of the above, i.e., palms facing backward

Inversion: rotation of the foot to turn the sole inward

Eversion: rotation of the foot to turn the sole outward

Muscle Fibers. Muscles, which constitute approximately one half of the body, are arranged in bundles of fibers. These fiber bundles, called fasciculi (singular, fasciculus), are arranged in various ways to afford maximum efficiency. In some muscles they are parallel; in others they converge to a center line, and in yet others they are arranged to lie in several different directions. Since the fibers in the muscles resemble the forms in a feather, the word "penniform" is used to describe them (Fig. 5–2).

The reason for the various arrangements of fibers is to provide a maximum amount of force or direction with a minimum amount of volume. Tendons add necessary area for attachment of fibers, since bone itself would not provide half the surface area necessary. The fibers may insert into a central tendon running through the length of the muscle, or they may terminate in a tendon.

Attachments. Attachments of muscles are described on the basis of which end is stationary and which movable. The origin of a muscle is the stationary attachment, while the more mobile end is the insertion. In the biceps, for example, the origin is the end closer to the shoulder, and the insertion is the end closer to the elbow. It should be noted that this naming is arbitrary. If one is hanging suspended from a bar and pulls himself upward as in a chinning exercise, the shoulder end of the biceps becomes the mobile portion, and the fixed attachment is now the elbow. This does not, however, change the accepted nomenclature of origin and insertion.

Names of Muscles. Muscles are named according to their shape, size, function, situation, direction, structure, or attachment. The following list illustrates this:

Shape: trapezius—shaped like a trapezoid

Size: gluteus minimus—the smallest gluteal muscle

Function: pronator teres—the round muscle causing pronation

Situation: pectoralis—the muscle of the breast

Direction: levator scapulae—the muscle that lifts the scapula

Structure: triceps—a muscle with three heads or origins

Attachment: sternocleidomastoideus—the muscle attached to the breast bone (sternum) and clavicle (cleido) and to the mastoid process

Nervous Stimulation. Nerves to the muscles contain motor (activating) and sensory (feeling) fibers in equal proportions. Each bundle of muscle fibers is supplied by a small branch from the main nerve. The branch ends in a motor end plate on the surface of each muscle cell. In some muscles like the buttocks (gluteus maximus) there may be 200 muscle cells in a group. In others such as the fine muscles that

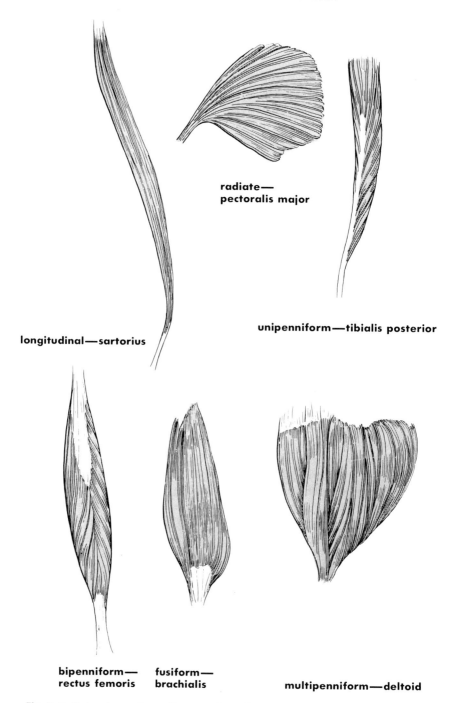

radiate—
pectoralis major

unipenniform—tibialis posterior

longitudinal—sartorius

bipenniform—   fusiform—
rectus femoris   brachialis

multipenniform—deltoid

Fig. 5–2. Various types of penniform muscles. (Crouch, J.E.: Functional Human Anatomy. 3rd Edition. Philadelphia, Lea & Febiger, 1979)

move the eye, there may be as few as five. The nerve cell, its axon or arm, and its group of muscle cells form a motor unit.

The all-or-none law indicates that once a group of muscle cells is stimulated it must contract fully or not at all. Each motor unit obeys this law. Thus the activity of the whole muscle is geared by the number, size, and power of its stimulated units. If a small number of units are stimulated, only a weak contraction is possible; if a large number, a strong contraction results. In holding an egg, one needs to exert enough force to keep from dropping it, but not enough to crush it. This means that only a very few groups of muscle cells are operating, but they are contracting to their maximum. Control is more precise in muscles in which there are fewer fibers to each motor unit.

By working in relays or shifts, motor units in a muscle can give continuous activity without fatigue during light work. As work gets heavier, more motor units are called into action simultaneously until, for a maximum effort, all are called into play at once. Then the muscle fatigues very quickly.

The sensory nerve fibers have special endings called muscle spindles situated near the tendon of muscle. These sensory endings receive signals that are sent *out* of the muscle and to the brain. These signals initiate reflexes that coordinate and control muscular activity. The brain, for example, must know how much tension exists in a muscle or how many degrees of flexion have taken place in a joint to gauge how much more or how much less effort must be made by the muscles involved.

The sensory nerves providing the feedback are termed *afferent*, while the motor nerves providing stimulation are termed *efferent*.

Blood Supply. The skeletal muscles are the most richly supplied of all tissues. Since the muscles burn the calories necessary for movement it is only fitting that they receive an ample food supply. The major arteries and nerves travel together in a neurovascular bundle (Fig. 5–3), and thus each group of muscle fibers is assured of both a blood and nerve supply.

At each joint in a limb and at some other sites there are anastomoses. These represent alternate routes for the blood should major arteries become plugged or damaged. At the knee, for example, there are several alternate pathways leading from the thigh to the ankle.

The veins returning blood to the heart travel with the arteries deep within the muscle. They appear on the surface of the body as well, but without the accompanying arteries.

Contractions. Muscles shorten their fibers to cause movement in the limbs. When this occurs the insertion is brought closer to the origin (in most cases). There are, however, several types of contraction (Fig. 5–4). The most common type of contraction is *isotonic*, and it is the type typical of most movements. Muscle fibers are drawn together because of nervous stimulation; the insertion is pulled closer to the origin; and the limb moves. Such is the process that occurs over and over again in the quadriceps and hamstrings, for example, in the act of walking. An isotonic contraction may be of two types—*concentric* and *eccentric*. The concentric contraction has already been described; the eccentric contraction is somewhat different. Lifting a heavy weight such as a suitcase uses a concentric contraction. Putting the suitcase down carefully requires an eccentric contraction of the same muscles. An eccentric contraction is one in which a muscle is slowly lengthened rather than shortened. The principle is used in weight training to put maximum load on a muscle group by having the lifter slowly lower a greater weight than he can lift with a concentric contraction.

In some cases a muscle contracts, but no movement takes place. Such a contraction is *isometric*. This state may occur because an object cannot be moved. In some instances movement may not be possible in the limb. Muscles cannot push; they can only pull. A person in a cast, for example, will be asked to contract the muscles

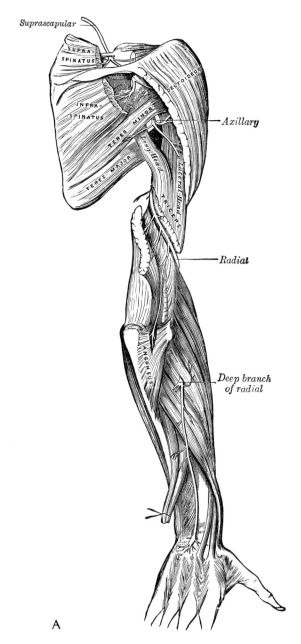

Fig. 5–3. Nerves and arteries of the arm. *A,* Posterior view: Supracapsular, axillary, and radial nerves. *B,* Posterior view, showing surface markings for bones, arteries, and nerves. *C,* Cross section through forearm. (Goss, C.M., Editor: Gray's Anatomy of the Human Body. 29th Edition. Philadelphia, Lea & Febiger, 1973)

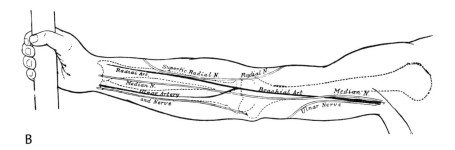

B

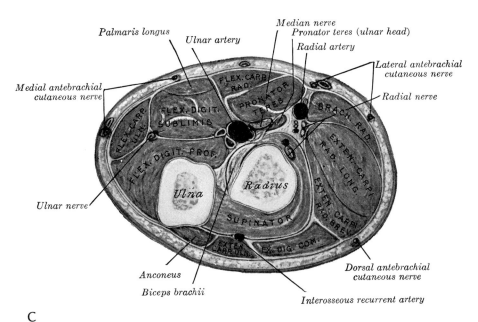

C

Fig. 5–3 (continued).

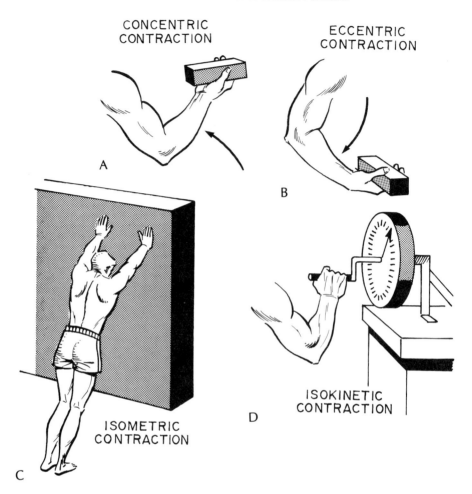

CONCENTRIC
CONTRACTION

ECCENTRIC
CONTRACTION

A

B

ISOMETRIC
CONTRACTION

C

ISOKINETIC
CONTRACTION

D

Fig. 5–4. Four different types of muscular contraction. *A*, concentric; *B*, eccentric; *C*, isometric; *D*, isokinetic.

even though he cannot move his leg or arm. The isometric contraction helps maintain strength in the muscle despite the lack of movement.

The final type of contraction is *isokinetic*. It is a laboratory-contrived type of contraction because it can be achieved only with a special machine, an isokinetic exerciser. In an isokinetic contraction the speed of movement of the limb is controlled throughout its range of motion. When a limb moves under normal circumstances, as when the elbow is flexed, the first part of the movement is more difficult than the latter. Anyone who has performed the exercise known as a curl with a dumbbell can attest that the first few degrees of flexion are much harder to achieve than the last few. Thus in an isotonic concentric contraction, the greatest load is placed on the muscle at the beginning of the movement. An isokinetic contraction seeks to retain the same degree of resistance or load at any point in the movement, so that the last few degrees of flexion are just as difficult as the first few.

Lever System. The muscles move limbs according to a lever system that is based on a principle that muscles cannot push, they can only pull. Thus in any work or movement performed the muscle pulls (exerts force or power on) a bone (lever), which revolves around a joint (fulcrum); the weight (resistance or load) is at some point distal to the muscle.

There are three types of levers (Fig. 5–5), only two of which appear in any significant number in the body: Levers of class 2 are very rare; most of the levers are class 1 or class 3. In a class 1 lever the fulcrum is between the pull and the weight. The force applied is near the fulcrum and the weight is not far from the fulcrum; power is lost, but speed is gained.

In a lever of class 2 the weight is between the fulcrum and the pull. These levers have great mechanical advantage (a wheelbarrow is a good example), but they are often slow. The fact that muscle insertions are usually close to the joints they move precludes most muscles from acting in a second-class lever, i.e., with the power acting far from the fulcrum.

In a lever of class 3 the pull is between the fulcrum and the weight. These are the most common levers in the body. The muscle in a class 3 lever operates at a mechanical disadvantage, but it is a lever of speed. The muscle is inserted close to the point (fulcrum) about which it moves; a rapid movement is produced even with little shortening of the muscle fibers.

Muscle Roles. Muscles usually act in concert with others in a group. In fact, the body is established with the muscles grouped in mutually antagonistic sets. This means that for every flexor there is an extensor, for every abductor an adductor, etc., although this is not strictly true—there seldom being exactly three extensors opposing three flexors. It is only sensible that one should be able to return a limb from a flexed state to an extended one and vice versa.

Muscles are categorized as prime movers or agonists, antagonists or opposite movers, synergists or coordinators, and fixators.

Prime movers or agonists are primarily responsible for a particular movement. In flexion of the elbow the prime movers are the biceps and brachialis.

Antagonists act in opposition to the prime movers. In flexion of the elbow the antagonist is the triceps, used to extend the elbow.

Synergists are used to prevent any unwanted movement from occurring and to make fine adjustments necessary for accuracy and precision. In flexion of the elbow the forearm might pronate (turn over) were it not for the synergistic action of certain muscles to prevent it.

Fixators have nothing to do directly with the action but "fix" the body or the limb. In flexion of the elbow it is often necessary to fix the shoulder joint to steady the elbow. Thus the shoulder muscles contribute to the working of the elbow flexors by holding the shoulder solid and providing a base against which the elbow flexors might work.

BASIC STRUCTURE OF THE UPPER LIMB

The human machine is capable of movement only because of the muscles acting on the articulated (jointed) skeleton. The most important body segments concerned with locomotion are obviously the arms and legs.

The study of the arm commences at the shoulder. The clavicle (collar bone) and scapula (shoulder blade), comprising the shoulder girdle, and humerus (bone of the upper arm), all function in movements at the shoulder. The attachments of ligaments (Fig. 5–6) and fascia as well as muscles insure that the arm is held in place.

The shoulder joint is classified as a ball-and-socket joint, but the socket, or glenoid fossa, of the scapula is very shallow (Fig. 5–7). There are no ligaments of any significance attaching the humerus to the scapula; the main support of the joint comes from a capsule of heavy fascia that encloses both the head of the humerus and the perimeter of the socket. While the shoulder has lost most of its stability by virtue of the very shallow glenoid fossa, it has gained great mobility. Study of the shoulder

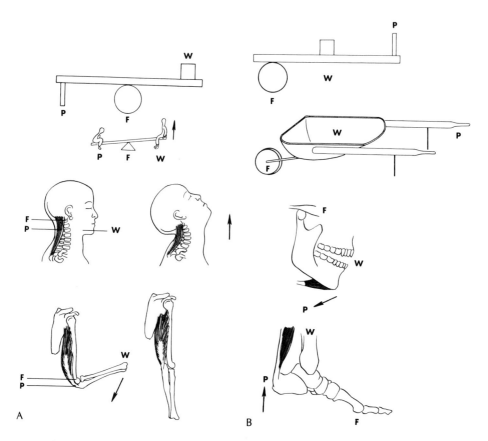

Fig. 5–5. The different classes of levers and examples of how they are represented in the body. *A,* class 1; *B,* class 2; *C,* class 3. F, Fulcrum; P, pull or force; W, weight or resistance. (Crouch, J.E.: Functional Human Antomy. 3rd Edition. Philadelphia, Lea & Febiger, 1979)

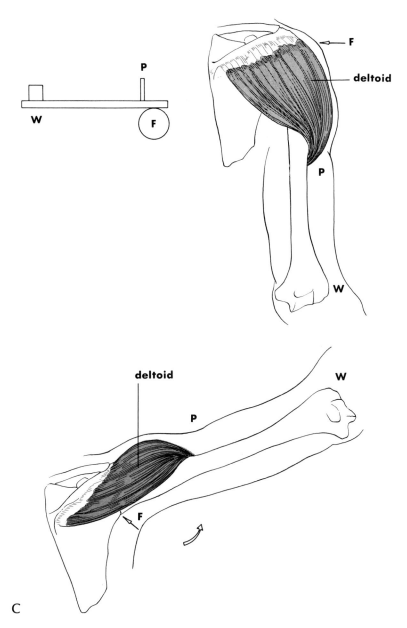

C

Fig. 5–5 (continued).

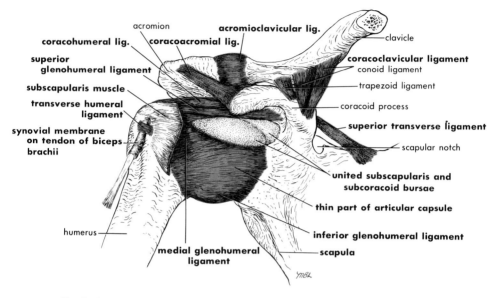

Fig. 5–6. Ligaments and capsule of the shoulder. (Crouch, J.E.: Functional Human Anatomy. 3rd Edition. Philadelphia, Lea & Febiger, 1979)

joint and the hip joint will contrast the effects of a shallow socket (the shoulder) and a deep socket (the hip).

The shoulder joint, like all synovial joints in the body, is enclosed in a capsule lined with a special membrane called a synovial membrane. This membrane releases a thin fluid called synovia, or synovial fluid, that lubricates the joint much as oil lubricates moving parts in a machine. Also, the portion of the humerus and the glenoid fossa that articulate (come into contact) are coated with a very thin layer of cartilage, called hyaline cartilage, designed to protect the bony surfaces from the effects of friction.

Movement at the Shoulder Joint

The mobility at the shoulder is considerable. Swinging the arm in a circle is ample illustration. The movement forward is *flexion* of the shoulder, while movement backward is *extension*. Raising the arm laterally or sideways in *abduction,* and returning it to the body is *adduction*. Furthermore, the arm may be rotated on its long axis. Turning the thumb inward with elbow extended is *medial rotation;* turning it outward is *lateral rotation.*In swinging the arm in a wide circle, all of these movements are utilized; the combination of flexion, medial rotation, abduction, lateral rotation, and extension is *circumduction.*

Musculature of the Shoulder

The muscles that cause these movements are many, but the prime mover for all shoulder action is the deltoid (Fig. 5–8A). It is a large muscle, and coarse (making it suitable for injections), and it has three somewhat distinct sets of fibers (i.e., it is multipennate). These three sets of fibers allow it three distinct movements: (1) anterior fibers provide flexion; (2) posterior fibers provide extension; and (3) middle fibers provide abduction.

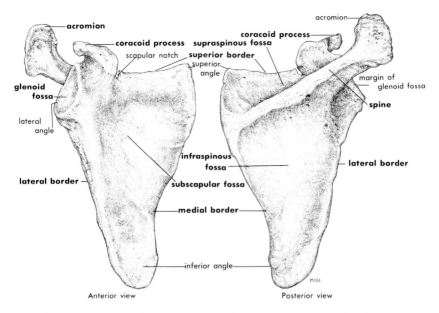

Fig. 5–7. Right scapula. (Crouch, J.E.: Functional Human Anatomy. 3rd Edition. Philadelphia, Lea & Febiger, 1979)

The origin of the deltoid is the clavicle, acromion, and spine of the scapula. The insertion of the deltoid is the deltoid tuberosity of the humerus.

Other muscles, of course, contribute to movement at the shoulder. Among the contributing muscles are the *rotator cuff* group. These muscles act as synergists (these are the muscles that prevent noncontributory movements) and have a special function. They act as dynamic ligaments to give the relatively weak shoulder joint support, which in other joints is furnished by the strong ligaments present. In addition, they help movement by acting as synergists (coordinators). A lone person attempting to put a ladder into a vertical position has difficulty. As he attempts to lift one end higher, the opposite end moves away. An assistant, standing on the end of the ladder, can hold it down, allowing the lifter to walk toward the assistant under the ladder and push it upward rung by rung as he advances. The rotator cuff muscles act in the manner of the assistant holding the end of the ladder; they hold the humerus in the glenoid fossa while the deltoid lifts the humerus. Were they not to do this job, the deltoid could pull the humerus straight up before the arm could be abducted.

It should be noted that adduction of the arm at the shoulder does not always involve the muscles antagonistic to the deltoid. Standing in anatomical position, one can abduct the arm and then simply relax the deltoid. Gravity will return the arm, or adduct it, to the side of the body. The antagonists (principally the pectoralis major and the latissimus dorsi) are used only when adduction is resisted. A gymnast performing the "iron cross" on the still rings must use the adductors to maintain his position.

Since the four rotator cuff muscles are beneath (or deep to) the deltoid, they must be relatively small (Fig. 5–8). All originate on the scapula and insert on the head of the humerus. The four muscles are the supraspinatus (above or superior to the spine of the scapula); infraspinatus (below or inferior to the spine of the scapula); teres

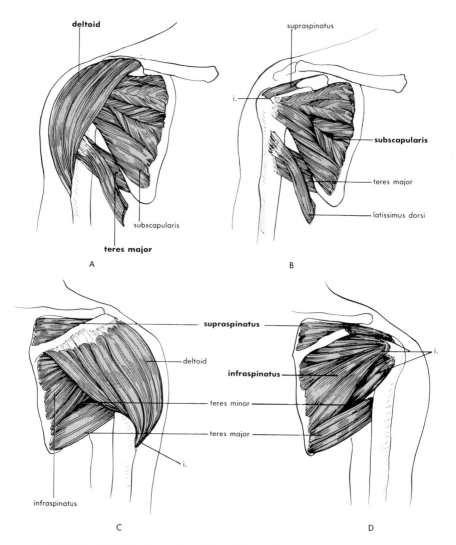

Fig. 5–8. The deltoid and muscles of the rotator cuff. *A* and *B,* Anterior view, *C* and *D,* posterior view. (Crouch, J.E.: Functional Human Anatomy. 3rd Edition. Philadelphia, Lea & Febiger, 1979)

minor (a round muscle and smaller than the teres major); and subscapularis (beneath the scapula).

Taking the first letter from each muscle provides a mnemonic, S I T S. In addition to their function in assisting the deltoid, the rotator cuff muscles also provide medial and lateral rotation (i.e., on the long axis of the humerus).

Movement of the Scapula

Since the scapula is quite mobile, it must have opposing sets of muscles to move it and to return it to its original position. The following movements are those the scapula can assume:

1. Protraction. The scapula is drawn forward and around the rib cage as when reaching with the right hand to grasp the left shoulder.
2. Retraction. The scapula is returned from the above position or drawn back even farther as when standing at military attention.
3. Elevation. The scapula is raised as when hunching the shoulders.
4. Depression. The scapula is depressed or pulled downward as when trying to close an overfilled suitcase.

Almost all of the motions of the arm and shoulder entail the scapula in one of the above ways or in a combination thereof. Reaching upward for a book on a high shelf, for example, requires protraction and elevation of the scapula. These movements place the glenoid fossa facing the area of activity, thus permitting the arm and hand to be used to best advantage.

Muscles Acting on the Scapula

In addition to the muscles of the rotator cuff and the deltoid, 11 other muscles are attached to the scapula:

Coracobrachialis. The muscle arises from the coracoid process and inserts to the shaft of the humerus. This muscle assists the deltoid in flexion of the arm.

Levator Scapulae. This muscle originates on the transverse processes of the first four cervical (neck) vertebrae and inserts on the medial border of the scapula. It assists in "hunching" the shoulder.

Long Head of the Biceps Brachii. The muscle originates on a tubercle superior to the glenoid fossa and inserts on a radial tuberosity of the radius (forearm). It assists in flexion of the arm at the shoulder.

Long Head of the Triceps Brachii. Like the long head of the biceps, this muscle originates on a tubercle; however, this tubercle is on the inferior aspect of the glenoid fossa. It inserts into the olecranon. It assists in extension of the arm at the shoulder.

Pectoralis Minor. This muscle originates on the chest wall and inserts onto the coracoid process. It helps depress the scapula as well as protract it.

Rhomboideus Major. This muscle originates on the spines of thoracic vertebrae and inserts onto the medial border of the scapula. It retracts the scapula or "squares" the shoulders.

Rhomboideus Minor. It has the same general origins and insertions as the major except it is superior to the major. It retracts the scapula.

Serratus Anterior. This muscle arises from the first eight or nine ribs and then reaches posteriorly under the scapula and the subscapularis to insert on the medial border deep to the rhomboids. It is a powerful protractor of the scapula and is known as the fencer's muscle.

Short Head of the Biceps Brachii. Like the pectoralis minor and the coracobrachialis, the short head of the biceps originates on the coracoid process. It shares the insertion of the long biceps. It also helps flex the shoulder and provides some adduction.

Teres Major. Arising from the inferior angle and the lateral border of the scapula (Fig. 5–8, A and C), the teres major inserts onto the humerus at the medial lip of the bicipital groove. It acts to adduct the humerus.

Trapezius. This muscle of the back is shaped like a trapezoid, hence its name. It attaches to the clavicle, acromion, and spine of the scapula, but it originates on the spinous processes of the seventh cervical and all twelve thoracic vertebrae as well as the ligament of the neck, the ligamentum nuchae. Like the deltoid the trapezius has three sets of fibers and each provides a different function. The upper fibers elevate the scapula, the middle retract, and the lower third depress the scapula.

Muscles of the Brachium

The brachium or arm is that area of the upper extremity from shoulder to elbow. It is divided into anterior and posterior compartments by tough fascia (septa) (Fig. 5–9). This division is based on the innervation as well as on the septa (walls) between the two. The anterior compartment muscles are innervated by the musculocutaneous nerve and the posterior by the radial nerve.

Muscles of the Anterior Compartment

The anterior compartment is comprised of the biceps (long and short heads), the coracobrachialis, and the brachialis. The short head of the biceps and the coraco-brachialis arise jointly from the coracoid process and cross the·shoulder. The coracobrachialis runs from the coracoid process to a point midway down the humerus on the medial side; the biceps inserts on the tuberosity of the radius. The brachialis originates on the lower third of the humerus and inserts on the tuberosity of the ulna.

The muscles of the anterior compartment provide mainly flexion of the elbow, as well as flexion of the shoulder. The workhorse is the brachialis, which may come into play only when the load being moved is very heavy.

The two heads of the biceps, having a common point of insertion on the radial tuberosity, also have a second function, to provide additional power for supination. Changing the hand from the normal anatomical position, i.e., thumb lateral, palm

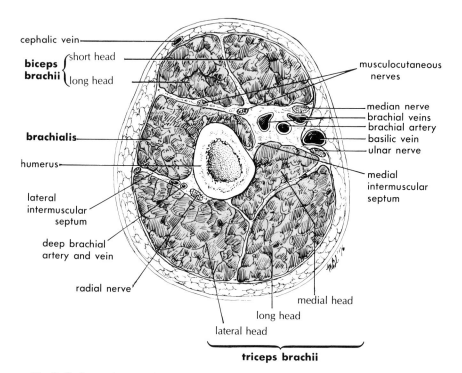

Fig. 5–9. Compartments of the left arm. Tough fascia (septa) separates the anterior from the posterior compartment. The coracobrachialis is not shown because the section was made below the point on the humerus where the short coracobrachialis inserts. (Crouch, J.E.: Functional Human Anatomy. 3rd Edition. Philadelphia, Lea & Febiger, 1979)

forward, to a position with the thumb touching the thigh, i.e., thumb medial, is *pronation;* returning the hand to the normal anatomical position is *supination.* When resistance is met during supination, as when one turns a balky doorknob or opens a screw-top jar, additional power is supplied by the biceps.

Muscles of the Posterior Compartment

The posterior compartment is comprised of the three heads of the triceps muscle—the long, lateral, and medial. They have different origins but a common insertion on the olecranon. The principal action of the triceps is extension of the elbow, although the long head crosses the shoulder joint and extends the shoulder as well.

The long head of the triceps arises from the infraglenoid tuberosity of the scapula; the lateral head originates about one third of the way down the humerus; and the deep (medial) head originates slightly lower and deep to the other two heads.

The Elbow

The elbow is the joint between the arm and the forearm, consisting of articulations between the humerus and the radius and ulna (Fig. 5–10). The articulations are covered with hyaline cartilage, and the joint is encased in a synovial capsule. The elbow joint has a hinge action; it may flex and extend. No other action is possible at the elbow joint because of the tight closure between the humerus and the ulna. The fitting of the proximal end of the ulna on the humerus is shaped much like the open jaws of a wrench. The articulation between the radius and humerus is minimal, but the head of the radius is solidly attached to the ulna (Fig. 5–10).

A second movement takes place in this region, although it is not of the elbow joint. It occurs at the radioulnar joint during pronation and supination. In these movements the ulna stays relatively stable while the radius rolls over across the ulna.

The ligaments of the elbow joint are strong, especially laterally where the articulation with the radius is so shallow. The ligaments are found only on the medial and lateral aspects and are called collateral ligaments. "Collateral" is a general term applied to the ligaments of hinge joints such as the elbow and knee. The ligaments of the elbow are the collateral radial and collateral ulnar ligaments; the ligament joining the head of the radius to the ulna is the annular (circular) ligament.

Muscles of the Forearm

The muscles of the forearm are divided into anterior and posterior compartments. The muscles of the anterior compartment are innervated by the median nerve, while those of the posterior compartment are stimulated by the radial nerve. The muscles in both groups are further subdivided into superficial and deep. Some of both groups are two-joint or multijoint muscles; that is, they originate above the elbow joint on the humerus and insert distal to the wrist joint. In such cases the muscles can act upon both joints.

The muscles of the anterior compartment can be termed (with certain exceptions) the flexor group, while those of the posterior compartment can be called the extensor group.

Muscles of the Anterior Compartment

The superficial muscles of the anterior compartment of the forearm include the pronator teres, flexor carpi ulnaris, flexor carpi radialis, flexor digitorum superficialis, and palmaris longus (Fig. 5–11A).

Actions of the Superficial Muscles. The actions of the superficial muscles are diverse. The major function is flexion of the hand and fingers; however, the pronator teres serves to pronate the wrist. In addition, since the muscles originate above the elbow, they contribute to flexion of the elbow as well.

The principal wrist flexors are the two carpi (wrist) muscles, one on the radial side

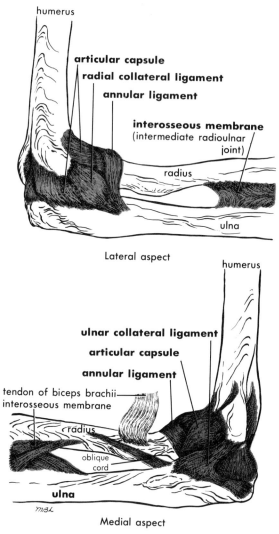

humerus

articular capsule

radial collateral ligament

annular ligament

interosseous membrane
(intermediate radioulnar
joint)

radius

ulna

Lateral aspect

humerus

ulnar collateral ligament

articular capsule

annular ligament

tendon of biceps brachii

interosseous membrane

radius

oblique
cord

ulna

Medial aspect

Fig. 5–10. Right elbow joint. (Crouch, J.E.: Functional Human Anatomy. 3rd Edition. Philadelphia, Lea & Febiger, 1979)

and one on the ulnar side. The palmaris longus is inserted into a broad sheet of fascia covering the palm, and it would seem to be an important wrist flexor also; however, not only is the muscle very weak, it is absent altogether in some people. It is therefore not an important muscle.

The flexor digitorum superficialis is an important muscle of the hand. As its name implies, it flexes the digits. Since its major bulk is outside the hand, it is termed an extrinsic muscle of the hand. The principal characteristics of this group of muscles (i.e., the extrinsic muscles of the hand) is that they supply power and have long tendons (as opposed to the intrinsic group that provide precision of movement and have relatively short tendons).

Tendon Sheaths. Throughout the body there are muscles with the same characteristics as those of the flexor digitorum superficialis—long tendons. These tendons move with great frequency and can be likened to the transmission on a car. Like a transmission, they must be lubricated, and this function is carried out by the synovial sheaths that encase each tendon (or sometimes a set of tendons) much as a scabbard protects a sword. The inner lining of the sheath is similar to that in a synovial joint. The lining secretes synovial fluid so that the tendons sliding back and forth inside will not suffer from friction.

Occasionally athletes or laborers suffer from inflammation of the tendon. This condition, known as tendinitis, can prevent function for several days or longer. It occurs most often in the tendons associated with the ankle joint, but it also occurs in the tendons of the wrist.

Action of the Deep Muscles. The deep muscles of the anterior compartment are the flexor digitorum profundus, flexor pollicis longus, and pronator quadratus (Fig. 5–11B).

The flexor digitorum profundus (deep) is obviously a muscle similar to the superficialis. Both muscles run to the fingers (first, second, third, and fourth digits) and insert there. The profundus muscle inserts at the end of the finger or the distal phalanx, and its action is as its name suggests—flexion. The flexor pollicis (thumb) longus is analogous to the flexor digitorum but goes to the thumb. The pronator quadratus is the deepest of the group and is situated just above the wrist. Its function is to pronate the hand, i.e., turn it from a facing-forward position to a facing-backward position.

These extrinsic muscles of the hand provide power—power for gripping, which is essential. It is interesting that a champion weight lifter, lifting over 1000 pounds, relies on his fingers to grip the bar while his arms, shoulders, back, etc., do the lifting. The fingers must withstand the 1000-pound pressure first.

The Retinaculum. The tendons of the extrinsic muscles would have a tendency to "bowstring" during strong flexion were it not for the flexor and extensor retinacula. A retinaculum is a sheet of tough fascia found at the wrist (and ankle) that holds the tendons down to the bone beneath to keep them in place (Fig. 5–12).

Muscles of the Posterior Compartment

There are 12 muscles in the posterior compartment. Like the anterior group, they are subdivided into superficial (seven) and deep (five) muscles. If the principal function of the anterior compartment is flexion, then the opposite action, extension, is the major responsibility of the posterior compartment. There are, of course, other actions that the muscles of the posterior compartment supply. The seven superficial extensors are the brachioradialis, extensor carpi radialis longus, extensor carpi radialis brevis, extensor carpi ulnaris, extensor digitorum, extensor digiti minimi, and anconeus (Fig. 5–13A).

Action of the Superficial Muscles. The action of the brachioradialis is flexion. The muscle may be considered an oddity, since it seems to be in the wrong group or compartment. It does not cross the wrist joint so its flexing action is exerted on the elbow joint. All the remaining muscles are extensors of the elbow and wrist, and in the case of the extensor digitorum and extensor digit minimi, of the fingers.

To note the action of the brachioradialis, hold the hand and forearm as though you were about to use a tennis racquet. Press downward on your wrist with the opposite hand and resist this pressure. The brachioradialis will contract and show as a ridge along the surface of the radius.

The two extensor carpi radialis muscles lie medial to the brachioradialis. Taking the same position of the forearm as indicated above, cock or extend the wrist back fully, and the extensor carpi muscles will be seen to contract at the lateral aspect of the elbow joint. In individuals with well-developed muscles the extensor carpi radialis

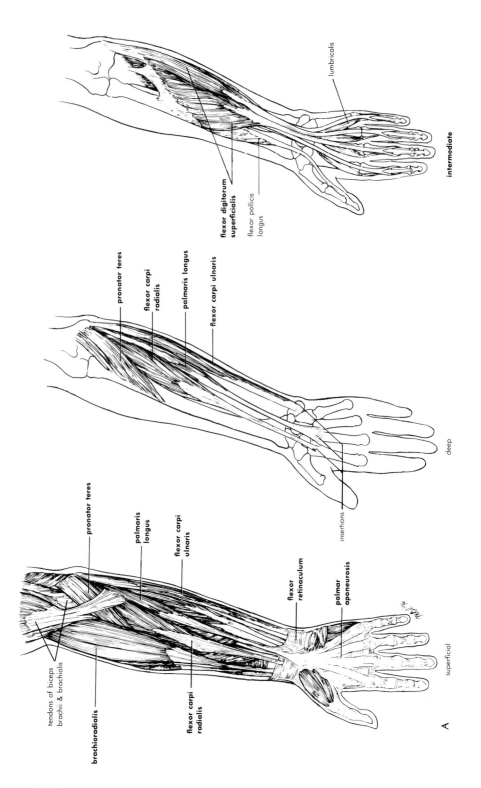

lumbricalis

flexor digitorum
superficialis

flexor pollicis
longus

intermediate

pronator teres

flexor carpi
radialis

palmaris longus

flexor carpi ulnaris

deep

insertions

pronator teres

palmaris
longus

flexor carpi
ulnaris

flexor
retinaculum

palmar
aponeurosis

tendons of biceps
brachii & brachialis

brachioradialis

flexor carpi
radialis

A

superficial

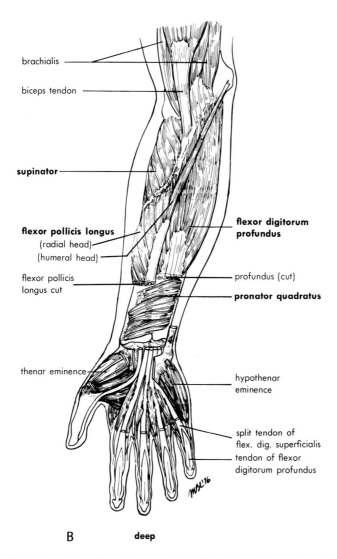

brachialis

biceps tendon

supinator

flexor pollicis longus
(radial head)
(humeral head)

flexor pollicis
longus cut

thenar eminence

**flexor digitorum
profundus**

profundus (cut)

pronator quadratus

hypothenar
eminence

split tendon of
flex. dig. superficialis

tendon of flexor
digitorum profundus

B   **deep**

Fig. 5–11. Origin and insertion of the superficial *(A)* and deep *(B)* muscles of the anterior compartment of the forearm. (Crouch, J.E.: Essential Human Anatomy. Philadelphia, Lea & Febiger, 1982)

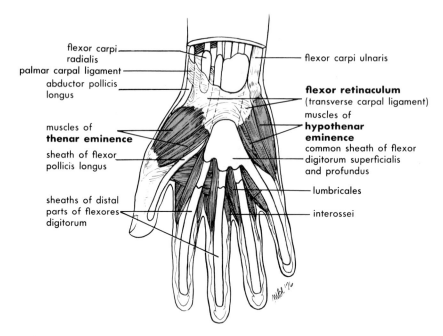

flexor carpi radialis

palmar carpal ligament

abductor pollicis longus

muscles of **thenar eminence**

sheath of flexor pollicis longus

sheaths of distal parts of flexores digitorum

flexor carpi ulnaris

flexor retinaculum (transverse carpal ligament)

muscles of **hypothenar eminence**

common sheath of flexor digitorum superficialis and profundus

lumbricales

interossei

Fig. 5–12. The attachment of the flexor retinaculum provides a roof over the carpal tunnel through which most of the tendons, nerves, and blood vessels travel. (Crouch, J.E.: Functional Human Anatomy. 3rd Edition. Philadelphia, Lea & Febiger, 1979)

longus will appear about the size of a golf ball under the skin when the wrist is extended. These extensor muscles are obviously important in gripping and in actions of the hand and wrist such as playing tennis or other racquet sports and hockey.

The extensor carpi ulnaris acts, as do the two extensor carpi radialis muscles, to extend the wrist. If one thinks of the wrist as a square, there is a muscle or muscles, two flexors and three extensors, attached at each of its four corners. If both ulnar muscles contract (the flexor carpi ulnaris and the extensor carpi ulnaris), a new movement is created—adduction. Similarly if the flexor carpi radialis and extensor carpi radialis longus and extensor carpi radialis brevis are contracted, abduction occurs. These two movements, abduction and adduction, provide the action in hammering or in throwing a javelin.

The extensor digitorum inserts into a special area of fascia covering the posterior surface of each finger. It is called the extensor expansion or hood. The most important action of the extensor digitorum is to extend the fingers at the knuckle or metacarpalphalangeal joint.

The extensor digiti minimi is simply a separate slip of muscle that sends a tendon to the fifth digit or little finger.

The deep muscles of the posterior compartment are the supinator, abductor pollicis longus, extensor pollicis longus, extensor pollicis brevis, and extensor indicis (Fig. 5–13B).

Actions of the Deep Muscles. The supinator takes its name from its action (Fig. 5–14A). It supinates the hand. To do so, it must wrap around the radius as it proceeds from its origin on the ulna to its insertion on the radius. If supination is resisted (e.g., in using a screwdriver), then the biceps brachii assists.

The three pollicis (thumb) muscles are sometimes termed "outcropping" muscles since they proceed downward toward the hand and then make a sharp turn over the

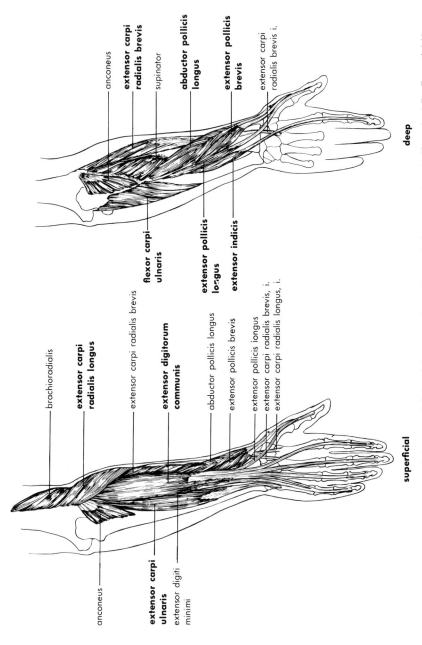

Fig. 5–13. Origin and insertion of the superficial and deep muscles of the posterior compartment. (Crouch, J.E.: Essential Human Anatomy. Philadelphia, Lea & Febiger, 1982)

deep

anconeus
extensor carpi radialis brevis
supinator
abductor pollicis longus
extensor pollicis brevis
extensor carpi radialis brevis i.
flexor carpi ulnaris
extensor pollicis longus
extensor indicis

superficial

brachioradialis
extensor carpi radialis longus
extensor carpi radialis brevis
extensor digitorum communis
abductor pollicis longus
extensor pollicis brevis
extensor pollicis longus
extensor carpi radialis brevis, i.
extensor carpi radialis longus, i.
anconeus
extensor carpi ulnaris
extensor digiti minimi

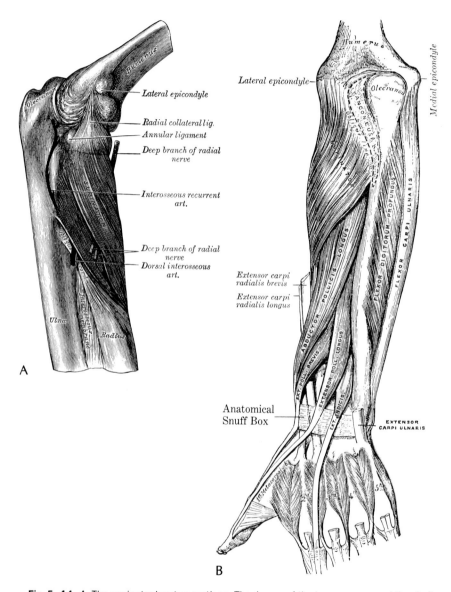

Fig. 5–14. *A,* The supinator has two portions: The deeper of the two wraps around the shaft of the radius from behind. *B,* The tendons of the three pollicis muscles form the anatomic snuffbox. (Goss, C.M., Editor: Gray's Anatomy of the Human Body. 29th Edition. Philadelphia, Lea & Febiger, 1973)

carpal bones to attach to the thumb. The reason for this is found in evolution. As man developed, his thumb moved from its original alignment beside the fingers (where it still remains in nearly every mammal, including the ape and monkey) to a new position that placed it at a right angle to the fingers. This gave man an opposable thumb and thus the ability to use tools. The tendons followed the thumb in its migration; hence they outcrop from the other muscles of the posterior compartment. The three pollicis muscles also combine to form a landmark called the anatomical snuffbox (Fig. 5–14B).

The extensor indicis is simply a second muscle going to the index finger.

The general action of the entire posterior compartment is extension, principally of the wrist. This action, paradoxically, is very important in gripping. To exert maximum grip pressure, one must not only flex the fingers but must cock back (extend) the wrist. Extending the wrist slightly allows the finger flexors to contract fully. (This can be tested by the following experiment: Flex the wrist as far as possible and clench the fingers. Then extend the wrist as far as possible and flex the fingers. Note the difference in the pressure exerted.)

Muscles of the Wrist and Hand

The bones of the wrist and hand are arranged to permit a wide variety of movements (Fig. 5–15). There are eight carpal (wrist) bones arranged roughly in two rows. They are held one to another by a web of interosseous ligaments that does, however, allow them some degree of movement. Only two of these bones, the scaphoid and lunate, articulate with the radius. That articulation represents the wrist joint proper. There is no bony articulation with the carpals and the ulna.

The five metacarpals form the palm of the hand. They have a limited degree of movement and serve as the origin of some of the intrinsic muscles of the hand.

The phalanges are highly mobile; there are three to each digit except the thumb, which has only two, a total of 14. The joint between two phalanges is the interphalangeal joint (often referred to as the IP joint), while the joint between the carpal bone and the proximal phalanx is the metacarpophalangeal joint (or the MP joint).

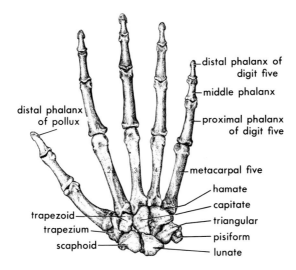

distal phalanx of digit five
middle phalanx
distal phalanx of pollux
proximal phalanx of digit five
metacarpal five
hamate
capitate
trapezoid
triangular
trapezium
pisiform
scaphoid
lunate

Fig. 5–15. Right wrist and hand, posterior view. (Crouch, J.E.: Functional Human Anatomy. 3rd Edition. Philadelphia, Lea & Febiger, 1979)

The Intrinsic Muscles of the Hand

The muscles of the hand proper are the precision muscles. They are divided into groups: the lumbricals, palmar interossei, dorsal interossei, muscles of the thenar eminence, adductor pollicis, and muscles of the hypothenar eminence.

Action of the Intrinsic Muscles. The four *lumbricals* (worm-like) are unique in that they originate from the tendons of the flexor digitorum profundus rather than from a bony structure (Fig. 5–16A). The insertion is also different from normal. Like several intrinsic muscles of the hand, the lumbricals insert into the extensor expansion and thereby are able to produce two actions—flexion of the metacarpophalangeal joint and extension of the interphalangeal joint. These actions are used in writing.

The *dorsal and palmar interossei* originate on the inner-facing surface of the metacarpal bones and insert into the extensor expansion. Their actions are the same as the lumbricals (i.e., flexion of the MP joint and extension of the IP joint). In addition, the interossei can abduct and adduct the fingers. The dorsal (muscles) abduct (DAB is a mnemonic for the action) and the palmar adduct (PAD is the mnemonic here).

There are four dorsal and three palmar interossei muscles (Fig. 5–16 B and C). When abduction and adduction of the fingers take place, the movement is relative to a line down the length of the middle digit. Taking the fingers away from the midline or spreading them is abduction and returning them is adduction. The middle finger (third digit) may be abducted from this imaginary midline by its two abductors. Note that the third digit has no adductors.

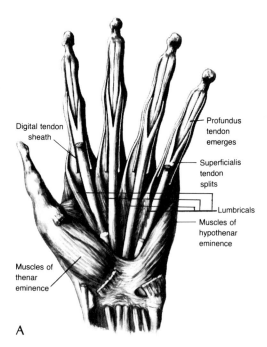

Digital tendon sheath

Profundus tendon emerges

Superficialis tendon splits

Lumbricals

Muscles of hypothenar eminence

Muscles of thenar eminence

A

Fig. 5–16. *A,* Lumbricals, all of which insert from the radial side. (Gardner, W.D., and Osburn, W.A.: Structure of the Human Body. 2nd Edition. Philadelphia, Saunders, 1973) *B,* and *C,* Dorsal interossei and palmar interossei. (*B* from Crouch, J.E.: Functional Human Anatomy. 3rd Edition. Philadelphia, Lea & Febiger, 1979; *C* from Hollinshead, W.H., and Jenkins, D.B.: Functional Anatomy of the Limbs and Back. Philadelphia, Saunders, 1981.)

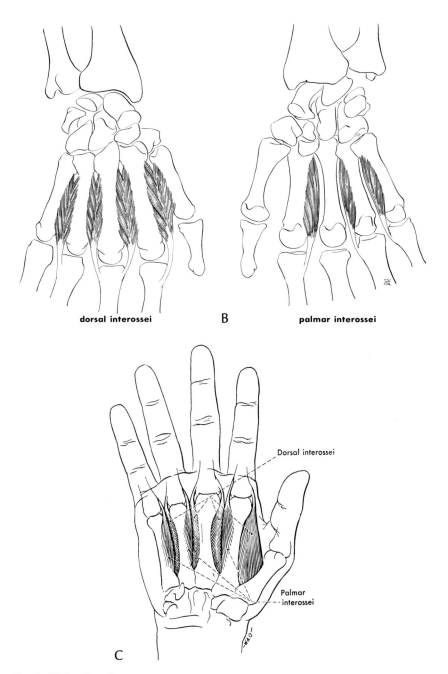

dorsal interossei   B   palmar interossei

C

Fig. 5–16 (continued).

The *thenar eminence* is the bulge of muscle at the base of the thumb. It is comprised of three muscles: the flexor pollicis brevis, abductor pollicis brevis, and opponens pollicis (Fig. 5–17).

To understand the functions of these muscles it is first necessary to appreciate that the thumb operates on a plane at right angles to the fingers. If the hand is palm up on a desk and the thumb is moved to point to the ceiling, that movement is abduction. Returning the thumb to its normal anatomical position is adduction. Scraping the thumb nail down and across the palm is flexion, while holding it out as in hitchhiking is extension. Pressing the tip of the thumb to the tip of the little finger is opposition.

The muscles of the thumb in the thenar eminence act as their names suggest (i.e., the flexor pollicis brevis provides flexion, the abductor provides abduction, etc.).

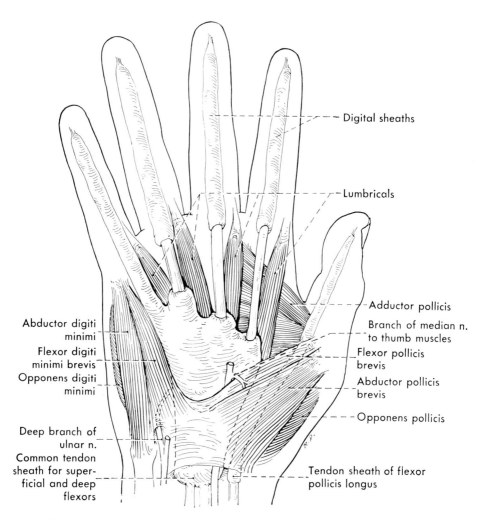

Fig. 5–17. Muscles of the thenar eminence and hypothenar eminence. (Hollinshead, W.H., and Jenkins, D.B.: Functional Anatomy of the Limbs and Back. Philadelphia, Saunders, 1981.)

Another muscle of the thumb, the *adductor pollicis,* is not of the eminence. It is deep to the flexor pollicis in the web between the first and second digits. The adductor pollicis is important in gripping.

The *hypothenar eminence* is the bulge of muscle at the base of the little finger. The muscles are named like those of the thenar eminence and have a similar function. They are the flexor digiti minimi brevis, abductor digiti minimi, and opponens digiti minimi (Fig. 5–17). These act to flex, abduct, and oppose the fifth digit.

BASIC STRUCTURE OF THE LOWER LIMB

The structure of the lower limb is a somewhat analogous to that of the upper limb; however, modifications have been made through evolution that sacrifice the mobility of the upper limb to give greater stability to the lower. The pelvic bones, and indeed all the bones of the lower limb, are more massive than the shoulder girdle and arm bones by virtue of the function of weight bearing.

The hip joint is extremely well supported by ligaments, and the basic bone structure of the pelvis is vaguely similar to that of the shoulder girdle except that the bones are fused to give greater stability. The hip bone consists of three bones, the ilium, ischium, and pubis, that join in the acetabulum to form the deep socket that contains the head of the femur (Fig. 5–18A and B). This ball-and-socket joint, the hip joint, is reinforced by a capsule and three broad, strong ligaments. Its movements are rather restricted in comparison to those of the shoulder joint.

Movement at the Hip Joint

The movements of the hip are flexion (bringing the knee to the chest), extension (taking the knee back as far as possible), abduction (raising the limb laterally), adduction (squeezing the legs together), lateral rotation (turning the foot outward), and medial rotation (turning the foot inward).

Ligaments of the Hip Joint

The three strong ligaments of the hip are the iliofemoral, pubofemoral, and ischiofemoral. The iliofemoral is the most important; it prevents overextension. The pubofemoral prevents overabduction, and the ischiofemoral prevents overadduction.

When a person is standing at rest the center of gravity pulls downward posterior to the hip joint. The joint is held in extension by the force of gravity, therefore, and the burden is taken by the iliofemoral ligament. Since ligaments have no contractile powers, holding the hip joint steady does not expend any caloric energy; yet this function is carried on for hours daily.

Musculature of the Hip

Gluteal Muscles

Study of the muscles of the hip and lower limb usually begins with the buttocks. There are three separate gluteal muscles, the gluteus maximus, gluteus medius, and gluteus minimus (Fig. 5–19). The gluteus maximus may be compared somewhat to the deltoid of the shoulder. The gluteus maximus is a large coarse-grained muscle (making it suitable for injections) originating on the crest of the ilium and the sacrum and inserting into a tuberosity on the femur as well as into the fascia of the lateral aspect of the leg, the fascia lata. Its major function is to extend the hip. This movement is normally that of stretching the leg posteriorly; however, if the legs are held fast, the trunk may be extended, at least in part, by the gluteus maximus. This is the position used for chest raises, an exercise. The gluteus maximus is not needed in the act of walking on level ground, but climbing stairs, jumping, sprinting, etc., all require strong contraction of the gluteus maximus. The final action of the gluteus

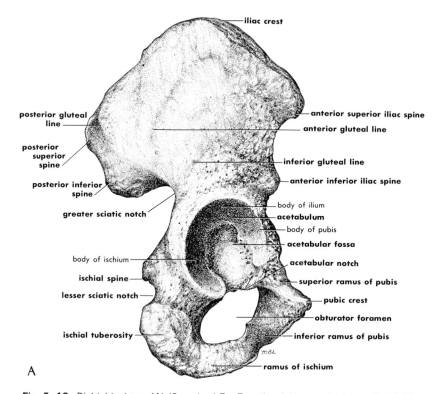

Fig. 5—18. Right hip bone *(A)* (Crouch, J.E.: Functional Human Anatomy. 3rd Edition. Philadelphia, Lea & Febiger, 1979); pelvis and hip joint *(B)*.

maximus is external rotation of the femur. The muscle is innervated by the inferior gluteal nerve.

The two smaller gluteal muscles, the medius and minimus, underlie the maximus, sharing the winglike spread of the ilium as their origins. They insert into the greater trochanter of the femur. Their special function is concerned with walking. When a step is taken, one side of the body is unsupported for a short period. The smaller glutei in the *opposite* hip contract and thus prevent the unsupported side from falling or sagging. In a sense, the two smaller gluteal muscles abduct the trunk away from the unsupported side. In addition, the gluteus medius and gluteus minimus rotate the femur medially and abduct it. They are innervated by the superior gluteal nerve.

Lateral Rotators. While the gluteus medius and minimus medially rotate the thigh (because of the "offset" head of the femur and the forward-facing acetabulum), the maximus assists a group of very small muscles to laterally rotate the thigh. These muscles of lateral rotation, in descending order from superior to inferior, are the piriformis, gemellus superior, obturator internus, gemellus inferior, obturator externus, and quadratus femoris (Figs. 5–19 and 5–20).

All originate somewhere on the ilium or ischium and insert on the greater trochanter deep under the two smaller glutei. The quadratus femoris inserts onto the shaft of the femur just inferior to the greater trochanter. They are innervated by nerves from L-4 to S-2.

The lateral rotators are quite small, relatively speaking, compared to the other muscles of the hip and so are of less significance than the rotator cuff muscles of the

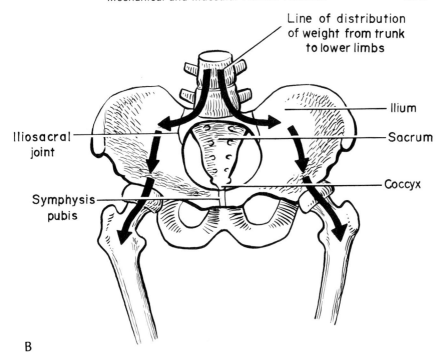

Line of distribution
of weight from trunk
to lower limbs

Ilium

Iliosacral
joint

Sacrum

Coccyx

Symphysis
pubis

B

Fig. 5–18 (continued).

shoulder to which they distantly relate. To understand their relationship it is necessary to form a three-dimensional concept of their position. The obturator externus,
for example, originates on the obturator membrane (*obturator* means "plug" or
"stopper") on the outer surface and proceeds backward and laterally to its insertion
on the inside of the greater trochanter. The obturator internus comes from the inside
of the pelvis, through the lesser sciatic notch, to its insertion on the greater trochanter.

The major hip flexor opposing the extension of the gluteus maximus is a compound
muscle called the iliopsoas. The psoas major muscle originates on all five lumbar
vertebrae and runs through the pelvis where it joins with the iliacus to form a common
tendon that inserts on the lesser trochanter (Fig. 5–21). As it passes over the brim
of the superior pubic ramus, the iliopsoas makes a sharp, nearly right-angled, turn
backward to its destination. This turn gives the muscle a certain mechanical advantage
much like a rope running over a pulley. The psoas is important in hip flexion. If the
legs are held down, the trunk can be flexed by the action of the iliopsoas—but at
risk to the lumbar vertebrae. It is worth noting that, for this reason, all sit-ups should
be done with bent knees to prevent injury to the lumbar spine. The iliopsoas is
innervated by nerves from L-1 to L-5.

The tensor fasciae latae is generally included with the gluteal muscles because it
is innervated by the superior gluteal nerve. Arising from the anterior superior iliac
spine, it inserts into the iliotibial tract, a broad sheet of tough fascia that attaches to
the fascia below the knee.

Muscles of the Anterior Compartment of the Thigh

The components of the quadriceps femoris are the bulkiest muscles in the body;
as the name implies, there are four, the largest of which is the vastus lateralis.

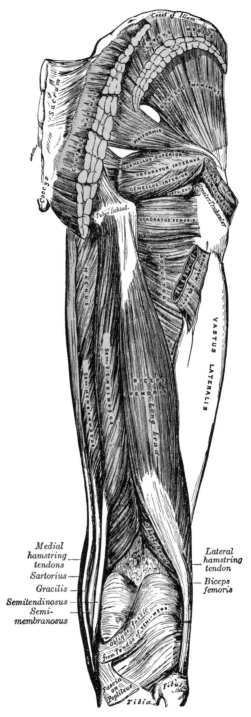

Fig. 5–19. Muscles of the gluteal and posterior femoral regions. (Goss, C.M., Editor: Gray's Anatomy of the Human Body. 29th Edition. Philadelphia, Lea & Febiger, 1973)

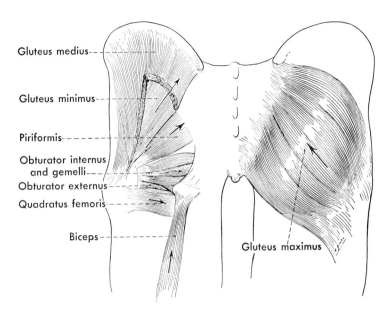

Gluteus medius

Gluteus minimus

Piriformis

Obturator internus
and gemelli

Obturator externus

Quadratus femoris

Biceps

Gluteus maximus

Fig. 5–20. Lateral rotators of the femur. Note that the obturator externus runs behind the head and neck of the femur to reach the greater trochanter. (Hollinshead, W.H., and Jenkins, D.B.: Functional Anatomy of the Limbs and Back. Philadelphia, Saunders, 1981.)

Accompanying this group in the anterior compartment is the sartorius, which is the longest muscle in the body. All the muscles of this compartment are innervated by the femoral nerve.

The muscles of the anterior compartment are, from lateral to medial, the vastus lateralis, vastus intermedius, rectus femoris, and vastus medialis, which comprise the quadriceps femoris, and the sartorius (Figs. 5–22 and 5–23). Only two of the group are two-joint muscles—the rectus femoris and the sartorius. All the others originate on the femur and insert just below the knee joint on the tibia. The principal function of the quadriceps is to extend the knee. Thus, these muscles are very important in all forms of locomotion—e. g., walking, running, swimming,—as well as in jumping, lifting, etc. The rectus femoris, which originates on the anterior inferior iliac spine as well as on the upper rim of the acetabulum, is known as the kicker's muscle since it aids in knee extension and hip flexion.

The components of the quadriceps have a common tendon that encases a sesamoid bone, the patella or knee cap. After passing the patella, the tendon is known as the patellar ligament, and it inserts at the tibial tuberosity.

Because of the size and strength of the quadriceps, it is not unusual, in adolescents who are very active in sports, for the muscles to pull loose a portion of the tibia to which they are attached. The tibial tuberosity is a growth center and, until it becomes completely ossified or bony, it can be damaged by the strong contraction of the "quads," whose maturity may have outstripped that of the skeleton. This condition is known as Osgood-Schlatter's disease.

The sartorius, while long, is not a particularly strong muscle. It is used chiefly to flex the hip and knee as in assuming a cross-legged sitting position such as tailors once used (*sartorius* means "tailor").

The bulky vastus lateralis in well-developed individuals projects both laterally and anteriorly. The vastus medialis is the only one of the group with fibers pulling

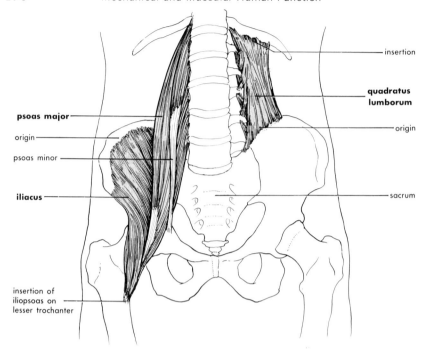

Fig. 5–21. Quadratus lumborum and iliopsoas muscles. Although considered as part of the posterior wall of the abdomen, these muscles actually function on the vertebral column. (Crouch, J.E.: Functional Human Anatomy. 3rd Edition. Philadelphia, Lea & Febiger, 1979)

medially. A strong medialis is important for stability of the knee. It is used only in the last 15 degrees of extension; thus if one walks with a limp, the medialis may not be used and it will atrophy. This atrophy and subsequent weakness will then affect the stability of the knee joint.

The majority of the fibers of the quadriceps run upward and laterally, following the 10° offset of the femur. They therefore tend to pull the patella somewhat laterally. As a result, most dislocations of the patella are in a lateral direction.

Muscles of the Posterior Compartment of the Thigh

The muscles of the posterior compartment are innervated by the sciatic nerve, of which there are two major motor branches—the common peroneal and the tibial. The latter is the more widespread.

The muscles of this compartment are also called hamstrings. They are important in flexing the knee and extending the hip. When the leg and thigh are held, they extend the trunk. Except for the short head of the biceps femoris, which originates on the femur, they have a common origin on the ischial tuberosity. If the knee is fully flexed, the hamstrings are so shortened that they cannot act on the hip to extend it. Similarly, if the hip is fully extended, the hamstrings cannot flex the knee.

The hamstrings comprise the long head and short head of the biceps femoris; the semitendinosus; and the semimembranosus (Figs. 5–22 and 5–23). The biceps inserts on the head of the fibula and makes up the lateral aspect of the popliteal (knee) space. The semitendinosus and semimembranosus are medial and can be felt on the medial side of the popliteal space. The tendons are easily palpable behind the knee joint in a person sitting with feet flat who raises the heel while pressing down with the toe of the same foot.

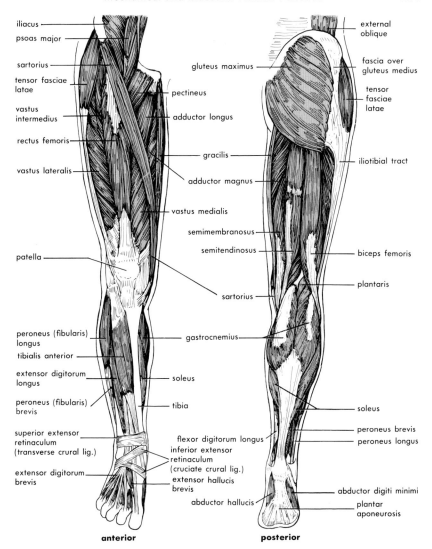

iliacus

psoas major

sartorius

tensor fasciae latae

vastus intermedius

rectus femoris

vastus lateralis

patella

peroneus (fibularis) longus

tibialis anterior

extensor digitorum longus

peroneus (fibularis) brevis

superior extensor retinaculum (transverse crural lig.)

extensor digitorum brevis

gluteus maximus

pectineus

adductor longus

gracilis

adductor magnus

vastus medialis

semimembranosus

semitendinosus

sartorius

gastrocnemius

soleus

tibia

flexor digitorum longus

inferior extensor retinaculum (cruciate crural lig.)

extensor hallucis brevis

abductor hallucis

external oblique

fascia over gluteus medius

tensor fasciae latae

iliotibial tract

biceps femoris

plantaris

soleus

peroneus brevis

peroneus longus

abductor digiti minimi

plantar aponeurosis

anterior

posterior

Fig. 5–22. Muscles of the lower limb. (Crouch, J.E.: Functional Human Anatomy. 3rd Edition. Philadelphia, Lea & Febiger, 1979)

The semitendinosus sits atop the semimembranosus and inserts into the medial aspect of the tibia. It is rather undistinguished as a muscle. Its cousin, the semi-membranosus (as its name implies, it is approximately one-half membrane) has a rather novel insertion; a superficial portion is reflected upward and laterally to become the oblique popliteal ligament running from the posterior medial aspect of the tibia to the lateral condyle of the femur. The deep part of the tendon attaches to the medial condyle of the tibia, and a short slip attaches to the tubercle just below.

The short head of the biceps arises from the linea aspera and from the lateral

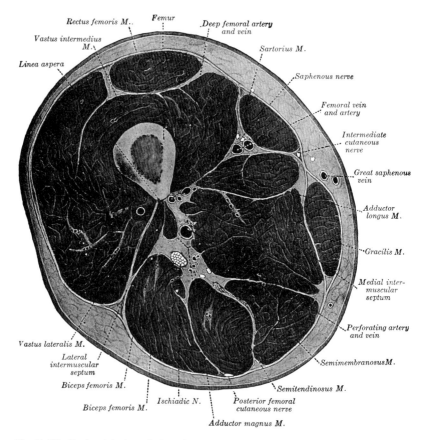

Fig. 5–23. Horizontal view of the left midthigh, showing the three compartments, their muscles, and one major nerve in the posterior compartment. (Goss, C.M., Editor: Gray's Anatomy of the Human Body. 29th Edition. Philadelphia, Lea & Febiger, 1973)

intermuscular septum separating it from the vastus lateralis. The biceps femoris inserts on the head of the fibula.

Muscles of the Medial Compartment of the Thigh

The muscles of the medial compartment are innervated by the obturator nerve and comprise the pectineus, adductor longus, adductor brevis, adductor magnus, gracilis, and obturator externus (included with the gluteal group) (Figs. 5–22 and 5–23).

Essentially the action of the muscles of the medial compartment is to adduct or draw the legs together. Anatomists of old referred to the gracilis as the "guardian of virginity." It is a weak muscle. The obturator nerve exits from the trunk via the obturator foramen, divides into two branches (anterior and posterior), and supplies all the muscles of the medial compartment. In addition to the obturator, the sciatic nerve (tibial portion) supplies part of the adductor magnus. The pectineus, being "fickle," sometimes is supplied by the obturator and at other times by the femoral.

Generally the muscles of this compartment arise somewhere on the inferior aspect of the pelvis and insert on the medial or posterior shaft of the femur. The pectineus (comb-like) assists in crossing the legs, an action that is a combination of flexion and adduction.

The adductor magnus, the largest of the group, has two portions. The upper portion, whose fibers run obliquely, adducts the thigh. The lower portion, whose fibers run more vertically, extends the thigh. Only the gracilis in this group is a two-joint muscle, arising as it does from the ramus of the pubis and inserting into the medial shaft of the tibia.

The gracilis, sartorius, and semitendinosus (one muscle from each compartment) have a special combined insertion called the pes anserinus ("goose's foot") and that they have on the medial-anterior aspect of the tibia. Athletes and others who suffer damage to the medial ligaments of the knee often have this common insertion lifted and moved surgically. The increased tension in the muscles gives the support of dynamic ligaments to the knee. Since they are from separate compartments, any imbalance is rather insignificant.

The Knee Joint

The knee joint (Fig. 5–24) is probably the most vulnerable of all the joints in the body. Despite having strong collateral ligaments the joint is susceptible to injury because of its mechanical structure and the uses and strains to which it is subject.

Being for the most part a hinge joint, with only a limited amount of medial and lateral rotation possible, the knee suffers when rotational forces act on it. This occurs when a person changes direction quickly while running or simply slips on a patch of ice. Any such force is compounded, of course, by the fact that the knee joint supports the body weight. In addition, there are two semicircular wedges of cartilage called menisci inside the joint that can be damaged and that deteriorate with age. They, too, cause knee problems.

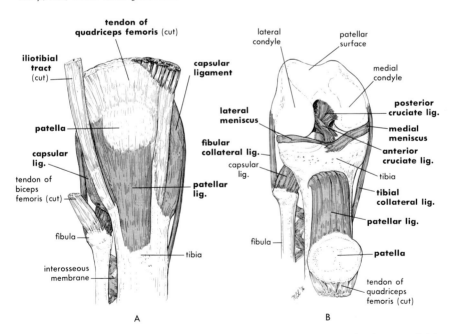

Fig. 5–24. Anterior (A) and posterior (B) views of the right knee joint showing superficial and deep ligaments and related muscles. (Crouch, J.E.: Functional Human Anatomy. 3rd Edition. Philadelphia, Lea & Febiger, 1979)

Movement at the Knee Joint

The basic movements are extension (provided by the quadriceps), flexion (provided by the hamstrings plus additional muscles of the leg), lateral rotation (provided by the biceps femoris), and medial rotation (provided by the semitendinosus and semi-membranosus).

Ligaments of Knee Joint

The four strong ligaments of the knee joint are the lateral and the medial collateral, the cruciate (inside the knee joint), and the oblique popliteal (at the posterior aspect). When a person is standing at rest, the center of gravity pulls downward anterior to the knee joint, thus holding it in extension. In this position (knee locked) the ligaments provide most support. They provide least support when the knee is flexed. Because of incongruities between the surfaces of the tibia and femur, the femur normally rotates medially a few degrees when the knee is fully extended while a person is standing. (This does not occur in walking and running.) This action "locks" the knee, and there is a special muscle, the popliteus, that "unlocks" the knee by rotating the femur laterally before the knee is flexed. It is significant to note that if the knee is extended while a person is sitting, the knee will lock. However, in a non-weight-bearing situation the tibia rotates laterally, instead of the femur rotating medially. This situation occurs during rehabilitative exercises.

Musculature of the Leg

The leg is the portion of the lower limb below the knee. It is divided into three compartments that are separated by septa of tough fascia and innervated by three distinct nerves (Fig. 5–25). The actions of the muscles provide movement at the knee, the ankle, and the foot.

Muscles of the Anterior Compartment

The anterior compartment has three muscles that lie between the lateral aspect of the tibia and the fibula: the tibialis anterior, extensor hallucis longus, and extensor digitorum longus, part of which is the peroneus tertius (Fig. 5–26A).

The muscles of this compartment are innervated by the deep peroneal (anterior tibial) nerve and act principally to dorsiflex the foot, that is, to pull the toes and foot toward the face. The tibialis anterior also helps invert the foot, while the extensor digitorum everts the foot.

These muscles originate from the tibia and the interosseous membrane and insert well down on the foot. They are extrinsic muscles of the foot.

The tibia is triangular to provide a solid flat surface for muscle origin. The sharp edge of the shin bone can be palpated quite readily. It is vulnerable to damage such as "barking" and also to "splints." This condition occurs in association with hard running on a hard surface, especially after a long layoff.

Muscles of the Lateral Compartment

The lateral compartment contains only two muscles, the peroneus longus and peroneus brevis (Fig. 5–26B), and is innervated by the superficial peroneal nerve. The muscles lie between the anterior and posterior septa lateral to the fibula.

The longus, as its name implies, is the longer of the two. It runs behind the lateral malleolus (little hammer) of the ankle, diagonally across the sole of the foot to the first metatarsal. It can thus act to plantar flex (point the toes) the foot and to evert it. The peroneus brevis inserts on the opposite side of the foot on the fifth metatarsal and does not cross the foot. It is responsible for eversion only. Eversion of the foot is important in walking as it helps the toes clear the ground when the foot is swung forward.

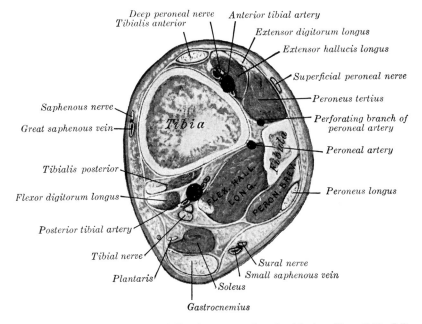

Fig. 5–25. Cross section of the calf: The three compartments of the leg. (Goss, C.M., Editor: Gray's Anatomy of the Human Body. 29th Edition. Philadelphia, Lea & Febiger, 1973).

Muscles of the Posterior Compartment

The posterior compartment, innervated by the posterior tibial nerve, is the largest of the three groups. Since the primary function of this group is plantar flexion, and against the full body weight as a class 3 lever, it develops into a powerful group of muscles. The muscles in the compartment are the gastrocnemius, soleus (Fig. 5–26C), plantaris, popliteus, flexor digitorum longus, flexor hallucis longus, and tibialis posterior (Fig. 5–26D).

The two heads of the gastrocnemius and the soleus together form the triceps surae; its tendon of insertion, easily palpable at the posterior of the ankle, is the tendo calcaneus or Achilles tendon. The triceps surae is important in walking, dancing, running, etc.

Since the gastrocnemius is a two-joint muscle, it flexes the knee as well as plantar flexes the foot; however, it cannot do both simultaneously. If the knee is fully extended, the lengthened gastrocnemius tends to pull the foot into plantar flexion and vice versa.

The plantaris is analogous to the palmaris longus of the forearm. It has little function and is often used by plastic surgeons for replacement of material elsewhere in the body.

The popliteus, as its name implies, is a muscle of the knee. Its specific function is to unlock the extended knee. Since it is a knee flexor it contracts at the start of flexion. At the same time it rotates the femur laterally at the start of the flexion movement.

The flexor digitorum longus, as its name implies, plantar flexes the toes and, since it crosses the ankle joint, plantar flexes the foot also.

The flexor hallucis longus functions in a manner similar to the flexor digitorum longus, but of course, it is inserted on the great toe.

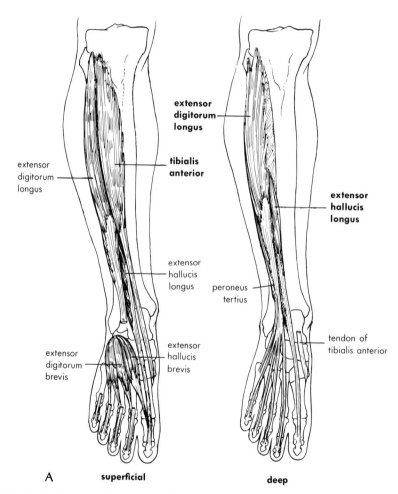

extensor
digitorum
longus

extensor
digitorum
longus

**extensor
digitorum
longus**

**tibialis
anterior**

**extensor
hallucis
longus**

extensor
hallucis
longus

peroneus
tertius

extensor
hallucis
brevis

tendon of
tibialis anterior

extensor
digitorum
brevis

A   **superficial**   **deep**

Fig. 5–26. Muscles of the anterior *(A),* lateral *(B),* and posterior *(C* and *D)* compartments
of the leg. (Crouch, J.E.: Essential Human Anatomy. Philadelphia, Lea & Febiger, 1982.)

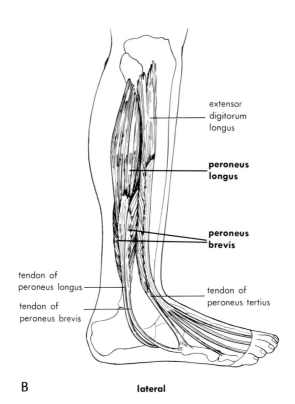

B   lateral

Fig. 5–26 (continued).

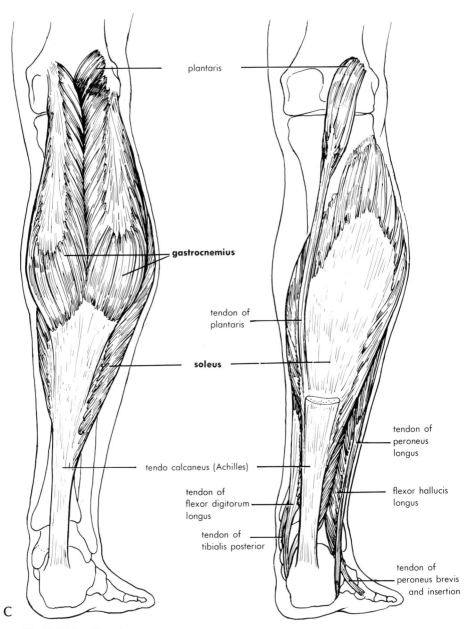

plantaris

gastrocnemius

tendon of
plantaris

soleus

tendo calcaneus (Achilles)

tendon of
flexor digitorum
longus

tendon of
tibialis posterior

tendon of
peroneus
longus

flexor hallucis
longus

tendon of
peroneus brevis
and insertion

C

Fig. 5–26 (continued).

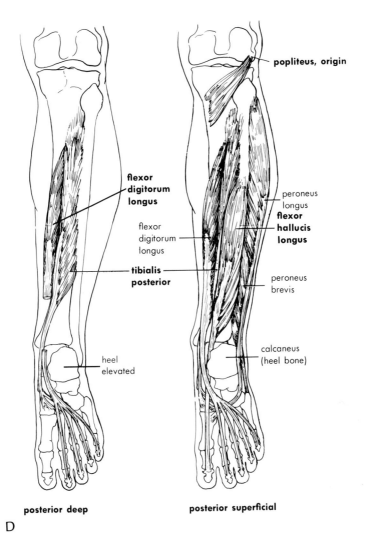

popliteus, origin

flexor
digitorum
longus

flexor
digitorum
longus

tibialis
posterior

heel
elevated

peroneus
longus

flexor
hallucis
longus

peroneus
brevis

calcaneus
(heel bone)

posterior deep   **posterior superficial**

D

Fig. 5–26 (continued).

The tibialis posterior is the deepest muscle of this compartment; it passes behind the medial malleolus to insert on eight of the bones of the foot. The tibialis posterior is the major invertor of the foot and also acts as a dynamic ligament for the arch of the foot.

The Ankle Joint

The ankle joint is a hinge joint involving the tibia, fibula, and talus. The major weight-bearing component is the talotibial joint. All the remaining movements of the foot are found in subtalar joints. The movements of inversion and eversion are very important in walking on uneven ground, since they permit the body to remain upright and steady while the subtalar joints make all the adjustments to the terrain.

The two malleoli clamp the talus between them and act as pulleys, giving mechanical advantage to the muscles of the posterior and lateral compartment passing behind them. The talus itself is wedge shaped, being wider in front than behind and convex from front to back. This shape facilitates the hinge action and also makes the joint solid in dorsiflexion and much looser in plantar flexion.

There is a vast web of ligaments holding the seven tarsal bones in position (Fig. 5–27). Among the more significant are the medial and lateral collateral ligaments of the ankle joint—the large deltoid ligament on the medial side joining the medial malleolus to the navicular, calcaneus, and talus—and the lateral series of ligaments—the calcaneofibular and the anterior and posterior talofibular ligaments. The majority of ankle injuries are to the lateral side, partly because of the weaker lateral structures of the joint.

Musculature of the Foot

The foot, although analogous to the hand, does not have the mobility or dexterity of the hand. The muscles can be dealt with in less detail since they contribute as groups to locomotion rather than individually to discrete functions as do the muscles in the hand.

On the dorsal (extensor) surface there is only one muscle, the extensor digitorum brevis. It has little discrete function and assists the extensor digitorum longus. With a sprained ankle, the foot is often everted, causing the muscle to contract. This contraction is often mistakenly diagnosed as a swelling of the ankle.

The muscles of the plantar surface are generally considered in four layers (Fig. 5–28). The unique feature of these muscles is that they act in close harmony with the heavy ligaments that hold the arch of the foot. In a normal foot the ligaments bear the load and preserve the arch in a quiet standing position. During activity the foot muscles, including some of the extrinsic muscles, especially the peroneus longus and tibialis posterior (the cross-strap muscles, so called because they come from opposite directions and cross deep on the sole of the foot), contract not only to provide locomotion but to aid the ligaments in maintaining the arch of the foot.

The muscle groups or layers of the foot are considered from superficial to deep:

1. Abductor hallucis, flexor digitorum brevis, abductor digiti minimi
2. Quadratus plantae, lumbricales, and long tendons of extrinsic muscles
3. Flexor hallucis brevis, adductor hallucis, flexor digiti minimi brevis
4. Interossei and long tendons of extrinsic muscles

The muscles are innervated by the medial and lateral plantar nerves. The one unique muscle in the sole of the foot is the quadratus plantae, or flexor accessorius, which arises in the calcaneus and inserts into the tendon of the flexor digitorum longus. The quadratus plantae straightens the pull of the diagonally placed flexor digitorum longus.

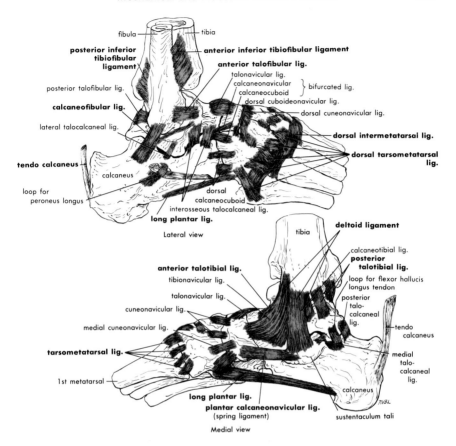

Fig. 5–27. Ligaments of the right ankle and foot. (Crouch, J.E.: Functional Human Anatomy. 3rd Edition. Philadelphia, Lea & Febiger, 1979.)

IMPLICATIONS FOR GENERAL EDUCATION

The study of the structure and function of the human body is central to a good general education, especially if one views that education as a means to enhance the quality of life. There is no doubt that an understanding of the body and its workings is a subject that each one lives with daily. Accurate knowledge of the body permits one to make decisions that are appropriate in regard to diet, dress, exercise, general health, etc. Additionally, a better grasp of many other subjects is held by those with a background in anatomy. In psychology, for example, one area of study is motor learning. A more complete understanding of that area of study is possible by those with a background in anatomy.

IMPLICATIONS FOR PROFESSIONAL PRACTICE

For anyone interested in a career in physical education and sport, a study of human mechanical and muscular function is mandatory. How could a study of *physical* education not include a study of how the human body works? Certainly, all biomechanical analysis, treatment and prevention of injuries, physiology, coaching, and other topics bear heavily on a basic knowledge of bodily function. In a sense, the

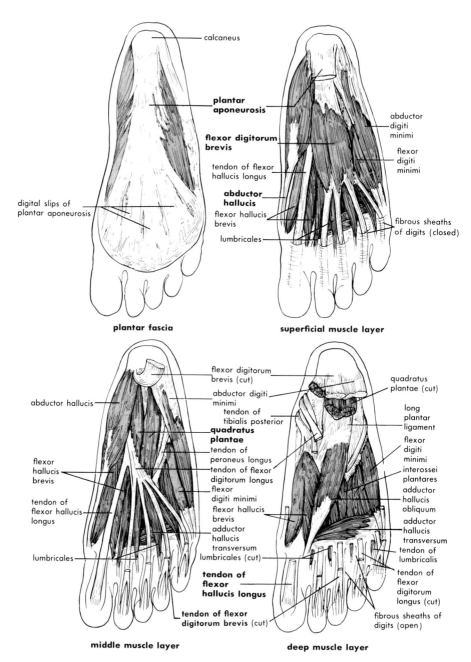

plantar fascia

superficial muscle layer

middle muscle layer

deep muscle layer

Fig. 5–28. Muscle layers of the foot. (Crouch, J.E.: Functional Human Anatomy. 3rd Edition. Philadelphia, Lea & Febiger, 1979)

study of the body is central to the study of virtually all other subdisciplines of physical education and sport.

PROFESSIONAL OPPORTUNITIES

The opportunities to pursue a career in physical education and sport in the subdiscipline involved with the functioning of the human body are on a par with other subdisciplines. There is great potential in the areas of physical education, coaching, biomechanics, athletic injuries treatment, and the like for those with a sound background in human mechanical and muscular function.

The study of the human body is a fascinating field for it is one in which every student provides his own study specimens. A knowledge of one's own physical capacities and liabilities and of one's own structures and their functioning can be a never ending source of wonderment.

REFERENCES

Basmajian, J.: Muscles Alive. 2nd Ed. Baltimore, Williams & Wilkins Co., 1967.
Crouch, J.E.: Essential Human Anatomy. Philadelphia, Lea & Febiger, 1982.
Crouch, J.E.: Functional Human Anatomy. 3rd Edition. Philadelphia, Lea & Febiger, 1979.
Gardner, E., Gray, D., and O'Rahilly, R.: Anatomy. 2nd Ed. Philadelphia, W.B.Saunders Co., 1966.
Gardner, W.D., and Osburn,W.A.: Structure of the Human Body. 2nd Edition. Philadelphia, Saunders, 1973.
Goss, C.M., Editor: Gray's Anatomy of the Human Body. 29th Edition. Philadelphia, Lea & Febiger, 1973.
Hollinshead, W.H., and Jenkins, D.B.: Functional Anatomy of the Limbs and Back. Philadelphia, Saunders, 1981.
Leeson, C., and Leeson, T.: Human Structure. Philadelphia, W.B. Saunders Co., 1972.
Leyshon, G.: Programmed Functional Anatomy. St. Louis, C.V. Mosby Co., 1974.
Lockhart R., Hamilton, G., and Fife, F.: Anatomy of the Human Body. Philadelphia, J.B. Lippincott Co. 1969.
Skinner, H.: The Origin of Medical Terms. Baltimore, Williams & Wilkins Co., 1949.

CHAPTER SIX

Management Theory and Practice

Daniel G. Soucie

Organizations come into existence when people get together and unite their efforts to achieve a common goal. Essentially the concept of organization means people working together for a given purpose.

> If the accomplishment of an objective requires collective effort, men set up an organization designed to coordinate the activities of many persons and to furnish incentives for others to join them for this purpose. (Blau and Scott, 1976, p. 16)

One must recognize that, in society as a whole as well as in the world of sport and physical education, organizations abound. Everywhere groups of people join forces and form associations, societies, and committees of all kinds to achieve objects of mutual concern or interest. In Canada the number of associations listed in the Directory of Associations published by the University of Toronto Press has increased to more than 7500. Additionally, the same individuals belong to more than one organization. A recent Canadian survey shows that "individuals relate to 3.6 groups, be they associations, societies, church organizations, bowling leagues or whatever" (Bullied, 1978, p. 7).

Our North American society is indeed characterized by many bureaucratic organizations that constantly affect our very own lives. Some authors go even further and postulate that "society is adaptive to organizations, to the large, powerful organizations controlled by a few, often overlapping, leaders" (Perrow, 1972, p. 199). In the world of sport, amateur as well as professional, and to a lesser degree, in the field of institutional physical education and athletics, the situation is no different. Sport clubs, sport-governing bodies, professional teams, minor baseball leagues, interscholastic and university athletics are all subject to the same basic bureaucratic principles. In all such cases the goals to be achieved, the rules organizational members are expected to follow, the hierarchical delegation of authority, the task descriptions and the specialization of duties have all been "consciously designed a priori to anticipate and guide interaction and activities" (Blau and Scott, 1976, p. 16). Organizations have purposes, and for these to be accomplished a minimum of coordination is required. Coordination is essential to determine who does what and when and how things are to be done within the organization. Coordination means to harmonize or to act together in a concerted way so that collective efforts are all oriented toward the realization of the group's objectives. Those responsible for effecting this coordination are usually referred to as administrators, managers, or supervisors.

Whether it is viewed as a leadership role, as a set of specified tasks, or as the sum total of the planning, organizing, controlling, and evaluating processes, administration (in the sense of "to administer") essentially consists of governing or orienting the cooperative efforts of people toward the objectives defined by the organization. In

Dr. Soucie is from The University of Ottawa, Ontario.

a few simple words, to administer is to strive toward the attainment of the effectiveness and the efficiency of the organization. Effectiveness refers to the accomplishment of the cooperative purpose, whereas efficiency refers to the satisfaction of individual and personal needs of the members of the organization (Barnard, 1938, p. 60). Effective administration therefore lies within a proper orientation of human behavior and performance in organizations.

Of all the tasks of administration, writes Likert, "managing the human component is the central and most important task because all else depends on how well it is done" (1967, p. 1). However, orienting the organizational behavior of people does not constitute an easy task, since individuals making up organizations differ in many ways and consequently think and react differently under various circumstances. People differ in personality, character, and previous experience in an organizational environment. They have different needs, interests, and levels of aspiration and therefore assign often radically different priorities to the many objectives under consideration in an organization. These individual differences inevitably lead to organizational goal displacement, often opposing role expectations, and various situations of conflict. Participants in an organization will often disagree over means and ends because they hold opposing views about what is good and desirable for them and for the organization of which they are an integral part.

As we head for the year 2000, the role of the administrator will become even more complex. The fact is, people have changed considerably since the days when workers were considered cogs that had to fit in the industrial machine (Taylor, 1947). Managing through rigid rules and punishment threats is no long possible or desirable. Scientific management and overrationality had destroyed individuality, a concept so dear to present-day behavioral scientists. Whereas effectiveness and output of goods or services were the prime objectives of yesterday's industrial organizations, efficiency and satisfaction of human interests are now considered priorities in the "matrix of organizational purposes" (Gross, 1968, p. 298).

Our society has indeed shifted toward more people-centered organizations in which objectives, policies, and procedures cannot be decided upon unless the individuals who make up the organization have their say in the matter. Recent democratic trends have brought about a new set of definitions for organizational concepts such as chain of command, delegation of authority, control, evaluation, communication, and decision making. Participative management and decision making today require that each member of the organization play his role and contribute, to the best of his ability, to the optimization of decisions.

> The organization, through compartmentalization of tasks and responsibilities, circumscribes for each member the domain of environmental factors with which he must be concerned and permits a match to be established between the complexity of the environment, the type of role and the modalities of decision-making which are appropriate in the functions performed by the members. (McWhinney, 1971, p. 435)

Largely because of the increasing democratization and bureaucratization in North American society, new functions and interrelations have emerged in the social structure of organizations. Specialization and professionalization have then resulted. In bureaucratic structures, specialization is required for organizations to attain their objectives in the most rational manner. Accordingly, responsibilities are delegated to persons holding competence (specialists, professionals) in the respective areas of specialization that are a part of an organization's mission. In this fashion this past decade has witnessed the emergence of a great diversity of administration specialists, ranging from planning strategists to communication experts to organizational development consultants.

Similarly, in sport and physical education new leadership roles and responsibilities have become available to professionals as well—fitness experts, sport managers, sport consultants, etc. As specialists and professionals, physical education people are "vitally concerned with the management of organizations" (Zeigler and Spaeth, 1975, p. 29), and jobs are becoming increasingly more numerous and diversified in this field. However, it is sad to realize that an apparent myth still exists that seniority and past membership within sport organizations constitute the major if not the only criteria for selecting administrators (Soucie, 1976, p. 87). Indeed, in most cases in the field of physical education, sport, and athletics, administrators are appointed not on the basis of their management training but solely because of their long association with that particular physical education or sport organization. One must agree with Parkhouse when she writes that: "one of the incongruencies in the multi-billion dollar business of athletics is the willingness to turn over the administration of this enterprise to these individuals who have had little, if any, formal preparation for the job" (1978, p. 22).

According to the now very well-known Peter principle (Peter and Hull, 1969), many individuals reach their level of incompetence when they get promoted to an administrative position. Indeed, it happens quite often in our profession that a person, because he was the best worker, the best teacher, or the best coach, will be elevated to the rank of manager, supervisor, or administrator. From one day to the next, these individuals are asked to do something at which they are usually very inexperienced and for which they have probably never been prepared—that is, to plan, organize, direct, and control the work of their peers or co-workers. There is, in fact, a great difference between doing a good job (as a subordinate) and making others do a good job (as a superior), between being responsible *to* and being responsible *for*.

Administration requires knowledge of and experience with effective planning strategies and organizational techniques, as well as proper communication skills, decision-making capability, and know-how. Administration is a science as well as an art, and administrators of physical education and sport must be properly trained and carefully selected if our organizations are to become effective. As Sprandel explains it, "We physical educators must be encouraged to give up our practitioner ways—no matter how uncertain those first steps, we should begin to move toward a more accountable and scientific approach to administration" (1974, p. 46).

There exists a vastly increasing body of knowledge called management theory that is being utilized more and more in schools and departments of physical education across the United States and Canada for the professional preparation and in-service training of administrators in our field. For over a decade now, research studies of the theory of physical education and sport organizations have multiplied and, while our profession is still far away from management models we could call our own, the efforts expanded in this direction are quite encouraging.

This is then what this chapter is all about, management theory as it applies to physical education and sport organization. First, the basic terminology specific to management will be presented to the reader, and then an inventory of the present state of theory and scholarly thought in the discipline will be introduced. Then, implications of this field of study for general education and for professional practice will be discussed. Finally, interrelationships between management theory and practice and the allied professions will be examined, and opportunities for professional careers in sport management and administration of physical education will be presented.

DEFINITIONS

For better appreciation of the material presented in this chapter the reader should have a clear understanding of some of the terminology basic to the field.

Management, Administration, and Supervision

The act of leading a group of people toward the attainment of objectives in an organization has been called many different things over the years. Similarly, people involved in management have also been called many things (e.g., director, supervisor, principal, head, general manager). Basically, however, three active verbs have emerged: administer, manage, and supervise. Individuals involved in these roles are identified as administrators, managers, and supervisors. To avoid becoming a prisoner of any one of these three terms, it is possible and acceptable to equate them. Administrative scientists may disagree with this equation and would want to make fine differentiation among the three concepts. However, even though subtle differences probably exist, they are more useful in theory than in practice. Therefore, in this chapter, management, administration, and supervision are considered synonymous. In all three there is a basic connotation of activating, directing, or leading the group (the organization) toward its goal.

Generally speaking, management consists of orienting human, material, and financial resources in dynamic and structured units that will attain their objectives to the satisfaction of those for whom the work is accomplished (effectiveness) while achieving the best possible morale among the participants (efficiency). More specifically, management can be viewed in three perspectives: leadership, task, and process.

Management in a Leadership Perspective. It is unfortunately evident that many physical education administrators or sport managers possess relatively large amounts of legally based authority and yet never really get things done because of lack of leadership ability.

> But leadership is complicated. It is intellectual; it is emotional; and it is physical. It is inherited, and it is learned. It is the summation of the total man which must square with myriad desires of the group. (Wilson, 1966; p. 50)

Leadership is difficult to define. Essentially it is equivalent to power or influence within the group that stems from informal sources of authority. If formal authority is power granted by the organization because of the position occupied (e.g., director), informal authority belongs only to the individual. Informal authority stems from characteristics that are outstanding in the personality of the individual. Charisma and expertise (expert knowledge) are two good examples of such personal traits.

Ideally, sport or physical education administrators should be able to rely on both formal and informal forms of power to arrive at decisions within their organizations. In other words, legally based forms of authority (status, position) and personal reference forms of authority (charisma, expertise) are both essential. Management cannot be viewed as absolutely equivalent to leadership, but it cannot be conceived without considering the personal leadership qualities of the manager. Leadership styles are very much a part of the act of managing, and management has to be envisioned as a leadership responsibility.

Management in a Task Perspective. The task perspective is one that approaches the field by defining and describing the responsibilities inherent to, and essential for, successful administration. Management can be viewed as a precise listing of various tasks to be performed. Obviously there can be many different classifications of the functional and operational areas of sport and physical education administration (i.e., not everyone agrees with its components or emphasizes the same elements or both). Additionally, these tasks' descriptions of managers or administrators would of course vary with each geographical environment and organizational level. Traditionally the following tasks of physical education and sport administrators have been recognized: staffing, budgeting, programming, scheduling, buying and caring for equipment, purchasing, accounting, public relations, consulting, and the like. Within each of those categories, many more subduties could be listed, depending on the specific situation and level of the job.

Most taxonomies will be derived from socially desired definitions of sport and physical education management. It then becomes easier for the administrator to evaluate the effectiveness of his administrative behavior (Sachs, 1966, p. 213). The task approach to management serves as a check list and reminds the administrator of certain critical aspects of his role that he may be neglecting. On the other hand, a normative statement of tasks has to be flexible enough so as not to place too great demands on the administrator who, in the final analysis, is confronted by "real-life" situations.

Management in a Process Perspective. Webster's dictionary defines *process* as "a series of actions or operations conducing to an end . . . a continuous operation . . ." Just as there are many tasks to be performed, there are many processes to manipulate.

The basic management processes are shown in Figure 6–1. In this perspective, management is viewed as the summation of planning, organizing, directing, and controlling the work to be accomplished in the organization. As the manager is called

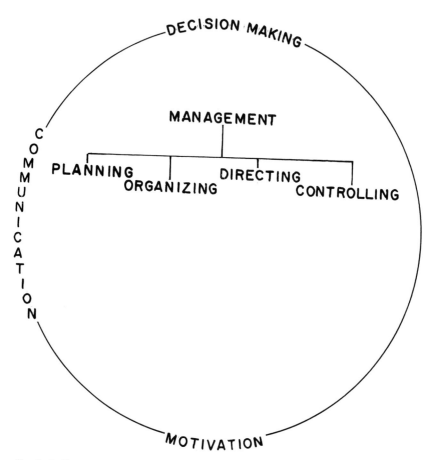

Fig. 6–1. The basic management processes.

upon to plan, organize, direct, and control, he makes use of three other general management processes (i.e., decision making, communicating, and motivating).

Planning is the thinking process that precedes any action. It is a continuing process by which the administrator determines and evaluates, before action, the decisions necessary to realize a given objective. It is essential since it allows the manager to clearly spell out what he wants and how he wants to get there. Planning is an attempt to answer the following questions: what, why, who, how, when, where, and how much? Specific planning tools are available to the administrator. Some of these techniques include CPM (Critical Path Method), PERT (Planning and Evaluation Review Technique), PPBS (Planning, Programming, Budgeting System), RAMP (Review Analysis of Multiple Projects), Gantt diagrams, and flow charts of all kinds. Planning is the first function of management and, if it is faulty, all the other functions may be affected. Plans of any type are only as good as the thinking that produces them.

Organizing is the process that guarantees that all the resources are properly arranged and used so that the job gets done effectively. The function of organizing is carried out by analyzing the job, setting up an organizational structure, and allocating the resources. Essentially it consists of determining who does what. Organizational manuals are often used to that purpose; functions and responsibilities are clearly established, relationships between functions are spelled out, and the formal flow of authority is clearly delegated. Organizing is essential to avoid duplication of roles and, evidently, to properly channel all the efforts toward a single goal and satisfactory functioning of the whole organization.

Directing may be defined as the application of leadership and issuing of proper orders and directives to derive the best results from the available resources and, ultimately, to attain the objectives established.

Controlling is a technique or method used to establish the means that will permit execution of the plans. It is the act of gathering and evaluating information to find out if the accomplished action (what is *or* the actual performance) is the same as the planned action (what ought to be *or* the ideal performance) in the organization. For various reasons the control function traditionally carries a negative connotation in the minds of subordinates in organizations. However, as a management process, the concept of control does not mean to "hold in check" or to "regulate" but rather refers to the act of determining accuracy by measuring against standards of comparison. Two forms of control are available to the administrator: continuous or preventive control and occasional or corrective control. Preventive controls aim at forechecking problems and making sure that everyone does what is expected of him. Preventive controls take two forms: *standards of performance*, which are established criteria (usually quantity, quality, cost, and time) against which actual results are measured, and clearly delimited and written *task descriptions*. Corrective controls consist of occasional (systematic or random) spot checks or visits to determine or identify discrepancies between work completed and objectives planned. In the final analysis, however, self-control on the part of subordinates is the best form of control, and the manager should concentrate on problem cases and exercise "management by exception." Evaluating and subsequent improvement are the essence of good controlling.

Decision making is a universal management process inasmuch as it is constantly used by administrators when planning, organizing, directing, and controlling. Decision making is the essence of the art of management and is the mark of an administrator's activity. It is, in fact, the only true task of the manager. The decision-making process is a technique used to decide, that is, to make a conscious choice between many alternate solutions for the purpose of solving a problem.

Communication is another universal management process essential for efficient administration. Better decisions should inevitably result from sharing of information and frequent exchanges among the individual members of an organization. A good communication system in organizations also leads to a better organizational climate, open discussions, and group cohesiveness. It is the simple fact of talking to each other that allows interactions and reciprocal influences to take place in organizations. Communication is essential for the administrator who has to plan, organize, direct, and control the work of organizational members. It is essential for informing members about plans and objectives and in motivating them toward the attainment of goals. It is also required for proper feedback from subordinates. As a management process, communication can be defined as exchange of information from one person to another for the purpose of encouraging a climate of trust and cooperation within a team of workers, and encouraging everyone to offer his resources, his knowledge, and his experience for the benefit of the entire organization.

Motivation in management is the effort of creating conditions (an environment) such that, at all levels, the members of the organization can reach their own objectives while orienting their efforts toward the objectives of the organization. Motivation is that drive within each one of us that initiates a will to reach an objective or to satisfy a need. Needs are diversified and vary from one individual to another. Needs will also fluctuate in intensity in everyday life and at various times in our lives. An administrator must then consider these variations in needs within the same individual and from one person to another when he works at motivating his subordinates. One must manipulate work-related factors intelligently to enhance job satisfaction. The administrator must realize the importance of delegating authority, of allowing the members of the organization to participate in decision making, and of exercising self-control, all of which give a feeling of worth and importance to the individual. He must answer to the subordinate's desire for self-fulfillment and self-actualization. Motivation is then an essential element of management requiring that the administrator exercise judgment since there exists no miracle recipe. Listening to subordinates and understanding them are the true ingredients of the art of motivation in management.

Planning, organizing, directing, controlling, decision making, communication, and motivation are general management processes in that they apply to all administrative functions and to any type of organization (Litchfield, 1956, p. 28). These management processes become operative and meaningful when applied to specific task areas and should be considered essential tools to the actualization of tasks. Another observation that should be made concerning management processes is that the operations are cyclical. One process leads to another. The act of planning, for example, will spin the wheel and engage the administrator into more actions. This cyclical aspect of management is characteristic of open and dynamic systems. "Decisions do not occur within a static environment where the goals are fixed, but they take place in a changing context" (Lane et al., 1967, p. 137). It is also obvious that at all times in the life of an organization many such management cycles take place simultaneously; they are initiated at different levels of the organizational structure; they are concerned with various administrative matters; and they may vary in length. Regardless of these characteristics, and the size and nature of the organization, management processes are used universally and understanding them is essential for people interested in management theory and practice.

Theory and Practice

If management practice is oriented toward the solution of immediate, specific, and concrete problems in the real world of organizations, management theory focuses on an understanding of administrative phenomena in general. "A theory," writes Silverman, "is a statement, in broad terms, on the probable relationship between two or more phenomena" (1971, p. 169). Theory, in management, suggests hypotheses to be confirmed or rejected about the functioning of organizations. It attempts to explain why organizations are the way they are and determine what to do to change them. However, as Griffiths explained, a theory is not a law (1959, p. 28). There are, in fact, many theories of management, since there exist many hypotheses on the most effective and efficient approaches to managing and changing organizations.

Since many theories of management describe, in a certain way, the nature of reality, they may be of some important use when applied to "real-life" situations. It is certain, as Zeigler and Spaeth point out, that theoretical principles and concepts related to, for instance, human behavior in organizations can be of great assistance in understanding the implications of effective and efficient management (1975, p. 12). Theory then serves as a frame of reference and puts order in the body of knowledge concerning management practice.

PRESENT STATE OF THEORY AND SCHOLARLY THOUGHT

Organizational phenomena have been examined from many points of view. "Indeed a major characteristic of the literature is the variety of theoretical angles from which organizations are studied" (Mouzelis, 1967, p. 1). Some studies, most notably those of Likert (1961) and McGregor (1960), scanned the organization from the top down, finally offering new strategies for management. Others approached the problem from another standpoint, inquiring into the process of individual self-actualization in an organizational setting (Argyris, 1959). Still others focused their attention on specific organizational processes and studied organizational behavior from various perspectives. Decision-making models (Simon, 1957) and leadership models (Fiedler, 1957) constitute examples of such approaches to organizational theory. Finally, a trend in studying organizations now consists of applying open-system strategies to better understand organizational phenomena as they relate to the environment (Thompson, 1967).

For the purpose of reviewing the present state of theory and scholarly thought in management, this section will focus on two aspects. First, a synopsis will be presented of the development of administrative thought that led to present-day theoretical models of management. Second, the major research efforts accomplished in the area of administrative theory in physical education and sport will be summarized.

Development of Administrative Thought

Management is one aspect of organizational activity, and management of organizations has been a major concern of man for many centuries. However, it was not until the beginning of the nineteenth century that the myths of "ultimate authority" and of "central omnipotence," which were deeply embedded in the political philosophy of previous centuries, were finally refuted and gave way to more flexible thoughts concerning the management of organizations. As a result of the administrative revolution, much literature appeared on the art and science of managing organizations, and many different managerial ideologies were identified.

In the twentieth century *scientific management* was designed by Taylor to increase organizational productivity, particularly at the workshop level in industry (1947). Taylor believed that there was one best way of performance for each process or task in industry. He attempted to determine scientifically, through the use of time and motion studies and job analysis, the best method of work. He then proceeded to the selection and training of the best workers for the job so that the highest production could be achieved. His wage-incentive system (the differential piece-rate system) was designed to motivate workers to keep up with management's scientifically established standards of production.

At approximately the same time *classical theories* of management shifted emphasis from the workshop level to the entire structure of the industrial organization. As the initiator of this "universalist" approach, Fayol believed that there were a number of general principles applicable to any kind of organization, such as unity of command, specialization, and small span of control (1949). He was the first to propose five elements of administration: planning, organizing, command, coordination, and control. Gulick and Urwick were two main contributors to this approach and suggested additional administrative principles (1937).

Bureaucratic theory, which is often classified with the classicist approach, deserves special attention because of its still prevailing influence on today's more complex organizations. Influenced by Marx's and Hegel's philosophy in the nineteenth century, Max Weber, a German sociologist, formulated his theory of domination, which refers to a "power relationship in which the ruler, the person who imposes his will on others, believes that he has a right to the exercise of power, and the ruled consider it their duty to obey his orders" (Mouzelis, 1967, p. 16). Also, Weber's notion of the administrative apparatus holds that, "when exercised over a large number of people, domination necessitates an administrative staff which will execute commands and which will serve as a bridge between the ruler and the ruled" (Mouselis, 1967, p. 16). Weber identified three types of domination found in organizations: legal, traditional, and charismatic. Finally Weber defined the ideal type of bureaucratic organizations, or the "formal organizations," and specified their characteristics: (1) high degree of specialization, (2) systematic division of labor, (3) hierarchical authority structure with limited areas of command and responsibility, (4) written rules, imposed or enacted, (5) impersonality of relationships between organizational members, (6) recruitment of officials on the basis of ability and technical knowledge, and (7) differentiation of private and official income and fortune (Mouzelis, 1967, pp. 38–43). Post-Weberian theoreticians attempted to point out the dilemmas and dysfunctional aspects associated with the bureaucratic model of organizations.

The *human relations school of thought*, that began somewhat later, must be credited with the notion of "informal organization." "Here attention is focused on variables that are not included in any of the rational models—sentiments, cliques, social controls via informal norms, status and status striving, and so on" (Thompson, 1967, p. 7). Here the emphasis shifts from a concern for productivity to a more efficient and sociopsychological approach to managerial problems. Follett was among the first to recognize the importance of human interaction on the work place; she recognized the inevitability of conflicts in organizations and introduced the concept of power as a resultant of the "law of the situation" (1942, pp. 25–29).

The famous studies that took place at Western Electric's Hawthorne plant are considered the starting point of all subsequent empirical studies in the area of human relations (Roethlisberger and Dickson, 1939). The major findings of these studies were that social relations are an important dimension in the satisfaction of workers and contribute to their motivation at work, which in turn, leads to higher productivity. It has since been shown, however, that employee satisfaction is not necessarily linked with higher productivity (Maslow, 1954).

Along with the earlier Weber, Chester Barnard remains as a leading theorist whose influence dominated the field of *organization theory* for many decades.

> The Barnardian model went beyond the pious statements that labor and management should cooperate or that conflict would be reduced or productivity raised by cooperation. Barnard was the first to insist, at length, that organizations by their very nature, are cooperative systems and could not fail to be so. (Perrow, 1972, p. 75)

For Barnard, organizations are nonpersonal and consist of forces rather than individuals. As cooperative systems, organizations have a common goal or moral purpose, which is service to society. Barnard's further contributions include his definition of the role of the executive in decision making; his inducement-contribution plan for organizational members; his distinction between the formal and informal forces of the organization; and his notion that authority is granted by subordinates at the bottom of the organization (1938).

Leadership theory, which stated that effective leadership will result in higher productivity and better performance by the employees, branched off from the human relations school of thought. Basically, three approaches have been utilized to examine organizational leadership. Trait theories were used to attempt to explain leadership from the standpoint of what the leader is; behavioral theories, from what the leader does; and situational or contingency theories, from the situation within which the leader operates.

The trait approach is based on the hypothesis that leaders have similar personality traits (inherited or acquired). Long lists of qualities and characteristics have been identified, but only a few may be common to all good leaders: intelligence, initiative, and self-confidence (Stogdill, 1948).

The behavioral approach has been the most popular. It emphasizes research of the various dimensions that can be used to describe and delineate leadership behavior. Many theoreticians belong to this school of thought. Management styles have been classified as defensive or participative (Gibb, 1954); as nomothetic and ideographic (Getzels and Guba, 1957); as initiating structure and as consideration (Halpin, 1967); and as mechanistic and bureaucratic versus organismic and professional (Hage, 1965). Management systems have been classified as: exploitative-authoritative, benevolent-authoritative, consultative and participative (Likert, 1967), and as based on theory X (effectiveness) and theory Y (integration of the individual) (McGregor, 1960). Styles of management have been classified on a continuum ranging from superior-centered to employee-centered (Tannenbaum and Schmidt, 1958) and from considering the employees as in the infancy stage and considering them as fully matured (Argyris, 1957). Others have classified managerial leadership on a grid describing various styles deriving from a combination of more or less interest for production or human relations or both (Blake and Mouton, 1964).

Situational theorists maintain that leadership is always related to the variables affecting the situation, such as formal authority status of the leader, the nature of the tasks to be performed, and the relationships between the leader and the group members (Fiedler, 1967). Situational theory therefore proposes to alter the situation (adapt the environment to the leader) instead of changing the leader (adapt the leader to the environment).

Motivation theory looks at organizational factors that lead to employee satisfaction. Lawler and Porter looked at employee attitudes and empirically determined that, when rewards accompanied high performance, satisfaction resulted from high performance rather than being a cause of it (1967, pp. 20–28). Herzberg's theory stated that satisfaction results when motivators are perceived positively but that their absence does not necessarily lead to dissatisfaction. Obviously there are many variables that may account for individual satisfaction and, as Maslow states, the higher the level of the need, the greater is the power of that need to give enduring satisfaction (1954, pp. 63–69). Nevertheless, Herzberg has made a great contribution in stressing the significance of working conditions as possible sources of motivation.

Scientific management, classical theory, bureaucratic theory, human relations theory, organization theory, leadership theory, and motivation theory constitute some of the scholarly areas in management in which researchers in physical education and sport have oriented their efforts.

Management Theory in Physical Education and Sport

While research is being done in the general area of management, the physical education profession also has a responsibility to engage in research to add to this body of knowledge and to make it available to physical education and sport administrators in the field. "We should not expect to be able to continue successfully with our management assignments by parasiting, so to speak, from other scholarly contributions carried out elsewhere" (Zeigler, 1979, p. 36). Up to this date, and in comparison with completed investigations in other disciplinary areas of physical education, a limited amount of research has been done in management theory as it relates to our field.

> At the present time, the academic work in sport management is still very much in the embryonic stage. In other words, we lack a body of knowledge in sport management. The work will remain embryonic until we can get students into the trenches to research the existing structure and conduct of programs in sport management. (VanderZwaag, 1980, p. 4)

Potential for Research. There is a great potential, however, for research in this field and there exists an identifiable body of knowledge that is specific to sport and physical education. Parkhouse and Ulrich express the opinion that sport management is a unique cross-discipline that is "constituted of portions of such related disciplines as journalism, business administration, educational administration, physical education, public administration and law" (1979, p. 269). Indeed the avenues for research in sport and physical education administration are tremendous in that the field offers a unique opportunity for analyzing the organizational behavior of sport administrators, of coaches, and of athletes, and, in so doing, of "relating to scholars in other disciplines that make up what have been called the behavioral sciences" (Zeigler, 1973, p. 141). In addition to experimental and descriptive research possibilities in the behavioral sciences, historical, philosophical, and comparative studies have great potential as they relate to the nature of sport and physical education organizations.

Nature of Management Research in Sport and Physical Education. A study completed in 1967 that reviewed a sample of doctoral dissertations written between 1940 and 1966 illustrated that most of the administrative research in physical education had been designed primarily to solve immediate and practical problems (Spaeth, 1967). The author concluded that there was little evidence of contributions to the theoretical body of knowledge in physical education administration useful for professional preparation and practice. The need for greater attention to the development of meaningful concepts and models in sport and physical education administration was further demonstrated in 1968 in another study that revealed that "professors of educational administration view the concepts in administrative theory as being generally more contemporary and potentially meaningful than physical education administrators and faculty" (Penny, 1968). Finally, in 1970, a third study showed that there was a significant lack of theoretical orientation in graduate administration courses and doctoral dissertations in physical education (Paton, 1970). Paton recommended that the emphasis be redirected from the current focus on principles of management to a focus on organization theory, management analysis, and human relations (1973, p. 73).

Figure 6–2 shows the evolution in the number of doctoral dissertations in physical education and athletics administration over 30 years. It appears obvious in this illustration that (1) the popularity of management as a field of investigation in physical education and athletics at the doctoral level in American universities is constantly increasing, and (2) the call for a need for more theoretical studies in physical education administration by researchers like Paton and Spaeth at the end of the 1960s did not go unanswered. A closer look at the curve depicted in this figure reveals that a substantial increase in the number of doctoral dissertations in this field started in approximately 1969–1970, reaching a peak of 28 completed doctoral studies in the year 1975. It also appears that, along with a continued interest in the 1980s for the field of management as a career and as an area of study in American universities, a similar trend seems to hold in physical education as well, considering that a total of 69 doctoral students completed their studies in administration in 1976–78.

Altogether a total of 318 doctoral studies has been reported since 1949, and this clearly supports the results obtained in a more recent study that revealed that "the

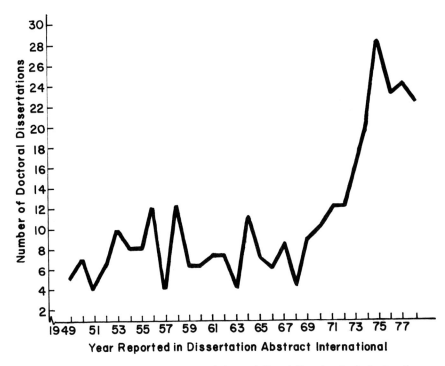

Fig. 6–2. Evolution of the number of doctoral dissertations in physical education and athletics administration over 30 years.

graduates' major areas of doctoral study represented an almost equal division between the disciplinary and professional areas, exercise physiology being the most popular disciplinary area and administration being the most popular professional area" (Knight, 1974). Although one could question the classification of administration as strictly a professional area, the results of this study support the notion that management has been and remains a popular area of investigation in our profession.

Following a pattern similar to business and educational administration, earlier management research in physical education made use of status surveys and job analysis techniques for the main purpose of suggesting "general principles" and solving immediate problems confronting administrators of physical education. In that sense, Zeigler wrote:

> Interestingly enough, it is true that there have been more master's and doctoral studies in physical education that, broadly speaking, could be called "administrative" in nature than in any other area of investigation within the field. However, neither these investigations nor almost all the texts and monographs that have appeared have gone beyond the listing of prescriptive policies and procedures. (1979, p. 36)

Figure 6–3 indicates the nature of administrative concerns in completed doctoral studies from 1940 to 1980. The histogram is divided into two segments: The one on the left depicts the major areas of *practical* and *technical* concerns that have been the object of doctoral dissertations; the right segment lists the major topics of theoretical and behavioral concerns. Even though some "hard" decisions had to be made in classifying these research studies, it is felt that this figure accurately represents the research field as it presently stands.

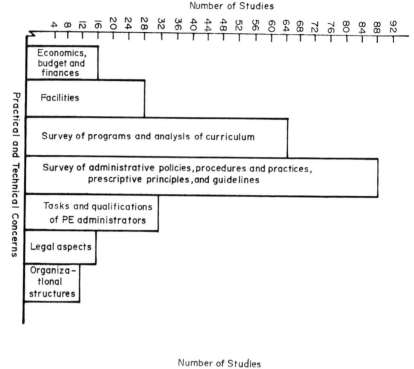

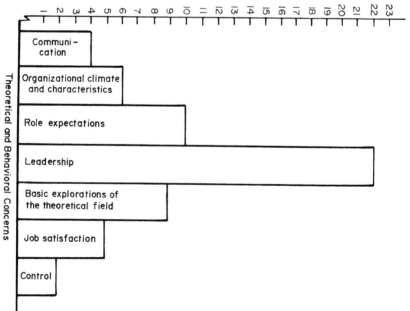

Fig. 6–3. Nature of administrative concerns in doctoral dissertations.

As stated earlier, the most popular domain of investigation at this level has been related to surveys of administrative policies, procedures, and practices, the majority of which were completed for the purpose of prescribing principles and guidelines for action; 88 studies can be classified in this category. Another often selected domain of doctoral investigation has been surveys of existing programs of physical education and athletics at various educational levels. The major acknowledged purpose of such studies has been the analysis and evaluation of program offerings in physical education, sport, and athletics; 64 studies of that nature were found. Job (tasks) analyses of administrators of physical education and athletics, and analyses of the qualifications of heads and directors in this field, have been grouped together and form the next largest area of investigation. The area of facilities has also been extensively (27 studies) investigated. Analyses of economic and financial aspects (16 studies), of legal aspects (16 studies), and of existing organizational structures (12 studies) constituted the other major areas of practical and technical concerns.

The majority of theoretical concerns in doctoral studies have been mostly all behavioral in nature; that is, they have been particularly concerned with analysis of organizational behavior in physical education and athletics. Although a few investigations have been completed at the elementary and secondary school levels, most studies were done on two types of physical education organizations: departments of physical education and departments of athletics in colleges and universities. Most studies may be considered as partial attempts at empirically testing theoretical models of management, even though the majority of them constituted applied research in that they had practical orientations.

The most investigated organizational variable in physical education has been leadership (Fig. 6–3, right segment); 22 studies were classified as such. Most of these studies have been concerned with identifying perceived administrative behavior, often situational behavior, of physical education and athletics leaders. The most popular research instrument has been the LBDQ (Leadership Behavior Descriptive Questionnaire). Broadly speaking, professional leaders have been identified mostly as democratic and participative and as scoring high on both "consideration" and "initiating structure" dimensions of leadership. Some discrepancies appear to exist between perceptions of leadership styles between superiors and subordinates.

Role expectations on the part of physical education and athletics superiors and subordinates have been the object of ten studies. These investigations have dealt with perceived ideal and actual role expectations. In general, there appears to be agreement on ideal role dimensions, but some incongruences exist concerning actual role dimensions as perceived by administrators and organizational members.

Six studies have been classified as concerned with the concept of organizational climate and characteristics. For the most part, organizational environments in physical education and athletics are perceived as open and participative even though, again, discrepancies do appear to exist between perceived actual and ideal climate organizational environment characteristics.

Job satisfaction has been investigated in five studies. Again, broadly speaking, physical education and athletic personnel appear to be more satisfied than dissatisfied, but in most studies findings reject the Herzberg hypothesis that sources of satisfaction are found only in the work content and those of dissatisfaction are related to the work environment.

Other variables investigated in physical education have included communication and control. It appears risky at this point in time, with a limited number of studies on these topics, to generalize from the findings. Finally, a number of studies have been conducted for the purpose of exploring and defining the field of management theory in physical education.

If doctoral studies can be a true indicator of professional involvement in management, it now appears evident that a major shift of emphasis in scholarly investigations in physical education administration has taken place since 1967. Before that year, with maybe a few rare exceptions, professional scholars had very little interest in management theory as it relates to physical education and sport. It must, however, be added that many scholars at the doctoral level are still conducting studies with "technical and practical" concerns in mind. It can be roughly estimated that only slightly more than half of the doctoral studies reported in physical education since 1967 have had "theoretical and behavioral" orientations. Professional areas such as the planning and management of sport facilities, legal aspects of the profession, and financial dimensions of physical education and sport management still constitute popular sectors of investigation. Aa far as management theory is concerned the profession of physical education and sport has now started to make its contributions. As Zeigler and Spaeth wrote:

> Obviously, the whole idea of a Ph.D. specialization in administrative theory and practice in physical education and athletics is that those following this endeavor will continue to spend at least a portion of their time in the future carrying out further studies along this line, tending in direction of tenable theory at some not-too-distant point-in-time. (1975, p. 422)

The development of management theory in physical education and sport is now on course.

IMPLICATIONS FOR GENERAL EDUCATION

People do not have a choice about interacting or not interacting in social and formal organizations. As social animals, human beings need to be a part of groups. They need to belong; they need to be wanted and included by their peers. On the other hand, humans are exposed to formal organizations as soon as they enter nursery schools or kindergartens. From then on, they will be interacting in organizational environments of every shape and form. As pointed out earlier, we do live in a highly organized society.

Whether a person is a student in engineering, arts, law, education, or whatever field, he should know about how organizations function and how they can affect people's behavior. After all, he will spend his whole life interacting with others in social and formal organizations. Many of these may be sport organizations. Who, in this so-called leisure society of ours, does not belong to a racquet club, or to a fitness group, or does not go to the local Y?

For some students, for example those in business, education, or law, a knowledge of management theory and practice in sport and physical education would become essential if they eventually have to work within a professional sport organization, a private health and fitness facility, a marketing agency, institutional athletics, or whatever.

Management theory and practice of physical education and sport organizations has become of interest to scholars and educators in other fields, particularly the social sciences, law, and business administration, as evidenced by jointly offered programs and courses in our field by colleges and universities and by an increasing number of studies completed by task forces that include experts from various sectors, including physical education. Hence, this field of study may be important for prospective students interested, for example, in the social psychology of team sports, the legal aspects of professional and amateur sports and institutional physical education, or the plannng and management of major sport events.

It can then be stated that understanding the field of management theory and practice in sport and physical education can be of value in the general education of all, and it is almost a necessity for those contemplating a career in areas in which sport may be the focal point in their employment.

IMPLICATIONS FOR PROFESSIONAL PRACTICE

Following the rationale exposed in the preceding section, the necessity of possessing knowledge in management theory and practice for professional students in physical education and sport is evident. In fact, most colleges and universities in North America offering professional programs in physical education have traditionally offered courses in this area.

> Evidence at hand points to the offering of a course in the organization and administration of physical education and athletics as far back as 1890, and by 1927 such courses were typically included in professional curricula throughout the country. (Zeigler and Spaeth, 1975, p. 22)

A survey in Canada revealed that 88% of universities offering professional preparation programs offer at least one course in the area of physical education/sport/athletic administration (Bedecki and Soucie, 1980). Many institutions of higher learning in the United States and Canada offer structured undergraduate and graduate programs of studies in physical education/sport/athletic administration. In the United States a study by Parkhouse revealed that 20 of 244 institutions were offering a graduate course of study in athletic administration and sport management. (1978, p. 23). In Canada a similar study by Soucie and Bedecki indicated that ten undergraduate programs (six at university level and four at college level) currently exist in physical education/sport/athletic administration, while nine universities offer a master's degree and two universities offer a doctorate with a possibility of specializing in this field (1980, pp. 4–6). Presently many more institutions may be considering such curricular offerings in this "relatively new classroom pursuit" (Geis, 1974, p. 14), which will be urgently needed in the future for more adequate professional preparation.

There appear to be marked differences in the designs of such specialization programs, but Carroll's study revealed a constant: "the propensity toward curricula that prepared students as generalists in the field of athletic administration" (1978). This concern for preparing "generalists" in sport management is in agreement with the conclusions of another study which, from a job analysis of a number of athletic administrators, concluded that degree programs in this field, in addition to being competency based and interdisciplinary, should prepare competency for a wide range of positions (Kinder, 1975). Closer analysis of currently offered programs in this area does confirm these basic trends: (1) field work constitutes a major component of the program; (2) undergraduate programs emphasize exposure to functional areas of administration while graduate programs appear to have more theoretical orientations and be research oriented; and (3) previous administrative experience appears to be highly desirable for admission to such programs (Soucie and Bedecki, 1980, p. 8).

Lack of Adequate Management Training

Even though physical education and sport management programs are apparently now becoming more numerous throughout North America for tomorrow's administrators, the lack of adequate preparation of current administrators, particularly in the area of professional and amateur sport, has been often pointed out.

> In the modern complexity and high technology of industry, management in sport has long been looked down upon. Often staffed by persons who have entered through the player-coach-manager route, the sport manager has been dubbed as being of the "Jock" mentality. (Mullin, 1980, p. 5)

As stated in the introduction to this chapter, there is quite a difference between being the "administrator" and the "administered." Management is a profession that requires not only experience but also leadership qualities and a good understanding of managerial techniques and processes. Unfortunately, many administrators in our field have never received the necessary training in management theory and practice.

> It is also readily apparent that most of these people (sport managers) were trained through some form of apprenticeship in which they learned to pursue their tasks in a manner which had been established by tradition. (VanderZwaag, 1980, p. 4)

Need for a Scientific Basis

Managerial practice in sport and physical education is in desperate need of a scientific basis. Research that leads to management theory can have two fundamental applications. First it may, as is the case for all other fields of research, aim at satisfying our curiosity. The researcher in management science wants to know. He wants to know why people behave the way they do in organizational environments. He wants to know the consequences of the application of different managerial approaches and styles—how to plan, organize, direct, control, and evaluate human effort in organizations. He seeks to know how to arrive at organizational effectiveness and efficiency. Second, management research can be of great service to practicing administrators confronted by "everyday" managerial difficulties. If there is one sector in which it is vital to link theory and practice, to bridge the gap between researchers and practitioners, it is indeed in the field of management.

Parkhouse and Ulrich claim that there is a need for us to inductively develop a mid-range theory:

> A mid-range theory is to a discipline what a coach's strategy or "play book" is to the actual game. The coach's strategies are not the play itself, but a conceptualization of it. The mid-range theory of sport management is not the discipline but its conceptual foundation. (1979, p. 272)

Such a theoretical framework for management practice will derive from "action" research as conducted by SIR-CAR (Sports Institute for Research through Change Agent Research) at the University of Windsor. SIR-CAR is based on the premise that

> the collaborative efforts of theoreticians (scholars, scientists and community experts) and practitioners (amateur and professional executives, coaches, officials, sponsors, spectators, and participants) is superior to the two-step process wherein a middleman attempts to communicate between theoreticians and practitioners. (Moriarty, 1976, p. 123)

SIR-CAR is a unique research approach that combines organizational analysis, organizational development, and organizational research in an effort to identify problems in physical education and sport and to suggest alternate management approaches. In this action approach, communication-feedback workshops and participative clinics are used following the collection of data to induce the desired changes. Action research of this nature is required to build up scientific foundations for the practice of management in our profession.

> As administrators in athletics and physical education learn to use action research they will find more fulfillment within their organizations, be more helpful to their clientele, and be more effective in dealing with their environments. (Parkhouse and Holmen, 1979, p. 520)

Numerous and Unique Research Opportunities

Opportunities and avenues for conducting action research in management theory and practice are exceptional. Some of the "technical concerns" in which research can be conducted may include such areas as facilities and equipment, public relations, budgeting, marketing, curriculum and programming, legal liability, selection and recruitment of personnel, and many others covering the entire gamut of specific tasks that are the responsibility of managers and supervisors in sport and physical education. Some of the "theoretical" concerns that may be the object of investigation are as varied as there are organizational variables and management processes (for example, conflicts; goal setting; goal displacement; motivation; job satisfaction; role differentiation and role expectation; planned change; change agents; organizational development; leadership; authority-power relationships; organizational climate; and in areas of managerial processes such as effective planning strategies, organizational structure, effective control and evaluation, decision making, and communication). In summary, there are as many possibilities for research in management theory as one can imagine hypotheses about the relationships of variables in the management of sport and physical education organizations.

Just as the researcher needs the assistance of the practicing administrator in identifying specific problems of more immediate concerns, the practitioner requires the insight and the research know-how of the theoretician. Just as research is not possible without action, action is not possible without research.

RELATIONSHIP TO AFFILIATED PROFESSIONS

In the same fashion as scholars in management theory and practice have a responsibility toward the general education of college and university students, management experts and theorists have a commitment toward affiliated professions from the world of sport and physical education. Interrelationships should be obvious between the field of management theory and practice and our allied professions such as health education, safety education, recreation, dance, competitive athletics, sports medicine, and physical therapy.

These allied professions can provide excellent opportunities to management scholars for conducting research. Whether in hospitals, public health units, recreation agencies, dance studios, or on the playing field, participants in rehabilitative, recreational, or competitive programs, or whatever, all have one thing in common, that is, their involvement in physical activity. The organizational environment within which these individuals are physically active represents a unique laboratory for management scientists to study and analyze organizational behavior and interactions as well as leadership processes. Also, some very interesting opportunities exist for studying the organizational structures within which these allied professions operate and in conducting comparative studies. Finally, management scientists should be interested in analyzing the various management approaches utilized in those professions for planning, organizing, directing, and controlling their various programs of physical activity.

Management theory and practice scholars have, in return, a commitment to provide the theory and the scientific background to the practicing administrators involved in these allied professions. Not only do they have to assist them in conducting their own research, but they also have to make research information readily available to them for immediate consumption. Management theorists can also play a major role in designing and implementing professional leadership tι..ining programs, seminars, and workshops for managers and supervisors involved in those various allied sectors. In brief, it should be evident that the professions allied to sport and physical education need the knowledge of management scientists for management practice as much as the management theoreticians need the experience and insights of allied professional administrators for developing management theory.

PROFESSIONAL OPPORTUNITIES

In the past decade, prospects for careers in administration of sport, physical education, and athletics have increased tremendously.

> The phenomenon of organized physical education, including competitive athletics, that has taken place in the United States within the past one hundred years has today become a vast enterprise that demands wise and skillful management. (Zeigler and Spaeth, 1975, p. 3)

If, in general, the North American job market is quite delicate and uncertain these days, the fact remains that more jobs in physical education and sport management are created every day. Paralleling the movement toward equal opportunity for women and the introduction of Title IX, more jobs are available for women administrators (Gibson, 1978). As Ley expresses it, when she writes about intercollegiate athletics, "Men must not take over for women in some areas of function just because women have had limited experience in the area" (1973, p. 52).

Many major sectors for employment opportunities in physical education and sport management have been identified (Jackson and Love, 1978). A close analysis of all forms of social and formal organizations dealing with physical education, athletics, and sport reveals that, indeed, many professional opportunities do exist.

There are job opportunities in *educational settings* as physical education super- visors and department heads, as directors of intramural programs and interscholastic sports, as head coaches, and as athletic directors. At the university and college level, there are, in addition, teaching and research possibilities in management theory and practice for the more scholarly oriented students who wish to continue through the doctoral level.

There are job opportunities in the *sport industry* in major and minor professional sport leagues as finance manager, publicity director, marketing and promotion agent, and player-contract negotiator. There are also possibilities at the amateur sport level as coaches, executive directors, and technical directors of sport-governing bodies.

There are job opportunities within *commercial firms* in the manufacturing and merchandising of sporting goods and in *private clubs* such as fitness and health centers, tennis and racquet clubs, resorts, and summer and outdoor education camps. Career opportunities also exist in facility (arena, stadium, fieldhouse, etc.) manage- ment, and as consultants in planning and designing sports facilities and equipment.

There are employment opportunities in *recreation agencies* in park management, camping, therapeutic recreation; in the management of agency programs for children and of activity/fitness programs for the aged in nursing homes, retirement centers, and Ys. There are career possibilities in municipal recreation as recreation director and playground supervisor.

Finally, there may eventually be full-time job opportunities in *professional as- sociations* (as editors, technical assistants, and executive directors) such as AAHPERD (American Alliance for Health, Physical Education, Recreation, and Dance) and its affiliated association for Research, Administration, Professional Councils, and Soci- eties; CAHPER (Canadian Association for Health, Physical Education and Recreation) and its affiliated Management Theory and Practice Committee; SMARTS (Sport Management Art and Science Society).

In brief, job opportunities in this professional area are developing quickly as various forms of organizations and associations of physical education and sport emerge in North American society.

SUMMARY AND CONCLUDING STATEMENT

The existence of a vast number of organizations and associations in today's society cannot be denied. People live and work all their lives within organizations. Because leisure time available to North Americans will most likely continue to increase in the 1980s—as it did in the 1970s—it can be speculated that the end of the twentieth century will witness further emergence of sport organizations, particularly in the area of participative sports.

It takes someone to head and run these numerous sport and physical activity organizations and associations, regardless of their size, nature, and purpose. Orga- nizations need to be managed. They need to be directed by the best-qualified in- dividuals our profession can offer. So far the profession of physical education and sport has not done too well in this area. Our best "qualified" administrators have always been, and still are, those who have "come up through the ranks," the ones with "experience" and "seniority." While these variables have great importance in the selection of administrators in sport and physical education, as well as in any other field of endeavor, specific professional training in management is essential. In today's increasingly more complex organization, knowledge and understanding of the theory of organizations is indispensable. Awareness of organizational behavior and leadership theory is essential.

Scholars in our profession have a responsibility to develop a scientific basis and a theoretical framework for the management of physical education and sport organizations. Human organizational behavior in sport and physical education settings is unique and constitutes a challenging research opportunity for scholars from the behavioral sciences. There are very few such scholars in North America who are currently devoting time and efforts in this vast domain. If professionals and scholars in physical education and sport do not want to get "bumped" by individuals from other fields, they will have to seriously consider getting quickly involved in investigating management theory and practice in our field. There are really no other alternatives.

QUESTIONS FOR POSSIBLE DISCUSSION AND TESTING

1. Define the following concepts as they relate to management theory: management, management as leadership, management as a set of tasks, management as a series of processes, organization (group), planning, organizing, directing, controlling, communication, decision making, motivation, and theory.
2. Provide some examples of formal organizations in physical education, athletics, and sport.
3. Identify the basic characteristics of the general management processes.
4. What characterized the following schools of thought in management theory: scientific management, classical theory, bureaucratic theory, human relations theory, leadership theory, and motivation theory?
5. Historically, which "practical" and "theoretical" concerns have been the object of scholarly investigations in physical education and sport management?
6. Why is 1967 identified as a turning point in management theory and practice in physical education and sport?
7. What are some of the current generalizations that may be emerging as a result of theoretical investigations in management of sport, physical education, and athletics organizations?
8. What are the implications of management theory and practice in physical education and sport for general education?
9. What appear to be some of the current characteristics of professional preparation programs in North American colleges and universities for sport and physical education administrators?
10. What are the implications of management theory for professional practice in physical education and sport administration?
11. Why is there a need for a scientific basis and action research in sport and physical education management?
12. Which unique research opportunities are available to the scholar interested in management theory and practice in physical education and sport?
13. Which relationships should exist between the field of management theory and practice and the allied professions?
14. What are some of the professional opportunities for careers in physical education and sport management?

REFERENCES

Argyris, C.: Personality and Organization. New York, Harper & Row, 1957.
Argyris, C.: The individual and the organization. Adm. Sci. Q., 4, 2:145–167, 1959.

Barnard, C.: The Functions of the Executive. Cambridge, Mass., Harvard University Press, 1938.

Bedecki, T., and Soucie, D.: Trends in physical education/sport/athletic administration in Canadian universities and colleges. Paper presented at the 26th Annual Conference of the Canadian Association for Health, Physical Education and Recreation, St. John's, Newfoundland, July, 1980.

Blake, R., and Mouton, J.: The Managerial Grid. Houston, Gulf Publishing Co., 1964.

Blau, P.M., and Scott, W.R.: The concept of formal organization. *In* Management, Organizations, and Human Resources. 2nd Ed. Edited by H.G. Hicks and J.D. Powell. New York, McGraw-Hill, 1976.

Bullied, A.: Associations . . . a long history and broad reach. Sport Ontario News, 7, 5:7–8, 1978.

Carroll, J.W.: A comparison of developmental processes and designs of athletic administration programs at six institutions of higher education. Doctoral dissertation, University of Pittsburgh, 1978.

Fayol, H.: General and Industrial Management (translated by Constance Storrs). London, Pitman, 1949.

Fiedler, F.: A Theory of Leadership Effectiveness. New York, McGraw-Hill, 1967.

Follett, M.P.: Dynamic Administration—The Collected Papers of Mary Follett. Edited by H.C. Metcalf and L. Urwick. New York, Harper & Row, 1942.

Geis, J.: Sports administration programs. Athlet. Adm., 8, 3:14–20, 1974.

Getzels, J.W., and Guba, E.G.: Social behavior and administration process. School Rev., 65, 4:423–441, 1957.

Gibb, C.A.: Leadership. *In* Handbook of Social Psychology. Edited by C. Lindzey. New York, Addison-Wesley, 1954.

Gibson, K.D.: Changing nature of women's athletic administration. Scholas. Coach, 48, 5:67–90, 1978.

Griffiths, D.E.: Administrative Theory. New York, Appleton-Century-Crofts, 1959.

Gross, B.M.: Organizations and Their Managing. New York, Free Press, 1968.

Gulick, L., and Urwick, L. (eds.): Papers on the Science of Administration. New York, Institute of Public Administration, 1937.

Hage, G.: An axiomatic theory of organization. Adm. Sci. Q. 10, 3:289–320, 1965.

Halpin, A.W.: Theory and Research in Administration. New York, Macmillan Co., 1967.

Herzberg, F.: Work and the Nature of Man. Cleveland, World Publishing Co., 1969.

Jackson, J., and Love, B.: Sport as a Career. Ottawa, CAHPER Sociology of Sport Monograph Series, 1978.

Kinder, T.M.: Criteria for a graduate program in athletic administration based on a job analysis of athletic administrators in selected south-eastern states. Doctoral dissertation, George Peabody College, Nashville, 1975.

Knight, W.J.: Specialization in physical education doctoral programs as it relates to the eventual professional-vocational responsibilities of doctoral graduates. Doctoral dissertation, Ohio State University, 1974.

Lane, W.R. et al.: Foundations of Educational Administration. New York, Macmillan Co., 1967.

Lawler, E., and Porter, L: The effect of performance on job satisfaction. Indus. Rel., 6:1–28, 1967.

Ley, K.: Philosophical considerations in the administration of intercollegiate athletics for women. *In* Administrative Theory and Practice in Athletics and Physical Education. Edited by P. Hunsicker. Chicago, Athletic Institute, 1973.

Likert, R.: The Human Organization, Its Management and Value. New York, McGraw-Hill, 1967.

Likert, R: New Patterns of Management. New York, McGraw-Hill, 1961.

Litchfield, E.H.: Notes on a general theory of administration. Adm. Sci. Q. 1, 1:3–29, 1956.

Maslow, A.H.: Motivation and Personality. New York, Harper & Row, 1954.

McGregor, D: The Human Side of Enterprise. New York, McGraw-Hill, 1960.

McWhinney, W.H.: Organizational form, decision modalities and the environment. *In* Readings in Organization Theory, Open-Systems Approaches. Edited by J.G. Maurer, New York, Random House, 1971.

Moriarty, D.: Avoiding organizational self-destruction in amateur sport or professional athletics by SIR-CAR. Can. J. Appl. Sport Sci. 1, 2:123–131, 1976.

Mouzelis, N.P.: Organization and Bureaucracy, An Analysis of Modern Theories. Chicago, Aldine-Atherton, 1967.

Mullin, B.: Sport management—The chicken and the egg. Sport Man. Newslet. 2, 2:5–6, 1980.

Parkhouse, B.L.: Professional preparation in athletic administration and sport management—Graduate programs in the United States. J. Phys. Educ. Recr., 49, 5:22–27, 1978.

Parkhouse, B.L., and Holmen, M.G.: Action research and development: Utilizing sociometric analysis in physical education and athletic departments. Res. Q. 50, 3:511–520, 1979.

Parkhouse, B.L., and Ulrich, D.O.: Sport management as a potential cross-discipline: A paradigm for theoretical development, scientific inquiry and professional application. Quest, 31, 2:264–276, 1979.

Paton, G.A.: An analysis of administrative theory in selected graduate administration courses in physical education. Doctoral dissertation, University of Illinois, Champaign, 1970.

Paton, G.A.: Administrative theory and graduate physical education. *In* Administrative Theory and Practice in Athletics and Physical Education. Edited by P. Hunsicker. Chicago, Athletic Institute, 1973.

Penny, W.: An analysis of the meanings attached to selected concepts in administrative theory. Doctoral dissertation, University of Illinois, Champaign, 1968.

Perrow, C.: Complex Organizations, A Critical Essay. Glenview, Ill., Scott, Foresman and Co., 1972.

Peter, L. and Hull, R: The Peter Principle. New York, Bantam Books, 1969.

Roethlisberger, F.J., and Dickson, W.J.: Management and the Worker. Cambridge, Mass., Harvard University Press, 1939.

Sachs, B.M.: Educational Administration, A Behavioral Approach. Chicago, Scott, Foresman and Co., 1966.

Silverman, D.: The Theory of Organizations. New York, Basic Books, 1971.

Simon, H.A.: Administrative Behavior. New York, Macmillan Co., 1957.

Soucie, D.: La théorie administrative au service de la gestion de l'éducation physique et du sport. Can. J. Appl. Sport Sci. 1, 1:87–92, 1976.

Soucie, D. and Bedecki, T: Professional preparation programs in physical education/sport/athletic administration in Canada. Paper presented at the Sport Management Art and Science Conference, Boston, June, 1980.

Spaeth, M.J.: An analysis of administrative research in physical education and athletics in relation to a research paradigm. Doctoral dissertation, University of Illinois, Champaign, 1967.

Sprandel, D.: A crisis in athletic administration. Phys. Educ. 31, 1:44–46, 1974.

Stogdill, R.M.: Personal factors associated with leadership. J. Psychol. 25, 1:33–66, 1948.

Tannenbaum, R. and Schmidt, W.H.: How to choose a leadership pattern. Harvard Bus. Rev., 36, 2:95–101, 1958.

Taylor, F.: Scientific Management. New York, Harper & Row, 1947.

Thompson, J.D.: Organizations in Action. New York, McGraw-Hill, 1967.

VanderZwaag, H.: Degree programs and management needs in sport. Sport Man. Newslet. 2, 2:4, 1980.

Zeigler, E.F.: Administrative theory and practice: A conference summary. *In* Administrative Theory and Practice in Athletics and Physical Education. Edited by P. Hunsicker. Chicago, Athletic Institute, 1973.

Zeigler, E.F.: The case for management theory and practice in sport and physical education. J. Phys. Educ. Recr., 50, 1:36–37, 1979.

Zeigler, E.F. and Spaeth, M.J. (eds.): Administrative Theory and Practice in Physical Education and Athletics. Englewood Cliffs, N.J., Prentice-Hall, 1975.

SELECTED READINGS

Bennis, W.: Beyond Bureaucracy: Essays on the Development and Evolution of Human Organization. New York, McGraw-Hill, 1973.

Eble, K.E.: The Art of Administration. San Francisco, Jossey-Bass, 1978.

Etzioni, A.: A Sociological Reader on Complex Organizations. New York, Holt, Rinehart and Winston, 1969.

Hicks, H.G, and Powell, J.D.: Management, Organizations, and Human Resources. New York, McGraw-Hill, 1976.

Hunsicker, P. (ed.): Administrative Theory and Practice in Athletics and Physical Education. Chicago, Athletic Institute, 1973.

Maurer, J.G.: Readings in Organization Theory. New York, Random House, 1971.
Sergiovanni, T.J., and Starratt, R.J.: Emerging Patterns of Supervision: Human Perspectives, 1979.
Toffler, A.: Future Shock. New York, Random House, 1970.
Zeigler, E.F., and Spaeth, M.J. (eds): Administrative Theory and Practice in Physical Education and Athletics. Englewood Cliffs, N.J., Prentice-Hall, 1975.

CHAPTER SEVEN

Program Development

Ann E. Jewett

Program development in sport and physical education necessarily emphasizes both scholarly and professional dimensions. Program development draws its theory from current theories of human development and learning and from contemporary theories of curriculum development and instruction. Program decisions are based on the theoretical insights of each of the subdisciplines discussed in preceding sections. The improvement of curriculum and instruction in any particular context requires intelligent application of management theory and practice and of evaluation and measurement theory and techniques. In highlighting key concepts of program development in sport and physical education, this section attempts to integrate the best of professional wisdom acquired through the experience of our past with the disciplinary insights of the present and to look to the future with a social relevance perspective.

In this spirit the introductory paragraphs present certain admittedly biased conclusions with regard to the present state of theory in physical education curriculum and instruction. Discussion of the practice of human motor performance in sport, dance, and exercise is focused primarily on programs developed within educational institutions. It is assumed that a liberal education or a general education in sport and physical education is the predominant goal of educational programs. Guidelines for such programs are detailed through illustrations from elementary-school physical education, middle-school physical education, secondary-school physical education, and adult physical education, with supplementary commentary on special physical education programs, intramural and physical recreation programs, and educational athletics.

In the latter part of the chapter, professional preparation program development is spotlighted. Guidelines for teacher education programs are suggested. It is recognized, in addition, that the future directions of sport and physical education will require opening new career fields that will emphasize not only teaching and scholarly productivity but also social service, sports medicine and health-related fitness, and professional athletics, sports communication, and sports-related business. Consequently suggestions are offered for professional preparation for future opportunities envisioned in each of these areas.

THEORY IN PHYSICAL EDUCATION CURRICULUM AND INSTRUCTION

What is theory? What is the role of curriculum theory in program development? There is general agreement that a theory is a set of related statements explaining

Dr. A. E. Jewett is from the University of Georgia, Athens.

The basic ideas in the section on curriculum and instruction theory were presented in a paper delivered to the Curriculum Academy, New Orleans, Louisiana, March 17, 1979. A revised version of that paper was subsequently published in *Quest*.

Certain portions of the content of this chapter have been adapted from Nixon and Jewett, *Introduction to Physical Education* (9th Ed.). Appreciation is expressed to Dr. Nixon and to W. B. Saunders Co.

some series of events. Those interested in theory building are engaged in defining, classifying, and describing phenomena of interest and in establishing relationships among the identified phenomena. The role of curriculum theory in program development is to provide planners with a description of available alternatives. Curriculum theory provides a systematic basis for decision making in selecting, structuring, and sequencing content. Curriculum theory describes alternative criteria for these activities and predicts their impact upon the instructional process. Instructional theory focuses upon describing the teaching process and predicts the impact in terms of student learning outcomes.

The first systematic comprehensive formulation of theory in physical education was the 1963 classic authored by Brown and Cassidy entitled *Theory in Physical Education: A Guide to Program Change*. Brown and Cassidy initiated theory building with two major emphases. Their theoretical formulation of the field of knowledge of physical education reflected Metheny's earlier foundational work directed toward a theoretical analysis of the discipline of human movement (Metheny, 1965). The school program development component was viewed much more pragmatically.

Nearly 10 years later, following the direction initiated by Metheny, AAHPERD encouraged and supported the theoretical structure project, a significant achievement in the national professional effort to identify and describe "a theoretical structure of physical education as an area of scholarly study and research." Ulrich and Nixon prepared a report of this project and formulated a broader theoretical perspective published as *Tones of Theory: A Theoretical Structure for Physical Education—A Tentative Perspective* (1972).

AAHPERD also supported the development of a conceptual framework for physical education curricular decision making. *Curriculum Design: Purposes and Processes in Physical Education Teaching-Learning* (Jewett and Mullan, 1977) narrows the scope of the broad theoretical structure for physical education to conceptualizing focused on the planning of educational programs dealing with human movement phenomena. The Purpose-Process Curriculum Framework is based on two key assumptions: (1) that physical education is concerned primarily with the individual moving in interaction with the environment and (2) that each individual person may seek personal meaning through any combination of potential movement goals. The primary components of the theory are key purpose concepts and a movement process category system.

Haag made a major contribution to theory building in his publication entitled *Sport Pedagogy: Content and Methodology* (1978). This unique work deals with current theoretical concepts and research findings. Emphasis has been placed upon definition and classification; a highly useful thesaurus of sport pedagogy terminology is included. Haag identifies two basic aspects of sport pedagogy: curriculum theory (problem of decision—problem of aim) and instructional theory (theory of teaching—theory of learning) (1978, p. 236).

Bressan proposes a theory describing physical education as a productive discipline (1981). Her theory proposes three primary structures for the productive discipline of physical education: substance, syntax, and performance. Her theory appears to have considerable power for clarifying relationships among the components of the total theoretical structure. It may well lead to a new paradigm for viewing sport and physical education.

What is the current state of development of theory in physical education? Prior to the 1960s, theory was almost nonexistent, but there has been genuine progress since the publication of Brown and Cassidy's *Theory in Physical Education*, in 1963, and continuing effort and increased sophistication can be expected in the near future.

First of all the importance of theory building in physical education has finally been acknowledged. The significance of alternative value orientations and the need for diverse theories have finally been recognized. There have been some scholarly contributions to the development of genuine physical education theory within the overall realm of curriculum theory. Curriculum and instructional specialists are increasingly aware of the need for academic training in philosophy and sociology as well as psychology. Physical education needs a sociological perspective as well as a sound theoretical base in motor behavior. Bain argues that we need both prescriptive and descriptive theory in physical education curriculum. "Scientific description should precede value based prescription" (1978, p. 25).

A second area in which progress has been made in theory building is in clarification of the phenomena of interest. It is generally agreed that physical education theorists are building theory to define, classify, and describe human movement phenomena and to establish relationships among these phenomena. They seek to describe and to prescribe approaches to curriculum and instruction relevant to personal interaction within the natural and social environment.

Present-day physical education theorists have learned to distinguish between curriculum theory and instructional theory. Curriculum is an educative agency's plan for facilitating learning. Instruction is a delivery system or the educative transactions that constitute the teaching-learning process for implementing the plan. Macdonald views curriculum as a purposefully selected cultural environment. "Curriculum is a study of 'what should constitute a world of learning and how to go about making this world' "(1977, p. 11). Instruction facilitates learning by persons in the process of becoming. Curriculum tends to focus more on ends, while instruction tends to emphasize means. Curriculum theory describes alternatives for making decisions about scope, structure, and sequence of content. Instructional theory details the range of potential teacher behaviors and teacher-learner interactions.

In reporting on the present state of theory building in physical education curriculum and instruction, it is important to emphasize the progress that has been made in identifying key questions to guide investigation, research, and analysis. Curriculum theory tries to answer the *why* and *what* questions. Instruction theory emphasizes the *how* questions. *What happens* is the evaluation question. It is relevant for both curriculum and instruction. For purposes of defining the fields of inquiry for curriculum theorists and instruction theorists, four categories of curriculum questions and six categories of instruction questions are listed:

Curriculum
   1. Values
   2. Aims/Objectives/Goals
   3. Content (including clustering and major decisions of sequence)
   4. Evaluation

Instruction
   1. Strategies (including pupil grouping and specific content progressions)
   2. Materials and learning resources
   3. Teaching behaviors
   4. Teacher-learner interaction
   5. Class management
   6. Assessment

Theorists investigating alternative value orientations for curriculum development have offered a variety of analyses. Four excellent analyses of different approaches to curriculum development are those by Eisner and Vallance (1974), Macdonald (1975), Pinar (1975), and Orlosky and Smith (1978). Eisner and Vallance detailed five conflicting conceptions of curriculum: cognitive processes, technology, self-actualization, social reconstruction, and academic rationalism. Macdonald's scheme classifies three types of curriculum theory as control, hermeneutic, and critical. Pinar's collection of curriculum readings reflects three designated groups of curriculum scholars, the traditionalists, the conceptual empiricists, and the reconceptualists. Orlosky and Smith labeled the four styles of curriculum theorizing as humanistic, discipline, technology and futuristic.

Among physical education curricularists, Jewett has proposed a classification of three types of models: disciplinary, social interaction, and personalized (1972). More recently she proposed value orientations identified as performance, fitness, and transcendence (1977). In a 1978 review Bain identified movement form, movement analysis, discipline of human movement, developmental stages, motor learning task analysis, and student motives or purpose theories. A year later she contributed an unusually promising analysis of physical education curriculum theory from a sociological perspective, examining structural functionalism and conflict theory as bases for curricular research (1979b). At the 1979 Conference on Curriculum Theory in Physical Education, Ulrich, Bain, and Studer reexamined physical education's commitment to fitness, play behavior and movement (Jewett and Norton, 1979, pp. 3–20).

A primary concern of those who are developing curriculum theory in physical education is the question of personal meaning or individual significance in movement. The Purpose-Process Curriculum Framework provides for the selection of content in terms of its meaning to individual persons (Jewett and Mullan, 1977). The 22 purpose elements are conceptualized as unique ways of finding or extending personal meaning through movement activities. Personal meaningfulness may also be increased by viewing the Movement Process Category System as curriculum content. The seven movement processes serve not only to facilitate the development of instructional objectives directed toward motor skill acquisition but also to extend the potential of physical education for heightening perceptions and personal awareness and for facilitating the development of individual creativity.

Bressan's work appears to offer outstanding potential for extending physical education theory in the direction of describing variables related to personal meaning and significance. Presentations such as "Making Movements that Matter—The Structure of a Productive Discipline for Physical Education" (1979) clearly emphasize this concern.

> Pursuit of significance is viewed within the performance structure of the discipline as a personal discovery or encounter with personal meaning available only to actual participants in sport, dance and exercise. . . . In this view teaching . . . requires an understanding of the general meaning of movement followed by a skillful translation into instructional actions which promote a student's ultimate discovery of significance. (Bressan, 1981, pp. 262–263)

Bain has also indicated concern for questions relating to personal meaning in teaching-learning contexts. Her studies of the hidden curriculum identify meanings implicit in the educational environment (1975, 1976). One of her studies investigated college students' motives for participation in sport, dance, or exercise activities and their perceptions of the appropriateness of specific activities for satisfaction of these motives (1979).

Most researchers in physical education have been more interested in instruction than in curriculum. In the last decade there has been a great flurry of activity in studies of teacher effectiveness; special emphasis has been given to descriptive studies of teacher behaviors. The current generation of studies on teaching is based largely on the work of educational psychologists. Key references are Gage (1978), Smith (1971), Joyce and Weil (1972), and Dunkin and Biddle (1974).

In the *Second Handbook of Research on Teaching* (1973), Nixon and Locke contributed a landmark review of the research on teaching physical education. Probably the most comprehensive work focusing on instruction in physical education is that presented by Heitmann and Kneer (1976). Others who have made important contributions in the development of particular aspects of instructional theory include

Mosston, Anderson, Cheffers, Siedentop, Singer, and Dick. Mosston's spectrum of teaching styles is a classic in physical education literature (1966). Anderson provided the first influential report on descriptive analytic research on teaching physical education and continues to contribute to building instructional theory (1971). Singer and Dick advocate a systems approach model of teaching (1974). Cheffers and Siedentop have reported data-based research findings on instruction and have synthesized their findings in textbook presentations (Cheffers and Evaul, 1978; Siedentop, 1976). While there is significant progress in research on teaching physical education there has been little integration into comprehensive instructional theory. There is need for continuing effort to advance theory formulation in the instructional component as well as in curriculum.

In summary, while there has been important progress in theory building, both in curriculum and instruction, too few physical education scholars have given priority to the formulation of theory. Few theorists have addressed the problem of broad comprehensive theory building. Those engaged in theoretical work are, for the most part, focusing their efforts in areas of limited scope. At this time there are large gaps in dealing with the total range of curriculum theory and almost no theoretical formulations to provide insights into relationships among theoretical elements. The needs for both speculative and empirical investigation, for collaborative models for physical education curriculum and instruction, and for efforts in theory building are compelling.

GENERAL EDUCATION IN SPORT AND DEVELOPMENTAL PHYSICAL ACTIVITY

Developmental physical activity and education for sport participation are general education in the truest form. Everyone needs learning opportunities in this broad field of knowledge to fulfill individual developmental potential, to enjoy a meaningful life, to develop abilities and competencies to contribute effectively as a citizen of a particular community, and to facilitate the shaping of a better future world by cooperative human beings on a global scale. Persons of all ages need the stimulation of educational programs in sport and physical education. They need access to learning environments rich in movement education possibilities. They have a right to expect that public resources will be available to assist them in achieving and maintaining health-related fitness and satisfying involvement in physical recreation activities. General education in sport and physical education is essential to these ends.

Educators became aware of the real importance of human growth and development in curriculum planning in the 1940s and 1950s. The concept of developmental tasks that provided guidance in sequencing instructional goals made its greatest initial impact on educational programs for young children. Now it is recognized that developmental tasks face individuals at all stages of life and that developmental physical activity is important for the infant and the senior citizen as well as for persons who happen to be enrolled in formal school programs. Sport and physical education is an essential phase of the curriculum in all schools. Physical activity programs need to be available to persons of all ages. School programs need to provide the learning that will make it possible for persons no longer in school to benefit from programs that depend on voluntary participation. Informal learning settings including physical activity as an essential aspect of general education probably will continue to increase in order to keep pace with the growing appreciation of the role of motor performance in human growth and development.

Preschool and Elementary-School Physical Education

Infants and preschool children are dependent upon their parents for environmental stimulation to facilitate sequential motor development. For this reason secondary-school students need physical education that prepares them as future parents to guide the early movement education experiences of their children. Optimum motor development for young children requires a family environment in which exploratory movement is encouraged and physical activity is not unduly restricted. Parents need to ensure that young children have the opportunity for extensive and varied movement challenges, that they are provided with positive reinforcement in the motor development process, and that the pediatrician is consulted if there are symptoms of unsatisfactory progress in motor development. Parents need to be particularly aware of appropriate guidelines for selecting and purchasing toys that will stimulate educationally sound play and present no safety hazards.

All day-care and educational programs for children of preschool age should provide for a significant amount of vigorous physical activity and guided movement education. Parent education and involvement will be necessary to support these programs. Once they recognize the importance of appropriate environmental stimulation for healthful physical activity in the overall process of human growth and development, the vast majority of parents will want to enroll their children in programs that give attention to sound motor development.

Parents also need to be aware of the importance of avoiding sex stereotyping in the play of young children. One of the reasons that women today typically lack upper body strength is that in our culture girls as young as 4 or 5 years of age have been discouraged from using their arms and shoulders. While their male counterparts were being encouraged to participate in activities emphasizing shoulder development, the girls have traditionally been conditioned not to participate in these activities and not to display strength. Until parents learn to encourage vigorous physical activity and optimum physical development in their daughters, girls and women will continue to be disadvantaged as sport participants and persons desiring to enjoy optimum health-related fitness. Appropriate nonsexist guidance of developmental motor performance must begin early; the major responsibility thus falls directly upon the shoulders of parents.

The focus of the elementary school has typically been placed upon the development of basic cognitive skills. It is now recognized that the fundamental developmental motor performance skills are just as basic to the whole child's functioning as the cognitive skills. Thus, every elementary school needs to provide for a daily instructional program in physical education for all children. Today's educators generally accept some variation of the Laban analysis of movement as a framework for elementary-school curriculum planning of movement education (Stanley, 1977). The major elements are body awareness in the performance of nonlocomotor, locomotor, and object manipulation activities and the development and refinement of movement patterns through attention to factors of time, space, effort, and flow.

The activity content of the elementary-school physical education curriculum emphasizes educational gymnastics and self-testing activities, dance, and games. Gymnastic activities will include stunts, tumbling, trampoline activities, and movement challenges on the balance beam, box, poles, ropes, ladders, stegels, stall bars, and creative types of hanging and climbing apparatus. Dance activities offer a wide variety of expressive rhythms, folk dances, ethnic dances, and creative dances.

The elementary-school curriculum should make minimal use of traditional children's games in which only one or two children are really active while others wait their turns. Games that emphasize competition by systematically eliminating the less successful players should also be discouraged. Instead, the games selected for instructional purposes should be games that keep all children actively involved in practicing fundamental motor skills; in refining throwing, striking, and kicking skills within changing game situations; and in constantly more demanding movement challenges presented in novel and interesting settings. Teachers are now creating new games specifically designed to achieve movement education objectives and to emphasize desirable social interaction among the children. Games are now designed to encourage responsibility to and caring for a partner and to teach cooperation with other children as equally or more important than competition that focuses attention on excelling by "beating" others. Self-direction, responsibility, and creativity are stimulated through encouraging children to create their own games. Everyone's goal in playing the new games is to have fun together.

The overall goals of the elementary-school physical education curriculum are:

1. Facilitation of optimum motor development through extensive movement experiences
2. Competence in spatial orientation abilities, including body awareness, consciousness of position in time-space, and identification of a dynamic self-environment of moving objects and other persons
3. Development of expressive abilities and creative movement
4. Group-interaction skills based on concepts of partner, teammate, group goal, captain, game rules, sharing
5. Personal confidence in motor performance based on individual success in meeting progressively more difficult movement challenges
6. Positive attitudes toward physical education growing out of intensive involvement in meaningful and enjoyable physical activities

Effective elementary-school physical education teachers use a variety of instructional methods. Movement exploration is stressed, particularly in the primary grades. Guided discovery in a wide variety of activities with and without equipment is a key strategy. A consistent supportive environment is essential. One of the most important skills of the teacher is the ability to establish movement tasks to stimulate problem solving by the children. These movement tasks need to be planned as individualized challenges that will provide for the involvement and success of each child. Teaching methods should be selected to encourage the development of self-direction by individual learners. Group activities should be organized to stimulate cooperative abilities. Motor skill development activities should emphasize partner and small group activities. "Perhaps most important, teachers provide frequent guidance in individual awareness of the body in motion and of personal response to this inner being that compels the student to actively fight to retain and extend the feeling of human joy in physically demanding and psychologically exhilarating movement" (Nixon and Jewett, 1980, p.267).

Middle-School Physical Education

In most progressive educational systems the traditional junior high school has now been replaced by the middle school. Organizational patterns vary, but the typical middle-school program is a 3- to 4-year program for children in the age range of 9 through 13 years. It is designed to provide a less arbitrary curriculum pattern and a more sympathetic environment for these children than the junior high school, which, for all practical purposes, was a "watered-down" high-school setting for younger children. Middle-school educators aim to provide an appropriate curriculum for the preadolescent who is no longer a child, but who is not yet striving to be independent of the significant adults in his life, and not yet capable of being totally self-directing. The middle school provides for general education of all preadolescents through the organization of five or six core curriculum areas, one of which is developmental motor performance or physical education. The Society of State Directors of Health, Physical Education and Recreation recommends that middle-school students be scheduled in some combination of at least 250 minutes of physical education per week, distributed over 3 or more days (1972).

The movement activity content emphasized in the middle school includes aquatics, gymnastics, dance, adventure activities, track and field, fitness activities, popular sports, and new games. Each child needs to increase his vocabulary of motor performance skills and to refine to a higher level those motor skills previously learned. Students need to expand their understandings of movement principles in situations emphasizing modifications of environmental media.

Emphasis on aquatics results in increased understanding of movement principles, while at the same time developing essential survival skills and desirable recreational skills for participation in many popular forms of recreation. Many middle schools plead lack of facilities as an excuse for not offering aquatics instruction. Beginning instruction in aquatics is more appropriate for middle-school youngsters than for students of secondary-school age. Board of education and educational facilities planners need to recognize that general education in aquatics deserves a higher priority than opportunities for interscholastic competition for a selected few students. School districts that cannot provide for the construction of a swimming pool should seek cooperative arrangements with other public agencies or private businesses to facilitate swimming instruction for middle-school students.

Emphasis on gymnastics activities should continue in the middle school. The basic gymnastics skills acquired during elementary-school years serve as a foundation for increasing self-mastery. Students at a wide range of individual performance levels can achieve satisfaction in skill achievement and extend concepts of spatial awareness, relocation, balance, and movement creativity.

One of the advantages of the acceptance of coeducational physical education in the middle school should be the strengthening of dance experience for boys as well as girls. Students should have opportunities to develop free and expressive movement as well as to learn dances that require precision, control, and endurance. Opportunities for rhythmic experience should extend beyond structured dance forms to include rhythmic gymnastics, improvisation, and the design of creative activities to be performed with rhythmic accompaniment.

Positive self-concept and concern for ecology can both be enhanced through outdoor adventure activities. The natural environment should be used to design movement activities that provide special challenge and unique satisfaction. Games can be adapted and created to play on the sand, in the snow, on the ice, on grassy slopes, or in the woods. Activities requiring cooperation with others such as scaling cliffs, crossing streams, transporting survival equipment, and human rescue skills can heighten self-awareness, increase feelings of individual worth, and develop useful skills for individual survival and group cooperation. Outdoor adventure activities are becoming increasingly popular among middle-school children.

Track and field activities should be emphasized in middle-school programs. In addition to their universal appeal to both boys and girls, they permit continuing emphasis on individual skill achievement and on fitness development. Long-range fitness goals can be fostered by planning for enjoyment of vigorous physical activity in middle-school physical education. Children of this age can be predisposed to positive attitudes and habits through the enhancement of self-knowledge concerning their individual physiological functioning. Understanding of the immediate and short-range effects of exercise provides the foundation for more sophisticated concepts of conditioning to be developed during the secondary school years.

Team activities and skills of the popular team sports clearly have a place in middle-school physical education. Socialization skills and teamwork concepts are essential to the middle-school child's education. However, it is important that the curriculum not be dominated by the concerns of high-school athletics. At this age there are many sport and athletic possibilities to explore. Each child should be introduced to some of the popular individual and dual sports. New games should continue to be emphasized, providing novel challenges appropriate to the needs of preadolescents.

The overall goals of the middle-school physical education curriculum are:

1. Refinement of personal motor performance skill, providing increasing self-mastery, and a broad base for personal recreational involvement
2. Enhancement of life-activity skills, including efficient body mechanics, survival aquatics, and competency for the enjoyment of outdoor adventure
3. Basic understanding of key fitness concepts and personal awareness of individual fitness status
4. Socialization leading to individual concern for others, cooperative group skills, team involvement, and increased cultural understanding

Appropriate instructional methods for middle-school physical education include emphasis on challenge activities, individual task completion, and circuit, station, and learning-center organization, supported by flexible grouping practices. Students should have opportunities for individual selection from among alternative educational activities. They should be given extensive opportunities for developing self-direction and personal creativity. Individual profiles should be established and kept by the students. Elementary concepts of physiological conditioning and safe and healthful participation should be taught as an integral part of all movement activities included in the physical education program. Instructors should have available, in addition to sufficient quantities of the usual supplies and equipment, extensive technological aids to maximize learning in an individualized and personalized physical education environment. Culminating activities developed with student involvement in the planning should be utilized frequently to maximize the integration of specific knowledges and skills. Together, students and teachers plan for project adventure, a new games day, a track meet, a camping experience, dances in which parents participate with children, creative performance, fitness clinics, and other activities to highlight key physical education learnings.

Secondary-School Physical Education

The primary focus for the secondary school, as for every educational institution, is the individual learner in his or her ultimate unity and personal coherence. Realization of personal potentials requires a breadth of physical education offerings, courses designed to challenge learners at different skill levels, and experiences that focus on the personal search for what is satisfying and rewarding in physical activity and sport. At the secondary level there is also increased urgency for emphasizing concepts of community service and group responsibility. The curriculum must incorporate the EFGs of *ecological education, futures education,* and *global education.* In order to serve secondary-school students most effectively, the physical education curriculum will include a few core courses, selective offerings to fulfill the local physical education requirement, and elective offerings for individual program enrichment. A secondary-school physical education program should include approximately 100 hours of instruction at each grade level in addition to individualized community service activities and intramurals, recreational, and club sport activities selected for personal participation.

The curriculum content for secondary-school students should emphasize lifetime sports, fitness activities, awareness activities, and high adventure pursuits to maximize lifetime commitments to voluntary participation in physically active recreation. Secondary-school physical educators should provide instruction in a wide variety of individual and dual sports in addition to the traditional popular gymnastics, dance, aquatics, and team sport activities. Individuals seeking the satisfaction of skill achievement may choose to develop their abilities to genuinely advanced levels in any of these activities. Competence in an activity is usually accompanied by enthusiasm and pleasure in participation and may well lead to the selection of any given activity as a lifetime or carry-over leisure activity.

The curriculum should include a core course in fitness for life that encompasses individual assessment of the key aspects of health-related fitness, self-monitoring of fitness achievements, self-directed prescription of exercise, and intensive participation in selected fitness activities. Selected popular sports and such fitness activities as weight training, jogging, circuit training, and developmental exercise programs may also be used to achieve appropriate levels of muscular strength, circulorespiratory endurance, and flexibility.

Awareness and expressive activities need much more emphasis in secondary-school physical education curricula. Traditional activities can be taught so as to maximize self-awareness and individual expression. Tennis or golf or skiing can focus on inner awareness through sports. "Run-for-awareness" programs can bring youth in touch with their own feelings and the realities of the environment. Aquatics can bring persons new experiences in relatively unknown realms of awareness in diving, surfing, and scuba diving. Dance can be openness to existence and full awareness, an attitude toward life that restores perspective. Greater conscious awareness, body balance, and centering can be achieved through the addition of activities such as yoga, karate, aikido, and skating.

High-adventure or risk sports have become increasingly popular and should definitely have a place in the secondary-school physical education curriculum. Rock climbing, sky diving, skiing, surfing, hang gliding, and orienteering all have the appeal of bringing the individual into closer touch with the natural environment. Perhaps they aid the personal search for what Leonard has termed the ultimate athlete because they share not only an element of risk but also aspects of boundaries crossed, limitations transcended, and perceptions gained (1975). It is not unreasonable to believe that regular participation in high-adventure sports develops a more efficient, more creative, and more productive person.

The overall goals of the secondary-school physical education curriculum are:

1. Development of the competencies and the commitment required to achieve individual physical fitness and to plan and maintain personal fitness programs throughout life
2. Lifetime sports competence enabling the individual to participate in several sports at a personally satisfying performance level in different seasons, climates, and circumstances
3. Understanding of the major societal roles of the movement arts and sport sciences, the development of democratic group skills through movement activities, and a willingness to modify movement activities and to utilize personal movement skills to create a better global future
4. Guidance for each individual in seeking personal meaning in movement, through providing for the achievement of effortlessness and excellence in performance, increased awareness and expressiveness, or the pursuit of high adventure in accordance with individual preferences and potentialities

The key to a successful secondary-school physical education curriculum may well be emphasis on individual assessment. Students should be encouraged to set their own goals and should be involved in decision making related to class procedures and long-range planning for physical recreation and fitness. The processes for learning to facilitate, extend, and fully utilize movement capabilities are exceedingly important. Physical education curriculum designers should include plans for experiencing, understanding, and gaining competence in perceiving, patterning, adapting, refining, varying, improvising, and composing in movement. To the individual high-school graduate these process learnings may be even more important than the specific product outcomes represented by a high fitness test score or superior achievement in particular sport skill tests. Secondary-school teaching-learning must be based on the best current scientific knowledge of human growth and development, perceptual motor learning, kinesiology and biomechanics, exercise physiology, and measurement and evaluation. For maximum effectiveness, however, scientifically based instruction must be supported by flexible scheduling, independent study, open laboratory options, and other opportunities for individualizing and personalizing learning.

Adult Physical Education

The concept of lifelong learning is now widely accepted. It is universally agreed that education is not limited to school settings. Education may take place in any location, formal or informal, with or without the assistance of a teacher. We have long known that much learning takes place during the preschool years. This is especially evident in the field of motor development in which dramatic changes occur during the early years.

The post-secondary-school years are also exceedingly important from an educational perspective. More and more adults are enrolling in credit and noncredit courses of instruction. For all adults, including those who do not formally enroll for instruction, educators must encourage continuing learning throughout life. Educational opportunities in physical education and sport should be available to adults on a continuing basis from the time they leave the secondary school well into old age. Adults should have the opportunity to achieve and maintain optimum physical fitness as a condition for individual fulfillment. In addition, it is important to make a successful adjustment to aging, to find meaningful substitutes for former activities, and to minimize deterioration in physical abilities. Although the aging process is characterized by gradual reduction in dynamic fitness qualities of muscular strength, flexibility, endurance, and neuromuscular coordination, sensible exercise regimens throughout life decelerate these changes. Active individuals find life more satisfying than do those who withdraw from the mainstream of society. This generalization applies to senior citizens as well as to younger persons.

Many adults today are discovering that they can "find themselves" in a physical activity setting. Adults who had only limited physical education opportunities in school are finding the potential for achieving personal well-being and self-satisfaction in activities not taught in the school. Adults whose prior experiences have been restricted by age, sex, and ethnic stereotypes are discovering genuine enjoyment in learning, pleasure in gaining skill competence and increased fitness, and depth of interest in learning more about themselves as functioning organisms with the capacity for growth and continuing learning. Physical educators probably face a great deal of remedial work during the next quarter of a century in assisting these adults who have been disadvantaged in their school physical education, in addition to the challenge of revising and strengthening current school programs to ensure that future secondary-school graduates receive a sound physical education, equivalent in quality to their educational achievement in other core curricula.

Physical education programs for adults should provide instructional opportunities at beginning, intermediate, and advanced levels in the total range of activities appropriate for secondary-school students. Only through extensive breadth of offerings can individual differences be accommodated. Adult fitness programs require increasing emphasis. Instruction needs to be provided including valid and reliable information on exercise physiology. Physical education programs for adults should also include innovative offerings specifically designed for adults and for future planning. Instructional programs should be developed to deal with such topics as effective movement for meeting the demands of new occupational tasks, exercise and fitness in gravity-less environments, survival and quality living in underwater communities, senior citizens as a resource for community recreation, biofeedback analysis, movement notation, and the impact of popular recreational activities on the biosphere.

The overall goals of adult physical education are:

1. Achievement and maintenance of long-term health-related fitness, including the abilities to be self-directing, physically independent, and capable of minimizing unavoidable deterioration in physical abilites and capacities
2. Development of the adult "inner athlete" who seeks active recreation and enhancement of the quality of life through personal fulfillment in challenging and satisfying achievement in physical activity

Designers and leaders of adult physical education programs must constantly emphasize individualization and be ever mindful of the importance of developing and encouraging self-direction by the individual participant. Group activities lending psychological support to the participants need to be emphasized. This is particularly true for those who have not developed their physical abilities to the full potential during the adolescent and young-adult years. Those who need to be convinced of the acceptability of adults learning at beginning skill levels, especially adult women who have been conditioned to consider vigorous physical activity as inappropriate, particularly need to share their experiences with others who face similar difficulties in making initial adjustments. Even adults who have developed skills at the intermediate level enjoy the social benefits of participation as members of groups with like interests. Adult learners appreciate prompt, specific, and detailed feedback relevant to individual performance. They are interested in receiving personal fitness status information and in knowing how to progress toward performance skill goals as rapidly as possible. Leaders of adult physical education programs must also accept the responsibility for continuing consumer education. Adults are keenly interested in specific information on the effects of exercise, sound warm-up techniques, selection of appropriate sports equipment, evaluating commercial health and recreation services, nutrition, ergogenic drugs, and new recreational opportunities available to the public.

Adult physical education programs are available in a wide variety of settings. Although many colleges and universities no longer require physical education, most provide elective physical education courses with a variety of offerings. Continuing education and public recreation agencies are expanding their offerings in physical education. An increasing number of firms are now providing fitness and recreation programs for their employees. Many adults are joining private sport clubs emphasizing such activities as tennis, badminton, racquetball, golf, handball, and swimming. Private social agencies such as the YMCA offer excellent physical education programs for adults. Many commercial enterprises are also drawing adults into physical activity. It is probable that all of these programs will continue to expand and that the next 20 years will see the extension of adult physical education into an even broader spectrum of both organized and informal settings.

Intramural Sports and Physical Recreation

Most school and college physical education programs provide for noncredit intramural sports and physical recreation in addition to courses of physical education instruction offered for academic credit. Intramural sports and physical recreation programs are made available for voluntary participation by all interested students. Intramural programs serve two major goals:

1. Provision of wholesome recreational opportunities for students from middle school through college and university and for nonschool adults belonging to identifiable organized populations
2. Offering supplementary opportunities for application of learnings and practice of skills taught in physical education instructional courses

Intramural sports and physical recreation programs are designed to serve everyone who desires opportunities for active participation. In contrast to interscholastic and intercollegiate athletics, which are restricted to the most talented athletes, intramural sports and physical recreational programs provide opportunities for all who desire to participate regardless of their level of performance ability in a particular activity. In order to respond to this goal of maximum participation, intramural sports and physical recreation programs must provide for a wide variety of activities to be accessible for individual selection and participation.

Concepts of cooperation and competition are fostered through intramural programs. Opportunities for satisfying experiences in teamwork and for rewarding competitive experiences are necessarily limited in the physical education class program. The potential of intramurals for extending those experiences is one of the main attractions for participants. Program leaders need to be aware of the potential for intensive involvement and the consequent requirement that cooperation, competition, and sportsmanship be taught as interrelated concepts in programs structured to provide for sound educational outcomes in this regard.

With few exceptions, intramural sports and physical recreation programs are coeducational in organization. In order to provide for satisfying recreation and fair competition, ability-level grouping is most frequently used. The goal of maximum participation dictates that groups be formed for all ability levels and that as many teams or functional units be provided as the number of participants demands. In the vast majority of programs, participants are organized into leagues of competing teams or tournament flights in individual and dual sports. In organizing leagues and flights, efforts are made to equalize competition.

There has been a rapid increase in sport and physical recreation clubs. Sport clubs have been especially successful on college and university campuses, although they are also popular in high schools, community colleges, and in public and private adult recreation programs. Clubs generally include individuals with a common activity interest and provide for participation of members with a wide range of abilities. Most frequently they are organized around sports not in the formal institutional sports program and are more informal in their organization. Popular club sports include sailing, karate, judo, skiing, mountain climbing, cycling, lacrosse, volleyball, bowling, rugby, and fencing. Nonschool adults have been enthusiatic about organizing clubs for participation in racquet sports, handball, gymnastics, swimming, and soccer as well.

In addition to intramural leagues and sport clubs, adults have been particularly interested in the provision of open recreation opportunities. Many college and university students and nonschool adults prefer unstructured physical recreation. There is a growing demand for opening up gymnasia and other physical recreation facilities for voluntary workouts. Many adults desire the opportunity for participation that does not require making a schedule commitment. Activities particularly in demand for open recreation are swimming, weight training, running, handball, racquet sports, bowling, basketball, and softball.

Instruction should be provided as desired by the participants in intramural sports and physical recreation programs. Not all participants will have received recent or relevant instruction needed for successful and satisfying participation. The amount of formal instruction desired will vary with the activity, the type of program organization, and the background of the participants. Instructional resources of some sort should be part of the planning of all such programs. It is important that instructors, coaches, officials, and leaders be well qualified to perform their roles within the intramural sports and physical recreation programs. Appropriate physical conditioning should be a required aspect. High standards should be maintained for necessary protective equipment and safety practices. Sports etiquette and true sportsmanlike behavior should be expected of all who participate.

Educational Athletics

Are competitive athletics educational? This topic has been debated by educators and athletic promoters for more than a century. Since this is a textbook dealing with theory and practice, it seems appropriate to examine interscholastic and intercollegiate athletics from both points of view. Theoretically the rationale for including competitive sports programs within education is that these programs provide a culminating experience for athletically gifted students. For several decades professional physical educators regarded the competitive sports programs as a logical extension of the physical education instructional program. Physical education programs utilizing a symbolic pyramid were described. The class instruction program formed the base of the pyramid; the intramural sports and physical recreation program represented the second level; and interscholastic and intercollegiate athletics formed the peak of the educational pyramid.

The overall goals of educational athletics are:

1. Provision of opportunity for the athletically talented to develop their full potential in motor performance
2. Establishment of models of excellence in motor performance providing for inspiration, motivation, and emulation of all students
3. Fulfillment of a need of all members of the student body, and in some cases, members of the local community, for affiliation and belonging, group cohesion, and community identity

Programs of competitive athletics cannot be considered educational unless they serve to reach educational goals. If interscholastic and intercollegiate athletic programs are to contribute to the achievement of educational goals they must indeed be educational in their organization and conduct. Ample opportunities must be made available for would-be participants to become qualified and demonstrate their qualifications. Trials must be organized to provide fair consideration for all. Competitive sports programs must provide for maximum participation by fielding more than a single team in a sport. Educational institutions that provide for junior varsity, lightweight, and reserve teams are attempting to meet this goal. All teams should have challenging and satisfying schedules; all team members should participate in athletic contests. A sound interscholastic or intercollegiate program provides for teams in a wide variety of sports such as gymnastics, wrestling, swimming, field hockey, soccer, and cross-country in addition to the typical most popular spectator sports. Equal opportunity for participation is provided to athletes participating in the so-called minor sports as well as to women and members of ethnic minorities.

Good programs can maintain their educational orientation only if competent leadership is provided. Coaches have often been credited with providing the very best quality of instruction in the performance of motor skills. They are usually selected because of their own high level of performance skill and their depth of knowledge of the chosen activity. They work with students under much more favorable conditions than the average physical education instructor. The teacher-student ratio is much better; facilities and equipment are superior; and time allocations are much greater.

The major challenge in guiding athletic programs within an educational context, however, is to ensure that overemphasis on competitive sports programs is not permitted to undermine educational goals. Typical problems include the diversion of facilities from the instructional and intramural programs for almost exclusive use by the athletes; disproportionate budgets for competitive athletics by comparison to class programs; preoccupation of physical educators with coaching responsibilities that results in neglect of other instructional responsibilities; and exploitation of athletes through demanding an unreasonable amount of their time and energy and thereby depriving them of educational opportunities essential to their gaining the full benefits of the school's educational programs. Furthermore, it is often difficult to ensure that the individual participant's experience in a competitive program is, in fact, educational, that it is shaping his development in socially desirable ways. Health and safety concepts, sportsmanlike behavior, skills of self-direction and decision making, concern for others, and loyalty to the group do not automatically result from participation in interscholastic or intercollegiate athletes. Desirable behaviors are taught only if programs are conducted in accordance with sound educational goals and principles.

In practice the evidence is growing to support the view that competitive athletics should be separated from education. When the overall goals of these programs become winning and entertainment, they cease to be educational in a positive sense. This position has been clearly stated by Scott:

> Interscholastic and intercollegiate programs do not "belong" to the profession of physical education and they do not belong to public education. These competitive sports programs belong to our culture and thus to everyone. They will continue to exist regardless of who or what attempts to control them. . . . The responsibility for these competitive sports programs does not belong with education. To attempt to keep them within the school setting does a disservice to the programs themselves and to education. . . . The most cogent reason for the separation of competitive sports programs from education is that the two programs have little in common. In competitive sports programs winning is the major goal for the producers or players and entertainment is the major goal for the consumers or spectators. . . . Education isn't structured to entertain. . . . Education does place emphasis on winning in the sense that it rewards success, but this is a product of education, not a process of education. (1979, p.5)

For the reasons summarized by Scott, most intercollegiate athletic programs cannot be regarded as educational. On the other hand, it is still possible to identify secondary-school interscholastic programs that appear to serve educational goals. Many Canadian programs, for example, appear to provide genuine educational experiences for the participants without dominating the school curriculum. Only in the United States are secondary-school athletic programs in flagrant conflict with educational goals maintained under school sponsorship.

Special Physical Education Programs

Schools exist to facilitate the development and learning of individual persons. Individual differences of importance in physical education exist in physical, motor, academic, cognitive, and perceptual abilities and capacities. Those children who are impaired, disabled, or handicapped—designated as exceptional children—often exhibit severe developmental lags in one or more of these areas. These lags may occur as a result of human deviance or of lack of opportunity for nurturing. Specific motor disabilities may be minimized directly by physical education learnings. Children with other types of handicaps frequently find movement experiences helpful in dealing with their disabilities. When developmental lags in any of these areas may be ameliorated by movement experiences, it is important that such experiences be provided.

The needs of special children are special only in degree. Their basic needs are the same as those of all other children. Physical education programs for special children should be planned individually to accommodate, and to ameliorate when possible, their unique disabilities. Special physical education programs must be responsive to the needs of those with visual and auditory handicaps; mental retardation, specific learning disabilities, and emotional-behavioral disabilities; and orthopedic, neurological and neuromuscular, and other handicaps. In identifying the overall goals of special physical education, three components are recognized:

1. Adapted physical education emphasizes the modification or adaptation of physical education activities in order that impaired, disabled and handicapped children may participate safely and with success.

2. Developmental physical education emphasizes total development through appropriate physical activities for children exhibiting developmental lags.
3. Corrective physical education emphasizes the correction or rehabilitation of specific conditions through movement activities. (Winnick, 1979, pp. 4–5)

Physical education is primarily concerned with the development of physical and motor abilities. However, movement experiences are also used to achieve other educational objectives. The physical educator works as a member of a team of educators, and the program emphases are placed where needed by the particular children participating. Program models for physical education for the impaired, disabled, or handicapped should be developmental and educational rather than medical or pathological (Winnick, 1979, p. 6).

The abbreviation IEP is now widely used to designate an individualized education program for a handicapped child. Special children are an extremely heterogeneous population, and educational programs must be designed to meet unique needs. The Education for All Handicapped Children Act (United States Public Law 94–142) requires that an IEP be developed for each handicapped child. The IEP must include a statement of present levels of educational performance, a statement of goals, a description of specific educational services to be provided, projected dates for a child's participation in the selected programs, and appropriate evaluation procedures and schedules.

Individual assessment is important as a basis for developing and conducting any educational program. It is perhaps even more important in developing individualized education programs for the impaired, disabled, or handicapped. The most basic and most important assessment is that provided through a comprehensive medical examination administered by a physician. The physical educator begins with prescriptions and recommendations provided by the physician, most often on a standardized form required in the particular school district. Height and weight measures are usually provided. These should be supplemented by body composition measurements. Underwater weighing procedures are the most accurate for assessing body composition but are elaborate to administer and expensive to provide. Consequently the most satisfactory technique for estimating leanness or fatness in most situations is the skinfold test. The needs of the individual child as identified by the medical examination, including or supplemented by a measure of percent body fat, are further assessed by the physical educator through tests that deal with physical fitness, basic motor development, motor skills, and perceptual-motor development. Tests developed for general physical education populations may be used when appropriate. In addition, a number of test scales and inventories have been developed specifically for use in programs for the impaired, disabled, or handicapped (AAHPER, 1975).

As recently as the 1950s and 1960s it was generally believed that handicapped children were served best in special classes. Today, however, it is agreed that individuals with impairments, disabilities, or handicapping conditions should function in the mainstream of society to the highest degree feasible. In the United States, federal legislation requires that all handicapped children be provided with a free appropriate public education in the least restrictive environment possible. As a consequence of this philosophy and the supporting legislation there are fewer classes in adapted physical education. A larger proportion of children with impairments, disabilities, and handicaps are attending regular public schools. A great many more of them are "mainstreamed" in regular physical education classes.

Whether the special child is mainstreamed or served in a tutorial or small-group setting, the physical education program is based on an individually developed IEP, and a few general suggestions for optimizing the instruction should be followed. The handicapped child's physical activity program must be developed on the basis of the child's medical status and in accordance with medical advice. Special children will need even more individual attention than it is possible to accord to the average child. The teacher must be aware of the need to provide environmental security. This includes particular attention to safety precautions, greater structure and more routine in the learning environment, and teachers who maintain calm but are clearly in control of the situation. Special emphasis should be given to arranging for success for each child, for building on small successes, for positive reinforcement, and for utilizing personal performance improvements rather than competition with others as a motivating factor. In most instances, learning progressions can be similar to those the teacher uses with others, but the pace needs to be modified for the special child. Instructors should be sensitive to the desirability of providing for education through a variety of sensory modalities in order to capitalize fully on the abilities of handicapped children. A key strategy in special education is to assist the individual to focus on unique abilities rather than disabilities.

Adults with impairments, disabilities, or handicapping conditions also have the same needs as their counterparts who need not learn to live with these types of limitations. Physical education and physical recreation have special importance. The disabled adult requires opportunities to function effectively in a work environment as well as to enjoy living within the mainstream of social activities. Thus handicapped adults need free access to all public buildings; transportation assistance to permit full participation in educational, social, and service programs; and the services of physical educators in making the best possible use of their physical abilities. In an important sense, all senior citizens develop disabilities of some degree as they grow elderly.

Persons of all ages should be encouraged to participate in the mainstream of society. They are entitled to receive free public education in the least restrictive environment possible. They should never be deprived of any individual benefit that current knowledge, technology, and the caring of others can make accessible to them. Those who can be mainstreamed in intramural sports and physical recreation programs as well as physical education instruction should enjoy movement experiences alongside persons free of impairments, disabilities, and handicaps. When success in movement experiences and positive responses to participation in typical competitive sports situations are not possible, special programs should be provided. Physical recreation clubs that bring together individuals with similar impairments—wheelchair basketball leagues, skiing contests for amputees, and Special Olympics—are examples of successful programs providing healthful competitive sports opportunities for persons with disabilities.

PROFESSIONAL PREPARATION AND OPPORTUNITIES

Traditionally physical education has been viewed as a professional specialization for those interested in teaching careers. Teaching is still the first occupational choice of most persons holding baccalaureate degrees in physical education. However, greater understanding of the significance of human movement phenomena in contemporary living has opened up new career fields for physical educators. Today there are at least four broad career fields for those with professional specialization in physical education. In addition to careers in teaching the professional choices include occupations in social service, in sports medicine and health-related fitness, and in professional athletics, sport communications, and sport-related business. Preparation for vocations in all of these fields requires a core of common educational experiences in addition to specialized professional education.

Core Educational Experiences

Professional preparation curricula in physical education have three major components: (1) liberal studies or general education, designed to extend the individual's familiarity with the major fields of organized knowledge, to permit a search for deeper personal meanings in areas of individual interest, and to prepare the student to function effectively as a citizen of society; (2) disciplinary studies, designed to develop knowledge and competence in the field of human movement phenomena; and (3) specialized professional education, designed to prepare for responsibilities as a specialist utilizing human movement as a focus and medium (Nixon and Jewett, 1980, pp. 368–369). Core general education requirements are usually established by a college or university for all undergraduate students in all academic majors. Typically these requirements include studies in the biological and physical sciences, the social sciences, and the humanities. Students majoring in physical education in most universities are required to complete certain prescribed courses within these general education areas to establish sound foundations for professional careers in physical education. Core experiences within the discipline of human movement include human growth and development, physiology of muscular activity, neural bases of movement, human anatomy, kinesiology, perceptual-motor learning, sport psychology, sociology of sport, rhythmic structure of movement, philosophy of sport, dance philosophy, and history of dance, sport, and related movement activities. Study of the basic concepts in these areas of knowledge, participation experience in many forms of physical activity, skillful laboratory analysis of human movement phenomena, and acquisition of skill in selected sport, dance, and exercise forms are all required to achieve disciplinary competence. Specialized professional studies, on the other hand, should vary with the individual's selected career emphasis and should be kept as flexible as is consistent with maintaining high-quality educational standards.

Teaching

As inflation and living costs have skyrocketed in North America, and as growing economic difficulties have threatened tax-supported services, concern for security of employment has increased. Many interested in careers in education have worried about future opportunities in teaching. While it is true that the overwhelming teacher shortages no longer exist, the outlook for physical education teaching positions now and in the immediate future is still bright. Inexperienced teachers will probably have a narrower range of choice of positions, and teachers who are not fully qualified will have more difficulty in finding employment, but the demand will continue for well-qualified, service-oriented physical education teachers. In fact, teachers are likely to have more job security than persons in other employment fields in times of economic recession or depression and high unemployment. There is no need for those who are attracted to the uniquely stimulating, demanding, and rewarding challenge of physical education teaching to seek alternative careers.

Students preparing for teaching careers need to assess realistically future demands upon professional educators. This is an age of specialization. A teacher needs to select a specialization. It is no longer enough to select physical education as a teaching field. The successful teacher needs special abilities and competence to work effectively with particular populations. It is also appropriate to develop particular subdisciplinary specializations. There are fewer positions that put equal emphasis on the dual roles of teaching and coaching. It is probably necessary today to orient one's career toward an emphasis in teaching with the coaching of educational athletics viewed as a secondary responsibility, or to decide that athletics will be the major source of livelihood, and seek to develop supportive competence beyond the realm of physical education teaching certification.

Teaching opportunities are expanding at both ends of the educational continuum. Programs for preschool children are increasing rapidly; such programs require a significant component of movement experiences. The mainstreaming of the impaired, disabled, and handicapped will continue to require more teachers of adapted physical education at all school levels. The rapid growth of continuing and adult education is expected to counterbalance decreasing enrollments in elementary and secondary schools.

Organization of elementary schools for physical education varies. Whether elementary-school physical educators work directly with young children or whether they serve as consultants in guiding classroom teachers in the improvement of physical education instruction, responsibility for movement education in the elementary-school years offers unique teaching opportunities. The trend has been toward increasing demand for elementary-school physical education specialists. The professional preparation of the elementary-school physical educator emphasizes depth studies in motor development and child psychology. This curriculum option includes considerable emphasis on the philosophy, content, and instructional strategies of movement education. Specific materials and teaching techniques in creative dance and thorough knowledge of educational gymnastics are needed. The elementary educator must learn to analyze and modify games and to guide children in designing and playing new games; must be knowledgeable and skillful in teaching the exceptional children who are mainstreamed into the physical education class; and must be prepared to work with other educational specialists as a member of the elementary-education team.

As school district organization plans have incorporated the upper elementary-school grades into middle-school or junior high school units, the demand for physical educators at the middle-school level has increased. The middle school offers particular job satisfactions for teachers who enjoy working with preadolescents. Middle-school physical educators need professional preparation similar to that required of the elementary-school specialists, with additional emphasis on the sensory, motor, intellectual, and socioemotional development of the preadolescent. Special attention must be given to the developmental rationale and educational philosophy underlying the middle-school concept. Skills and knowledge relating to the popular team games, dances, gymnastic activities, and individual sports activities appropriate for boys and girls of this age group are also important. Competence in organizing and coaching intramural and competitive sports activities is also expected.

The secondary school is the level at which physical education teaching opportunities are not expanding. At the same time it is the level most suitable for choice for the physical educator who wishes to be a teacher-coach. The educator who views interscholastic sports as an extension of instructional experiences, as physical education for the gifted athlete, will find a satisfying career at the secondary-school level. The secondary-school physical educator, whether male or female, has the opportunity to provide leadership through a complete program of movement activities.

Professional preparation for secondary-school teaching should emphasize adolescent development and learning, sociology, psychology of sport, and leisure counseling. While preparing to meet state certification in physical education the undergraduate student should achieve, in addition to broad preparation in the field, a specialization that will permit supplementing the particular strengths of other physical education staff members effectively. This specialization may be expertise in a selected activity area for teaching and coaching; a special competence such as the organization and administration of intramurals; or qualification as an adapted physical education specialist to provide educational services to exceptional children.

All secondary-school physical educators should develop basic competence in health education, safety education, and guidance. All will need minimum coaching skills and competence in a variety of different teaching and evaluation skills. During the 1980s particular attention must be given to the physical education of the handicapped and to the development and administration of coeducational programs that assure equal educational opportunities for all secondary-school boys and girls.

The successful college or university physical educator must be an effective teacher, a scholar, and a productive researcher. Opportunities for positions in which duties are limited to the teaching of activity classes are decreasing. The university physical educator should be prepared to teach lifetime sports, dance, or fitness activities for adults. Additional responsibilities may include teaching professional courses for undergraduate majors in physical education, graduate teaching, undergraduate and graduate advising, and university and community-service activities.

Increasingly it is expected that the college or university faculty member will be engaged in research, writing, and editorial activities. It is more and more difficult to combine coaching and academic responsibilities. Such joint assignments place the faculty member at a genuine disadvantage in earning academic promotion and tenure within the institution. Students who are interested in developing careers in higher education need to be aware that graduate study is a prerequisite. Tenured positions in universities offering graduate study ordinarily require an earned doctoral degree and continuing evidence of scholarly productivity.

Graduate physical education curricula should be tailored to individual student career goals. The student interested in becoming a college or university professor will select a specialization that will permit development of an area of scholarly expertise in which the individual can teach courses for undergraduate students, conduct research, and ultimately teach graduate students and guide their research. Graduate specialization in physical education may be developed in areas such as curriculum, instruction, supervision, administration, history, philosophy, sport psychology, sport sociology, motor development, perceptual-motor learning, kinesiology, biomechanics, physiology of exercise, and measurement and evaluation.

Included in the graduate program will be education in methods and techniques of research as well as seminars offering advanced work in areas of specialization. In addition the program should include studies in curriculum development since most faculties are charged with decision making relative to courses and curricula. Teaching effectiveness, instructional strategies, and educational evaluation should be studied to strengthen individual teaching competence. Each graduate student should become sufficiently familiar with the organization and administration of higher education to function effectively as a member of the college or university community of scholars.

Graduate study in physical education may also be directed toward educational administration. Public-school administrative positions include opportunities to serve as department chairperson; curriculum consultant; physical education supervisor; director of health, physical education, and athletics; or school principal. At the college and university level, administrative positions include opportunities to serve as department and division chairperson, dean, and other leadership positions, including college president.

Many graduate-degree programs currently emphasize research preparation. It is anticipated that greater opportunities will become available for primary contributions in physical education research in university, private foundation, commercial industry, and government contexts. The emphasis on research productivity for career advancement in academia has increased interest among physical education graduate students in developing research specializations, although full-time university research positions in physical education are limited in number.

All career fields in which teaching is a significant responsibility are placing increasing emphasis on field-based experiences. The trend in undergraduate teacher education and certification is toward competency-based programs and requirements. Physical education teachers need experience and competency required by all teachers in areas such as human development, learning, school and society, communications, and media and technology. They share, with other physical education specialists, interests and undergraduate preparation in movement analysis, movement performance, and study of the foundations of human movement. As physical education teachers they require extensive professional laboratory experience in working with individuals in groups in both movement and nonactivity settings and specialized competence in the guidance of movement learnings.

All physical educators making their careers in teaching need to be committed to continuing education and scholarship. The elementary-, middle-, or secondary-school teacher is expected to be continuously involved in in-service education. The individual career physical educator is expected to take the initiative to enroll in graduate programs, to become actively involved in the work of professional associations, to read and contribute to professional publications, and to participate in workshops, seminars, and professional conferences. The college and university physical educator is also continuously engaged in advanced study, research, professional writing, and other forms of scholarly productivity.

Social-Service Options

Teaching is generally viewed as a social-service profession. Because sport and dance are such pervasive aspects of all societies, there are also many opportunities for persons with physical education backgrounds to serve disadvantaged individuals and groups of persons with unique needs outside school settings. Career opportunities are open through private social agencies and through governmentally supported programs. Social agencies established to provide services to preadolescent and post-adolescent youth typically utilize organized physical activity programs as an important feature of their group meetings, conference or youth rallies, and summer camping programs. Youth sport programs use a combination of volunteer and salaried leaders. The scouting movement in the United States now reaches over 10 million young people. Over 5 million are currently being served by 4-H Club programs. The primary factor in making social-agency programs a strong positive influence for youth is effective leadership.

Inadequate leadership is a major criticism of many of the youth sports programs that have become so popular throughout the United States. The total number of participants in various organized youth sports programs in the United States is estimated at 20 million. While Little League baseball and similar programs have drawn criticism from professional physical educators, it is generally acknowledged that these programs fill a genuine need for participation in athletic competitions. Important research studies such as the Michigan Youth Sports Study are seeking to find useful data for directing youth sports programs toward appropriate developmental and educational goals (Seefeldt, 1978).

Sport and recreation programs are often designed to provide healthful and socially acceptable activities for disadvantaged youths, potentially delinquent young persons, and juvenile offenders. Social service in communities recognizing the need for positive peer group identification and responsible adult supervision for disadvantaged youths frequently includes physical recreation programs sponsored by groups such as the Boys Clubs of America. Vigorous sport and exercise programs are an accepted component of rehabilitiation programs. Correctional institutions now serve inmates with programs of supervised physical activity that provide needed physical exercise and help to develop healthy self-respect, better relationships with peers, and recognition that rules and regulations are necessary.

Undergraduate physical education majors interested in social-service careers should select substantial supporting study in sociology, psychology, political science, economics, social work, and public administration. In addition, those who are looking forward to working in programs for children and youth will include advanced study in motor development, child and adolescent psychology, perceptual-motor learning, and special education.

Ageism is increasingly recognized as a critical social problem. Today one American in nine is over 65 years of age. As people live longer, and as inflation results in lack of financial security for more retired persons, more attention must be given to providing needed health, recreation, and social-welfare services to senior citizens. Trained leadership is needed to provide programs that educate older persons to the importance of remaining active.

The realization that many medical problems associated with aging can be prevented, minimized, or at least delayed has led to the development of interdisciplinary studies of gerontology and the expansion of programs and career opportunities in working with the aging. Of special interest to physical educators is the need for qualified individuals to direct low-stress exercise activity programs for the elderly. Leslie suggests the following academic content for a specialization option within an undergraduate physical education program: biology of aging, sociology of aging, health and aging, fitness and therapeutic programs for the elderly, and recreation programs for the elderly (1975). He further recommends field experience in such settings as nursing homes, retirement centers, golden age type of organizations, recreation departments, and area agencies on aging.

Important social problems that result in systematic disadvantage to particular population groups have seldom been solved through education alone. Since the era of the New Deal during the administration of Franklin D. Roosevelt, it has been widely accepted that the federal government is responsible to the American people to provide leadership and substantial financial support in national efforts to resolve major social problems and to improve the welfare of disadvantaged citizens in whatever geographical region they live. Official support is designated for particular social problems. The programs supported by public funds will vary with each political administration. In many programs now receiving major federal allocations, sport and recreation play an important role.

The Civil Rights movements of the 1950s and 1960s helped Americans to understand better the importance of competence and skill to the self-image of those struggling for self-worth, identity within an ethnic minority, and belonging to a larger group. Physical skill or athletic excellence became a primary goal for many black youths. At the same time it became apparent that racial and ethnic discrimination existed within sport. Similarly the Women's Rights movement brought to light much discrimination and inequity in sport and physical education operating to the disadvantage of girls and women as well as ethnic minorities. Increased knowledge and understanding of the handicapped or exceptional person as an individual with normal needs, interests, and desires has led to the search for better ways of integrating these individuals into society and diverse human activities. Attitudes are changing and services are expanding to facilitate the movement of exceptional persons into the mainstream of American life. Programs to help the poor such as Volunteers In Service To America (VISTA) and the Comprehensive Employment and Training Act (CETA) change frequently; it is probable, however, that opportunities for physical educators to provide social service through such federally supported programs will be available for the so-called foreseeable future.

Physical educators interested in providing services to minorities, women, the handicapped and disabled, and the poor, or any other group needing special assistance, may tailor the elective portions of the undergraduate curriculum to their unique special interest. Some of the most relevant courses are those in social work, community planning, public administration, law and social problems, crime and delinquency, special education, ethnic studies, and women's studies.

International sport competition has been viewed for many years as a vehicle for increasing international understanding. So significant have sport and dance become in international affairs that governments have made them deliberate instruments of national policy. From the earliest beginnings, educational exchanges have involved American physical educators, sport leaders, and dance companies. The Peace Corps was established in 1961 and has been highly successful in providing volunteer service to people in the developing countries. Physical educators and sport specialists have always been included among Peace Corps volunteers. Undergraduates interested in preparing for service in an international context need to develop to a high level skills that may be of interest in other countries. In addition, they should engage in inter-disciplinary studies emphasizing language, cultural anthropology, political science, economics, sociology, social psychology, ecology, and regional area studies.

Many young people with social-service career orientations will choose teaching as a profession. However, it is important to recognize that there are many other alternatives for serving society utilizing physical education preparation. It is also probable that many individuals who prefer to work outside school settings will elect to major in recreation, just as individuals interested in social service through teaching may prefer to emphasize other related subject areas and complete certification programs in dance, health education, or safety education. All of these individuals would share common core educational experiences as undergraduates and develop the professional studies components in unique ways according to their career directions.

Sports Medicine and Health-Related Fitness

Sports participation by the general public continues to increase, and exercise has become fashionable. Consequently, many additional career opportunities are now available. There is need for professional leadership in the development of exercise programs and in expanding opportunities for participation in fitness programs. Qual-ified specialists are needed to plan and conduct exercise programs and to assist with the prevention and treatment of sport injuries. Fitness leaders may seek employment in private agencies, in corporate health centers, and in health clubs and spas. Qual-ified exercise physiologists are employed in sports medicine clinics to perform fitness assessment responsibilities and then to provide individual counseling in planning fitness programs, in selecting physical recreation activities, in purchasing appropriate sportswear and equipment, and in engaging in sound conditioning programs. If properly qualified they may also conduct research activities and assist in preventive medicine programs.

Athletic training is a rapidly expanding career field. The goal of the athletic trainer is crucial in preventing injuries, in recognizing and evaluating injuries, and in pro-viding appropriate paramedical services when injuries occur. The demand for qual-ified athletic trainers is evident in that every major league professional sports team and every major university athletic program employs at least one full-time athletic trainer. Increasingly, the importance of employing athletic trainers to serve on high-school athletic department staffs is becoming accepted. Trainers also work in sports medicine clinics, student health centers, and with athletic training supply companies.

Physical activity has been found to be an effective therapeutic modality for many disabled, disadvantaged, and exceptional children, youth, and adults. Therapists are needed in many career specializations, including physical therapy, corrective ther-apy, occupational therapy, dance therapy, and recreation therapy. All are potential directions for professionals in movement arts and sport sciences desiring careers focusing on health-related fitness.

Undergraduate students who prepare for careers as fitness specialists, exercise physiologists, athletic trainers, or therapists need to emphasize additional study in the biological sciences. Additional study in psychology and in health and safety education will also be needed. Individual students will enroll in professional courses specific to the desired specialization, including an appropriate type of internship.

Specialized professional studies for the fitness specialist include body mechanics, conditioning, weight training, fitness exercise, care and prevention of injuries, aquat-ics, motor learning, and physiology of the aging. Desirable electives might be selected from departments of business administration, marketing and advertising, leisure studies, sociology, psychology, and journalism.

Professional preparation for the athletic trainer includes qualification for certification by the National Athletic Trainers Association. Courses specifically required, in addition to those already listed as requirements for all preparing for health-related fitness careers, include remedial exercise, therapeutic exercise, adapted exercises or corrective exercise, first aid and safety, nutrition, and techniques of athletic training. Also recommended are laboratory physical science, pharmacology, histology, pathology, and coaching psychology.

Professional preparation of therapists occurs primarily at the graduate or postbaccalaureate level. An undergraduate physical education major is recommended for admission to physical therapy and corrective therapy programs. Potential recreation therapists should earn the bachelor's degree in recreation and leisure studies. The dance therapist should select dance as the undergraduate specialization. The occupational therapist may choose any of several undergraduate majors, including both physical education and recreation. Prospective therapists may be encouraged at the undergraduate level to develop skills and competence related to the assessment and analysis of motor function and movement patterns, a general orientation to disease and disability, and an overview of characteristics of special populations. Professionals in these fields will need many movement skills, familiarity with all types of physical recreation, and ability to use a wide variety of teaching methods, especially those appropriate for independent learning and small-group settings.

Professional Athletics, Sport Communications, and Sport-Related Business

Coaching may be viewed as a specialized form of teaching. Those who are interested in the coaching of educational athletics will prepare themselves through teacher certification and will view the coaching assignment as but one responsibility in a full-time teaching role. In reviewing all potential career options, however, those interested in athletics should consider professional athletics and athletic administration as business roles. Sport is big business in America today. The administration of sports and other leisure ventures provides steady cash flows and substantial employment, including some of the highest personal salaries negotiated each year.

Sport administration according to VanderZwaag "encompasses the administration of those programs involving games of sport and/or sport skills" (1975, p. 17). It includes not only activities, the active participants, and spectators but also the administration of professional sport, collegiate sport, private sports clubs, commercial recreation, and public recreation.

Professional sport is a large industry employing many as athletes, coaches, trainers, scouts, officials, agents, medical and paramedical specialists, financial managers, ticket sales persons, sports information specialists, concession operators and field personnel, security guards, and maintenance personnel. Professional athletics stimulate consumer spending and generate industry income through seasonally scheduled league games; playoffs, bowl games, and other types of championship contests; tournaments and exhibition tours; television contracts; and sales of programs, souvenirs, endorsements, and advertising. The big money-makers are baseball, football, basketball, hockey, boxing, wrestling, golf, tennis, automobile racing, and horse racing.

The universities with the most successful intercollegiate athletic programs now have annual athletic department operating budgets above $2 million. They are clearly in the entertainment business since athletic contests are a major factor in the economies of their universities and their local communities. Those engaged in the administration of intercollegiate sport must carry out most of the business functions associated with professional sport: budgeting and accounting, scheduling and ticket sales, contest management, sport information, personnel management, facilities management, and governmental paper work.

Professional preparation for coaches in educational settings has traditionally been an undergraduate major in physical education. Most jurisdictions require that secondary-school coaches be certified teachers. It is recommended that coaches who do not select physical education as an undergraduate major include in their preparation background in the medicolegal, sociological, and psychological aspects of coaching, theory and techniques of coaching, and kinesiological and physiological foundations of coaching (AAHPER, 1974).

Athletic directors require practical experience in coaching. In addition to coaching, officiating, athletic training, and directing athletic programs, career opportunities in sports administration include many business positions. VanderZwaag (1975, pp. 17–27) has proposed that undergraduate professional preparation for sports administrators include basic sport studies and seminars in history, philosophy, psychology, and sociology of sport; business administration courses in accounting, finance, marketing, management, and economics; an integrating sports administration seminar and an internship in a sports organization such as a collegiate athletic department, collegiate intramural sports program, high-school athletic program, professional sports team or league office, or a professional sport commissioner's office.

Because sport is a major interest of the North American public, sports communication is a growing specialization within the mass media. Newspaper, magazine, television, and radio coverage of sports events continues to increase. Many career opportunities are available in sports journalism and sportscasting.

Professional preparation for sports communication is best organized through interdisciplinary curricula made up of physical education, journalism, and communications. A number of institutions have developed programs that permit the student to receive a major in one department and to include in the undergraduate program a substantial number of courses in the cooperating department. To these interdisciplinary programs physical education contributes such traditional offerings as sport history, sport philosophy, sport psychology, sport sociology, and coaching courses. Typical journalism courses are reporting, broadcasting, mass communications, public relations, and advertising. Curriculum patterns also show titles such as photo journalism, film for television, persuasive communication, and factual television. Courses jointly developed specifically for new programs in sports communication include sports information, sports literature, and sportscasting. Practicum experiences are essential.

Our economy can be described as a leisure economy; it can also be described as a consumer economy. Sport-related businesses are thriving. Tourism has an increasingly important role in the U.S. economy; although physically active recreation is only one of several major categories of attractions promoted, many trips and vacations are planned around sporting spectaculars and special events. Retail sales find big markets in sports equipment and clothing, and the development of facilities for public or private enjoyment of active leisure interests supports the construction industry and many related businesses.

Most of the early private sports clubs were exclusive country clubs. A more recent development is the private sports club with open membership designed to promote a single sport. Popular sports organized in the private-club sector include swimming and diving, tennis, golf, gymnastics, squash, handball, racquetball, badminton, boating, sailing, scuba, skiing, judo, and karate. Many positions are available in the administration of private sports clubs and in the administration of both commercial and public recreation programs. From bowling alleys and skating rinks to organized summer camps and white-water rafting, physical recreation has resulted in scores of successful businesses providing financial profits and employment for many. Public recreation programs now provide a broad scope of varied activities such as outing clubs, nature hikes, dance instruction, jogging groups, weight training, and yoga as well as comprehensive programs of competitive sport. The administrator of a public recreation program may be employed in a municipal facility or in a state or national park offering camping, backpacking, mountain climbing, skiing, and aquatic activities.

Young persons interested in the management of a private sports club, the operation of a sporting goods business, the development of a commercial recreation facility, or the promotion of tourism are apt to find the best undergraduate preparation in a school or college of business or in a program sponsored jointly by business administration and health, physical education, and recreation. Typical courses to be included in the program, in addition to those required by the major selected and by the specific leisure or sport interest, include design, construction and maintenance of athletic and recreation facilities, public relations, sales, economics, environmental education, leisure counseling, marketing and advertising, management of conventions and trade shows, organization of special events, and consumer education. An appropriate on-the-job internship is required.

SUMMARY AND CONCLUDING STATEMENT

Observation of current practices in physical education program development reveals clearly that most programs are not built on a consistent theoretical base. On the other hand, study of the emerging literature in physical education curriculum and instructional theory does provide some encouragement to those concerned about theory building. While the present number is limited, a few scholars are investigating the theoretical realm of physical education, and many others are reporting data-based research into specific aspects of physical education curriculum and instruction. It is hoped that these efforts will continue, and new theoretical insights and research findings will gain more application to the processes of curriculum development and instructional innovation in physical education. Only if this occurs can more effective physical education programs at all educational levels be anticipated.

This chapter has given primary attention to the concerns of the career-oriented physical education teacher. While the job market for teachers tightens in periods of economic recession as a factor in the overall unemployment rise, it is important to recognize that outstanding opportunities will continue to be available for well-qualified physical education teachers. At the same time, greater appreciation of the significance of human movement phenomena in contemporary living is already opening up new career fields for those who wish to prepare themselves to be competent human movement specialists working in different occupational roles.

QUESTIONS FOR POSSIBLE DISCUSSION AND TESTING

1. Why is theory important in physical education? Discuss the present status of theory in physical education curriculum and instruction.
2. Why should physical education be included in the general education of all learners?
3. What are the overall goals of elementary-school physical education? What changes in present practices are needed to achieve these goals?
4. Discuss the concept of the middle school. What are the most important contributions of physical education to children of middle-school age?
5. Identify any special problems you anticipate in coeducational instruction in secondary-school physical education classes. How might these difficulties be resolved?
6. Discuss the changing status of adult education and the needs of adults that should be addressed through physical education. Describe what a continuing physical education program might be like in your community.
7. Discuss the pros and cons of "mainstreaming" handicapped children in regular physical education classes.
8. Distinguish between intramural and interscholastic programs. What are the primary contributions of intramurals and sport club programs to youth of secondary-school and college age?
9. Discuss the concept of 'educational athletics.' In what respects do "big time"

intercollegiate athletics violate the concept of educational athletics? To what extent is your local interscholastic or intercollegiate athletic program educational?

10. What are the purposes of each of the three major components of the physical education student's curriculum?

11. Identify your particular specialization interest and discuss the job opportunities and professional preparation within the specialization.

REFERENCES

American Association for Health, Physical Education and Recreation: Professional Preparation in Physical Education and Coaching. Washington, D.C., AAHPER, 1974.
American Association for Health, Physical Education and Recreation: Testing for Impaired, Disabled, and Handicapped Individuals. Washington, D.C., AAHPER, 1975.
Anderson, W.: Descriptive analytic research on teaching. Quest, 15:1–8, 1971.
Bain, L.L.: The hidden curriculum in physical education. Quest, 24:92–101, 1975.
Bain, L.L.: Description of the hidden curriculum in secondary physical education. Res. Q. 47:154–160, 1976.
Bain, L.L.: Status of curriculum theory in physical education. JOPER, 49, 3:25–26, 1978.
Bain, L.L.: Perceived characteristics of selected movement activities. Res. Q., 50, 4:565–573, 1979a.
Bain, L.L.: Physical education curriculum theory: A sociological perspective. *In* Curriculum Theory in Physical Education Conference Proceedings. Edited by A. Jewett and C. Norton, Athens, University of Georgia Press, 1979b.
Barker, J.A.: Three concepts for re-unifying K-12 curriculum. Futurics, 3, 2:129, 1979.
Bressan, E.S.: Making movements that matter—The structure of a productive discipline for physical education. Paper delivered at the SAPECW Fall Conference, Nashville, Oct. 26, 1979.
Bressan, E.S.: Human Movement and Physical Education: Meaning and Significance. 1981. Unpublished manuscript.
Brown, C., and Cassidy, R.: Theory in Physical Education. Philadelphia, Lea & Febiger, 1963.
Cheffers, J., and Evaul, T.: Introduction to Physical Education: Concepts of Human Movement. Englewood Cliffs, N.J., Prentice-Hall, 1978.
Dunkin, M.J., and Biddle, B.J.: The Study of Teaching. New York, Holt, Rinehart and Winston, 1974.
Eisner, E.W., and Vallance, E.: Conflicting Conceptions of Curriculum. Berkeley, Calif., McCutchan, 1974.
Gage, N.L.: The Scientific Basis of the Art of Teaching. New York, Teachers College Press, 1978.
Haag, H.: Sport Pedagogy: Content and Methodology. Baltimore, University Park Press, 1978.
Heitmann, H.M., and Kneer, M.E.: Physical Education Instructional Techniques. Englewood Cliffs, N.J., Prentice-Hall, 1976.
Jewett, A.E.: Humanistic programming: Paradox or paragon? Paper delivered at the NAPECW Biennial Conference, Dixville Notch, N.H., Aug. 25, 1972.
Jewett, A.E.: Relationships in physical education: A curriculum viewpoint. Acad. Papers, 11:87–98, 1977.
Jewett, A.: Relationships between curriculum development and instruction. Paper presented to the Curriculum Academy, New Orleans, Mar. 17, 1979.
Jewett, A., and Norton, C.: Curriculum Theory in Physical Education Conference Proceedings. Athens, University of Georgia Press, 1979.
Jewett, A.E., and Mullan, M.R.: Curriculum Design: Purposes and Processes in Physical Education Teaching-Learning. Washington, D.C., AAHPER, 1977.
Leonard, G.: The Ultimate Athlete. New York, Viking Press, 1975.
Joyce, B.R., and Weil, M.: Models of Teaching. Englewood Cliffs, N.J., Prentice-Hall, 1972.
Leslie, D.K.: Fitness programs for the aging. *In* Careers in Physical Education, NAPECW and NCPEAM, 1975.
Macdonald, J.B.: Curriculum theory as intentional activity. Paper delivered at Curriculum Theory Conference, Charlottesville, Va., October, 1975.
Macdonald, J.B.: Values bases and issues for curriculum. *In* Curriculum Theory. Edited by A. Molnar and J.A. Zahorik. Washington, D.C., ASCD, 1977.

Metheny, E.: Connotations of Movement in Sport and Dance. Dubuque, Iowa, William C. Brown, 1965.

Mosston, M.: Teaching Physical Education: From Command to Discovery. Columbus, Ohio, Charles E. Merrill, 1966.

Nixon, J.E., and Jewett, A.E.: An Introduction to Physical Education. Philadelphia, W.B. Saunders Co., 1980.

Nixon, J.E., and Locke, L.F.: Research on teaching physical education. *In* Second Handbook of Research on Teaching. Edited by R.M.W. Travers. Chicago, Rand McNally, 1973.

Orlosky, D.E, and Smith, B.O.: Curriculum Development: Issues and Insights. Chicago, Rand McNally, 1978.

Pinar, W.: Curriculum Theorizing. Berkeley, Calif., McCutchan, 1975.

Scott, P.: Reflections (The Thirteenth Amy Morris Homans Lecture). Champaign, Ill., National Association for Physical Education in Higher Education, 1979.

Seefeldt, V.: Competitive athletics for children—the Michigan study. JOPER, 49, 3:39–41, 1978.

Siedentop, D.: Developing Teaching Skills in Physical Education. Boston, Houghton-Mifflin, 1976.

Singer, R.N., and Dick, W.: Teaching Physical Education: A Systems Approach. Boston, Houghton-Mifflin, 1974.

Smith, O.B.: Research and Teacher Education—A Symposium. Englewood Cliffs, N.J., Prentice-Hall, 1971.

Society of State Directors of Health, Physical Education, and Recreation: School Programs in Health, Physical Education and Recreation: A Statement of Basic Beliefs. Kensington, Md., 1972.

Stanley, S. Physical Education: A Movement Orientation. Toronto, McGraw-Hill Ryerson, 1977.

Ulrich, C.: Tones of theory revisited. *In* Curriculum Theory in Physical Education Conference Proceedings. Edited by A. Jewett and C. Norton, Athens, University of Georgia Press, 1979.

Ulrich, C., and Nixon, J.E.: Tones of Theory: A Theoretical Structure for Physical Education— A Tentative Perspective. Washington, D.C., AAHPER, 1972.

VanderZwaag, H.J.: Sport administration. *In* Careers in Physical Education. NAPECW and NCPEAM, 1975.

Winnick, J.P.: Early Movement Experiences and Development: Habilitation and Remediation. Philadelphia, W.B. Saunders Co., 1979.

SELECTED READINGS

American Association for Health, Physical Education and Recreation: Professional Preparation in Physical Education and Coaching. Washington, D.C., AAHPER, 1974.

Haag, H.: Sport Pedagogy: Content and Methodology. Baltimore, University Park Press, 1978.

Jewett, A.E., and Mullan, M.R.: Curriculum Design: Purposes and Processes in Physical Education Teaching-Learning. Washington, D.C., AAHPER, 1977.

Jewett, A.E. and Norton, C.: Curriculum Theory in Physical Education Conference Proceedings. Athens, University of Georgia Press, 1979.

Kneer, M.E.: Curriculum: Theory into practice. J. Phys. Educ. Rec., 49, 3:24–37, 1978.

MacDonald, J.B., Wolfson, B.J., and Zaret, E.: Reschooling Society: A Conceptual Model. Washington, D.C., ASCD, 1973.

Molnar, A., and Zahorik, J.A.: Curriculum Theory. Washington, D.C., ASCD, 1977.

National Association for Physical Education of College Women and National College Physical Education Association for Men: Careers in Physical Education, (Briefings 3), 1975.

Nixon, J.E., and Locke, L.F.: Research on teaching physical education. *In* Second Handbook of Research on Teaching by R. M. W. Travers. Chicago, Rand McNally, 1973.

Nixon, J.E., and Jewett, A.E.: An Introduction to Physical Education. Philadelphia, W.B. Saunders Co., 1980.

Winnick, J.P.: Early Movement Experiences and Development: Habilitation and Remediation. Philadelphia, W.B. Saunders Co., 1979.

CHAPTER EIGHT

MEASUREMENT AND EVALUATION

B. Don Franks

Physical educators are often asked their opinion about the fitness, skill, knowledge, and form of other persons. These opinions are used for evaluation of self, teachers, programs, professional players, and students. The worth of the opinions depends on an understanding of both the activity being analyzed *and* the procedures used for the evaluation.

Other professional and disciplinary areas included in this book help those studying sport and physical education to know the factors that are important for skill, fitness, movement forms, and the knowledge desired for different levels of activity. Testing, measuring, and evaluating are the focus of this chapter. The goal is to provide information about the process by which an appropriate test is selected, administered, scored, and analyzed to allow assessment of the characteristic(s) being tested.

DEFINITIONS

A *test* is the instrument used to assess a variable. For example, the vertical jump test.

The *measurement* is the score assigned to a response to a test item. For example, 10 cm was measured between the height that the student could reach while standing and the chalk mark made during the jump.

Evaluation is the value judgment placed on the test score. For example, "good," "within the normal range," or "indicated a weakness"—each could be an evaluative statement comparing the person's score with some standard.

EVALUATIVE PROCESSES

The early approach to testing in sport and physical education often resembled the first part of this old native American saying:
"Give me a fish and I will eat today; teach me how to fish and I will eat for a lifetime."
Physical educators were taught about certain tests of fitness, sports skill, and knowledge. The professionals could do well as long as they needed tests solely in those areas covered in their test and measurement class. The more recent approach is to teach the basic evaluation procedures that can be utilized in any situation in which evaluation is desired. The major components of evaluation are:

Dr. B. Don Franks is from the University of Tennessee, Knoxville.

Many of the concepts in this chapter are included in expanded form in Franks and Deutsch (1973). (My thanks to Dr. Helga Deutsch for her assistance in my education in evaluation.)

Knowledge of:
    Goals (Derived from disciplinary and professional aspects of sport and physical education)
    Variables to be tested
    Factors that affect test scores

Ability to:
    Select/construct a suitable test
    Administer test(s) efficiently and accurately

Provide information as a basis for:
    Current status
    Realistic goals
    Next steps for improvement

To determine:
    Relationship between variables
    Difference between groups

Objectives

One cannot evaluate anything unless it is clear what the teacher/coach/program is trying to accomplish. These goals have to be translated into specific objectives that can be clearly described. This information plus an understanding of the nature of the characteristics to be tested is provided by the bodies of knowledge in the other disciplinary and professional aspects of sport and physical education.

Test Selection and Construction

After the objectives are clearly perceived, the testing/measuring/evaluating processes can be used. The first task is to find appropriate tests for all of the objectives of the person or program. A good test is defined by the extent to which it meets the criteria listed in Table 8–1.

Validity. Does the test give us information we want about the person being tested? Does the test measure what it is supposed to? A valid test will have a yes answer to these questions. There are essentially three ways that one can determine the degree to which a test is valid.

The first way to explore validity is to ask the question, Does the test seem to be a good way to measure this characteristic of a person? Is it a logical test? Do experts in this area use it? Does the test appear to give the information that is desired? This approach to validity is called *content*, or face, *validity.* For very concrete variables, content validity is the only type of validity that is needed. For example, measuring the number of centimeters from the bottom of a person's feet to the top of the head when standing straight would seem to be a logical way to test standing height. It is also the way that has been used by experts in height testing. There is no need to provide additional evidence of validity for this test of height. However, more abstract

Table 8–1
Criteria for Test Selection/Construction

Criterion	Purpose
Validity	Relevance to purpose of test
Reliability	Consistency of test
Objectivity	Consistency of testers
Accuracy	Absolute score
Appropriateness	Differentiation of abilities
Cost	Time, personnel, facilities, and equipment available

variables, such as cardiorespiratory function or attitude toward physical activity, would require additional checks on validity before one would accept the validity of a particular test. The tester would start with something that seemed logical and is utilized by experts, but additional evidence of validity would be needed before selection of a test. There are important elements to analyze in each of the types of validity. The quality of content validity depends on the initial logic in selecting appropriate test items. The extent of validity based on expert opinion obviously is as good as the experts involved.

A second way to determine the degree of validity is to compare the proposed test with an accepted (valid) test. *Concurrent validity* is established if the new test has a high positive relationship (correlation) with the test that is known to be valid (criterion test). For example, it would appear logical that a person's ability to continue to run (hop, swim, jump, step, cycle) for 9 minutes would depend, in part, on cardiorespiratory function. Thus there is some content validity for the endurance run as a test of cardiorespiratory function. To establish concurrent validity, the endurance run needs to be compared with an established test of cardiorespiratory function. It is generally agreed among exercise scientists that maximal aerobic capacity (highest ability to utilize oxygen during increasingly strenuous work) is a valid test of cardiorespiratory function. The high, positive relationship between the distance one can run in 9 minutes and the maximal oxygen intake provides concurrent validity for the use of the run as a test of cardiorespiratory function.

Concurrent validity depends on the validity of the criterion test. If test A is valid because it correlates with test B, which is valid because it is related to test C, eventually one has to accept validity of the original criterion test based on content and construct validity. A common, but questionable, method of establishing concurrent validity is to validate a single test item by comparing it with the whole test. Thus question 16 might receive a validity rating based on how well that test item was related to the entire test. Or a specific skill, performance, or fitness test is sometimes validated by comparison with the entire test battery of which it is a part. This approach to concurrent validity assumes that the entire test is valid. It may be that a single item measures an important objective that is not covered by any other item on the test. Thus that single item could have a low correlation with the entire test and still be a good test item. At the other extreme, a test item might have a high "validity" coefficient simply because it was one of several items testing basically the same thing, in which case it could be eliminated without decreasing the value of the test. Thus one must critically evaluate the criterion test in interpreting the concurrent validity value.

Another way to establish concurrent validity is to show that the test differentiates among groups who are known to be different on the variable being tested. A valid test of golf ability would produce higher test scores for par golfers than for bogey golfers, who would do better than "weekend hackers." Although this is a recommended procedure for establishing concurrent validity, it is difficult to find groups that are known to be different on a particular variable without also being different in other ways. For example, persons who are clinically judged to be in separate categories on anxiety might score differently on an anxiety test, but they might also have other psychological distinctions.

A third way to determine test validity is to decide if the test reacts to varying situations the same way the characteristic being tested should respond to those situations. This *construct validity* is based on theoretical understanding of the characteristic of interest. One aspect of construct validity involves the relationship between the variables being tested and other variables. We know that a particular variable should be positively related to some variables, negatively related to some variables, and not related at all to some variables. For example, a valid test of cardiorespiratory function should have positive association with the components of cardiorespiratory function, such as stroke volume, oxygen transport, and ability of the muscle to use oxygen. A valid cardiorespiratory test would have negative relationship with low-density cholesterol, amount of obstruction in the blood vessels, and hypertension. At the same time, it would not have any relationship to variables such as arm strength, height, weight, IQ, and a host of other noncardiorespiratory variables. Thus there would be evidence for construct validity if the distance run in 9 minutes had a high positive correlation with stroke volume and other components of cardiorespiratory function; a high negative correlation with cholesterol and other cardiorespiratory problems; and a close-to-zero relationship with noncardiorespiratory variables such as strength and intelligence.

Another way to demonstrate construct validity is to show that the test changes in the same way the characteristic being tested would change. Again with cardiorespiratory function as an example, it is well known that cardiorespiratory function is decreased by prolonged bed rest and increased by appropriate endurance-running conditioning. Therefore, if the subject's mile-run time improves after several weeks of a conditioning program and deteriorates after a few weeks of bed rest, then these results would provide additional construct validity for the endurance run of a mile as a test for cardiorespiratory function.

The person establishing construct validity must have a thorough knowledge of the characteristic being tested, statistical techniques, and research design. A theoretical understanding of the variable and how it should be related to other variables and how it should respond to various situations and treatments is necessary to determine construct validity. In addition, the evaluation specialist must be able to design studies in such a way that the research will show to what degree the test being validated is related appropriately to other tests and the effects of various experimental conditions on the test. Either lack of knowledge about the variable being tested or faulty research design would lessen the evidence for the test's validity.

A valid test is one that logically tests the variable of interest. It compares favorably with good tests of the same variable. It has positive, negative, and near-zero relationships to the same things that the variable would or would not be associated with. It changes in response to different stimuli and situations in the same ways that we would predict the characteristic being tested would change. It can differentiate among persons who have different levels of the variable being tested. Every test used should have the highest degree of validity possible within the limitations imposed by the situation. The amount of validity evidence that is needed increases as the variable becomes more abstract and less concrete.

Reliability. Does the test give consistent results? Would I get the same score for this person today, tomorrow, and next week? A reliable test would provide a yes answer to these questions. A reliable scale for body weight would indicate time after time the same weight for a person whose weight had not changed.

Reliability is determined by testing the same group of persons two different times under the same conditions. A reliable test will give similar absolute scores for each person and will rank the persons in the same relative order both times. Thus the persons who score in the 80s on the test battery will continue to score in the 80s and will continue to score better than those who scored in the 70s and worse than those who scored in the 90s. The reliability of using skinfold calipers to measure the amount of fat at the triceps and subscapular sites (used in the AAHPERD health related physical fitness test) could be determined by having the same person measure the millimeters of fat at these two sites on the same groups of students on two different days. It would be important that both days be within a short time so that the actual amount of fat would not have changed. In this way, any differences in score would reflect either the unreliability of the instrument or the tester. To the degree that the same amount of fat was measured on the two separate days the test would be considered reliable.

Although giving the test twice is used in the examples for simplicity, one may want to estimate reliability by giving the test a number of times to determine if consistent results are obtained across a series of administrations.

There are some situations in which a person's score would change simply by retaking the test. In these cases, obviously the same test could not be given a second time for reliability. The reliability in these cases is estimated by having the person take two versions of the same test of equal difficulty, style, and length. Reliability is determined by the degree of correlation between the two versions of the test. This is sometimes done by comparing one half of a test with the other half. Since students might do better on a written test of soccer rules if it were given a second time (i.e., they would have had a chance to think about answers, read the rule book again, and discuss the test with friends), the reliability could be determined by dividing the test into halves for analysis. It would be important for the halves to be as equal as possible in content, style, and difficulty. Then the students' scores on each half can be compared. The more nearly the two halves differentiate among the students in the same way on both halves, the more reliable the test.

Accuracy. Reliability does not indicate the absolute accuracy of the test score. In the example of the scale for body weight, it could be a highly reliable scale (i.e., consistent), but everyone could have a weight that was too high. The purpose of calibration of equipment is to ensure its accuracy. This is done by comparing a known standard with the reading of the testing instrument. Thus, known weights of 20, 40, 60, 80, and 100 kg might be placed on the scale. Then the scales can be adjusted to these known standards (or a correction factor can be computed to adjust the observed score to the actual score).

In some cases there is no "known standard," and in other cases the absolute scores are not essential. For example, we do not have a known standard for a highly positive attitude toward physical activity that can be compared with the self-report scale for attitude. If one is interested only in the *change* in body weight caused by physical conditioning, then any reliable scale will indicate the change. However, in those instances in which a known standard is available and it is important to have a score that is accurate in the absolute sense, then careful calibration of the equipment is essential. For example, one would hope that the radar used to determine speeding is both reliable and accurate.

Objectivity. Would different testers give the same score to the individual for the same performance? The degree to which this happens reflects the objectivity of the test. Whether or not the basketball went through the goal would be completely objective (all would agree); however, there would be less agreement (objectivity) whether it was in the air before or after the buzzer sounded ending the game. For those tests that are completely objective (e.g., multiple choice with only one correct answer, number of baskets made, number of strokes taken to get the golf ball in the cup), there is no need to provide evidence for objectivity. However, for those tests in which different scorers might rate the same performance differently (e.g., overall ability, form, ethical behavior), then one should know how objective the test can be with trained testers.

Objectivity is determined by having two testers measure the same test performance independently of each other. The degree to which their scores are the same indicates the degree of objectivity. An obvious example would be the judges at a gymnastics or diving meet. They observe the same performance and then rate it independently on a predetermined scale. Although all the judges will not rate all performances exactly the same, there is a high degree of objectivity among well-trained judges. In the earlier example of skinfold fat measurement, the reliability is established by comparing the same tester's results of administering the test twice to the same group. The objectivity would be determined by having two testers test the same group. The degree to which they measured the same amount of fat on the same persons would reflect the objectivity of that test.

Appropriateness. Can the cost of the test be afforded? Do we have enough time, personnel, facilities, and equipment for the test? Is it appropriate for my group? An appropriate test will provide a yes answer to these questions. Test decisions have to be made within the external restraints that are placed on professionals. Often, the question is, What is the most valid test that can be administered to 60 students in 20 minutes with no testing assistants, limited equipment, and in one half of a small gymnasium? The costs of tests in terms of money, time, personnel, facilities, and equipment severely restrict the choices that many physical educators have. The importance of establishing concurrent validity for shorter, simpler tests that can be used for large groups in small spaces in a short time continues to be one of the important contributions that measurement specialists can make to the profession.

The other aspect of the appropriateness component of testing deals with abilities and differentiation. It may be that the type of muscular endurance tested by pull-ups is important for a particular physical activity that is being used for a group. However, if the group is made up of young children of whom only 2% can do even one pull-up, that test would not provide much information about the muscular endurance of these children. A test of self-concept that is constructed for mature adults would not be appropriate for young children or mentally retarded persons of any age simply because of the vocabulary. These persons could not understand either the instructions or the terms used to describe many of the concepts being tested. At the other extreme, a test designed for beginning golfers would be inappropriate for advanced golfers if they all scored the maximum number of points on the test. To give the tester the best information about the relative ability of the persons in the group on a test, that test needs to be easy enough that nearly everyone can get some score and difficult enough that almost no one gets the maximum score.

Reliability, Objectivity, and Cost Related to Validity. One additional point needs to be made regarding the relationship of validity to other components of test selection and construction. A test cannot be valid unless it includes the other desirable criteria of a test. This point is routinely made with regard to reliability but really needs to be made for all other components of testing. How can a test give information about a person's ability if it yields inconsistent results? Unless the test would give the same results for the same level of ability time after time, it is not giving reliable information, and it cannot be valid if it is not reliable. In a similar way, unless the same person who scored the test in the original validity and reliability studies is going to score all the tests for all people at all times, then it cannot be a valid test without a high degree of objectivity. If qualified persons with training and practice cannot provide similar scores for a person's performance, then the test lacks objectivity, and it cannot be giving valid information if the score depends on the tester rather than the level of performance. If a test is not appropriate for a specific group in terms of instructions, ability level, developmental level, personnel, facilities, or equipment, then the evidence supporting the test for other types of groups in other situations cannot ensure that this group will respond with the same degree of validity.

At the same time it must be stressed that just because a test is reliable, objective, and appropriate for selected persons does not prove that it is valid per se. Validity requires these attributes of reliability, objectivity, and appropriateness plus additional information that the test measures what it is supposed to test. Thus reliability, objectivity, and appropriateness are prerequisites, i.e., necessary ingredients, for validity, but they are not sufficient for establishing validity. To use an absurd example, one could test standing height in a reliable and objective way appropriate to a particular group, but that would not be enough to indicate that standing height is a valid test of cardiorespiratory function. On the other hand, if an endurance run were not reliable, objective, and appropriate for a group, it could not be a valid test of anything. If it were reliable, objective, and appropriate and had content, concurrent, and construct validity, only then could it be selected as a valid test.

Locating Tests

After deciding what variables are to be tested and the qualities desired in a test, it is helpful to find tests that have been used for the same purposes. There are several sources that can be used to locate tests.

The most comprehensive review of tests in many areas is the *Mental Measurement Yearbook* (Buros, 1978), which was initiated in 1938. Additional volumes are published intermittently. This source includes a listing of different tests designed to measure a particular characteristic with a critical review of the qualities of each test. Individual volumes are not comprehensive, so one might need to search several volumes to find a review on a particular area. For example, if one wanted to test anxiety, one would have to check the different volumes of *Mental Measurement Yearbook* to determine which had the most recent review of tests on anxiety.

Textbooks in testing, measuring, and evaluating frequently include lists of tests, with some review of their qualities. Several of these textbooks are included in the references for this chapter.

Contacting experts in the area to be tested will provide information about tests that can be used. Similarly, tests that have been used in research studies to test selected variables can be identified. One of the helpful guides in locating these studies is the AAHPERD *Completed Research in Health, Physical Education, and Recreation*, which has been published annually since 1959. *CRHPER* includes an extensive index for health, physical education, and recreation with references for published articles found in numerous journals, and titles (with some abstracts) of theses and dissertations completed in major universities.

Review articles that synthesize the literature in a selected area often include a section on methods. The ACSM *Exercise and Sport Science Research Review*, published annually since 1973, would provide information on testing in some areas of our field. Other journals that include review articles and indices are available in related fields.

Improving Testing

The use of the criteria for improved test construction and selection will enhance the accuracy of assessment in sport and physical education. Providing concurrent validation for practical tests that can be used in mass testing is a continuing contribution that can be made by evaluation specialists working with persons in the disciplinary and other professional areas, as well as by practitioners in the field.

There are additional ways physical educators can more accurately and more efficiently use the tests selected. A well-conceived testing plan is an integral part of the teaching/coaching or other professional plan. It is tied directly to the goals, learning experiences, and evaluation of the outcome. The good teacher includes testing and learning experiences throughout the year. Although there will be days when more of the time will be used in testing, it is not necessary to do all the testing, then all the learning, then all the testing. Some testing can be done initially to help provide a baseline to evaluate individual improvement and to place persons in more homogeneous groups. Testing should be an important part of the learning process itself, so that students are given immediate feedback as they learn (formative evaluation). Finally, testing is used toward the end of a unit to determine the overall assessment of the extent the objectives have been accomplished (summative evaluation). Preplanning for testing is an obvious and important characteristic of good evaluators. Pretest instructions include what persons should and should not do on the day of the test. They are based on controlling factors that might influence the test results. A realistic testing plan minimizes standing in line and waiting. The plan involves having the equipment, markings, and needed assistants all in place in advance. The amount of time for each test is used to set up more stations for the longer test items. The instructions for the students are clear and provide for the best way for them to move from one testing station to the next.

In addition to the aspects of the testing plan that provide for the maximum use of the time spent in testing, it is important that accuracy not be sacrificed for efficiency. All students should be given enough practice on test items so that their scores reflect their true ability on the test, rather than how well they can "take the test." (Many performance test scores can be improved by learning how to take the test.)

A good test will indicate the number of trials that are optimal for the most reliable score. In general, two or three trials give a better estimate of the student's ability than a single trial. In most cases more than three trials is not necessary. The average of the two or three trials is more consistent than taking the best trial, but it increases the amount of teacher time in scoring, and the best of two or three trials is certainly preferred to the score on a single trial.

Subjective rating is essential for certain objectives (e.g., correct form), and it is time consuming when done well. Clear definition of each point on the rating scale, setting up game-like situations for the rating, and observing every student in a similar situation for the same amount of time, all increase the accuracy, objectivity, fairness, and efficiency of this necessary aspect of an overall evaluation plan. Video taping can be a useful aid in subjective ratings.

Scoring

Two aspects of scoring deal with how each item will be scored and the relative weight of different test items.

Individual Test Items. The scoring of each test item depends on the nature of the test. In written tests the answers are scored *correct, incorrect,* or *partially correct,* with a set number of points for each item. Objective skill tests are normally scored with a certain number of points for each skill. Often there are gradients so that more nearly accurate results are scored higher, with relatively less accurate performance receiving a smaller score. For example, more points might be given for a clear badminton serve if it hits within a certain number of centimeters of the back line, with fewer points being given for shorter serves.

The more difficult test items to score are the subjective ratings. Each thing being rated should have clearly defined components to differentiate between the ratings. Many beginning teachers try to include too many classifications for rating. Whereas one might be able to distinguish among a 3, 2, or 1, it might be impossible to clearly differentiate on a 5- or 10-point scale. Sometimes the rating is based on how many elements are included in the movement. Other ratings are based on the quality or how well each element is done. One might simply include whether the swing is in the correct plane (yes or no) or its degree of smoothness (very smooth, a little rough, or very jerky).

Relative Weight. Within any single test the relative weight of each test item is determined by setting an arbitrary score. A particular component can be emphasized by including more test items on that one aspect or by having higher scores for the test items on that aspect. In the overall evaluation of any objective it is necessary to determine which things are more important, and then this relative importance should be reflected in the scoring. The same point can be made about an entire program—the test(s) of the more important objectives should receive proportionally more points than the test(s) of less important objectives.

Analyzing Scores

Once the test items have been accurately scored with appropriate weight given to individual test items and various tests, then the score has to be interpreted. This interpretation includes breaking down the total score into its component parts and providing the basis for a value judgment concerning the scores in the various aspects of the total. To tell Sue or her parents that she had a total of 1486 points in physical education, with 182 in tennis, including 94 on tennis knowledge, 35 on the serve, 28 on the forehand, 16 on the backhand, 4 on volleying, and 5 on agility related to tennis would be meaningless without some additional information.

Improvement. One way that meaning is attributed to the score is to indicate how much improvement (or deterioration) has occurred over a time. Thus, to know what Sue scored at the beginning of the tennis unit would give some basis to judge her scores.

Comparison with Others. Another way to begin to understand an individual's test score is to describe some reference group. One could describe Sue's class or a larger group of similar persons (same age, same beginning skill level). Whether Sue scored above or below the "typical" student of her age and how she compared with most of these students could then be decided. This comparison would normally be done with some sort of norm table from which the percent of students who did better and worse than she did on each of the test items could be determined.

Comparison with a Standard. The score might be interpreted in terms of a particular standard (criterion) that is established for that test. Sometimes this standard is based on comparison with others who are similar or with persons who have achieved high levels of achievement. In other cases there is some other reason to establish a standard. For example, based on information about health related to obesity, it would be reasonable to indicate that all persons should have less than 10% *excess* fat. Thus, one would take the essential fat (about 5% for males and 15% for females) and set a standard that mature males and females should have less than 15% and 25% fat respectively. Thus the goal would be for everyone to at least reach that standard regardless of what percent of persons were above or below the standard.

Grading

Another way to interpret scores is to assign a grade. It must be emphasized that grading is only one aspect of evaluation. Testing and evaluation have numerous uses in addition to their traditional use as a basis for assigning grades in educational institutions. The following issues have to be addressed before a grade can be assigned to individual students.

Objectives. Everyone agrees that the first step in setting up a grading plan is to clearly establish the relative importance of the objectives for the class. The implication is that taking showers, being dressed for participation, and attendance are not used for grading unless they are included as objectives for the class.

Tests for the Objectives. The second step in grading is to select or construct a test for each objective. Each objective should be tested with the best test available.

Tests for the Grade. In theory, all of the tests used to evaluate the objectives should be used in the grading plan. However, there are some objectives that are important in the program that cannot be tested accurately enough to be included in the grade. For example, let us assume that the student's attitude toward physical activity is an important objective for a physical education class. Let us further assume that the best test available is a self-report pencil-and-paper test asking the student to indicate preferences among a number of activities, combined with a questionnaire concerning the individual's leisure time activities. The test might have evidence for validity and reliability when given to students who have no incentive to give false information, but if the results are going to become a part of the student's grade, it would be quite simple for students to provide dishonest answers simply to make it appear that they had a very positive attitude toward physical activity. Other objectives may not have valid tests available at this time. Thus the physical educator has to decide which objectives will be included in the grading plan on the basis of the availability of valid tests. These tests that are chosen are weighted in terms of relative importance.

Grading System. There are numerous grading systems. Most of those are different in terms of how many categories are included. Some include two categories such as pass/fail, satisfactory/unsatisfactory, credit/no credit. Others add a third category such as honors/pass/fail. A common system has five categories, A, B, C, D, F. At the other extreme there is the system with 100 categories in which the grade is reported from 0 to 100. In any case, there needs to be a clear description of what must be done to qualify for each category. Those supporting fewer categories argue that it puts less pressure on the student, and the learning atmosphere can be more positive with evaluation becoming less important. Those supporting more categories suggest that more precise and accurate evaluation information is given with more differentiation among students. Some physical educators have indicated that physical education should use the same grading system as other educational areas since all are attempting to set objectives, provide learning experiences, and determine to what extent the objectives have been achieved. Others indicate that physical education has unique objectives that are different in kind from other subjects and therefore should not use the same grading system that others use.

Another issue related to grading systems is the place of behavior, effort, and attendance. Many schools solve this issue by assigning separate grades for the content of an area, behavior, and effort, and record the attendance. There might be some school-wide objectives in terms of behavior, effort, and attendance, but the specific content grades are related to specific objectives of math, English, and physical education.

Final Performance or Improvement. This issue does not appear to be raised anywhere in the educational system except in physical education activity courses. Most people appear to agree that the reading grade should be based on the final-performance (i.e., at what level this student is reading). Final performance is also used in physical education theory classes. To use final performance in these situations is "unfair" to the students who do not have as good a background or who learn more slowly—they can try harder and still make poorer grades. Some physical educators argue that physical education activity classes should be graded on the same basis; thus the grade reflects how nearly the objectives have been accomplished—not how much effort one had to expend in a particular class. Others suggest that the grade should be based on the amount of improvement that the student makes during a certain time.

What Standards. Regardless whether one grades on final performance or improvement, certain standards have to be established for each grade category. One method that is inappropriate except for very large classes is to simply allocate a certain percentage of students to each grade category, such as 10%—A, 20%—B, 40%—C, 20%—D, and 10%—F. On the other hand, one could take such a percentage and apply it to scores that have been gathered over a number of years or based on some larger group. Some establish certain levels to be achieved on the basis of their understanding of the activity, knowledge, fitness, and group.

Handicapped. Normally the same objectives will be appropriate for handicapped students. Some of the objectives, learning experiences, and tests will not have to be modified at all. However, when the handicap would cause the student to score differently on the test, modifications of the test and grading standards are needed. Until there is much more information available on all types of handicaps, this has to be done on an individual basis. Persons in adapted physical education and special education should be consulted to assist in setting realistic goals.

Acceptance. The many issues in grading in which there are legitimate differences of opinion make it impossible to establish a grading plan that will gain complete acceptance by colleagues, students, and parents. However, a well-planned grading scheme can be an asset for the program. It is essential that the plan be clearly outlined at the beginning of each course so that it is understood by the students, parents, and school administrators. A plan in which students know exactly what has to be done for a particular grade, with well-organized learning activities to assist them in achieving these levels and valid tests carefully administered and fairly scored, will not only receive wide acceptance but will also help educate persons about the important elements of sport and physical education.

Feedback. Providing feedback concerning how well a student has accomplished certain goals can assist in additional learning and the setting of realistic future goals. The feedback should be provided not only in terms of what has been accomplished, but also the next steps in this activity and what could be accomplished with additional effort. The improvement that has been made and the potential of further improvement should receive more emphasis than the current status that will be reflected in the grade.

Description of Groups

One use of test scores is to describe various groups (e.g., tenth grade physical education students, college sophomores, athletes). Two characteristics of the test scores are needed to describe the groups—the typical score and the normal fluctuation.

Typical Score. If one score were chosen to represent the entire group on a particular characteristic, what score would be selected? Three different methods have been used to represent the group's central tendency: (1) the average score (mean); (2) the middle score, which divides the group into two equal halves (median); and (3) the score of the largest number in the group (mode). If the scores are normally distributed, all three of these typical scores would be the same. However, extreme scores in one direction affect the mean more than they do the other two indicators. Either the mean, which is more precise and has wider use mathematically, or the median, which is easier to determine, is appropriate in most educational situations. Either the mean or median would be preferable to the mode.

Normal Fluctuation. The variability of the group must be known along with the typical score to adequately describe the group. For example, two groups could have an average score of 75 on a 100-point test, but they would be quite different if one group had scores from 15 to 99 and the other group had scores between 65 and 80. Both the typical score and normal fluctuation would be needed to describe the group or interpret an individual's test score. The variability is sometimes described by the (1) range of scores (highest to lowest score); (2) the middle 50% of the scores (from the lowest quartile—25th percentile—to the highest quartile—75th percentile); or (3) the scores that one would expect to include two thirds of the population (one standard deviation above and below the mean).

One would normally use the mean and standard deviations together or the median and quartiles. The mean and standard deviation would be slightly preferred from a mathematical sense, but the median and quartiles are easier to compute and are quite acceptable for most educational situations. When either of these methods is used, the range is also often reported.

Relationship between Variables

Another area in which physical educators are assisted by the evaluation processes is in determining the relationship between different characteristics. For example, what physical and psychological variables will be most highly related to a person's enjoyment of playing a particular sport? If our aim is to have all persons enjoy participation in a sport, the characteristics that are highly related to that aim might get some emphasis in our classes. It must be stressed that just because two variables are highly related does not mean that one caused or was caused by the other, but the high relationship allows certain hypotheses to be made that can be studied in experimental research. As an illustration, if it was found that persons who can hit a backhand off the back wall more accurately seem to enjoy racquetball more than persons who do not hit the backhand as accurately, then that skill could be emphasized in the racquetball class to determine if improving on that skill also increased enjoyment of the game.

The relationship between variables is normally determined by some form of correlation that quantifies the relationship between the variables into a number between 0 and 1. Thus the more highly related the variables, the closer to 1 the correlation will be. The sign of the correlation indicates whether the relationship is positive (+) or negative (−). In the positive relationship, as persons tend to score higher on one variable, they also tend to score high on the related variable. For instance, one might find a correlation of + 0.7 between height and weight, since, in general, as persons tend to be taller, they also tend to be heavier in total body weight. In the negative correlation, as persons tend to score higher on one variable, they tend to score lower on the related variable. For example, one might find a correlation of − 0.8 between aerobic capacity and time in a mile run; that is, as the runner tended to have a higher maximal oxygen uptake, the tendency would be to run the mile in a faster (shorter) time.

The most common statistical technique used to determine the degree of relationship between two variables is the Pearson product moment correlation coefficient (represented by r). In general, the correlation is computed when each person in a group has two scores. In addition to determining the relationship between two different variables, it is also used to determine concurrent validity, reliability, and objectivity. Concurrent validity is established by finding the correlation between the new test and a criterion test of the same variable. Thus all persons in a group are tested on both the new and the established test, and those scores are correlated to find the degree of validity for the new test. In finding reliability, all the persons in a group are given the same test twice, and the two scores are correlated for the extent of reliability. Correlation is used to determine objectivity by finding the relationship between two scores given by two different scorers for the same performance for all members of the group.

Difference between Groups

Another question that is often asked is, Are groups different on a particular variable? Do athletes and nonathletes differ on certain physical or psychological traits? Does the group that has been running for the last 2 years differ from a similar group that has not participated in any physical activity?

These two questions represent the two types of group-difference questions. In the first case, two identified groups are compared. One can determine to what extent the groups are different, but not why. To illustrate, boys continue to improve on certain physical performance items from age 12 to 17 years, whereas girls do not. There is no question that a difference can be demonstrated, but the reason for the difference is not known (i.e., to what extent it is biological, early socialization, peer pressure, or some other reason). On the other hand, one could take a group of 13-year-old girls and have half of them be active for a certain time, while the other half remained sedentary. If the subgroups (samples) taken from the same larger group (population) were significantly different after a certain amount of activity for the one group, then it could be concluded that it was the activity that caused the difference. In both cases, the same statistical analysis would determine to what extent the groups are different, but the conclusions drawn from differences (or lack of differences) between groups would depend on the type of research design.

Although there are a number of statistical techniques that can be used to determine group difference, the two most commonly noted in the literature are a *t*-test to determine difference between two groups and analysis of variance (ANOVA) to determine difference among more than two groups.

Both of these analyses result in a probability statement ($p<$ some level less than 1), which should be interpreted that a difference this large between groups such as these on this variable would be expected to occur by chance less than the significance level. Thus, $p< .75$ would not show much difference between groups since a difference that large would be expected to occur by chance 75% of the time. However, $p < .01$ is such a large difference that it would occur by chance only 1% of the time, and most persons would conclude that it shows a real group difference. Many researchers use the .05 significance level to indicate whether or not they will conclude that these are "real differences" rather than chance differences. In those cases, if $p< .05$ the conclusion is that these are significant group differences. If $p> .05$ then the conclusion is that a significant difference is not shown in that study.

Current Status of Evaluation

In this century there have always been persons in sport and physical education who were making contributions in testing, measuring, and evaluating related to aspects of our field. We still refer to some of the tests developed by the name of the developer. In recent years the same thing has happened in evaluation in sport and physical education that has happened in many of the disciplinary areas; namely, our students have gained a new level of sophistication by studying the body of knowledge in measurement and evaluation and then applying that understanding to sport and physical education. The textooks, special conferences (e.g., those sponsored by the AAHPERD Measurement and Evaluation Council), and research articles exhibit the basic issues and techniques found in measurement and evaluation per se. Evaluation is used to improve the disciplinary and professional components of sport and physical education. In addition, physical activity is used as a medium to further basic understanding in measurement and evaluation.

Fitness. Although this term is still (mis)used to include numerous elements of physical activity and functional capacity, the new AAHPERD Health-Related Physical Fitness Test (1980) is a step toward a more focused approach, with recommendations for the best field tests available. In general, it is recommended that physical fitness items be related to positive health, associated with physical activity, and testable in field situations. Three areas are identified: cardiorespiratory function, body composition, and neuromuscular function in the mid-trunk and low-back areas. The tests recommended are the mile run (or 9-minute run), the sum of skinfold fat at the triceps and subscapular sites, and both sit-ups and sit-and-reach for the muscular endurance and flexibility in the mid-trunk, low-back region. Additional validity and reliability studies are needed; however, these tests have sufficient theoretical and evaluation support to be used until better tests are available.

Performance. It is time to declare the general motor ability search over. It was a noble effort but based on unsound ground. There is no need to determine "general" qualities of strength, flexibility, balance, agility, coordination, speed, power and muscular endurance. It appears that each of these things would have many subdivisions and would not be the same for different parts of the body. The evidence also reveals that they are uniquely related to specific activities, or work tasks. A better approach appears to be to emphasize movement in creative and exploratory ways for its own sake and to emphasize the various aspects of a particular sporting or vocational activity directly related to that activity. Thus one might walk, run, leap, jump, crawl, roll, and climb in various combinations to explore one's body and space and to create movement for enjoyment of self or others. One would also analyze and try to improve on the factors involved in tennis, volleyball, or being a fire fighter. Thus, strength, flexibility, balance, etc., would become important not for their own sake, but for that particular muscular strength and endurance, flexibility, agility, etc., that is important for an activity of interest.

There are a number of good tests of specific aspects of skill in various activities. There are also examples of ways that rating scales can be established to rate form. Written tests are available in some areas, as well as suggestions concerning how to construct one's own written tests. However, the complete analysis of what fitness, performance, skill, and cognitive factors are essential for specific activities, along with their relative importance, remains to be done. After these analyses are completed, then appropriate tests and weights given to each test can be selected and constructed. This is an unfinished job that sport and physical educators working with evaluation experts need to be about.

Affective. Many persons are interested in the psychological and sociological benefits of activity. We have long claimed that these benefits are among our objectives and resulted from sport and physical education. Important strides have been made in expanding the research body of knowledge in these areas, but most professionals have not evaluated such effectiveness in the affective domain. Once again, persons understanding the affective potential of sport and physical activity must work with evaluation specialists to provide usable tests and learning experiences for the practitioner.

Future. The continuing inclination to want to evaluate sport and physical education that has historically permeated our field and the increasing understanding of basic evaluation processes are the bases for some optimism about the future. As bodies of knowledge are increased in the disciplinary, professional, and other aspects of movement themselves, these scholars will be seeking out evaluation experts to work with them to provide more valid tests and better evaluation standards.

IMPLICATIONS FOR GENERAL EDUCATION

The need for evaluative processes in the professional application of the various disciplinary aspects of sport and physical education is apparent. The need for an understanding of the disciplinary foundations for all students in sport and physical education regardless of vocational goals is discussed in other chapters in this book. A legitimate question that is often raised in establishing the core curriculum for sport and physical education is, Do students who are studying sport and physical education for its own sake need to understand the bodies of knowledge contained in the professional aspects of the field? More specifically, is there a need for all persons in sport and physical education to know evaluative processes?

A thorough understanding of evaluation is less important for those students who essentially want a "liberal arts" education in sport and physical education with no professional application anticipated. However, the interrelationships between the disciplinary and professional aspects of the field make some understanding of the professional processes a necessary ingredient for full understanding of the underlying discipline. The evaluative processes also contribute to the general education goals of ability to critically analyze literature and to make intelligent decisions about one's personal life style.

Understanding the Discipline

The essential feature of a discipline is the body of knowledge that is known because of studies in that area. Thus the disciplinary aspects of sport and physical education provide many theories and concepts about human movement. One might study these truths as a foundation for one's education and one might study the disciplines in the humanities, natural, or social sciences in a similar way. The place of evaluation in the general study of a discipline is to assist the student in a better grasp of the fundamental knowledge of the discipline. One cannot dig very deeply into any aspect of sport and physical education without having to think about how things that form the basis for our theoretical understandings were tested.

For example, one part of the disciplinary body of knowledge is the relationship between arousal and performance. In general, as one becomes more aroused up to an optimal point, a better physical performance results. When aroused beyond the optimal point, performance decreases. The optimal point varies with the type of performance and perhaps with individuals. One cannot separate our knowledge of this relationship without dealing with how both arousal and performance are tested. Is arousal how people indicate their feelings? Is it the behavior patterns that best reflect arousal, or is it the physiological stress indicators? What about performance— is it a task performed in a laboratory, on an athletic field, with or without an audience? Is the performance tested in objective ways or with a subjective rating? Do the tests of performance include all important aspects of the ability in that activity? The point is that one cannot fully understand the relationship between arousal and performance, or critically evaluate the studies done in this area, without consideration of the testing processes. In fact, it may well be through improved testing that a more complete theory of arousal and performance will be developed. To ignore the evaluation procedures in studies in this area, or other aspects of the discipline, would be to acquire less than a complete understanding.

Analytic Thinking

The ability to critically analyze theories, textbooks, review articles, and research studies would appear to be an important outcome of general education. It would be impossible to adequately evaluate the quality of the oral and written literature without paying some attention to the testing and evaluation that were used. A position statement about exercise, nutrition, and obesity that was based solely on height/ weight tables would be suspect because of inadequate testing. Persons familiar with sport and physical education testing would recognize that more valid tests are available for determination of the amount of body fat.

Life Style

There are abundant examples of nonprofessional use of evaluation in a person's life. A physically educated person would make better judgments about the quality of evaluation seen in everyday life, whether in the judging of gymnastics seen on TV, the basis for support for a particular commercial item, the suggested benefits of a fitness program, or the adequacy of the device used to issue a speeding ticket. Persons understanding evaluation can assess levels of skill, fitness, knowledge, and other characteristics related to important areas of their lives for friends and themselves.

Processes of testing, measuring, and evaluating can therefore be helpful in the "pure" study of human movement to assist in understanding the disciplinary bodies of knowledge and in coping with survival within our society.

IMPLICATIONS FOR PROFESSIONAL PRACTICE

Many students of sport and physical education will have vocational aspirations for the use of their program of study. These professional applications of our field may include working with persons of different ages, physical abilities, and levels of health in educational, governmental, health, business, or voluntary institutions. The comprehension of the disciplinary and professional bodies of knowledge is essential for career success. Part of one's accomplishments and the ability to determine the extent of the success will depend on a mastery of the processes by which one tests, measures, and evaluates the various aspects of the job.

Professional Evaluation

Several of the professional responsibilities will involve evaluation. These include evaluation of the individual's work, the program(s), and the clients, whether students, athletes, or postcardiac patients. Any of the content areas of sport and physical education may be included as part of the evaluation. The following are examples of questions that need to be evaluated by a teacher/coach:

> Am I a good teacher?
> Am I a good coach?
> Do my students learn what I want them to learn?
> Do my students feel good about what they learn and how they learn?
> Do my students enjoy the activities used as learning experiences?
> How much have individual students achieved?
> How do these student achievements relate to realistic expectations?
> Are the athletes learning what I want them to learn?
> Which athletes should be played in which positions?
> Am I accomplishing what the school and community expect in my teaching
>   and coaching?
> What fitness, performance, attitude, and knowledge aspects of sport and
>   physical education need increased attention in this school?
> What alternatives to my teaching and coaching would more nearly achieve
>   what is desired within the limits of the situation?

Each of these broad questions would have many subdivisions that would require evaluation. For example, *Am I a good teacher?* would include defining the characteristics of a good teacher by using the body of knowledge from that professional area. Ways to test each characteristic of being a good teacher and assigning appropriate weights to the component parts would be the next step. Then one would need to measure himself on the tests. These scores on teaching ability would need to be interpreted in terms of comparison with other teachers and whether one's teaching is improving over time. Finally, the evaluation of the strength and weakness of one's teaching would provide a basis for recommendations of what could be done to improve teaching.

Regardless of the professional setting, physical educators will be asked to determine to what extent their objectives are being met, and thus they will be expected to evaluate themselves, their programs, and their clients. The evaluation will include different aspects of the disciplinary and professional portions of sport and physical education. Both a general understanding of evaluative processes and specific knowledge of the best tests available in each disciplinary and professional component of the position will be necessary for the dedicated professional. The general processes will help determine how to select (or construct) a good test. The specific knowledge will help decide the best way to test a specific performance skill whose evaluation is important.

RELATIONSHIP TO ALLIED PROFESSIONS

Persons in different professional settings and in fields related to sport and physical education will be assessing different types of variables. However, the basic steps in evaluation are similar whether the test subject is volleyball serving ability, health behavior, or the safety characteristics of a work task. It is important for physical educators to learn the underlying processes of testing, measuring, and evaluating rather than being trained only to utilize specific physical education tests. The person who knows evaluative processes can work with others in any field to assist in setting up appropriate programs, whereas the person who simply is familiar with a number of specific tests can function only in situations in which those tests are appropriate.

One of the aspects of sport and physical education that is somewhat frustrating for the beginning student in evaluation is the necessity of using many different types of testing (such as written, skill, fitness, subjective rating, attitude, or behavior). However, the application of evaluation processes through these diverse types of tests prepares a person to be a valuable consultant to a large number of related fields.

Bases for Cooperation

The main elements for cooperative efforts to achieve quality evaluation in related fields include:

> Persons working together who understand evaluation and the specific characteristics to be evaluated
> Location of available information
> Decision to use or modify current tests or construct new ones
> Decision how the tests will be administered and by whom
> Decision on the basis for evaluation of test scores
> Decision how evaluation will be used

Physical educators are asked to assist with the physical fitness and performance of persons in a variety of professions (e.g., fire fighters, coal miners). It is necessary to establish what fitness and performance levels are desired, based on knowledge of work requirements and physical fitness. The next step is to determine how to test for these fitness and performance levels, based on knowledge of physical fitness and evaluation. In most cases there is concern for those who are below the desired standards, which leads to the establishment of an appropriate conditioning program based on test evaluation, exercise physiology, and exercise prescription information. The results of the testing and conditioning might be evaluated in terms of better screening, in-service or on-the-job training improvements, and work productivity.

Benefits of Cooperation

Numerous professions have (and could) benefit from working together with persons in evaluation to set up testing, training, and evaluation programs. There has also been legal action asserting that certain requirements were not based on sound evaluation principles. For example, the absurd notion that females should not play baseball or full-court basketball or be employed in certain positions that require some muscular strength and endurance has been changed in some cases with the support of evaluation specialists.

PROFESSIONAL OPPORTUNITIES

There will be a few professional opportunities for evaluation specialists to conduct research in the area of measurement and evaluation and to teach and advise students solely in the body of knowledge in this area. Some major universities will select this as one of the areas of sport and physical education to develop depth so that students may receive major emphasis in this area. In most cases persons will be asked to teach in the evaluation area as one of two or three areas of interest. Scholars in this area are invaluable to persons in all aspects of sport and physical education, assisting with appropriate testing for research, program assessment, and accountability.

Evaluation experts will have opportunities to assist industrial, athletic, fitness, motor development, health, and community programs in setting up tests for screening and to assist with evaluation of the success of specific endeavors. There are also numerous internal and external program evaluations at all levels of education that need assistance from those who understand evaluation processes.

At the current time there are not many openings for persons with specialization in only measurement and evaluation. However, a good background in this area is often helpful in securing a position. Once a person with abilities in evaluation is established in a professional position, there are numerous informal and formal opportunities to assist colleagues and allied professionals throughout the community and region.

CONCLUDING STATEMENT

The major thrust of this chapter is that the first step in evaluation is to understand the underlying processes used in testing, measuring, and evaluating persons and programs. These procedures are presented with practical examples of how they are used in sport and physical education. The importance of this area is supported in terms of understanding other areas as well as various aspects of one's personal and professional life.

After the basic concepts involved in evaluation and in each of the other areas of sport and physical education are learned, the advanced learning involves cooperation between evaluation and these other areas of our field. As we learn more about evaluation, better ways to test variables can be devised that lead to better understanding of the disciplinary and professional concepts being studied. As better understanding of these other areas is developed, we can more clearly define what needs to be tested, which can lead to better evaluation techniques. By working together we can assist each other in moving forward in both the extension of the body of knowledge and its professional application.

QUESTIONS FOR POSSIBLE DISCUSSION AND TESTING

1. A. What are the criteria for selection of a test?
    B. Select a test for a particular objective within a specific situation.
    C. Analyze the test in terms of each of the criteria.
2. A. What decisions have to be made in establishing a complete grading plan?
    B. What is your opinion about each issue involved in grading?
    C. Justify the decisions you would make in grading.
3. Give specific examples of how evaluation would be used by a:
    A. Citizen
    B. Parent
    C. Person to improve individual life style
    D. Physical education teacher
    E. Coach
    F. Exercise leader
    G. Motor-learning researcher
    H. Department head
4. List particular improvements that could be made in sport and physical education with assistance of evaluation specialists.

SELECTED REFERENCES

American Alliance for Health, Physical Education, Recreation, and Dance: Completed Research in Health, Physical Education, and Recreation, Vol. 21, 1979. (Vol. 1–20, 1959–1978.)

American Alliance for Health, Physical Education, Recreation, and Dance: Health Related Physical Fitness Test, Washington, D.C., AAHPERD, 1980.

American College of Sports Medicine. Edited by R.S. Hutton and D.I. Miller. Exercise and Sport and Sciences Reviews, Vol. 7. Philadelphia, Franklin Institute Press, 1980. (Vol. 1–6, 1973–1979.)

Barrow, H.M., and McGee, R.: A Practical Approach to Measurement in Physical Education. 3rd Ed. Philadelphia, Lea & Febiger, 1979.

Baumgartner, T.A., and Jackson, A.S.: Measurement for Evaluation in Physical Education. Boston, Houghton-Mifflin, 1975.

Buros, O.K.: The Eighth Mental Measurements Yearbook. Highland Park, N.Y., Gryphon Press, 1978.

Franks, B.D., and Deutsch, H.: Evaluating Performance in Physical Education. New York, Academic Press, 1973.

Johnson, B.L., and Nelson, J.K.: Practical Measurements for Evaluation in Physical Education. 2nd Ed. Minneapolis, Burgess, 1974.

Phillips, D.A, and Hornak, J.E.: Measurement and Evaluation in Physical Education. New York, John Wiley and Sons, 1979.

Safrit, M.J.: Evaluation in Physical Education. Englewood Cliffs, N.J., Prentice-Hall, 1973.

Looking to the Future

Earle F. Zeigler

There should be no doubt in your mind about the complexity of the field of physical education and sport now that you have read the five subdisciplinary and three subprofessional sections of this introductory text. My objective in this final section will be to stimulate your thinking about the immediate present and to provide some incentive for you to move ahead with purpose into the open future in this interesting and challenging profession. I am anxious to point out the possible unique role of sport and physical activity in people's education throughout their lives. I want to point out further the persistent professional concerns (or problems) that the profession still faces and the ten philosophical stances that will have to be eliminated if we are to have the sort of future that can be envisioned. Here is truly a profession in which you can indeed develop a life purpose that will enable you to develop maximum energy for a truly worthwhile life.

SPORT AND PHYSICAL ACTIVITY WITHIN THE GOOD LIFE

Citizens of the United States and Canada are wont to say that they have the highest standard of living in the world. Someone from another continent might state that the Scandinavian countries have surpassed us both in several ways. This may thrust us immediately into debating what is meant by a high standard as opposed to a low standard—and how all of this may be measured. Any attempt to respond to this question with complete accuracy would be doomed to failure at present. Nevertheless such statements about the quality of life should cause us all to take stock as we conjure the spirit and tone of life on this continent between now and the magic year 2001. Where ought we to be by then?

Obviously we will need to think very seriously about the character and traits for which Americans and Canadians will educate in the years immediately ahead. Kateb, writing about *Utopia and the Good Life*, considers the problem of increased leisure and abundance very carefully (1965, pp. 454–473). Although at that time some of the dire future predictions about overpopulation and ecological disaster were not clear to most of us, he foresaw no fixed pattern of future perfection such as that often predicted by others. However, he did suggest a progression of possibilities as the good life: (1) *laissez-faire;* (2) the greatest amount of pleasure possible; (3) play; (4) craft; (5) political action; and (6) the life of the mind. His conclusion, not unexpected from a university scholar, is that the life of the mind offers the greatest potential in the world as we know it now or even may know it in the future.

Whatever conclusion you may have come to at this stage of your career regarding the good life and its various components, or how you will seek to improve the quality of life for yourself, your family, your friends, and your associates in the future, it may now be apparent to you that the level of future planning should be increased sharply. We simply must do better in preparing youth to learn how to adapt to change itself—an art that will not be acquired with the same facility that these words are written. Discussions about the future are entered into quite readily by many, but when an attempt is made to get people to do some concentrated and complex planning for the future, one learns soon that words are cheap.

Admittedly, Kateb's recommendations concerning the six possible approaches to the good life have merit. However, it occurs to me further that it should be possible in an evolving democratic society to strive for a very high quality of life through the correct blending, according to each person's choice, of these various approaches in such a way as to correspond most closely to the hierarchy of values that the individual determines for himself in a world undoubtedly characterized by continuous change. If the change and novelty mean in the final analysis that there are no immutable and unchangeable values in the fabric of the universe—a debatable point, of course— we must all necessarily keep open minds to avoid rigidity, stultification, and eventual decay.

My considered response to Kateb's various alternatives for the good life would be that the individual in our society should be allowed the greatest amount of freedom consistent with that encroachment upon personal freedom that seemingly has to be made within the context of an evolving democracy. This would have to be the amount of *laissez-faire* that can be allowed to any one person in this type of political state. Second, we should understand that there are different kinds of *pleasure*, ranging from the purely sensual to the more refined and abiding types. Within this orientation the greatest amount of pleasure will probably result from active and creative participation in the various facets or categories of activity that life has to offer. Here we should understand that the concept of a 'unified organism' implies that the human has the inherent capacity to explore successfully at least five types of interests— physical activity interests, as well as social, aesthetic and creative, communicative, and learning interests (e.g., educational hobbies).

Third, the idea that *play* represents one approach to the good life is momentarily appealing, but then one is faced with the prospect of determining what is meant by the concept 'play.' Some 30 years ago I recall stating, "Let play be for children, and let recreation be for adults." By that I was implying that recreation was some form of mature play in which intelligent adults engaged. Now a more analytical approach to this topic has shown that the word *play* has approximately 70 different meanings either as a noun or verb. Obviously this term merits careful analysis because of the confusion created by what appears to be a family resemblance term (philosophically speaking). In our society we speak of the play of kittens, and we use the word "play" also to describe the contest that takes place each fall between the Chicago Bears and the Detroit Lions (or in Canada between the Edmonton Eskimos and the Calgary Stampeders). I can argue, therefore, that all of us should seek to preserve some of the spirit of kittens' play in our daily lives to broaden the range of life's experiences and thereby to improve its quality. Conversely, it becomes apparent immediately that life and accident insurance rates would rise sharply if we sought to play games with our families and friends that employ the same spirit typically evident in professional football games in which high salaries are paid for performance and traditional grudges prevail.

Fourth, Kateb stated that *craft* represented a fourth approach to the good life. By this it is presumed that craft is defined as art or skill, and also that a person might use such craft as an occupation to make money. Keeping with the basic nature of the definition, then, I might argue that craft belongs in each person's life for the enrichment and satisfaction that it can bring.

Fifth, the concept of *political action* was presented. This proposal for achieving the good life may be the only one of the six offered by Kateb that bears little relationship to sport and physical activity (although even here politics and sport have been interwoven lately in what seems to be an inextricable manner, and conversely there are some who approach politics as a game with rules, strategy, goals, etc.).

Once again, however, I can argue that political action belongs in the life of each citizen in an evolving democratic state. This may sound like a truism, but such must become the case if we hope to preserve and develop this form of political state with its ideal of individual freedom. Failing this, other forms of monarchy, oligarchy, or fascistic dictatorship seem to be the only alternatives left for the twenty-first century.

The sixth and final approach recommended, and that which Kateb asserted is the best one, was that entitled *the life of the mind.* He felt that this approach offered the greatest potential in the world as it is presently known or as it may be known in the future. He concluded that "the man possessed of the higher faculties in their perfection is the model for utopia and already exists outside it. . . ." (p. 472). Once again, it seems that such an approach to life, that is, the pursuit of the life of the mind, should be part and parcel of the life of each person in our society. To me it is amusing to witness the attitude taken by many intellectuals in university circles as they go about their lives as presumably "disembodied spirits" in pursuit of the life of the mind. Such reasoning would seem to imply that the findings of psychology and closely related disciplines concerning the human being as a unified organism were never corroborated—that such theory is not tenable. Of course, it is possible to make a good case for the position that the so-called life of the mind can be improved in many ways—if such activity takes place within a healthy, physically fit body (to give such a state of well-being its minimum amount of credit).

PRESUMED "VIABILITY" OF A MULTIPLE TRANSCENDING APPROACH

What I am recommending to you, therefore, is that men and women now and in the future should combine all six of the approaches recommended for consideration into one presumably "viable," multiple, all-encompassing approach. Further, I want to stress that at least five of these six approaches to the good life are directly or indirectly related to the role that sport, dance, play, and exercise can fulfill within a society generally, as well as what it can mean *specifically* in the life of a mature person. Here is a way to truly "live in your body" (or *vivre dans son corps*) as you begin to truly comprehend, and then seek to do full justice to the vital importance of human movement with purpose in these activities characterized by motor performance.

Fine educational experience is usually related to the mastery of various subject matters. Somewhat less do we expect it to encompass all of the changes that take place in individuals on the basis of their total life experience. Somehow the quality human motor performance experience aspect of education, of recreation, of all life has been slighted historically down to the present day. Huxley designated this as the "education of the non-verbal humanities"—the education of the "psycho-physical instrument of an evolving amphibian" (1964, p. 31). If the kinesthetic sense of man and woman were prepared more efficiently through the educational process, the effects of such experience would inevitably influence subsequent behavior for better or for worse. Thinking, and who can deny that we "think with our entire body," has generally been characterized best as symbolic experience, the assumption being that the formation of habits results from direct experience. An interesting finding, for example, is that thinking tends to be facilitated when there is a general increase in muscle tone. In addition, as thought becomes more concentrated, general muscle tone becomes even greater.

THE UNIQUE ROLE OF SPORT AND PHYSICAL ACTIVITY IN THE EDUCATION OF "ECOLOGICAL MAN AND WOMAN"

No matter whether a man or woman elects to follow primarily one of Kateb's approaches to the good life or accepts my balanced, multifaceted, transcending approach to the improvement of the quality of life—and indeed this includes a greatly improved opportunity over the norm to live in your body—the field of physical education and sport must become fully aware as soon as possible of the environmental crisis confronting humanity. The field of education should be playing a vital role in the development of what might be termed ecological awareness.

Granting that this educational duty should fall to professional teachers at all educational levels who are specialists in all of the subject matters taught in the curriculum, the physical educator/sport coach quite naturally has a general education responsibility. This is true, of course, inasmuch as this person is directly concerned with the human's relationship with self, fellows, other living creatures, the remainder of the biological environment, and finally the physical environment. Specifically, the physical educator/coach and the recreation director are confronted daily with a population that has a very low level of what has been called *physical* fitness with a resultant decrease in overall *total* fitness.

In the next 25 years it will be imperative to affirm the priority of man and woman over athletics and other types of physical activity that may be employed detrimentally. The late Arthur Steinhaus argued that sport was created for man's use, and not vice versa. This sound dictum has been forgotten far too often in the United States, and to a lesser extent in Canada except in hockey, in which there has been vast overemphasis, and the violence has gotten almost completely out of control. Some are seeking to lead Canadians down the same questionable path the United States has followed in intercollegiate athletics. There is a very delicate balance that must be maintained between a program of healthful physical activity in sport, dance, play, and exercise and a type of program that leads a select few to the heights of successful international competition. We can and should adapt and shape reality to our own ends. Sport and physical activity can help to make our reality on this closed planet more healthful, more pleasant, more vital, and more life enriching.

PERSISTENT HISTORICAL PROBLEMS THE PROFESSION STILL FACES

We trust that you, the reader, have been at least somewhat convinced about the importance of the role that human motor performance in sport, dance, play, and exercise can and should play in people's lives now and in the future. It is on this basis that we feel young people can be challenged to make this profession their life work. Nevertheless, you have no doubt sensed the many difficulties that the profession has faced in the past, still faces in the present, and will undoubtedly still have to overcome in the future. This should not trouble you unduly, because every profession has its problems to a greater or lesser extent. Granted that we seem to have a few more than most, nevertheless the uniqueness of our field and its special problems has always been interesting to me.

During my professional career that began over 40 years ago, I have maintained a continuing concern for what I have called the persistent historical problems of physical education and sport, six of which were identified in the introductory chapter as social forces of a pivotal or somewhat lesser nature. They were designated as (1) values and norms, (2) the influence of politics (or *type* of political state), (3) the influence of nationalism, (4) the influence of economics, (5) the influence of religion, and (6) the influence of ecology. Education and sport were also mentioned as significant influences themselves. These persistent problems or social forces influence all of society, as well as the entire field of education. However, there are also other persistent problems of much greater professional orientation confronting the profession of physical education and sport, problems that have themselves been influenced by the various social forces. The last of these problems, the concept of 'progress,' may be considered to be both a social force and a professional concern. All of these problems are shown in Figure 1 with the final one ('progress') indicated in an overarching manner. Those indicated as professional concerns are explained briefly below:

Curriculum (7). Although this is the seventh persistent problem, it is the first

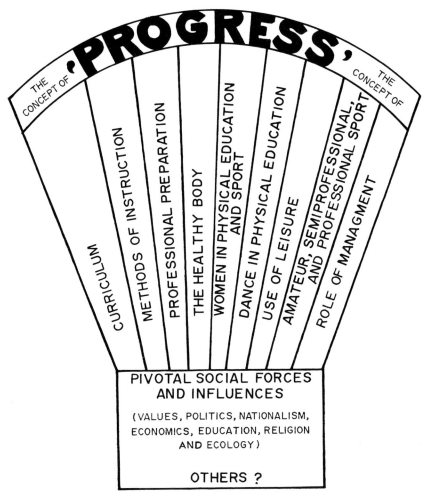

Fig. 1. Selected persistent, historical problems of physical education and sport. (Design advice from Glenda Dhillon)

professional concern. A primary task in curriculum instruction is to determine which subjects should be included because of their recurring interest to the public and to educators. Decisions must be made daily regarding the bases upon which a curriculum is selected. The curriculum has developed and expanded at a fantastic rate on this continent over the past few centuries, and many people now insist that this trend must be reversed so that the "essential" subjects can be taught adequately. The task of the physical educator/coach today is to ascertain the values and norms that are uppermost in the society, and then to attempt to implement them to the greatest possible extent through the medium of sport and related physical activities.

Methods of Instruction (8). We might argue that methods of instruction and curriculum should go hand in hand if effective education is the desired end product. Initially we should appreciate that effective instructional methods involve more than merely what a teacher "does" to a subject matter. If we are talking about sport skills instruction in tennis, for example, the teacher needs to know how to teach tennis, what is taking place within the learner as he seeks to learn tennis from the instructor, and, finally, what the end result is (i.e., what a learner does when he or she has learned to play the sport).

Professional Preparation (9). Professional preparation of teachers to any considerable extent began in the United States in the late nineteenth century. Starting with the normal school, this type of specialized professional preparation for teachers in the public schools progressed in the twentieth century to college and university status. Throughout the world, generally speaking, specialized professional preparation for physical education and sport has been included at the normal and technical school level. University recognition was achieved first in the United States at several universities shortly before the turn of the century. Such status did not come in Canada until the 1940s, but progress has been excellent since that time with the first Ph.D. in Physical Education being awarded in 1969. Although the first Ph.D. degrees were awarded in the United States and Germany in the 1920s, the systems of higher education function quite differently. Subsequently the German Ph.D. in our field was dropped in the 1940s, but it was then reinstated in the early 1970s. Progress has been made in countries such as England and the Scandinavian countries in regard to the granting of university status. Recently Japan made it possible for a person to earn a Ph.D. degree in physical education at one university.

The Healthy Body (10). A study of past and present civilizations indicates that times of war and peace have produced quite different emphases on health. When a country needs to win a war, freedom from disqualifying defects, strength, and endurance are important. During periods of peace, which have been fewer than one would think from an overall global standpoint, the emphasis in health can be placed on the related questions of longevity and environmental health. Much of the disagreement over the role that school health education should play in the educational pattern stems from differing educational philosophies and from the various concepts of health that prevail.

Women in Physical Education and Sport (11). (These statements apply also to what might be called "other minority and handicapped groups," although women have certainly not been a minority group numerically.) Throughout history women's physical education and sport has been hampered, not only by the place that such activity has held in a society, but also by the place that women themselves held in most societies. It had erroneously been concluded that women simply did not possess the intellectual capacity to profit from the higher types of education. Certainly one of the significant trends of the twentieth century—despite continuing efforts on the part of a significant number to slow down such progress—has been the social movement for women's emancipation. The ultimate goal in our field is, of course, an ideal program of physical education and sport at all levels and on into later life for both men and women. The evidence gathered now indicates that men's and women's programs should more nearly approximate each other in both scope and intensity.

Dance in Physical Education (12). In all ages people have danced for personal pleasure, for religious purposes, for expression of the gamut of emotions, and for the pleasure of others. An analysis of the dance forms of a civilization can tell a qualified observer much about the total life of that society. The twentieth century has witnessed truly remarkable development in the dance, as the body is being gradually rediscovered as a means of communication through the dance medium. As both an art and a social function, dance will probably always be with us and will further reflect the dominant influence of the age in which it is taking place. In recent years on the North American continent there have been varied opinions as to where a department or division of dance belongs on a campus. The usual place for dance instruction at all educational levels has been within the field of physical education, but there has been a move in some quarters to transfer dance into the arts or humanities faculty.

Use of Leisure (13). In primitive and preliterate societies there probably was not so sharp a division between work and play as in civilized societies. Early cultures developed certain folkways and ceremonials of a more controlled nature than were present previously. We are told that citizens in the industrialized (and so-called postindustrial) world now have more leisure than ever before, although inflation has forced many wives to seek work as well as husbands to take part-time jobs in addition to their regular employment (the Women's Movement notwithstanding). The promotion of the concept of 'education for leisure' depends a great deal on whether the prevailing educational philosophy will allow sufficient support for the inclusion of such programs in the educational system. What we decide as professionals, and what others will accept, will exert considerable influence on the place of physical education and sport in our educational systems and subsequently in the leisure patterns of our communities at large for mature citizens.

Amateur, Semiprofessional, and Professional Sport (14). Sport (sometimes viewed as a pleasurable diversion) and athletics (a highly competitive activity that brings a reward) are both part of the very lifeblood of our field and offer the possibility of great benefits and satisfaction to participant and coach alike. Primitive and preliterate people undoubtedly felt the urge to play, and they often took part in contests and games as part of religious observances. There is no denying that sport gave them the opportunity to practice skills upon which they relied for survival. Even in the earlier days the aspect of overspecialization because of the desire to win tended to tarnish the luster of the concept that has become known as 'the amateur ideal.' There is an urgent need today for recognition of a semiprofessional category in sport as well as in other areas of endeavor. There is further need for professional athletes who will recognize the need to devote their lives to a social ideal—to serve their fellow men through their contributions to the many phases of sports development.

Role of Management (15). Social organizations of one type or another are inextricably related to the history of mankind as human (and social) animals. Superior-subordinate relationships evolved according to the very nature of things. We are now facing a situation in which a steadily growing percentage of the manpower available has been necessary to cope with the management of the efforts of the large majority of the people in our society, a development that has been called the administrative revolution. Within this development, education has become a vast public and private enterprise demanding wise management based upon administrative theory. In many educational institutions the management of physical education and athletics is now big business within big education. The same can be said for the management of professional athletics and professional exercise establishments on a private basis. Unfortunately, although management science generally has been called on to some extent, there is very little theory that is tenable or ongoing research about the administrative task as it relates specifically to sport and physical education.

The Concept of 'Progress' (16). This persistent problem can be viewed as either a social force (influence) or professional concern or as both. It relates closely to the values that a society holds for itself. Any study of history inevitably forces a person to conjecture about human progress. Certainly there has been progression, but can this be called progress unless it is based on an acceptable criterion? Further, it is doubtful whether we as humans can be both judge and jury in this matter. In the field of physical education and sport we must search for further agreement continually—for the greatest consensus possible among the conflicting positions or philosophical stances extant today. There are undoubtedly some common denominators based on the field of physical education and sport that can be recommended at this time, as well as others that can be agreed upon through consultation with colleagues in the allied professions.

TEN STANCES THAT HAVE TO BE CHANGED

In addition to the 16 social forces and professional concerns enumerated above, the so-called persistent historical problems, there are a number of prevailing philosophical positions or stances that will have to be changed if we ever hope to eliminate the present credibility gap that exists between many practicing professionals and so many of the young people and adults that we hope to serve. My analysis of the profession of physical education and sport notably in the United States, and to a lesser extent in Canada, revealed that it is suffering from what Walter Kaufmann identified as "decidophobia"—the fear of making autonomous decisions without the aid of "crutches" such as religions, political ideologies, philosophical positions, microscopic deviational maneuvers, and other "Band-Aids of life" (1973, pp. 2–34). Finally, I concluded that there are at least ten prevailing ideas in the field of physical education and sport that have to be changed considerably if we wish to eventually bridge the gap that presently exists.

Idea 1: Generalized Professional Preparation. The public is having difficulty keeping up with the image that the field is projecting presently. The task for us right now is primarily to teach humans to move efficiently and with purpose in sport, dance, exercise, and related play activities. Our programs of professional preparation should reflect this emphasis precisely.

Idea 2: Athletics Are Separate from Education. Poor educational practices in competitive athletics at all levels are multiplying almost unchallenged, because the public is entranced with sport and because materialistic influences and general inertia seem insuperable. We must work tirelessly to correct this situation.

Idea 3: The Status of Women in the Field. Professional women physical educators have achieved equal opportunity in the various professional associations, and yet in many ways they are still second-class citizens within their own profession. Obviously this situation will not change overnight.

Idea 4: Embarrassment over the Term "Physical Education." Although the term "physical education" has evidently caused embarrassment and confusion to many in the field—and also seems to imply a mind-body dichotomy that we are seeking to overcome—the time is not ripe yet for complete elimination of the term. An interim solution appears to be the use of the term "physical education and sport" (or vice versa). In the meantime we should not be embarrassed by this name, and we should seek to build on its strengths.

Idea 5: Elementary Physical Education Will Somehow Improve By Itself. It is obvious to almost all professionals in the field that there is an urgent need for improvement of the program of physical education and sport at the elementary level. Somehow there is always rationalization that *others* ought to do something about this vexing problem that is so damaging to our field. We must take the lead in this matter.

Idea 6: The Present Curriculum Is Satisfactory. Professional preparation programs have often deserved a considerable amount of the ridicule that has been heaped upon them, although there are some aspects that are valid and for which the struggle for acceptance must continue. Some have made efforts to improve the situation by raising entrance requirements and grading standards. There is still much room for improvement, including development of alternative professional streams within major programs.

Idea 7: The Concept of 'the Required Program.' The concept of 'the required program' at the university level, and also at the upper-grade levels in high school, has been difficult to defend for several reasons. It is very difficult to defend a 'service program' concept also, especially when we ask for full academic credit for the teaching of a sport skill that could or should have been, and in some cases was, learned in the lower grades. We must strive for a set of standards for which we stand as professionals—a level of achievement of knowledge, skill, and competence in human motor performance in the theory and practice of sport, dance, play, and exercise. Thus a new approach is needed based on the social forces and influences of the time.

Idea 8: The Body of Knowledge Will Somehow Emerge. Despite continuing attacks against physical education and efforts to eliminate it from, or cut it down within, the curriculum, only a relatively small percentage of professional physical education and sport practitioners understand the great need for the development of a more solid body of knowledge upon which the profession can base its practice. This problem needs diagnosis and prescription so that the prognosis will look brighter for the years ahead.

Idea 9: A Struggle at the University Level. In addition to the ongoing problem at the university level that often results in an organizational split between physical education and organized sport, there now appears to be a struggle between faculty members teaching and carrying out research in the bioscience aspects of physical education and sport and those attempting to strengthen the core of undergraduate and graduate programs by adding course experiences in the social science and humanities aspects of the field. Because of the many as yet unrecognized subdisciplinary relationships possible, it is shortsighted and delimiting for the entire field if any group attempts to effect arbitrary exclusion of any seemingly worthwhile subdisciplinary area, not to mention the delimitation of the subprofessional areas (e.g., curriculum and instructional methods). There is often the self-defeating possibility of the denial of academic freedom to be considered as well.

Idea 10: Permanent Acceptance of Second-Class Status. For a variety of reasons, physical education and sport has not been considered academically respectable in the past, and it will have great difficulty achieving this status on a worldwide basis in the future. I explained above the ways in which I feel that this field can contribute to the improvement of the quality of life—if properly understood and implemented. The best way to make the grade would appear to be the steady improvement of the quantity and quality of scholarly endeavor, teaching, and professional service. First-class status is "out there," if we improve our effort to earn it (Zeigler, 1979b).

HOW TO DEVELOP A LIFE PURPOSE

Our task today is to motivate young physical education and sport professionals so that they may find a life purpose in their work in the field. Most of you may agree that potentially we have a unique role to fulfill in people's lives, but perhaps you are worried about these listings of 16 persistent historical problems and then another 10 ideas concerning positions or stances that "have to go" if we are to achieve our mission. I should like to point out that the 16 persistent problems—the 6 or more social forces, the 9 or more professional concerns, and the final concept of 'progress' that I argued may be regarded as either social or professional—would be present no matter what field you would be entering. By that I mean that the social forces are simply present in all societies, but each profession probably has a unique set of professional concerns. The important point, as I see it, is the enormous challenge that is present, that is inherent in physical education and sport by its very nature, and that if overcome can do so much to enrich the quality of life for all people everywhere. So that leaves the ten ideas that need to be implemented or, looking at it another way, the ten philosophical positions or stances that simply have to go. Granting that bringing about these changes may be akin to a superhuman task, I will now suggest that the only way to bring this condition about is to have a large group of young professionals in the field who are "supercharged"—young people who gradually but steadily find a life purpose in physical education and sport. "Impossible," you may say, "there is simply too much to be done, to be overcome." Perhaps you are right, but I refuse to accept that for an answer. I have seen so many fine people who have indeed found a life purpose in our work that I believe firmly in our future.

How then does a person find this life purpose? Also, what is meant by the term "life purpose?" These are good questions, and my response will be geared to making the answers clear—as clear as one can make the answers to basically subjective questions. The answer should be self-evident, but obviously one must be ever so much more precise and offer a step-by-step analysis of how one gets from here to there. The following are the steps that I recommend: (1) Determine your personal values; (2) place these values in some hierarchical order; (3) relate your personal values as best as possible to the values and norms of your culture within a world perspective; (4) analyze your own abilities and interests while ascertaining the needs and interests of the time; and (5) choose a life purpose for yourself and nurture it so that maximum energy for living will result.

It has been so difficult recently to decide upon *personal values*. The home and the church have run into serious difficulty coping with this problem, and the school and the university have been slow to fill the gap. Since the days of the ancient Greeks, savants have been plagued by whether education should be both rational and moral. Is a commitment to moral values taught or caught? Do you teach about it, or do you teach a commitment to value? (Brubacher, 1977, p. 73). Further, it is very easy to confuse means and ends along the way toward the achievement of a set of personal values. For example, are the following terms regarded as means or ends or both: sound health, religious faith, knowledge, truth, recognition, service to others, creativity, desirable personality traits, pleasure, and capacity and opportunity to profit from a lifelong education in an evolving democratic society?

For some unexplained reason we go at this most important aspect of our development in a typically haphazard manner. If a child has a mother and a father who are able to spend a large amount of time with him, and these people are intelligent, sensitive, and dedicated to the task, that young person is most fortunate indeed. This is true because it is during these formative years that a person's sense of life gets off to a good, bad, or indifferent beginning. Rand discusses this most succinctly in *The Romantic Manifesto* when she explains that religion offers humans a myth or allegory, stating that there is a supernatural recorder from whom none of man's deeds can be hidden. She states, "That myth is true, not existentially, but psychologically. The merciless recorder is the integrating mechanism of a man's subconscious; the record is his *sense of life*" (1969, p. 31).

To paraphrase Rand's sequence of ideas, this sense of life is a preconceptual, emotional, subconsciously integrated appraisal of existence, man, and that person's emotional response and character essence. Thus, before a person has a chance to study philosophy—if he ever does in today's world—choices are made, value judgments are formed, emotions are experienced, and an implicit view of life is acquired. If the person has the opportunity subsequently to develop his rational powers, the hope is generally that reason will act as the programmer of his "emotional computer," and then the earlier sense of life may develop into a rational philosophy. If we do not make the necessary effort to develop rationality, or never have the opportunity to understand that we need to develop such rationality as the basis for the possible future emergence of a life purpose, then chance takes over. The person then tends to become a machine without a driver that is "integrating blindly, incongruously, and at random" (p. 33).

The *hierarchy of values*, whether arrived at implicitly or explicitly, indicates what is important to a particular person, and thereby serves as a bridge between the individual's metaphysics and ethics. If a person's basic values are integrated, then a sense of life is integrated as well. The goal is "a fully integrated personality, a man whose mind and emotions are in harmony; whose sense of life matches his convictions" (Rand, 1969, p. 36). Of course, this sense of life continues on in an automatic fashion, but the hope is that thereafter the enlightened person will derive value judgments conceptually from an *explicit* metaphysics.

The third step involves *relating personal values* in the best possible fashion *to the values and norms of the culture* in which one resides, keeping it all within a world perspective, of course. The relationship between personal and societal values should be reasonably consistent or serious difficulties may arise. Proceeding on the assumption that the various subsystems of the general action system of a society together compose a hierarchy of control and conditioning, our cultural values (i.e., social, scientific, artistic, educational, sport) determine the state of our culture in the long run if the action system is functioning properly. Thus, our societal values in this evolving democratic society determine our so-called cultural pattern or configuration, which basically programs the entire societal action system.

In a classification of the fundamental values of the social system of the United States—an attempt to perceive the self-orientation in relationship to what is called a "collectivity orientation"—the United States is viewed as being more achievement oriented, universalistic, equalitarian, and self-oriented than, for example, Canada. However, the value differences are really not great, and any differences are probably due to "varying origins in their political systems and national identities, varying religious traditions, and varying frontier experiences" (Lipset, 1973, pp. 4–5). Our problem as individuals is, therefore, that we must work without *our* system and its ascribed values, or we should seek to change these values (or possibly move elsewhere).

In *analyzing one's own abilities and interests* while ascertaining the needs and interests of the time, the individual may move closer to the selection of a life purpose by asking such questions as (1) What is it that I want to do more than anything else in the world? (2) Will my work give me the greatest amount of satisfaction? (3) Will I be able to follow through with my initial decision tentatively before eventually making a final decision?

Here it seems appropriate to state that a life purpose is much more than the mere choice of and efforts to fulfill the demands of a job or occupation. It involves even more than the choice of and following through with a profession. A profession is a means to an end. We must ask what that end, that goal, is. Presumably, then, the term "vocation" would be more appropriate here, because it means a "calling" based on its Latin derivation. With a calling we encounter immediately the idea of accomplishing something of significance for the total movement of human life on this planet. I am still pragmatic enough to believe that this idea has validity even today despite the turmoil, inflation, and unemployment all around us. This type of philosophical meliorism—starting where you are and working with deep conviction and commitment to improve the quality of life—equates nicely with Berelson and Steiner's "behavioral science image" of man and woman. The image envisions him or her as a creature who is continually and continuously adapting reality to his or her own ends (1964, pp. 662–667). Within this context a person should inquire what kind of striving gives life its greatest meaning. (Here I point out that the idea of sacrificing yourself for some cause with no thought of enjoyment in the effort is definitely not the best approach; I believe it can be argued that you must really enjoy yourself, even if through vicarious satisfaction, to effect the most fruitful results from your work.)

Just before you attempt to narrow down the list of possibilities in your search for a life purpose, I would like to recommend that the following approaches be explored: (1) think reflectively; (2) observe as many different occupations as possible and ask questions; (3) enact a process of self-measurement and evaluation by reviewing the qualities necessary for entry and success in this book's Introduction; (4) review the needs and opportunities of this period in this field and others closely related; (5) read widely and as carefully as possible about career opportunities; and (6) listen to the thoughts of close relatives, friends, and associates who may have insights about you and who may have your best interests at heart.

At this point you should *choose a life purpose.* Keep in mind that you must begin immediately *to nurture it* to promote its effective development. We are confronted here at once with a "move-it-or-lose-it" ultimatum. Talk your choice through; even write it out so that you will comprehend it more thoroughly. (Try out the "What Do I Believe?" self-evaluation check list in the Appendix.) A life purpose ought to grow. It should be reviewed and revised yearly. A person needs to rededicate himself from time to time. The goal may change or alter somewhat, of course, but the purpose you have chosen needs to be fostered by the development of a strong, personal attitude. Possessing such an attitude will help to avoid any gradual surrendering to the shifting currents within the onrushing, changing society.

A young person will often find it difficult to hold true to a chosen vocation. The purpose may have to be guarded against a variety of ills that may appear from time to time along the way. Other career opportunities may present themselves that will seem to hold out greater material reward or more rapid success. It is true that success for some comes more quickly than for others. Further, there will be ways to make more money—or even just some extra money—that will in time detract from the accomplishment of your avowed life purpose. In the field of teaching and coaching, for example, success may come only after long years of dedicated effort to a cause. Youth may be long gone in such instances, and we all know of occasions when recognition came after a person's death. Although a statement such as this cannot be proved by mathematics, I believe that the course of human history has indeed been shaped by personalities who have held to high purposes on behalf of mankind over a period of years.

As we nurture a life purpose, we must guard that the means do not become confused with the end, that we do not become bogged down by so-called instrumentalities. So many people seem to spend time getting ready to live that they never quite get around to living. I am convinced that the joy comes from traveling hopefully along the way and that we should therefore enjoy ourselves because it's later than we think. We should be truly searching for the Aristotelean Golden Mean between fanaticism and egomania, on the one hand, and lackadaisical apathy, on the other. A person cannot ignore the conditions that must be met to fulfill a life purpose, and yet he should not ignore the important interests of his fellowman. The task, truly a case of delicate balancing, is to be sufficiently passionate about one's purpose in life while avoiding the sad pitfall of fanaticism. Particularly important in achieving this delicate and difficult golden mean that will allow accomplishment of one's life purpose is the attainment of a battery of knowledge, competence, skills, attitudes, and conditions. In this era of specialization, knowledge equates with power; competence is needed to meet both the general and specific demands of life; skills are required to solve the problems of varying complexity faced each day, not to mention the ability to distinguish between the extraordinary and what is ordinary (or even nonsense); an attitude is needed that exhibits care and concern for humanity—love for fellowman everywhere; and a condition of health is required that permits the vigor and endurance needed to accomplish one's chosen life purpose.

A FORMULA FOR HAPPINESS AND SUCCESS

What then might be a formula for happiness and success in this society? In offering this list of "ingredients," admittedly normative and unscientific, no effort has been made to present the eight aspects of the formula in any hierarchical order. My position is simply that the ingredients of this formula, applied to the degree or extent that must be personally determined, will enable a person to obtain the values desired from life. These values will accordingly contribute to the vague intangible goals of happiness and success. My belief is that competence (adequacy or sufficiency) in each of these eight aspects is possible and that still a life purpose may be fulfilled passionately and purposely.

1. A life purpose based on one's choice of profession (which should be fulfilled passionately but not fanatically)
2. A broad general education (which should result in an inquiring mind)
3. Desirable personality and character traits (which are the result of nature, nurture, and other experiences)
4. Intensive, specialized professional preparation (which should prepare the individual for the highest type of position available in accordance with his potential)
5. Successful human relations (which may involve the home and other social groups)
6. Active pattern of sport, dance, and exercise (which should achieve continuing physical fitness and bring enjoyment through play)
7. Creative educational/recreational participation (which may be carried out to a desired degree in social, communicative, aesthetic and creative, and "learning" recreational interests)
8. Community service (which should make a contribution to the goals of community living—interpreted as involvement locally, regionally, nationally, or internationally or in combinations of these) (Zeigler, 1979a, pp. 15–16)

CONCEPTS OF 'PROGRESS'

As we look ahead to the turn of the century, and to where the field of physical education and sport might be by then, we should appreciate the difficulty of obtaining true historical perspective about our present status. In this highly personalized epilogue, we have considered first the possible relationship of sport and physical activity to the good life. Then we traced the 16 persistent historical problems (identified as social influences and professional concerns). Third, we reviewed what I have concluded were ten philosophical stances or positions that had to go. Then, immediately above, we pondered over the various steps or stages that a person might follow to develop a life purpose within a profession or vocation. "All right, then," you may say, "I think I understand about the contribution to the good life that sport, dance, play, and exercise might make. I understand also the difference between the social influences and the professional concerns that you call persistent historical problems. Further, I appreciate that there are a number of ideas or stances that need to be changed in this field in the years ahead. Still further, I see the importance of developing a life purpose, and also how it requires a number of ingredients in the best possible formula for happiness and success. However, all of this notwithstanding, I am still puzzled by the concept of 'progress.' To play with words just a bit, *Where in the world are we going?*" (Zeigler, 1980).

This is really a good question, and I wish I could be truly definitive with an answer. "Futurology" (or "futuristics" as it is also called) can hardly qualify as a science, although much progress has been made. The best answer that I can give may not satisfy you. Our task, I believe, is to analyze the several meanings of the term "progress," and then to make our individual and professional determinations with the full understanding that our nonstatistical types of measurement are subject to errors of observation. To make matters even more difficult, we are not certain about the element to be measured, the motive force, the process of change, the route of change, the goals toward which the elements are moving, and how any goals can be measured. Except for these uncertainties, we are in good shape.

Schwartz, in his insightful but disturbing work, *Overskill*, states that:

The twentieth-century version of progress turns out to be a blindly hurtling technology that has carried man to the moon, split the atom, created a cornucopia of commodities for a privileged few of the earth, and holds out a promise to carry with it the remainder of mankind. Whereas flaws and dangers inherent in progress were becoming more apparent, in the twentieth century the "laws" of progress were becoming ever more elusive. . . . In the past two hundred years many attempts have been made to complete the edifice of the theory of progress, and on numerous occasions claims have been made that the elusive, universal law of progress has been discovered. But the "law" of progress is still undiscovered. Nor is it likely to be discovered, for in fact progress is a state of mind based upon faith rather than an element of nature. (1971, pp. 31–32)

I find it disturbing to be told that progress *in fact* "is a state of mind based upon faith rather than an element of nature." It is not that I am opposed to acting on the basis of faith, although I recognize that this itself is a controversial subject. For example, I have faith in scientific method, and I have faith that there will be eternal change—at least for the next few million years in our universe. Regardless of this uncertainty and keeping in mind that throughout much of our lives we "act on faith," I believe that there are several levels of progress that should be considered by us before this book is brought to a conclusion.

DEFINITIONS OF PROGRESS

Keeping in mind that a concept is a general notion or idea, we realize almost at once that the word "progress" is used generally to explain two different concepts— that of 'forward movement' and that of 'proceeding to a higher stage.' Thus, when we turn our attention to the human's progress in evolution, it is immediately obvious that human development on this earth has exhibited progress—progress, that is, when it is defined as forward movement or progression. However, Simpson stated over a generation ago that he had rejected "the oversimple and metaphysical concept of a pervasive perfection principle" (1949, pp. 240–262). We simply cannot assume that change is progress, unless we are prepared to reconsider a criterion by which our progress may be judged.

Next we are faced with the question whether men and women can dare to set their own criteria for human progress. Would we be exhibiting too much temerity to establish ourselves as both judge and jury in this regard? This question must be answered affirmatively, because to establish our own human criterion is to automatically assume that such is "the *only* criterion of progress and that it has a *general* validity in evolution. . . ." (Simpson, 1949, pp. 240–262). Throughout history (and prehistory, we must presume) there have been examples of progress and examples of retrogression. Presumably also, if it is a materialistic world, a particular species can progress and retrogress—and, fortunately for us, human beings give every evidence of being the organism that is progressing most rapidly on earth at present.

Today many of us take the notion of human progress for granted. Some think that the idea of progress is of relatively recent origin, although it may have begun with the early Greeks. However it may have begun, the idea gained some credence in the late seventeenth and early eighteenth centuries. It was Darwin's evolutionary theory that added a scientific base to the concept of 'progress' for mankind. We would need to make a careful analysis of each decade thereafter to understand whether the dominant social values and norms of a society were moving humans toward a better understanding of the idea of progress. Bury, in his definitive work on this topic, argues generally that it was not until the late Renaissance that men realized their capacity to structure their own world as skillfully as the citizens of the Classical World had controlled their destiny earlier (1955). Certainly the early Greeks gave some thought to the future, as evidenced by that phrase in the middle of the oath taken before the Council of Five Hundred by all young men at Athens: "I will transmit my native commonwealth not lessened, but larger and better than I have received it" (Durant, 1939, p. 290).

Durant, in one of his earliest works before he started his monumental world history, asked, "Is progress a delusion?" Seeking to encompass the problem of progress in a total view, he assessed all of history as follows:

> It is unnecessary to refute the pessimist; it is only necessary to enclose his truth, if we can, in ours. When we look at history in the large we see it as a graph of rising and falling states—nations and cultures disappearing as on some gigantic film. But in that irregular movement of countries and that chaos of men, certain great moments stand out as the peaks and essence of human history, certain advances which, once made, were never lost. Step by step man has climbed from the savage to the scientist. . . . (1953, pp. 249–250)

Then he delineates the stages of human growth as (1) the invention of speech; (2) the discovery of fire; (3) the conquest of the animals; (4) the gradual development of agriculture; (5) the gradual introduction of social organization; (6) a perhaps dubious rise in the level of morality; (7) the development of tools (machines) to assist us; (8) the victory of man over matter that has not yet been matched with any kindred victory of man over himself; (9) the growth of education—"the development of the potential capacity for the comprehension, control, and *appreciation* of the world"; and (10) the power of writing to unite generations and of print to bind civilizations together (pp. 249–257).

PROGRESS IN EDUCATION

Durant's quite optimistic assessment of human progress was written in the mid 1920s. Considering the events of the more than 50 intervening years, it was revealing to read the Durants' analysis of the world situation published more than 40 years later in what was intended to be a brief volume summarizing the world history series (1968). You may not wish to accept their definition of education as "the transmission of civilization" (p. 101), but keeping this phrase in mind, they asserted that "we are unquestionably progressing."

> Civilization is not inherited; it has to be learned and earned by each generation anew; if the transmission should be interrupted for one century, civilization would die, and we should be savages again. So our finest contemporary achievement is our unprecedented expenditure of wealth and toil in the provision of higher education for all. . . . Consider education not as the painful accumulation of facts and dates and reigns, nor merely the necessary preparation of the individual to earn his keep in the world, but as the transmission of our mental, moral, technical, and aesthetic heritage as fully as possible to as many as possible, for the enlargement of man's understanding, control, embellishment, and enjoyment of life. (p. 101)

Despite the Durants' cautious optimism, we are confronted with the fact that by the year 2000 the United States alone will in all probability have a population of more than 300 million. The threat of great strain and stress looms large in all of life's many aspects. We will undoubtedly have to devise better uses of leisure, especially if robots are gradually used more extensively in the hot, heavy, hazardous, and boring work that distinguishes much of our industry characterized by advanced technology. Where does education fit into this picture?

At present there are upwards of 60 million people enrolled at some level of the vast educational system in the United States, with a somewhat smaller percentage of the total population in Canada involved similarly. In the United States more than 50 billion dollars a year is being spent to finance this gigantic enterprise (perhaps a conservative estimate). And still the perennial questions remain: What is a good education, that is, what criteria shall we employ; how should the prevailing educational practice be modified by the current social and political scene; what type of environment should be provided to guarantee the best educational outcome; and, specifically, what is the function of the school?

Durant's ideas stated above may have answered the question for most people. We cannot really find many who would argue (along with educators like Counts and

Dewey) that the schools should serve a more creative function—to provide people of all ages with the knowledge, competence, skills, understanding, and attitudes whereby they could more effectively lead the way. Thus, even though there has been advancement, if not progress, the public is not willing to support education so that it can keep pace with the annual inflation factor. Operating funds are made available grudgingly; capital funding is really difficult to obtain; and there is obvious discontent with education, a most disconcerting fact to those who have devoted their lives to education while finding a life purpose therein. Regardless, the struggle will continue for us all as we seek to determine the ideal hierarchy of educational values in a pluralistic, evolving North American society.

THE NEED FOR CONSENSUS

If we hope to influence whatever we decide is progress in our society and in our profession, we must work for a greater amount of agreement about our professional goals—goals that are consonant with the values and norms in the society. Any evaluation of qualitative as opposed to quantitative progress would depend upon the extent to which our physical education and sport practice approximates an agreed-upon hierarchy of educational values. It is vitally important now that we speak out intelligently, honestly, and forthrightly regarding the many recurring problems that the profession is facing.

This means, of course, that we will have to assist in the establishment of criteria for the measurement of the goals that we set. Then we will have to state what elements of our work should show progress; what the causal factors are that will produce the desired result; what the route of change may be; how the elements of progress may change with time; and toward which objectives and long-range goals the elements we typically promote are moving; all in all, a prodigious task.

We should be able to agree on the following at least: (1) what a desired level of physical vigor and fitness is; (2) whether we believe that a reasonably standardized program of physical education and sport should be required, and to what educational grade or level; (3) what attitudes toward health and ecological problems are needed for survival; (4) what developmental physical activity is desirable in relation to other leisure activities; (5) who is responsible for therapeutic exercise for remediable physical defects; (6) what type of competitive sport experience is desirable for both sexes; and (7) to what extent sport and developmental physical activity can contribute to character and personality development. It is urgent that we agree on such a set of professional standards soon (Zeigler, 1977, p. 235).

To a considerable extent we are still being downgraded and shortchanged by our professional colleagues from many directions and from the public at large and the politicians as well. Why is this so, and what can we do to bring about progress toward our avowed goals? We know that a large segment of the population is sedentary with what Herbert Spencer more than a hundred years ago called "seared physical consciences." Scientists tell us that rapid behavioral evolution, that is, significant emotional, physical, and intellectual trait alteration, is at least possible with humans. Obviously our unique field can truly fulfill a significant role in any such future developments.

Undoubtedly there are many forces and influences threatening the old field of physical education at present. Much of our tradition, our cherished orthodoxy, and now hoary assumptions and myths will be challenged as never before in the years immediately ahead. How we confront this opportunity for professional consolidation and progress—the attitude that we will need to foster within our profession lest we be swept aside by the tidal wave of change that is threatening to sweep over us—is explained in an anecdote that described how Destiny came to an island some time ago and confronted three people—a *cynic*, a *mystic*, and a *physic*(al educator). Destiny asked, "What would you do if I told you that in exactly 30 days this island would be submerged because of the after-effects of a shifting of polar ice?" The first person, the cynic, said, "Why I would eat, drink, and make love for the whole month." The second person, the mystic, said, "I would go to our sacred grove with my loved ones, make sacrifices to the gods, and then pray ceaselessly for the entire 30-day period." But the third person, the physic(al educator), thought for a while, in a somewhat confused but definitely troubled state, and then stated, "Why I might eat, drink, make love, and pray when the occasion presented itself, but my immediate plan of action would be to assemble our wisest scholars, researchers, and practitioners, along with aquatic specialists and experts in wilderness-survival techniques. Together we would begin to plan, organize, staff, and work like mad 20 hours a day to figure out how to live under water."

I am not suggesting that prospective physical education and sport professionals take this story literally, and that we are indeed going to have to learn how to live under water. But I do believe that we are going to be inundated in the years ahead by all sorts of people from other trades, professions, and disciplines who will seek increasingly to "get into the act" that might be called "sport and developmental physical activity." I want *us* to be recognized as professionals who are leading the way in the research, analysis, teaching, coaching, and promotion of human motor performance in sport, dance, exercise, and play. Is this too much to ask?

If we wish to continue our progress, we will have to redouble our efforts to provide our profession with a sound body of knowledge at the same time as we sharpen our "conceptual lenses" as to exactly what our purpose is. Simultaneously we will need to improve our efforts in both undergraduate and graduate professional preparation. Finally, as a profession we will need to borrow marketing techniques with a strong psychological orientation. We will have to increase public awareness of their need for our product. While we improve the motivation techniques that we employ, we will need to strengthen our educational base and our instructional techniques. We should provide opportunities for sport and physical activity on an "easy-entry" basis, encourage continuation of vigorous activity regularly, and arrange for reinforcement reminders that carry a positive message with humor (Kisby, 1980).

A FINAL WORD

Finally, then, in the words of Durant,

> The heritage that we can now more fully transmit is richer than ever before. It is richer than that of Pericles, for it includes all the Greek flowering that followed him; richer than Leonardo's, for it includes him and the Italian Renaissance; richer than Voltaire's, for it embraces all the French Enlightenment and its ecumenical dissemination. If progress is real despite our whining, it is not because we are born any healthier, better, or wiser than infants were in the past, but because we are born to a richer heritage, born on a higher level of that pedestal which the accumulation of knowledge and art raises as the ground and support of our being. The heritage rises, and man rises in proportion as he receives it. (1968, pp. 101–102)

We in the profession of physical education and sport are part of this heritage. We now have a golden opportunity to enrich mankind's heritage through the involvement of a steadily increasing number of people to improve their quality of life through heightened experiences in sport, dance, exercise, and play. There will be many opportunities for eager and enlightened young men and women to find their life purposes in such an enormous undertaking.

Obviously our duty and responsibility in physical education and sport are to improve upon man's heritage through the experiences that developmental physical activity can provide for all people everywhere. We have an opportunity to transmit our field's body of knowledge and to develop the necessary accompanying attitudes to as many people as possible. We must work unremittingly toward the professional preparation of leadership that will permit our field to achieve its unique potential. This represents a concept of 'progress' that is very difficult to refute.

REFERENCES

Berelson B., and Steiner, G.A.: Human Behavior: An Inventory of Scientific Findings. New York, Harcourt, Brace and World, 1964.

Brubacher, J.S.: On The Philosophy of Higher Education. San Francisco, Jossey-Bass, 1977.

Durant, W.: The Pleasures of Philosophy. New York, Simon and Schuster, 1953.

Durant, W.: The Life of Greece. New York, Simon and Schuster, 1939.

Durant, W., and Durant, A.: The Lessons of History. New York, Simon and Schuster, 1968.

Huxley, A.: Tomorrow and Tomorrow and Tomorrow. New York, New American Library of World Literature, 1964.

Kateb, G.: Utopia and the Good Life. Daedalus, 94, Spring, 1965.

Kaufman, W.: Without Guilt and Justice. New York, Dell, 1973.

Kisby, R.: Conversation with Director, Sport Particip-ACTION, 1980.

Lipset, S.M.: National character. *In* Readings in Social Psychology: Focus on Canada. Edited by D. Koulack and D. Perlman. Toronto, Wiley Publishers of Canada, 1973.

Rand, A.: The Romantic Manifesto. New York, World, 1969.

Schwartz, E.S.: Overskill: Decline of Technology in Modern Civilization. New York, Times Books, 1971.

Simpson,G.G.: The Meaning of Evolution. New Haven, Yale University Press, 1949.

Zeigler, E.F.: Physical Education and Sport Philosophy. Englewood Cliffs, N.J., Prentice-Hall, 1977.

Zeigler, E.F.: Developing a life purpose in the profession of sport and physical education. *In* Theory into Practice. Edited by J.J. Jackson. Victoria, B.C., University of Victoria, 1979a.

Zeigler, E.F.: Issues in North American Physical Education and Sport. Washington, D.C,, AAHPER, 1979b.

Zeigler, E.F.: Physical education and sport philosophy: foundations and definitions. Asian J. Phys. Educ., 2, 3:151–164, 1979c.

Zeigler, E.F.: Concepts of progress. *In* Academy Papers, no. 13. Edited by G. Scott. Washington, D.C., AAHPER, 1979.

What Do I Believe?

A Self-Evaluation Check List for Professionals in Sport and Physical Education

Earle F. Zeigler

INSTRUCTIONS

Read each of the statements below carefully, section by section. Then indicate with an X that statement in each section that seems *closest* to your own personal belief. Keep in mind that you may not agree *completely* with any one paragraph.

Check your answers only after both sections have been completed. Then complete the summarizing tally form on the answer sheet prior to checking your position on the Freedom Spectrum at the end.

The concept of 'freedom'— "the condition of being able to choose and to carry out purposes" (Herbert Muller)—is basic to this approach.

Note: Many of the words, terms, phrases, etc., have been obtained from the works of philosophers, educational philosophers, and sport and physical educational philosophers (living or deceased). We wish to acknowledge this assistance, but we thought it best not to acknowledge them specifically in the course of the text so as not to influence the reader. A listing of names is provided at the end.

I. EDUCATIONAL AIMS AND OBJECTIVES

a.___Socialization of the child has become equally as important as his intellectual development as a key educational aim in this century. There should be concern, however, because many educational philosophers seem to assume the position that children are to be fashioned so that they will conform to a prior notion of what they should be. Even the progressivists seem to have failed in their effort to help the learner "posture himself." If it does become possible to get general agreement on a set of fundamental dispositions to be formed, should the criterion employed for such evaluation be a public one (rather than personal and private)? Education should seek to awaken awareness in the learner, awareness of himself as a single subjectivity in the world. Increased emphasis is needed on the arts and social sciences, and the student should choose his own pattern of education freely and creatively.

b.___Social self-realization is the supreme value in education. The realization of this ideal is most important for the individual in the social setting—a world culture.

Positive ideals should be molded toward the evolving democratic ideal by a general education that is group centered, one in which the majority determines the acceptable goals. However, once that majority opinion is determined, all are obligated to conform until such majority opinion can be reversed (the doctrine of defensible partiality). Nevertheless, education by means of hidden coercion is to be scrupulously avoided. Learning itself is explained by the organismic principle of functional psychology. Social intelligence acquired teaches people to control and direct their urges as they concur with or attempt to modify cultural purposes.

c.___The concept of 'education' has become much more complex than was ever realized earlier. Because of the various meanings of the term "education," talking about educational aims and objectives, or taking a specific stance or position, is almost a hopeless task unless a myriad of qualifications is employed for clarification. Education has now become what is called a "family-resemblance" term in philosophy. Thus, we need to qualify our meaning to explain to the listener whether we mean (1) the subject matter; (2) the activity of education carried on by teachers; (3) the process of being educated (or learning) that is occurring; (4) the result, actual or intended, or (2) and (3) above taking place through the employment of that which comprises (1); (5) the discipline, or field of inquiry and investigation; and (6) the profession whose members are involved professionally with all of the aspects of education described above. With this understanding it is then possible to make some determination about which specific objectives the profession of education should be directed toward as it moves in a collective effort to achieve long-range aims.

d.___The general aim of education is more education. Education in the broadest sense can be nothing else than the changes made in human beings by their experience. Participation by students in the formation of aims and objectives is absolutely essential to generate the all-important desired interest. Social efficiency in the broadest possible sense can well be considered the general aim of education. Pupil growth is a paramount goal; the individual is placed at the center of the educational experience.

e.___A philosophy that holds that the aim of education is the acquisition of verified knowledge of the environment. The value of content is recognized, as well as the activities involved in learning. Such a position takes into account the external determinants of human behavior. Education is therefore the acquisition of the art of knowledge utilization. The primary task of education is to transmit knowledge, without which civilization cannot continue to flourish. Whatever man has discovered to be true because it conforms to reality must be handed down to future generations as the social or cultural tradition. (Some holding this philosophy believe that the "good life" emanates from cooperation with God's grace and that development of the Christian virtues is obviously of greater worth than learning or anything else.)

f.___Through education the developing organism becomes what it latently is. All education may be said, in a sense, to have religious significance. This means that there is a "moral imperative" in education. As man's mind strives to realize itself there is the possibility of realization of the Absolute within the individual mind. Education should seek to aid the child to adjust to the basic realities (the spiritual ideals of truth, beauty, and goodness) that the history of the race has furnished us. The basic values of human living are health, character, social justice, skill, art, love, knowledge, philosophy, and religion.

II. AIMS AND OBJECTIVES OF SPORT AND PHYSICAL EDUCATION

a.___I believe in the concept of 'total fitness' that implies an educational design pointed toward the individual's self-realization as a social being. In our field there

---

This is an abridged and truncated version of a comprehensive, self-evaluation check list for professional practitioners in the fields of (1) sport and physical education, (2) health and safety education, and (3) recreation and park administration. Thus, this version covers educational aims and objectives as well as those for sport and physical education only. This 1980 check list was preceded by several earlier versions dating back to approximately 1960. I am appreciative of advice received from my associates.

should be an opportunity for selection of a wide variety of useful activities. Instruction in motor skills is necessary to provide a sufficient amount of "physical" fitness activity. The introduction of dance and art into physical education can contribute to man's creative expression. Intramural sports and voluntary physical activities should be stressed. This applies especially to team competition, with particular stress on co-operation and promotion of friendly competition. Extramural sport club competition should be introduced when there is a need. Striving for excellence is important, but it is vital that materialistic influence be kept out of the educational program. Relaxation techniques should have a place too, as should the concept of 'education for leisure.'

    b.___I believe that the field of sport and physical education should strive to fulfill a role in the general education patterns of arts and sciences. The goal is total fitness, not only physical fitness, with a balance between activities emphasizing competition and cooperation. The concept of 'universal man' is paramount, but we must allow the individual to choose his sport, dance, and exercise activities for himself, based on knowledge of self and what knowledge and skills he would like to possess. We should help the child who is "authentically eccentric" feel at home in the physical education program. Further, we should also find ways for youth to commit themselves to values and to people. A person should be able to select developmental physical activity according to the values he wishes to derive from it. This is often difficult because of the extreme emphasis on winning in this culture. Creative physical activities such as modern dance should be stressed also.

    c.___I believe that education "of the physical" should have primary emphasis in our field. I am concerned with the development of physical vigor. Such development should have priority over the recreational aspects of physical education. Many people who hold about the same educational philosophy as I do recommend that all students in public schools should have a daily period designed to strengthen their muscles and develop their bodily coordination and circulorespiratory endurance. Physical education must, of course, yield precedence to intellectual education. I give qualified approval to competitive sport, since such activity holds great appeal, and under good leadership helps with the learning of sportsmanship and desirable social conduct. However, all of this, with the possible exception of basic physical training, is definitely extracurricular and is not part of what is considered the regular educational curriculum.

    d.___I am much more interested in promoting the concept of 'total fitness' than physical fitness alone. I believe that physical education should be an integral subject in the curriculum. Students should have the opportunity to select a wide variety of useful activities, many of which should help to develop "social intelligence." The activities offered should bring natural impulses into play. To me, physical education classes and intramural sports are more important to the large majority of students than highly competitive sports and deserve priority if conflict arises over budgetary allotment, staff availability, and use of facilities. I can give full support to team activities under sound educational leadership, however, because such experience can be vital in the development of youth.

    e.___I believe that there is a radical, logically fundamental difference between statements of what the situation is and statements of what it ought to be. When people express their beliefs about sport and physical activity, their disagreements can be resolved in principle. However, it is logical also that there can be sharing of beliefs (facts and knowledge) with radical disagreement in attitudes. In a democracy, for example, we can conceivably agree on the fact that jogging (or bicycling, swimming, rapid walking, etc.) brings about certain functional responses in the human organism, but we cannot force people to get actively involved or to hold a favorable attitude toward personal involvement. We can prove the correctness of a belief, therefore, but we cannot prove the correctness of an attitude. Thus, I may accept the evidence that sport, dance, and exercise bring about certain effects or changes

in the body, but my attitude toward personal involvement—the values in it for me—
is the result of a commitment rather than a prediction.

f.___I am extremely interested in individual personality development. I believe
in education "of the physical," and yet I can believe in the idea of education "through
the physical" as well. Accordingly, I view physical education as important, but also
as occupying a lower rung on the educational ladder. I believe that desirable objectives for sport and physical education would include the development of responsible
citizenship and group participation. In competitive sport I believe that the transfer
of training theory operates in connection with the development of desirable personality traits. However, sports participation, except for the professional athlete, should
always be a means, not an end.

ANSWERS

Read only after both sections have been completed. Record your answer to each of
the two parts of this abridged check list on the summarizing tally form below.

I. EDUCATIONAL AIMS AND OBJECTIVES

a. Existentialistic (largely agnostic or atheistic)
b. Somewhat Liberal (Educational Reconstructionism)
c. Analytic (Analytic Philosophy)
d. Liberal (Pragmatic Naturalism)
e. Traditional (including Strongly Traditional elements) (Realism basically, including elements of Naturalistic Realism, Rational Humanism, and Catholic educational
philosophy)
f. Traditional (Idealism)

II. AIMS AND OBJECTIVES OF SPORT AND PHYSICAL EDUCATION

a. Somewhat Liberal
b. Existentialistic
c. Traditional (including Strongly Traditional elements)
d. Liberal
e. Analytic
f. Traditional

SUMMARIZING TALLY FORM

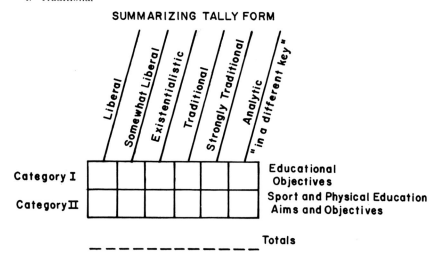

FURTHER COMMENTS

If you keep in mind the subjectivity of an instrument such as this, it should now be possible for you to make an initial determination whether your basic educational philosophy is in keeping with your ideas about the aims and objectives of sport and physical education.

At the very least you should be able to tell if your ideas are liberal, traditional, existentialistic, or analytic.

Now please examine the Freedom-Constraint Spectrum below. Keep in mind that Existentialism is not considered a position or stance in the same way as the others are (e.g., Traditional—Realism, etc.). Also, if you are Analytic, this means that your preoccupation tends to be with conceptual or language analysis as opposed to system building in a philosophical vein.

If you discover *Eclecticism* in your overall position or stance—that is, the checks are on opposite sides of the spectrum—closer analysis may be desirable to determine if your beliefs are philosophically defensible.

SOURCE MATERIAL

Recognition and appreciation are expressed to the following philosophers and educational philosophers whose work was gleaned in connection with determination of the various educational stances: John S. Brubacher, Abraham Kaplan, Morton White, William Barrett, E.A. Burtt, Van Cleve Morris, Ralph White, Herbert Spencer, J. Donald Butler, George R. Geiger, Theodore Brameld, John Wild, Harry S. Broudy, James Feibleman, Roy W. Sellars, Isaac L. Kandel, Alfred N. Whitehead, Mortimer J. Adler, Wm. McGucken, Pope Pius XII, Herman H. Horne, Theodore M. Greene, Wm. E. Hocking, and, of course, Paul Weiss.

From the fields of sport and physical education, as well as from health education and recreation in the complete version of this checklist, recognition and appreciation are expressed to the following people: R.B. Morland, J.F. Williams, C.H. McCloy, J.B. Nash, D. Oberteuffer, E.C. Davis, C. Brightbill, L. Joseph Cahn, Margaret C. Clark, Mabel Lee, Leona Holbrook, Bruce Bennett, Donn E. Bair, Barney Steen, R.J. Downey, Roger K. Burke, W.W. Wilton, D.B. Van Dalen, E. Metheny, H.J. VanderZwaag, J.W. Keating, L.J. Huelster, W.P. Fraleigh, and S. Kleinman. Ideas and phrases have been

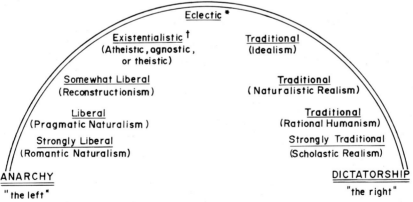

*The *eclectic* approach is placed in the center because it assumes that Xs have been placed in several positions on opposite sides of the spectrum. Most would argue that eclecticism is philosophically indefensible, while some believe that "patterned eclecticism" (or "reasoned incoherence") represents a stance that most of us hold.

†*Existentialistic*—a permeating influence rather than a full-blown philosophical position. Keep in mind that there are those with an atheistic, agnostic, or theistic orientation. This has been placed to the left of center because of emphasis on individual freedom of choice.

borrowed from them to express the various positions or stances in the allied professions. For the definition of the concept of 'freedom,' we express appreciation to Herbert J. Muller (see his *Freedom in the Ancient World.* New York, Harper & Row, 1961, p. xiii).

THE FREEDOM-CONSTRAINT SPECTRUM

Note:

The reader may wish to examine himself—his personal philosophical stance— on the basis of this spectrum analysis. Keep in mind that the primary criterion on which this is based is the concept of 'personal freedom,' in contrast to 'personal constraint.' Muller's definition of freedom is "the condition of being able to choose and to carry out purposes" in one's personal living pattern. Within a social environment, the words *liberal* and *traditional* have historically related to policies favoring individual freedom and policies favoring adherence to tradition respectively. (Traditional positions in educational philosophy are indicated in parentheses on the figure below.)

Analytic—philosophy "in a new key"—subscribing to a philosophical outlook with ancient origins, but which has moved ahead strongly in the twentieth century. The assumption here is that man's ordinary language has many defects that need to be corrected. Another objective is "the rational reconstruction of the language of science" (Abraham Kaplan). Preoccupation with analysis as opposed to philosophical system-building.

Index

Numerals in *italics* indicate a figure; "t" following a page number indicates tabular material.